BENGAL:

The Nationalist Movement   1876–1940

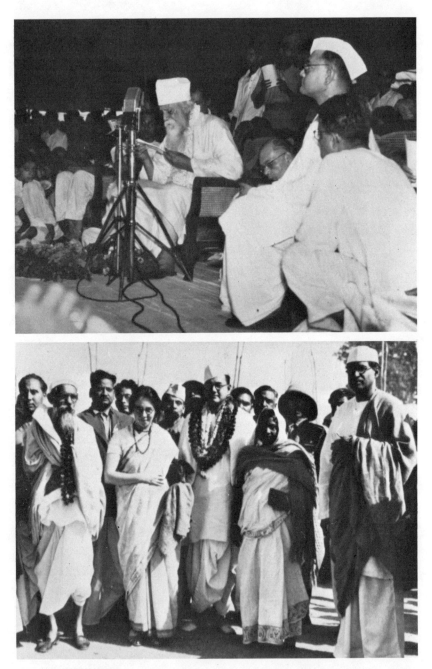

Top: Laying foundation stone at Mahajati, Sadan, 1939. Rabindranath Tagore speaking, Sarat Bose (head visible) and Subhas Bose to the poet's left. *Bottom:* Bengal Provincial Conference at Bisnupur, late 1930s. Front row, left to right: Jatindra Roy, Mrs. Ellen Roy, Subhas Bose, unidentified woman, M. N. Roy.

BENGAL:
The Nationalist Movement
1876–1940

Leonard A. Gordon

Columbia University Press
New York   London   1974

Publication of this book was made possible by support from the Frank Diehl Fackenthal Fund of the Press and the Department of History of Columbia University.

Library of Congress Cataloging in Publication Data

Gordon, Leonard A
   Bengal: The Nationalist Movement, 1876–1940. Newyork,
Columbia [1973]
   (Southern Asian Institute series)
   4070.
   Bibliography: p. 571—
   1. Bengal—Politics and government. I. Title.
II. Series: Columbia University. Southern Asian
Institute. Southern Asian Institute series.
DS485.B49G67   320.9′54′1403   73-12974
ISBN 0-231-03753-8

In memory of my Father
and of Kumar Goshal

Southern Asian Institute Series

The Southern Asian Institute seeks a deeper knowledge of that vast and tumultuous area stretching from Pakistan in the west to Indonesia and the Philippines in the east. To understand the problems facing its leaders and its diverse peoples requires sustained training and research. Our publications are intended to contribute to that better understanding.

Preface

රිෆ්රිෆ්ර Recently, Bengalis made world headlines as they fought through another major crisis in their existence. In the past generation their hard times have been extraordinary: a terrible famine, communal slaughter around the time of partition, periodic flows of refugees across the border of divided Bengal, a great tidal-wave disaster, communist-anarchist violence, brutal military suppression in 1971 by the Pakistani government, from which the people of eastern Bengal had become estranged, followed by a war for independence.

Following such turmoil, it seems but a small matter to offer a work of history. But the efforts of the Pakistan military to thwart Bengali culture and to kill some of its most creative exponents have shown how fragile culture is. Therefore, it has become even more important today for scholars, both South Asian and foreign, to continue to chart the history of Bengal. This work traces some developments in the nationalist period which help one to understand the complexity of the present.

Under British rule in India, Bengalis, for the first time in their history, were at the center of an all-India empire. Some high-caste Hindu Bengalis and a few Muslims quickly took to Western education and participated in the British Raj. The most politically conscious among them helped to found, lead, and sustain the nationalist movement during its first quarter century. Their centrality and early start led Bengali spokesmen in the later nineteenth century to develop a grandiose view of the role of Bengalis in Indian life relative to other regional groups. The cultural awakening, particularly of Hindu Bengal, the political activity, and even the land revenue settlement of Bengal were offered as models by Bengal to other regions.

Because the capital of British India until 1912 was Calcutta, Bengali leaders found the levers of power at hand and were able to convert regional and local issues into national ones. This process culminated during the Swadeshi agitation in the early twentieth century, when nationalist leaders from other regions joined Bengali nationalists in making the revocation of the partition of Bengal a general concern. During the Swadeshi years, Bengal was the cynosure of Indian politics, and Bengali leaders claimed that in spirit and in organization they were setting an example for other Indians to emulate. The agitation failed to sustain itself and did not lead to the building of successful parallel institutions outside the scope of the British Raj. This failure and the shift of India's capital to Delhi contributed to the loss of Bengali preeminence. The Bengali model lost its glow.

After World War I, Mahatma Gandhi and a corps of leaders selected by him, few of them Bengalis, took command of the Indian National Congress. The foremost political leaders from earlier dominant Bengal and Maharashtra usually were secondary figures in nationalist politics for the next generation. Two major revolts against the Gandhian nationalist leadership received strong support in Bengal. The first was the creation of the Swaraj Party in the 1920s, led by the Bengali Chittaranjan Das. The second was the challenge of the left in the 1930s, led by another Bengali, Subhas Chandra Bose.

The ultimate frustration of these attempts to break Gandhian supremacy, together with the failure of Hindu-Muslim alliances in Bengal, has contributed to the strong resentment against the national government still harbored by Bengalis in post-1947 West Bengal. The antagonism of Bengalis in the eastern half of the region against their national government culminated in an independent Bangladesh and grew out of a different but related history which also involves differences between Hindu and Muslim Bengalis. The declining role of Hindu Bengalis in Indian nationalist politics and their consequent revolts are major themes of the present work. The equally important but neglected history of Bengali Muslims before 1947 is a minor theme here but the focus of future research.

This book traces the changing place of Bengal and the growth of nationalism over three generations from the 1870s to 1940. I have concentrated on types of leadership and political organization, ideology and political strategy, case studies of leadership, and Bengali self-imagery. In most instances, I have not worked quantitatively. Rather, the study emerges in a more qualitative manner from strong impressions gained during immersion in many of the relevant sources.

My primary foci have been the Indian National Congress, its Bengal branch, the Bengal Provincial Congress Committee, and a small number of nationalist leaders whose careers have been examined in detail. The Congress was the leading nationalist organization and provided continuity for the movement as older leaders left and new ones came to the fore. Although it was a relatively small body through the first two nationalist generations and did not take practical steps toward becoming a mass organization until the 1920s, the Congress was recognized by the government of India from its inception as a most significant source of "native opinion." The Congress included under its umbrella a number of competing factions, and conflicts between differing ideologies, personalities, regional interests, and strategies were acted out within it. In the Congress arena we can see the changing role played by Bengalis and compare their actual part in it with their image of themselves and what they think their role should be.

To make my study more concrete and hopefully more vivid,

I have analyzed the life histories of a few Bengal leaders with some thoroughness. These men were chosen either because they played a large role in politics or because they had significant influence on the shaping of nationalist ideology. They were men of national as well as regional distinction, concerned with the problems arising from the fact that they were conscious of both a European and an Indian inheritance. They all tried to deal with this dual cultural tradition within themselves and their country. Of course, many Indians had to face similar problems; the Bengalis upon whom I have concentrated were among the few to whom other Indians looked for example and advice in dealing with the problems of conflicting values, legacies, and hopes. A number of psychological themes arose in studying these leaders, including the expression of aggression and ambivalence toward authority.

I have examined the different roles which each figure played and saw himself playing. The concept of role provides a useful link between organization and individual career. In this period we see the movement from amateur to professional politics worked out, inter alia, in the lives of these men. I have also examined the ideas these leaders formulated and spread, particularly their ideas about India and Bengal, and the past, present, and future of their country and region. An analysis of these ideas provides an understanding of what they saw as valuable in their own heritage, and what they meant by the Indian nation and by the Bengalis. Descriptions of Bengal and prescriptions for Bengalis, which I have called Bengali self-imagery, give a sense of the part they thought Bengalis should play in Indian life and is related to the contributions they actually did make. I have tried to compare the answers given by the leaders of the three nationalist generations as to the place of Bengal. As with other generational comparisons, I was looking for continuities and discontinuities which would give insight into the changing place of Bengal. The scrutiny of ideas and of the earthier workings of parties enables us to see how ideas function in politics. And it returns us to the major theme: changing problems and styles of leadership in declining and developing Bengal.

This study of Bengal and of Indian nationalism is the revised version of a doctoral dissertation submitted to the Department of History at Harvard University. Much of my work on Indian history was done at the University of Chicago, where I studied and later interned in the Indian Civilization Program. Professors Daniel H. H. Ingalls, Michael Brecher, Philip Calkins, Bernard S. Cohn, Dennis Dalton, Edward C. Dimock, Jr., Ainslie Embree, Warren Gunderson, H. J. Hanham, Stephen Hay, Ronald B. Inden, Richard L. Park, Edward Shils, Milton Singer, and the late David Owen read through parts of this manuscript at different stages of its preparation and offered useful criticisms and suggestions.

My research in India, supported by the Foreign Area Fellowship Program, was carried out mainly at the Netaji Research Bureau and National Library of India, Calcutta, the Indian Renaissance Institute, Dehradun, the Sri Aurobindo Ashram, Pondicherry, and the National Archives of India, New Delhi, and I am grateful to those in charge of these research facilities for their generous assistance. I would like to thank friends, associates, and relations of several of the leaders discussed here for patiently answering my questions.

My friends in India accepted me warmly into their company and society and thus enabled me to live and study there. In particular, I would like to thank Professor and Mrs. Sushabhan Sarkar and Miss Shipra Sarkar, Dr. and Mrs. Sisir Bose, Mr. and Mrs. Nirad C. Chaudhuri, Professor and Mrs. P. Lal, Mr. and Mrs. Abu Sayeed Ayyub, Mr. Bishnu Dey, Dr. and Mrs. M. K. Halder, Mr. Pradip Sen, Mr. Satyajit Ray, Mr. Anil Basu, Dr. and Mrs. Naresh Guha, the K. C. Chopra family of Bombay and New Delhi, the Sindhwani family of Dehradun, Mr. Keshub C. Sarkar, and the late David McCutchion and Jamini Roy. In addition, I benefited from discussions with Dr. and Mrs. J. K. Banerjee in London and talks with Frau Emilie Schenkl-Bose and her daughter Anita in Vienna.

Miss Judith Aronson helped me to revise the manuscript and Mrs. Mary Flower retyped it. Miss Karen Mitchell, my meticulous editor at Columbia University Press, has made every effort to tighten my writing style and avoid vagueness on crucial points. My mother, Mrs. Rose Gordon, and Miss Carol Meadows devoted many hours to reading the proofs. The Southern Asian Institute at Columbia University supported a summer's work of rewriting the original text.

My mother and my aunt, Mrs. Regina Berman, helped with my investigation of M. N. Roy's Mexican years. Finally I would like to express my love and appreciation to my two families-away-from-home: the Dimocks of Chicago and Calcutta, and the Dattas of Calcutta, Chicago, and West Branch, Iowa; and to my family at home as well.

Contents

PROLOGUE
Trends in Bengal, 1876-1904

Among the extraordinary creations of the British and of the Indians who worked and traded with them were the cities built in the three major coastal areas. Of these, Bombay and Calcutta developed into cosmopolitan centers of world importance. Calcutta grew from a few small villages in the seventeenth century to a large town of several thousand by the later eighteenth century; it numbered about 450,000 in 1871 and almost one million by the end of the century.

From 1773 to 1912, Calcutta served as the capital of British India, giving the city and the Bengal region a significance and centrality unique in their history. Calcutta was the administrative and political center of the British Empire in India and, during the later nineteenth century, it became both an industrial and a commercial center. Goods for export flowed into Calcutta from the whole of eastern and parts of northern India, and imports from Europe, East Asia, and the United States were carried to Calcutta and then inland. The European inhabitants of the city, ignoring Kipling's gloomy caricature, took great pride in their metropolis as the second city of the British Empire.[1]

But Calcutta was an Indian and Bengali as well as a European city, and concentrated the urban traditions of pre-British Bengal. The functions of the rajas' court-capitals and the Muslim commercial-administrative centers had been fused into one urban area which differed from the earlier centers simply in the degree of aggregation, not in the functions served. The wealthy and powerful families of nineteenth-century Calcutta, like the Debs and the Tagores, must be viewed partly in their resemblance to rajas of small kingdoms in earlier Bengal. Numerous high-caste families, Kayasthas, Vaidyas, and Brahmans, flocked to Calcutta, producing a much higher proportion of high-caste Hindus there than in Bengal as a whole.[2] Thus the Bengalis, especially those from the upper strata, had made Calcutta their own. It became a center of Bengali culture, wealth, and power. The countryside around the city, the "mofussil," contributed men and raw materials to the city and received back finished goods, ideas, and trained men. In Calcutta, the levers of imperial, provincial, municipal, and university power were close at hand. It was difficult for those who could not come easily or often to the metropolis to assume an important place in the British-Indian establishment. And from the last quarter of the eighteenth century, Calcutta was the arena in which those Bengalis who sought fame, fortune, and solid accomplishment had to climb the ropes of opportunity.

Bengal in this period was, and to a great extent remains, largely a rural society with a predominantly illiterate peasant population. Early compilers of the census (in 1872 and 1881) noted that after Calcutta the next largest urban area was Dacca, with somewhat more than 51,000 inhabitants, and that for an area that numbered more than 35 million in population, Bengal was remarkable for its absence of large or numerous towns. The rural population, by and large, was described as a stay-at-home one in which few left their district of origin. The picture is then one of a single great urban complex surrounded by a large agricultural area comprising mostly small villages, with a few towns slowly growing to city size. This rural population was more Hindu to the west, more Muslim to the east, and according to the first census there was an approximate demographic balance between these two major ethnic categories.[3]

The census takers noted that rural administration was decaying, but that some large zamindars continued to exert an influence. These zamindars whose landholding rights were to some extent a British creation, were heirs to the habit of authority descending from the Bengali rajas of earlier days. The peasant population, scattered, divided, and exploited, was generally obedient to the Bengali zamindars and to the district officials of the Raj.

The pattern of social, economic, and political organization and change within so large an area as the Bengali-speaking region is difficult to grasp. At present we must follow the lead of anthropologists and social historians who suggest that the operative social and political unit for rural Bengalis was one which has been called the "microregion" or "samaj." We may accept that the village or "gram" was generally not an effectively coherent unit in most spheres of life, but that it was nonetheless some sort of localized unit demarcating the important range of social connections. The "microcaste" or the local political factions might well be connected into wider networks for some purposes, but through the period under discussion, and even today, the smaller, basic units were those which were most meaningful to the majority of rural Bengalis.[4]

There were a variety of ties between local communities and units and the larger networks. These included, inter alia, links from microcastes to subcastes and regional caste groupings; economic relationships with markets and moneylenders which provided the means of supplying food and other rural products to the towns and cities and, in return, provided credit and some products to the rural population; and the administrative system of the Raj, which provided some judicial, peace-keeping, educational, medical, transportation, and communication services, and collected taxes.

Some changes in the structure of the Raj which followed the shift from East India Company to crown rule in 1858 offered new opportunities for young Indians. Although there was a shift to a generally more conservative policy in the generation after the revolt of 1857, the ways in which the government of India and the British government chose to respond to this upheaval allowed some Indians to enter new positions of responsibility within and in connection with the Raj. Clearly top places of responsibility were almost all held by Europeans into the twentieth century. But to meet growing Indian demands and their own desire to keep closely informed about their subjects, the rulers gradually allowed Indians into the Indian Civil Service (ICS), the senates of the newly constituted universities, the provincial and imperial legislative councils, local self-government institutions, and the bar and bench of the high courts.[5]

However, what A. P. Thornton has described as the "habit of authority" continued as an essential part of the Raj until its dissolution.[6] "We need to show," said Lord Elgin later in the century, "that we are the dominant race."[7] The influence of the permanent cadre of officials and of the nonofficial European community, particularly in Calcutta, was demonstrated a number of times during this period. The percentage of Indians in the ICS and lower services continued to be very low, and steps to favor the most conservative and aristocratic segments of Indian society marked the post-Mutiny period. A number of writers have sketched as well the growing racism of Europeans in India during the second half of the nineteenth century which followed the Mutiny and the estrangement in social life between Europeans and Indians.[8]

During the nineteenth century, vast areas of India came directly under British rule. The British needed trained officials to man the Raj, and many Bengalis, mostly Western-educated and high-caste Hindus, moved to areas outside Bengal with the expansion of British territory. This was the reverse of what had happened under Mughal rule, when Muslim officials had been brought from outside into Bengal to govern the region. The number of Bengalis was probably greatest in the adjacent regions of Bihar, Assam, and Orissa, which were parts of the Bengal Presidency at various times, but there were Bengalis in urban centers across northern India.[9]

As Western education became more common in these areas, resentment grew against the Bengalis who had come in the wake of British rule. Bruce McCully has described the economic and cultural motives underlying these feelings of antagonism:

> The employment difficulties of the small educated class of Upper India led them to resent the competition of domiciled Bengalis who were stigmatized as foreigners. The ensuing struggle for positions in public service provoked considerable ill-will and jealousy between the two classes. Bengalis, in turn, protested that competition within their own province had driven them to seek employment in other provinces and regions.[10]

The unprecedented movement by Bengalis out across northern India was an important element in their development of a self-image of preeminence among Indians. The Bengalis founded branches of organizations like the Brahmo Samaj and developed networks connecting Bengalis to other urban centers and to their Bengali base.[11]

The Bengal Presidency in the early nineteenth century covered vast territories beyond the Bengali-speaking region, and was gradually delimited. In 1836 Agra was separated from the Bengal Presidency, and

Assam was detached from Bengal in 1874 and given its own chief commissioner.[12] From 1833 to 1854, Bengal had a deputy governor and its
own small secretariat, but practically no political authority that was
separate from the government of India. This ad hoc arrangement was
changed in 1854, when Bengal was officially put under a lieutenant-
governor, and this last arrangement was retained until the partition of
Bengal in 1905. Throughout the second half of the nineteenth century,
Bengal was gradually granted its own officials and administration distinct from those of the government of India. But because Bengal and
Calcutta were at the center of imperial power, the Bengal government
was kept weak. Functions and departments which were managed by
the governments of Bombay and Madras were only slowly handed
over to the Bengal government, which remained weaker in its ability
to gather information and in manpower through the nineteenth century.[13]

One barrier to closer ties between Europeans and Bengalis may have
been the conception many Englishmen had of the Bengali character.
Englishmen found resemblances or contrasts to themselves in the Indians they encountered, and also, in the course of time, formulated categories to classify the Indians they had to deal with. Eventually these
categories came to serve certain practical functions, such as aiding in
the selection of Indians to serve in the army. One general typology
which the English commonly used in the nineteenth century was a dichotomy between the martial and the nonmartial races. The British
reserved admiration for the fiercer fighters and abler soldiers among the
Indians.[14]

Among the nonmartial races the English gave the Bengalis a special
place of scorn. As early as the eighteenth century, Luke Scrafton, an
official of the East India Company in Bengal, wrote of the Bengalis:

The Gentoos of the lower provinces are a slight made people. Rice is
their chief food. It seems to afford but poor nourishment; for strong
robust men are seldom seen among them. . . . Thus the spring of life is
but of short duration, and the organs decay before the faculties of the
mind can attain to any perfection. Is nature then deficient? . . . We
must rather look for it in that early indulgence in venereal pleasures,
their excessive abstemiousness, their sedentary way of life, and in Bengal and the conquered provinces, in the dejected state of their minds,

oppressed with the tyranny of their conquerors. No wonder then, that with such customs, such bodies, and such minds, they fall an easy prey to every invader.[15]

Some sixty years later, Thomas Macaulay came to Bengal to serve as a member of the governor-general's council and then as Law Member and member of the Committee on Public Instruction:

> The physical organization of the Bengalee is feeble even to effeminacy. He lives in a constant vapour bath. His pursuits are sedentary, his limbs delicate, his movements languid. During many ages he has been trampled upon by men of bolder and more hardy breeds. Courage, independence, veracity, are qualities to which his constitution and his situation are equally unfavourable. His mind bears a singular analogy to his body. It is weak even to helplessness for purposes of manly resistance; but its suppleness and its tact move the children of sterner climates to admiration not unmingled with contempt. . . . What the horns are to the buffalo, what the paw is to the tiger, what the sting is to the bee, what beauty, according to the old Greek song, is to woman, deceit is to the Bengalee. Large promises, smooth excuses, elaborate tissues of circumstantial falsehood, chicanery, perjury, forgery, are the weapons, offensive and defensive, of the people of the Lower Ganges.[16]

The view of the Bengali as weak, deceitful, oily, found its way into the writings of many Englishmen in the nineteenth century, visitors to Bengal and residents alike. Even Robert Carstairs, who served for many years as a district officer in Bengal, sketched a scene of a future "Bengal Republic" which the Bengalis had taken over with the departure of the British. All shortly descended into chaos and anarchy, and the Bengalis were soon calling for their former European rulers to return, because all the Bengalis can do in moments of difficulty is talk.[17] They are effete "babus." [18]

The Bengalis referred to by Carstairs, Macaulay, *Hobson-Jobson*, and numerous other sources that might be quoted, are for the most part urban, educated Hindus who worked with the Europeans and came to imitate them. This became especially galling when Bengalis began arguing that the same institutions and freedoms that the English had in England should be granted to the Indians in India. Carstairs and Kipling at the end of the century derided these urban Hindu Bengalis for grasping only the externals and formal structures of European political institutions, failing to see their essence, and for an inability to run such institutions themselves. They admitted that the Bengali could talk, that he could even talk just like an eloquent Englishman, but they asserted that he could never act or be one.[19] Although many English writers provided only one stereotype of the Bengali, some did begin to differentiate between Muslim and Hindu, rural and urban Bengali. Thus Carstairs, W. W. Hunter, and Kipling praised the rural, tribal Bengali from the far western or far eastern areas of the region.[20] The rural man was physically stronger, less educated, simpler, more honest, and no threat to the British in India.

British officials and contemporary scholars have used yet another stereotyping idea to deal with the educated high-caste Hindus, the concept of the "bhadralok." This term literally means the people of breeding or gentlemen. Although people from any caste theoretically could become bhadralok, in Bengali society most of them are high-caste, educated Hindus. But officials and then scholars have taken the term to refer to a closed class among the Bengalis, a group with a corporate sense of themselves with distinct interests and aims. And every political trend which the British officials did not like—nationalism, terrorism, communism—was blamed upon these same bhadralok. Indeed, the distinction between the bhadralok and others (sometimes "chotolok," or small people) is built into many records of the Raj and into the very survey techniques used by officials like J. C. Jack in his well-known analysis of a Bengal district.[21]

It has seemed to me better not to use this concept in describing and analyzing Bengali politics. Definitions of who is included among the bhadralok are very imprecise; those who seem to have been included in this category were often political adversaries. It does not correlate closely enough with economic indicators and has been used by some writers to deliberately denigrate those high-caste Bengalis who engaged in nationalist politics.[22] A major difficulty with the thesis of bhadralok plotting is that because this one tool of questionable sociological value is used to explain so much, in the end it explains little.

Whatever stereotyped ideas Europeans may have held concerning urban, educated Bengalis, the Raj found them useful as it spread its tentacles into the countryside. There would be a few British officials in each district, but a district might number several million, and Bengalis were needed to man the lower administrative posts.

A most important institutionalized change at work in the nineteenth century was the spread of Western education. Undoubtedly, most college students were of higher economic and social standing, but Pradip Sinha has suggested that an increasingly small percentage came from very wealthy families.[23] Drawing on information compiled by the Hunter Commission, the Calcutta University Commission documented the occupations of University of Calcutta graduates:

> By 1882 western education, with the affiliating university as its guardian, had fully taken root in India, and most completely in Bengal. The university degree had become the accepted object of ambition, the passport to distinction in the public services and in the learned professions. Of the 1,589 students who obtained arts degrees in the University of Calcutta between 1857 and 1882, 526 had in 1882 entered the public service, 581 the legal profession, and 12 had become doctors: the 470 who remained were, no doubt, largely employed as teachers in the colleges and the high schools. . . . A university career had obviously become the best career for the sons of the *bhadralok* to follow; and already the social value of western education was reflected in the fact that a man who had taken his degree, or even only passed the entrance examination of the University, had a definitely improved value in the marriage-market. Western education had made its way into the social system.[24]

Although thousands of Bengalis undoubtedly gained some knowledge of the English language and Western thought through formal education, individual contact, reading and discussions, and the ever-growing number of visits by Indians to Europe were also significant educational factors.[25]

Many writers on nineteenth-century education have pointed out that Muslims tended to lag behind Hindus in demanding and acquiring Western education. This disparity was particularly striking in the Muslim-majority province of Bengal proper, and the problem continued at least until the partition of 1947. This Muslim lag was a reflection of certain social factors and cultural dilemmas that faced the Bengali Muslims. Most were converted low-caste or untouchable Hindus. For the upper-class and wealthier Muslims, there were fear and doubt about Western education, since traditional Muslim education, which included training in Persian, Arabic, and Urdu, was for the few and was inseparably linked to religious training. Only slowly were some pupils permitted to study Western languages, science, and history.[26] Aristocratic Muslims tended to look down on the Bengali language, although it was the common language of discourse for most Bengalis, Muslim or Hindu.[27]

The desire for Western education grew as it became clear during the nineteenth century that this was the path to government service and the professions. In 1871, Muslims constituted 32.2 percent of Bengal's population, but only 14.4 percent of the enrollment in schools and 4 percent in the colleges.[28] Some progress was made in the following half-century, but Muslim education was still appreciably backward when the Calcutta University Commission prepared their report.

> [W]hile the Bengali Muhamadan is generally anxious that his community should reap the full benefits of secular education, he is not prepared to take the benefits at the price of any real sacrifice of Islamic tradition or custom. . . . The feeling of the Mussalman is tinged with a not unnatural pride. His traditional culture is the culture which was evolved during the great days of Islam. . . . It is something for a boy in a remote village in Eastern Bengal to find that he is following the same line of study as that taught in the Azhar Mosque in Cairo.[29]

The dilemma of the Bengali Muslim must be seen in the context of widespread cultural and political activity by Bengali Hindus. Alongside the Hindu ideologues of the nineteenth and twentieth centuries, there are few Muslims of comparable stature.

The paths open to new graduates were limited; Edward Shils has noted their "truncated possibilities." [30] Nonetheless, these young men were a privileged minority, surrounded by a relatively inert peasant society. The new careers were not altogether different from those open to comparable men of the previous generation, but they had a more Western shape and content to them. The ICS, the bar, and the academic profession seem to have been popular and available to the most successful. These choices were related to the establishment of Calcutta University in the late 1850s; the reform of the court system and the creation of high courts in the three major presidencies, which were soon opened to Indian barristers; and the competitive examination for the ICS, for which small numbers of Indians began to sit.[31]

Queen Victoria's 1858 proclamation of equality of opportunity for all races together with the shift to an open examination system for the ICS made it possible for a small number of Indians to begin to travel to

England for the examination. Some British officials were disturbed that a majority of the early successful candidates were Bengalis, whom they believed were innately unable to handle positions of executive authority. Discussions about the Indianization of the ICS continued for many years, and even those Indians in the elite service who proved themselves of superior ability were kept from the top positions of responsibility by the rearguard action of reactionary official and nonofficial Europeans.[32] The slow pace of entry of Indians into the ICS was controlled by the low age requirement and the government insistence that the examination could be given only in Great Britain. Indians secured 2.5 percent of the vacancies between 1878 and 1891 and 5.6 percent between 1892 and 1912.[33] Although the number was small, the ICS continued to be the vocational goal of young Indians for many decades.

Once company rule had ended, the government decided to consolidate its courts, and two separate systems were combined in the High Court and lower affiliated courts. Law was soon amalgamated into one ordered profession and practice, and a number of Indians began to seek legal training in Great Britain.[34] After some dispute, Indian lawyers were allowed to become barristers and solicitors on the original side and advocates and "vakils," or public pleaders, on the appellate side. At first the Indian practitioners had to struggle in a practice controlled by European law firms, but as Indian barristers and solicitors made their appearance, they were slowly employed by British firms. From the 1870s to the 1920s, at least, the legal profession was among the most lucrative livelihoods in India.[35]

Once the Calcutta High Court was established, at least one Indian usually sat on its bench. The earlier Indian justices were Hindus, but in the late nineteenth century Syed Mahmood and Syed Ameer Ali became justices. Ali's career as a lawyer and magistrate demonstrates that success was possible for a Muslim in Bengal, although it was not common. His assertion that Hindu control of the university, services, and judicial system kept Muslims out seems to have been overstated.[36] Muslims from Bengal were also sitting for the bar in London in increasing numbers.

In late-nineteenth-century Bengal there was a growing national and regional consciousness. Overlapping between the conceptions of India and of Bengal as nations exists in the Bengali terms for nation and people. Rabindranath Tagore wrote, "We have no word for 'Nation' in our language. When we borrow this word from other people, it never fits us." [37] The Bengali word "rashtra" is used to indicate the state or a large political unit but has no cultural connotations. By the late nineteenth century, at least in the writings of Tagore and urban, educated Bengalis, the term "desh" was often used to refer either to Bengal or to India. The term originally meant place of origin, place in a geographic, social, linguistic, and cultural sense, and the equivalent for our "country," "home," and "place." When someone said, "I am going to my desh," it would probably mean, especially for a worker or a villager, that he was going to his village or district. One informant has said that after about 1905, the term desh frequently meant Bengal.[38] In Tagore's essays, he often used the term "deshanayak" ("leader of the country") to mean first a leader of Bengal and then an all-India leader.[39] The term used to refer to the Swadeshi or "own-country" movement referred first to Bengal and then to all of India, which was to follow Bengal's lead in boycotting British goods. Further evidence could be offered to show the strength of identifications and feeling in Bengal, as well as the ambiguity in terms sometimes used to refer to India. For instance, "desh" and also the term "jati," (literally "birth," "family," or "caste") which may refer to a people, a nationality, or any group with whom one has an organic connection, came to be used more frequently with the regional or Bengali referents in the late nineteenth century.[40]

Part One

The First Generation: Early Nationalists 1876–1904

ONE
The Golden Age of the Moderates

ᏣᎿᏍᎻ᠑ᏍᏍ   In the last quarter of the nineteenth century, the first generation of Indian nationalists emerged in British India. During this formative phase of nationalist politics, British liberalism was seized upon by a relatively small number of English-speaking, articulate political spokesmen who organized regional associations and, in 1885, the Indian National Congress. It is to their credit that the steady flame of liberalism still burns in India today.

Their notion of the good polity and the good society was shaped by their idea of what existed in Great Britain. They wanted the same rights, in good time, that citizens of the Mother Country enjoyed. They wanted a parliament where representatives of the people could decide crucial questions of the day. At the same time, they believed in the legitimacy of British rule in India. More than one claimed he was loyal to the Raj to his backbone. They saw no contradiction between the aim of representative government and their faith in British rule. Their leading ideologues, Dadabhai Naoroji, R. C. Dutt, and G. K. Gokhale, marshalled evidence criticizing the drain of Indian resources to Britain, citing a disparity between Indian and British economic interests. They seemed to think that, ideally, British imperial and Indian interests were perfectly compatible. Only late in the nineteenth century did some begin to see the logic of nationalism: that only self-rule offered the possibility of eventually fulfilling national self-interest.

The most successful of the Western-educated, mainly professional men of Bengal in the generation following the revolt of 1857 formed a small, interconnected elite based in Calcutta. The full complement of those who participated in important official institutions and who dominated Indian political and cultural organizations during the period might total a few hundred.

The men I have called Bengali political leaders were almost uniformly Western-educated professional men of a high-caste Hindu background with many particularistic and cross-cutting ties to each other. They represented, inter alia, the first generation of graduates of Calcutta University, and a significant proportion had then furthered their education in England. They felt that because of certain processes at work in the social order, they had been chosen to speak for all their countrymen. They were the "natural leaders," not a hereditary aristocracy but educated middle-class men who represented the public interest whether or not they were elected. They did run in early elections for Bengal Legislative Council seats, for the Calcutta Corporation, the senate of Calcutta University, and local government bodies and often won. However, after the Morley-Minto reforms in the early twentieth century (see chapters 3–4), elections became increasingly difficult and contested. By then, their golden age was over.

They also described themselves as the "influential" men in Indian society. This meant to them that they could get interviews with officials both in India and England. In some cases these interviews and assistance from members of the House of Commons enabled them to make minor accomplishments: the Vernacular Press Act of 1878, Lord Lytton's attempt to limit extreme statements in the Indian press, was repealed; local self-government bills were passed; the Bengal Tenancy Act (see below, p. 31) was passed; the legislative councils were reformed in 1892 and 1909, although not satisfactorily; and the age for the ICS examination was raised. But they did not fully understand that their positions of influence were greatly dependent on the largesse of British officials. In this period, and even later, the recognition of the Raj was forthcoming for politicians who believed in the norms of restraint, tolerance, order, and slow political change.

This group included those who served in the ICS, all judges and practitioners on the Calcutta High Court, Bengali representatives in the legislative councils, the 177 Indians who served in the senate of Calcutta University between 1857 and 1904, leading professors, and businessmen.[1] The total number is drastically reduced by the fact that many of these men held three, four, or five of these positions, often simultaneously. A thorough study of the late-nineteenth-century establishment would consider the career patterns, interconnections, activity, and ideas of all these men. For the purposes of this brief account, 13 have been chosen (see table).

Of these 13, 10 are "kulin" (or highest ranking) Brahmans and Kayasthas, one is from a prominent Kayastha family, the last Hindu most likely also high caste, and the Muslim a Syed. None came from extraordinarily wealthy families, although most grew up in comfortable circumstances. Unlike the wealthy members of the British Indian Association, who were from Calcutta, several of these men came from East Bengal and from outlying districts in West Bengal. But their academic and professional achievements were made in Calcutta: 8 attended Presidency College, Calcutta, and 7 had further education in Britain at Cambridge, London University, or one of the Inns of Court. Many achieved academic distinction.

At least half met as young men and in some cases formed lifelong friendships. Ameer Ali knew Surendranath Banerjea and probably most of the others, but in his own memoirs and in the accounts of his life that have so far appeared he seems set apart. He mentioned his contact with Europeans, but no particular work with Bengalis in Calcutta. Many of the others often worked together, the similarity of caste, education, and career pattern contributing to their connections, cooperation, similar outlook and ideology. The Indian elite in Calcutta during the later nineteenth century, although always divided by factionalism, was a small, relatively homogeneous group with multiple personal and professional ties. Their success was a combination of ascription and achievement, with the latter predominating. S. N. Mukherjee and others have described the slow rise of men from lower castes into the elite of Calcutta,[2] but high-caste Hindus clearly continued to dominate. Whether they actively prevented the rise of low-caste Hindus and Muslims is still not evident; assertions have been made that they did.

Throughout the period, Bengali political leaders played an important role in forming and running nationalist political organizations and in agitating for the redress of Indian grievances. Because Calcutta was the capital of British India, Bengali leaders often tried to give and succeeded in giving matters affecting Bengal an all-India significance.

There is one other vital generational theme running through the late

TABLE MODERATES AND ESTABLISHMENT MEN

Name	Caste	Education	Academic Achievements	Profession	Positions
1. Ali, Ameer (1849–1928)	Syed Shiah Muslim	Hooghly College, Inner Temple (called to bar, 1873)	state scholarship to England	barrister, magistrate, Calcutta High Court judge, writer	founder & sec. Central National Mohammedan Assoc.; Calcutta High Court judge; member Legal Committee, Privy Council
2. Banerjea, Surendranath (1848–1925)	Brahman–K*	Calcutta U., University College, London (?)	college prizeman every year; passed ICS exam	ICS; college lecturer, journalist, politician	Congress pres. (1895, 1902) BLC (1883, 1895, 1897, 1900, 1901)
3. Banerji, Guru Das (1844–1918)	Brahman–K	Presidency College (1865)	gold medal in mathematics (1864)	legal practitioner, Calcutta High Court judge	Calcutta High Court judge; vice-chancellor, Calcutta University; Indian Universities Commission
4. Basu, Bhupendranath (1859–1924)	Kayastha–K	Presidency College (1879)	?	solicitor, Calcutta High Court	Congress pres. (1914) BLC (1903, 1905, 1906, 1907)

	Caste	Inns of Court / College	Distinctions	Profession	Career
5. Bonnerjee, W. C. (1844–1906)	Brahman–K	Middle Temple	R. J. Jeejeebhai scholarship to go to London to prepare for bar	barrister, Calcutta High Court	ILC; Calcutta Corp.; vice-chancellor, Calcutta U.; under-sec. of state for India Congress pres. (1885, 1892) BLC (1893)
6. Bose, Ananda Mohan (1847–1906)	Kayastha–K	Presidency College; (1863–1868) Cambridge	First Cambridge wrangler from India	barrister; tea investments	Congress pres. (1898) BLC (1885, 1895, 1901)
7. Dutt, Romesh Chunder (1848–1909)	Kayastha	Presidency College (1866); University College, London Middle Temple	school prizes; second in FA exam, Presidency College; second in final ICS exam	ICS, barrister writer and lecturer	Congress pres. (1899) BLC (1895) Royal Comm. on Decentralization; finance minister of Baroda
8. Ghose, Lal Mohan (1849–1909)	Kayastha–K	Middle Temple	first in entrance exam to Calcutta U. (in Bengal Presidency)	barrister, Calcutta High Court	Congress pres. (1903) BLC (1893)

TABLE MODERATES AND ESTABLISHMENT MEN (Continued)

Name	Caste	Education	Academic Achievements	Profession	Positions
9. Ghose, Man Mohan (1844–1896)	Kayastha–K	Presidency College?	?	barrister, Calcutta High Court	Congress rep. to England (1885, 1887, 1890, 1895)
10. Ghose, Rash Behari (1845–1921)	Kayastha–K	Presidency College (1861–1867)	first in FA exam, Presidency College, 1862; first class M.A., English and B.L., Calcutta U.; first Indian to get M.A. in English	vakil, Calcutta High Court	Congress pres. (1907, 1908) BLC pres., faculty of Law, Calcutta University
11. Mazumdar, Ambica Charan (1851–?)	?	Presidency College (1873)	?	barrister	pres., Bengal Prov. Conf. (1899); Congress pres. (1916) BLA BLC (1905, 1906)

12. Mookerjee, Asutosh (1864–1924)	Brahman–K	Presidency College (1881–1886)	1879, second in entrance exam to Calcutta U.; one of top in FA exam, 1881; paper published, Cambridge *Messenger of Mathematics*, 1881; first class; first B.A. 1884, M.A. 1885	barrister, judge, educator	judge, Calcutta High Court; vice-chancellor, Calcutta University; BLC (1900, 1902, 1903, 1904)
13. Sinha, Satyendra Prasanna (Lord Sinha) (1864–1928)	Kayastha–K	Presidency College (1879); one of Inns of Court, London	?	barrister	Congress pres. (1915) viceroy's exec. council; minister of Bengal government; under-sec. of state for India

* K: "kulin"

Sources: *Indian Nation Builder* (3 vols., Madras, n.d.); *Biographies of Eminent Indians* (Madras, n.d.); C. E. Buckland, *Dictionary of Indian Biography* (London, 1906); *Bengal under the Lieutenant-Governor* (2 vols.; Calcutta, 1901); biographies and autobiographies listed in bibliography by S. Banerjea, J. N. Gupta, N. K. Sinha, H. C. Sarkar, and S. Bonnerjee; *To the Gates of Liberty*, Congress Commemoration Volume (n.p., n.d.); K. K. Aziz, *Amer Ali, His Life and Work* (London, 1968)

nineteenth century, the growth of cultural and religious revivalism, although for the most part politics and religion were not yet intermingled. The main flow of politics was in the direction of sober liberalism. The more chauvinistic, cultural nationalism was still underground.

In long-term perspective, the moderate age marks one stage in the development of political organizations and roles, modes of agitation, and nationalist ideology. This is the period between the politics of a tiny group of aristocratic notables, the British Indian Association, and the politics of mass mobilization efforts which begin in the Swadeshi years after 1905.

The initiative of men from the Calcutta elite, what Karl Deutsch might call the "politically relevant strata," [3] led to the formation of cultural and political organizations in the capital, some of which reached out to the countryside and larger towns across India. The organizations and cultural movements combined selected elements of Indian traditions (as these existed in Bengal) with features of Western culture in eclectic syntheses. The Brahmo Samaj, the most renowned of these organizations and one that had considerable influence on a number of establishment men, will serve as a brief example.

The Brahmo Samaj grew out of a group founded by Rammohan Roy, the Atmiya Sabha, which in 1828 became the Brahma Sabha. The Brahma Sabha was organized to provide for proper worship of Brahma, who was in Rammohan's view the one true God of the Hindu scriptures. Rammohan believed that the pure Hinduism of an early golden age had become encrusted with degrading customs, and it was necessary to purge it of these encrustations to shape a purified religion compatible with Western learning. Such a faith was especially needed in Bengal, where religious immoralities, Rammohan thought, had contributed to indigenous weakness in resisting foreign conquerors. [4]

The Brahma Sabha languished until 1839, when it was merged with the Tattwabodhini Sabha, founded by Debendranath Tagore. The new organization was rechristened the Brahmo Samaj in 1842 and formed branches in the provincial towns of Bengal. "Samaj" in Bengali often means a group of families connected by caste and marriage ties, and the Brahmo Samaj gradually took on a number of caste and educational functions for its members, who were recruited from the high castes of Bengal. From the 1850s branches were organized in the major cities of northern and western India, recruiting primarily Bengalis who had taken up administrative, professional, and educational positions outside Bengal. The Samaj became associated with social service and a number of Brahmo preachers fanned out as full-time workers and pros-elitizers.[5]

The Brahmo Samaj split twice in the 1860s and 1870s, so that by 1880 there were three groups: the Adi Brahmo Samaj, with which De-bendranath Tagore remained associated; the Brahmo Samaj of India, headed by the ablest Brahmo preacher, Keshub Sen; and an offshoot of the latter, the Sadharan Brahmo Samaj. Sen's abilities attracted much new interest, but his controversial stands on a number of issues and his belief in himself as a prophet of a New Dispensation helped to faction-alize the organization. He incorporated Christian and Vaishnava features into the ritual of the organization and announced that India had a spiri-tual and moral mission in the modern world. He believed that all was sacred in Asia, the land of "introspection" and "flaming faith." Asia's spirituality and Europe's science were matched as the vital, comple-mentary components of the modern world. Thus colonial peoples, par-ticularly the Indians, were raised to the level of their imperial masters by a continental division of cultural labor.[6]

In carrying out India's mission, the Brahmo church should be a "source of real usefulness." Although Sen thought Bengalis were prone to "indolence, lethargy, and aversion to activity and enterprise," their "native meekness" could be transformed into moral principle worthy of being spread to the world.[7]

The Sadharan Brahmo Samaj was formed by members who broke with Keshub in 1878, and they were particularly active in missionary and social-service work. Like all the Brahmo organizations, it radiated out from Calcutta, recruiting members from the countryside and send-ing back trained preachers.[8] Work in the Brahmo Samaj prepared men for public life, imbued them with the idea of selfless labor, and sug-gested to them that reformed Indian traditions might have some special role to play in meeting the needs of modern men.

The Brahmo synthesis incorporated some Christian elements, like communal worship and the association of religion and social service, within a generally Indian framework. Other Western ideological cur-rents also had some influence on nineteenth-century Indians, including

positivism, utilitarianism, and liberalism. Indians also borrowed Western organizational structure and political pressure groups and made use
of advances in communication and transportation. Many writers have
described the phenomenon known as the Bengali Renaissance, which
included some of these changes of attitude and technology.[9] In almost
every case, Indians selected those cultural elements which they believed to be most valuable and reshaped them in an Indian environment.

THE POLITICS OF THE ESTABLISHMENT MEN

Those Bengalis whom I have called the establishment men engaged
in two related forms of political activity during the last quarter of the
nineteenth century. First, they participated in officially sponsored institutions like the Bengal and Imperial Legislative Councils, the Calcutta
University Senate, and the Calcutta Corporation. Second, they were
the organizers and leaders of Indian political organizations, such as the
Indian Association and the Indian National Congress. Their activity
was based on the assumption that Indians could gain an increasing
share in the rule of their country by taking every opportunity to work
with the British Raj. Although there were sharp criticisms of the Raj
from time to time, and even a wave of resignations from the Calcutta
Corporation in 1899, this assumption was left for later generations of
nationalists to doubt.

Lawyers were the most active occupational group in early nationalist politics. The phenomenon of lawyers in politics is well known in
many developed and developing countries. One writer on the legal
profession in India has suggested:

> Only the lawyers had the knowledge of the individual rights to which
> an Indian was entitled, the mastery of the English language, skills, and
> independence which enable him to "stand up to the bureaucracy of the
> day." Lawyers were in a better position to work for the cause of na-
> tionalism than were other men of their education level who were in
> government or government aided services. Their income and positions
> were independent from government pressure.[10]

They were skilled at negotiation and they had learned how to control
aggressive feelings toward their opponents. Many had trained for the
bar in England and had witnessed the party system, pressure groups,

and widening political participation. As they gained equality with British barristers, they came to expect that Indians would eventually have equal political rights as well.

Just after the revolt of 1857, the British established the universities of Calcutta, Bombay, and Madras as affiliating institutions. Calcutta University was set up with a strong measure of official control. The government appointed members of the university senate for life; between 1857 and 1904, 388 Europeans and 177 Indians served as members, including officials, judges of the High Court, businessmen, lawyers, and professors. Reforms were instituted after 1904, but official control continued. Members of the senate complained of a feeling of impotence because they knew that decisions could ultimately be reversed by the government.[11]

Other changes following 1857 included the opening of the governor-general's, governor's, and lieutenant-governor's councils to nominated members. Special provision was made in 1862 for the establishment of a Council of the Lieutenant-Governor of Bengal, which was to include 12 nominated members, of whom at least one-third were to be nonofficials. Under the Indian Councils Act of 1861 the body could discuss legislation; under the Indian Councils Act of 1892, it was enlarged and allowed to discuss the budget, ask questions, and consider and pass bills. The principle of election was indirectly recognized, but the lieutenant-governor still ran the meetings. The nonofficials, directly nominated by the government and after 1892 with tacit government approval, were infrequent guests in the official mansion.[12]

Nonetheless, the Bengal Legislative Council served a number of important functions. Like the senate, the bar association, and the Indian political organizations, the council was a meeting place for establishment men. It was, moreover, the one official forum where Indian spokesmen could confront the government with their recommendations, question administrative actions, and, as they put it, ventilate their grievances—although they might receive little satisfaction in official replies.[13]

Questions and comments in council during these years were revealing. Concern seemed to focus on opening more places in the government services to Indians, raising the salaries of those already so employed, and scrutinizing expenditures for higher education. Asutosh

Mookerjee mentioned during the 1901 budget debate that his special interests were education, law, and justice. In this forum and in the Calcutta Corporation, rural municipalities, and district boards, Indian members said they were setting forth the views and sentiments of the people. "People" meant all the Indians in Bengal, but sometimes meant the Hindus, the educated, or the "middle class." Muslims said they spoke for the Muslims of Bengal. Once there was a larger council, it was clear that no one man or organization spoke for all the people, or all the Hindus, or all the Muslims; [14] but the rhetoric of populism, borrowed from European politics, was often used.

The council also served as a training course in parliamentary method. Indians sat on select committees that reported on bills, entered the lists of the annual budget discussion, and learned to frame acceptable questions. Their British rulers often judged them on how well they did by the standards of British parliamentarians. The government also used the councils as a source of Indian opinion.[15] This worked while all important groups were willing to participate in the councils, but not after significant segments of the Indian political world decided to operate outside them.

The last quarter of the nineteenth century also saw formal advances in local self-government, including the Bengal Municipal Act of 1884 and the Bengal District Board Act of 1885, which provided for greater Indian participation. But as Hugh Tinker has pointed out,

> Indian local self-government was still in many ways a democratic facade to an autocratic structure. The actual conduct of business was carried on by district officials, with the non-official members as spectators, or at most critics.[16]

The impotence of Indian leaders in this period was also revealed by a crisis in the Calcutta Corporation in 1899. Sir Alexander Mackenzie, the lieutenant-governor of Bengal, felt that the corporation worked ineffectually and pushed through a bill reducing the proportion of elected councillors from two-thirds to one-half. Twenty-eight elected Bengali commissioners resigned; but a major reform of the corporation did not take place until 1923, in another era of Indian politics.[17]

Once we turn from the officially staged scene to the politics of the regional and national associations, we approach the more relevant and interesting questions of the age. Since mid-century, regional associations had been organized in Bombay, Madras, Calcutta, and a few other centers.[18] An examination of the regional groups and then of the Congress raises questions of Indian national identity: the extent of national consciousness, the relative strength of regional and national allegiances, the ways in which these associations were organized and for whom they spoke.

Charles Heimsath has suggested one definition of nationalism:

> an attitude of mind, or set of beliefs, that is shared by a group of people large enough to be influential, and that embodies ideas of the nation and the nation's goals, elevates those ideas to a prime position over other public values, and compels the assertion of the identity and aims of the nation.[19]

Heimsath, following Hans Kohn, emphasizes the configuration of attitudes in the populace involved. Another analyst, Karl Deutsch, points to cluster patterns of political organization, economy, literacy, and communication networks. These cluster patterns, he suggests, are affected by processes of assimilation and disassimilation which help to diminish or strengthen the cohesion of a given nation. The rise of nationalism, Deutsch argues, is related to a change of values, particularly to a new valuing of one's own kind.[20]

The organizational embodiments of growing political interest and consciousness in Bengal during the second half of the nineteenth century were the British Indian Association, founded in 1851, the Indian Association, begun in 1876, and the Bengali contingents in the Indian National Congress and the Central National Mohammedan Association. Throughout the period all these groups were almost totally made up of the urban, educated few.

The British Indian Association was a group of notables representing some of the wealthy and influential families in Bengal, almost all high-caste Hindu. They described themselves as a "middle class," but this term probably meant to them growing wealth, power, and respectability.[21] Their families had come to prominence with the Raj, often by working for it, and they resembled the rajas of the small kingdoms which had once composed Bengal. They claimed to speak for Indian society and were accepted in an advisory role by the government throughout the third quarter of the century. The association's membership was small and exclusive, with members of the Deb and Tagore

families often holding official positions. They stood, virtually unchallenged, at the top of a hierarchical society, and their positions of social
and economic power gave them a political role. They were not politicians in any modern sense, but rather amateur patrons whose credo did
not dictate extensive organization-building or gathering of supporters.
They initiated the politics of petitioning, acting as a small coterie of
influentials who reached the men in power when questions arose that
were of significance to them. The government of Bengal cooperated
by appointing a number of the association's members to the Bengal
Legislative Council.[22]

Their program included protection of their own economic interests
(e.g., the unquestioned continuity of the Permanent Settlement) and
the abstract support of other native groups on issues that did not interfere with those interests. Thus, they supported the peasants' indigo agitation, which was directed against European planters. They opposed
reforms which would have extended education, roads, and other kinds
of services to a large portion of Indian society at a cost to themselves.
Their loyalist stance made them "government men" in the eyes of new
political groups of the later nineteenth century. The government's alliance with urban and rural zamindars became one prop of stable British
rule.[23]

By the 1870s new men came to the fore to challenge these notables.
Surendranath Banerjea, the most able and persevering of the younger
men, explained that the older association could not do the tasks required of an Indian political organization in a new time. Sisirkumar
Ghosh of the *Amrita Bazar Patrika* was the catalyst in the formation
of the short-lived India League, which died of internal strife in 1876
soon after its founding.[24] But a year later, Banerjea organized a new
Indian Association which was to prove more durable. The younger,
mainly professional men who joined this latter group saw themselves as
middle-class, educated spokesmen who would represent the interests of
all Indians. Their rationale was that the illiterate masses could not
speak for themselves and the aristocracy spoke only for themselves. In
their three-tiered view of society, only the middle class, strategically
placed, could speak for all.[25]

The Indian Association and the life pattern of their "chief and
leader" Surendranath Banerjea mark an advance toward the formation

of a party and a political career.[26] Banerjea played a significant role in Indian politics for some fifty years. In his autobiography, *A Nation in Making*, he explained that he was specially fitted to assume leadership by his caste status, education, and personal talents.[27] He wrote that he felt a connection both with his traditional grandfather and with his father, "a modern man" and physician from whom he learned "disinterestedness," "sympathy for the poor," and "abhorrence of sordid means." Elsewhere Banerjea noted that he always liked to build on what went before rather than starting anew. Following Burke, to whom he acknowledged a debt, he said that in politics there was a need for a positive relationship between generations and a continuity of tradition.[28] The families of the early Indian Association and Congress leaders had often had connections to the Raj and Calcutta for two or three generations and were socially and economically interlinked with British Indian Association families like the Debs.[29]

Banerjea's autobiography contains a number of incidents which show he had an image of himself as a competitor, usually winning, infrequently losing, but never daunted. His first rebellion was against his private tutor, who Banerjea felt did not show him the respect due a kulin Brahman. He also believed in striving for social betterment and mentions the Brahmo movement, the temperance movement, and Vidyasagar's crusade for widow remarriage as archetypes of movements organized to serve idealistic ends.[30]

Banerjea went to England in the late 1860s to prepare for the ICS examination. Within a short time he was faced with two serious crises. The first was a dispute about his age which would determine his eligibility for the examination. He survived this predicament, with the aid of influential help in Calcutta and London, proving that he was a year younger than officials said he was. As a result, he began to see his own battles as an Indian cause, tied in with the fate of all his countrymen. The second crisis led to his dismissal from the ICS for what many thought inconsequential errors. This ouster closed a number of other career avenues, such as the bar. He was reduced, Indian friends told him, to death in life. But Banerjea transformed his dismissal into a lifelong cause, in which he sought to enlist all his countrymen.[31]

Within a short time Banerjea began to teach at Vidyasagar's Metropolitan Institution, joined in the work of Ananda Mohan Bose's Student Association, and together with Bose formed the Indian Association. Both a teacher and an extracurricular political guide, Banerjea linked together his educational and political work. He disagreed with critics who said that students should keep out of politics and became instrumental in shaping the role of future political leaders as he guided the students in public activity.[32] In the Indian Association, Banerjea found a role as guru and leader for older men. Working in both areas he also discovered a message to convey.

Banerjea instructed young and old that India was one and needed help, particularly from the devoted young, in rising from her divided and degraded state to new successes. He dwelt on India's achievements in learning, mathematics, morals, religion, and even war. The past greatness of India was primarily Hindu and Aryan, but the unity of the future would be built by all regions, communities, and religions. He likened himself to Mazzini raising a fallen and degraded Italy.[33]

Bose, who had amassed a modest fortune at the bar and from Assam tea investments, preferred to work behind the scenes, while Banerjea liked to be out front. For fifty years the Indian Association was dominated by a small group of men; like the British Indian Association and the Indian National Congress it was a caucus rather than a mass party.[34] It was the selector of delegates from Bengal to the Indian National Congress until about 1918. The leaders were based in and near Calcutta, but they made efforts to establish branches in mofussil towns. Several were founded in Midnapur, Pabna, Howrah, Hooghly, Nadia, and Jessore.[35]

As conceived by its leaders, the work of the association was petitioning the government and "educating public opinion." Banerjea was its foremost speaker and toured northern and western India giving his views on ICS requirements, freedom of the press, and representative government. To assist in shaping public opinion, Banerjea also determined to edit a newspaper. He bought the *Bengalee* with support from friends and began active work as a journalist, which he sustained until 1920. His many different activities, including positions in the Calcutta Corporation, the senate of the university, and legislative councils, were integrated with the roles of instructor, teacher, spokesman. His most critical function was the transmission of ideas, rather than creative thought. He could also be an able organizer and collector of the funds that were the practical accomplishment of his speaking.[36]

PUBLIC ISSUES AT STAKE

A number of public issues emerged in the early 1880s. The Ilbert bill concerned the right of Indian judges to try cases of Europeans in some circumstances. The European community in Bengal vigorously opposed it and together with Bengal's lieutenant governor, Rivers Thompson, they succeeded in rendering its provisions virtually meaningless. The liberal Ripon, then viceroy, could count on the support of all Indian political associations, but this was swept aside by the superior organization, passion, vituperation, and threats of the Europeans. In the course of the debate Rivers Thompson referred to "a want of nerve in the Native . . . in the presence of public excitement" and claimed that "reports before Government show innumerable cases in which a constitutional timidity had led natives to shirk duty because it is difficult." [37]

On a second issue, the Bengal Tenancy bill, Indian political organizations in Bengal were divided. The British Indian Association was opposed, while the Indian Association and Ameer Ali's Central National Mohammedan Association supported it. Like many passed in the nineteenth century, this bill tried to partially compensate the Bengali peasant for the neglect of his rights by the Permanent Settlement of 1793. The bill was passed, but did not significantly change the peasant's lot. By this time the British Indian Association was properly identified as the organ of large zamindars, while the associations of Banerjea and Ameer Ali, with a more populist line, claimed to speak also for the common peasant.[38]

Soon after the Ilbert bill debacle, Banerjea was arrested and tried for contempt of court; at issue was his attack on a judge who had brought a "salingam," a stone idol, into court. As a Brahman and as a spokesman for his countrymen, Banerjea said he objected. The court held that his language was too strong and he was sentenced to prison. He became one of the first of many nationalists to go to prison willingly; at a time when his popularity was not at its height, he suddenly became a martyr. Expressions of support came in from other parts of the country. As in the Ilbert and Bengal Tenancy bill events, the center of political activity was in Calcutta. The causes of Bengal, Banerjea and others asserted, were the causes of India. Using publicity gained from his court case, Banerjea started a national fund, and national conferences were held in Calcutta in 1883 and 1885.[39]

But Banerjea's efforts were too uniformly Bengal-centered to gain national support. Political leaders from other regions, a number of ex-civilians, and some other Bengalis joined in the first Indian National Congress session in Bombay in 1885. This was the beginning of a successful and enduring political organization into which the Indian Association and Banerjea soon knotted themselves.[40]

The Congress, particularly throughout its first twenty years, was dominated by a small group of men from Bombay, Bengal, and Madras and did not genuinely seek mass support until the Gandhian age. During its first few annual gatherings, resolutions were passed calling for reforms in the legislative councils and ICS and objecting to heavy military expenditures. But thereafter the leaders began to concentrate on defining the rules and membership regulations of the Congress and procedures for choosing leaders. Despite a number of changes and the organization of a kind of executive body, the Indian Congress Committee, in 1899, the Congress remained democratic in appearance and oligarchic in practice.[41] Looseness in its organizational procedures coupled with actual control by a number of powerful men did not present the best example from an association claiming to represent all groups in Indian society. Ironically, W. C. Bonnerjee, a wealthy Calcutta barrister, said in the first presidential speech to the Congress, "Surely never had so important and comprehensive an assemblage occurred within historical times, on the soil of India." [42]

The Congress itself did not elect representatives to any officially constituted bodies and did not represent any popular constituency in a direct way. However, it gradually gained recognition from officials both in India and in London as an important voice of Indian opinion, even though some labeled it a "microscopic minority." This denigrating attitude long continued among some Europeans.[43]

But the power bases were still in the presidencies, especially in their major cities, and the Congress organization was not yet a power base for its leaders. The Indian Association conducted Congress affairs in Bengal and formed a local standing committee of the Congress. The small group of men who dominated the Indian Association, plus a few other notables like W. C. Bonnerjee, represented Bengal; and from this relatively small circle, Bengal supplied 9 Congress presidents, 3 of whom served a second time. Through the first 32 years of the Congress, Bengalis served as president for 12 of them.[44]

The official historian of the Indian Association writes of its being "engulfed by Congress." But the organizations continued to be interlocked, assumedly both benefiting from the relationship, until the end of World War I.[45] The Indian Association organized the first Bengal Provincial Conference in 1888.[46] Annual provincial conferences began to be held more or less regularly from this period, and the Bengal conference served as a stimulus to other regions. The Congress had provincial bases, and the provincial organizations had a national center to coordinate their efforts with those in other regions. But the Congress was not yet the instrument of mass mobilization it could become. Much attention was still given to lobbying in London.[47]

The Bengalis' importance in the early leadership of the Congress went with a self-image which placed them at the center of Indian political activity and thought. Surendranath Banerjea told a public meeting of the Students' Association in Calcutta in 1878:

> Now, gentlemen, I think I speak the sentiments of my educated countrymen, when I say that we Bengalis do not aspire to occupy the position of leaders. We are only anxious that the light which is in us, that the light under which we have basked for so many long years, should spread over the whole of India and chase away that cimmerian darkness which has settled over the intellectual and moral atmosphere of this great country.[48]

Writing at the end of the period in which Bengal was seen by its Hindu political leaders as the center of Indian politics, Amvica C. Mazumdar said:

> As Europe is unthinkable without France, so India would be unthinkable without Bengal . . . Alert, keen-sighted, enthusiastic, acute, fiery, go-ahead Bengal is the fountainhead of ideas and the centre of patriotic inspiration . . . —where can you find a land so fertile and a people so sharp in intellect, so subtle in perception, so persuasive in eloquence, so cosmopolitan in ideas and so sanguine in patriotic fervour? With all her faults and frailties Bengal has always held the beaconlight to the rest of modern India and marched at the van of all movements religious, social and political.[49]

It would take a lengthy study to determine how widespread were the sentiments expressed by Mazumdar and his "chief and guru" Surendranath Banerjea. But it is fair to say that many in the politically alive circles felt them. It is equally clear that resentments rose against Bengalis and against the European community in Calcutta for what was felt to be their unfairly large voice in Indian politics.[50]

There were also a few disquieting notes in the symphony of moderate achievements during the last quarter of the nineteenth century. First, almost all Bengali peasants and most Muslims in Bengal were outside the Congress and Indian Association. Second, the politics of Calcutta was already divided into many sniping factions of which the Banerjea-Indian Association was only the most conspicuous. Third, though moderate leaders talked of representing all the people, they did not have a sense of the enormous task of developing from a small caucus party into a mass organization.

Among the Bengalis who took part in Indian Association work from the 1870s to the Swadeshi period there is scarcely a mention of a Muslim. Abdul Kasim of Burdwan enters briefly. The lack of Muslim participation was evident to association leaders. In a speech entitled "An Appeal to the Mohamedan Community" to a Congress meeting in Dacca, 1888, Banerjea argued that the Congress was open to all:

> I claim for the Congress that its programme is the most catholic, the most comprehensive, the most admirably suited to the varied requirements of the different sections of the great Indian community. Its concessions are such as will benefit Hindus and Mohamedans alike.[51]

His remarks point to a dilemma which the Congress leadership in Bengal (and elsewhere) never satisfactorily solved: the Muslims, educated or peasant, were not drawn to the Congress in large numbers except during the first Noncooperation movement, which was harnessed to the Khilafat agitation after World War I. There were Muslim members of the British Indian Association's delegation to the government in 1879 and a few Muslims in the Indian Association, but none in their inner coteries.[52]

Several reasons may be offered here and amplified later. First, as will be evident in the career of Ameer Ali analyzed in chapter 2, many of the aristocratic or middle-class, educated Muslims of Bengal did not consider themselves Bengalis. Their origins lay outside Bengal and they found it easier to join a Muslim organization that included many Muslims from different parts of the country, like Ameer Ali's Central National Mohammedan Association, than to play a secondary role in an organization dominated by Bengali Hindus. When Muslim leaders in Calcutta, Bengali or non-Bengali, did turn to politics their first interest was often to secure government help for the slowly developing Muslims of Bengal, who were primarily poor cultivators. This was never an important concern of the Indian Association and only briefly a concern of Bengali Congress members during the 1920s.

Second, from what we do know about Muslim political activity in Bengal, it appears that it was much easier to touch rural and poor Muslims with the cry of "Islam in danger," often in conjunction with a down-to-earth economic program. The Bengali national leaders of the period we are considering said they spoke for all Bengalis, but the symbols they used and the achievements they referred to were predominantly Hindu. There seems little in the words of Bankim Chandra Chatterjee, Vivekananda, Keshub Sen, Bipin Pal, Surendranath Banerjea, or Romesh Dutt that would appeal to Muslims. In fact, to Bankim Chandra and to some of the Swadeshi leaders, the Muslims were foreigners, intruders in India, who would be allowed to stay as the guests of temporary hosts, the British, and their long-term landlords, the Hindus. There is an insensitivity to the Muslims which continues through the nationalist period and is only occasionally dispelled.[53]

The Muslims had Abdul Latif's Mohammadan Literary Society, established in 1863, and Ameer Ali's Central National Mohammedan Association, founded in 1877; but these were concerned primarily with Muslim interests, although Ali often spoke on broader Indian and Islamic questions.

Bengali peasants as well remained outside early nationalist politics. In the nineteenth century some Bengali cultivators, both Hindu and Muslim, engaged at different times in protest movements which bordered on small-scale rebellions. Among these were the indigo disturbances; a rent revolt in Pabna; and the Fara'idi movement among Muslim peasants and craftsmen in the Faridpur, Pabna, Bakarganj, Dacca, and Noakhali districts in the 1830s to 1850s. In almost all these cases there were economic grievances which either precipitated the disturbances or were utilized by the leaders of the rebellions to marshal support. In the case of the Fara'idis an ideology of religious purity was spread in conjunction with the raising of economic grievances against Hindu zamindars and European planters. Although we now have a

useful study of this movement, it is still not clear how specific economic hardships helped to generate it. The general point to be made
about these diverse rebellions is that it was (and is) possible in some
areas and at some times to utilize economic distress in building a protest movement.[54]

There undoubtedly have been and continue to be serious problems
in building what some call a "national peasantry," and political leaders
in India are still wrestling with this task. In the light of the points
made about social organization in rural Bengal, it appears that those
who come from the outside in search of support and assistance might
encounter a number of difficulties in enlisting peasant support. The
process of census-taking in Bengal offers some insights into such problems. Each of the officials in charge of the census, from the first one in
1872, noted that the peasants were suspicious of outsiders, fearing that
they might be men sent to make investigations preliminary to raising
taxes. In some instances they even rioted to prevent the taking of the
census. It is also noteworthy that the number of enumerators needed to
carry out the census in 1901 was more than 400,000.[55] Granted that the
ideal of political organizing is the recruiting of local men who will
work at enlisting the support of their kinsmen and neighbors, the large
number of enumerators points to the magnitude of the population and
of the tasks involved in enlisting actual cultivators rather than a few
notables in each district.

The first generation of nationalist leaders in Bengal had a grandiose
vision of a bright future of representative government within the British Empire. Bengalis, they imagined, would play a significant role in
politics and administration, as they had under the rulers' shadow, particularly relative to other regional groups in the nineteenth century.

But the dark side was there too: constant and cutting criticism of
the Banerjea group from the *Indian Mirror, Amrita Bazar Patrika, Ban-
gabasi*, and from other groups.[56] The Banerjea group, of course, fought
back, and the continual infighting so well known in modern Bengal
was under way within and outside the nationalist movement. They
were simply a small caucus party of nationalists without power or
wide support. Making a national movement that included real participation by even a smattering of other sections of the population was a
task not yet envisioned. Some of these problems arise again in a consid-

eration of the Swadeshi period. But before turning to the next generation, consideration will be given to Bengali nationalist and Muslim ideology through an exploration of the lives of their chief articulators, Romesh Dutt and Ameer Ali.

TWO

Identity, History, Ideology: Romesh Chunder Dutt and Syed Ameer Ali

Romesh Dutt and Ameer Ali have usually been seen in separate lines of development in India, Dutt as a Congress ideologue, Ali as a modernizer of Islam and spokesman for the Muslim community.[1] But I suggest that in comparing the groups with whom they identified and the causes and concerns into which they threw their considerable life-energies, we will learn much about Indian and Bengali leadership in the early nationalist period, about Hindu-Muslim relations, and about the ways in which men of that time used historical analysis and cultural traditions for political purposes.

In such an examination it is important to see the total range of each man's activities and the timing of these activities as well as all the groups which were important to him. Therefore, it is necessary to look at Romesh Dutt's novels and school histories as well as his writings on social and economic questions; it is necessary to look at Ameer Ali's writings on law and on general political questions as well as his works on Islam.

It is necessary to note here that Ameer Ali represented one of several cultural and political trends current among Muslims in Bengal during the nationalist period. The trend he embodied was the pan-Islamic one eventually expressed in the Pakistan movement which at a crucial period of Bengal's history (1943–1947) had widespread support among Bengali Muslims. The other major trend, which had little meaning to Ameer Ali, emphasized the distinctiveness of Bengali Muslims both as Bengalis and as Muslims. This second trend, submerged for many years and shunned by the Urdu-speaking, upper-class leaders among the

Bengal Muslims, has now flowered in the creation of an independent nation of Bangladesh.

There are many similarities in the life-histories of the two men. Dutt was born in 1848, Ali in 1849, and both had their education in the Calcutta area. Both came from families associated with cultural achievements and with service to the Raj. Dutt went to England in 1868, passed the ICS examination, and was called to the bar in 1871. Ali went to England in 1869 and was called to the bar in 1873. Both read widely in English literature and history, identified with the Liberal Party, and developed a warm, enduring affection for the English. At some point early in life each determined to seek a literary reputation in England as well as in his native country. Dutt returned to India in 1871 and served with distinction in the ICS until 1897. At the same time he pursued a literary career in both English and Bengali. Ali returned to India in 1873 and had a distinguished career as a barrister and judge of the Calcutta High Court until he retired in 1904. Ali too followed a literary career concurrently with his public service, writing on Islam, Muslim law, and Saracenic history. At the end of their public service, both men retired to England. Dutt entered the service of the Gaekwar of Baroda a few years before his death in 1909. Ali lived on until 1928 much concerned with the fate of the Caliphate during his last years.

Both men served in the Bengal Legislative Council; Ali also served in the Imperial Legislative Council. Both of them were active in Indian political organizations, Dutt in the Indian National Congress, of which he was president for one year, Ali in the Central National Mohammedan Association of which he was the founder and long-time secretary. Both saw themselves in tune with the liberal, rational, and scientific trends of nineteenth-century Europe. They took similar positions on a range of political questions, including the Bengal Tenancy bill in the 1880s. Both believed in favoring Indian economic interests over British ones in the shaping of the policies of the Raj, and more extensive use of Indians in the various services of the government of India; they were opposed to those Indians advocating more extreme political actions against the Raj in the early twentieth century. Each saw himself as a man of intelligence and talent who had succeeded primarily through his own talents and hard work, although he had enjoyed advantages in social status and economic comfort. At times each saw himself as a spokesman for the Indian people, a member of the class most qualified to speak for all, not bound by any narrow class interest.

Again, in moving to the larger intellectual questions to which Dutt and Ali addressed themselves, we find many similarities. Each wrote works of history and studied the cultural traditions of people with whom he identified. Each searched for pasts which were relevant to his people in the present and tried to give an account of these traditions to a popular readership in India and in the West. Writing at a time when cultural apologetics and reform movements were under way in many parts of the non-Western world, Dutt and Ali wrote as selective justifiers and as critics of the past. Both were concerned with what one might call the cultural problem of East and West, or West and non-West: the need for non-Westerners in the age of imperialism to find cultural equivalency, equality of native and European traditions.[2]

The West and non-West theme may also be seen in the practical aspects of their literary careers. Both published their major works in London and wrote primarily in English. They saw themselves playing link roles; they wanted to bring the essential history of India, Bengal, Islam and the Saracens, to Western readers so that the Western public would confront these essential pasts and come to have greater respect and sympathy for India and for the Muslims in various parts of the world.

After a tour through the careers of each in turn, we will return to the comparison.

R. C. DUTT, ICS: INDIAN NATIONALIST

Romesh Chunder Dutt was the leading ideologue and writer among the early congressmen from Bengal. Although an ICS career man, he considered himself a member of the "band of patriotic workers" which dominated the Congress for a generation.[3] His novels, translations, histories, and writings on political and economic questions offer an extensive field for investigating the views and values of the early nationalists.

The Dutt family of Rambagan came from Burdwan district in western Bengal. His great-grandfather Nilmoni moved to Calcutta in the second half of the eighteenth century and became acquainted with such powerful Calcutta families as the Debs of Sobhabajar. Sons and grandsons of Nilmoni were employed in the Bengal Secretariat, the Accounts Department, and the courts. The family was active in the cultural life of the Bengalis in the city as well as in government service, and relatives of Romesh Dutt produced histories, poems, translations.[4]

Romesh attended the Hare School and then Presidency College, the elite college of Bengal, which both his father and his guardian had attended. He did well, placing second in the first Arts examination, and then traveled to England with his friends Surendranath Banerjea and Bihari Lal Gupta to sit for the ICS examination. The three young men went without parental consent and Romesh later described it as a momentous and difficult undertaking. His last thoughts upon leaving India were gloomy, lonely, melodramatic, but his prospects were good, and he was shortly tied into the Bengali network that bridged Calcutta and England.[5] Man Mohan Ghose had helped the young men to go to England and they were friendly with his younger brother Lal Mohan Ghose once they arrived. At Southampton they were met by W. C. Bonnerjee, who took them to London. They were later friendly with Ananda Mohan Bose, then a student at Cambridge. These few contacts give a sense of the close-knit quality of the Bengali establishment men in their young manhood.[6] In numerous cases friendships and alliances were made early in life which survived the decades ahead. The circle described in memoirs and letters includes only high-caste Hindus who had first achieved success in Calcutta and were moving out into the great world. All became establishment men and Congress leaders.

Dutt, Banerjea, and Gupta attended classes in London and passed the ICS examination, Dutt placing second among candidates in the final examination. He also spent eight terms at the Middle Temple and was called to the bar in 1871. During the same period, he read widely in English literature and history, traveled through Europe, and gained an intimate experience of English life and politics. Dutt and his compatriots witnessed the election of 1868.

> Every man in this country considers himself as a constituent of a great nation, prides himself on his nationality and the glory of the nation, and therefore keeps an eye on the welfare of his country . . . the people are the Government. Societies are formed by the persons desirous of bringing on some reform, they have their sittings, their lectures,

their pamphlets, they write articles in newspapers, they publish books to support their cause. Thus they go on influencing the public mind and convincing the people that a reform is needed. . . . They know that the will of the *people* is the law of the land, and if the people show increasing interest in their cause they are sure to succeed, otherwise their cause must of course be given up.[7]

It was during these years that the political socialization of Dutt, and presumably of his young fellow Indians, took place. Dutt's goals of national self-government and political participation by the people, the style of petitioning, forming societies, lobbying, and trying to shape public opinion owe much to the observations of these years; so, too, does Dutt's faith in the ultimate justice of the English public and enlightened English leaders.[8]

One might almost suggest that Dutt had an English identity interlaced with his Indian one. His writings, especially in these years, are filled with British literary and historical references. In politics, he supported the liberals against the conservatives. Later in life, he spent many years in England; it had been one of the dreams of his active years to retire to England. Writing of his travels, Dutt suggested that young Indians should all travel to Europe to see the freedom and the equality between men and women evident in the West.[9]

Returning to Bengal, Dutt served in many positions and had a distinguished career in the ICS from 1871 to 1897. He rose to positions which had not often been held by Indians before him. In 1894 he became officiating divisional commissioner of Burdwan and he might have risen even higher but for objections in the Anglo-Indian press to his ruling over Europeans. But his vigorous work in fighting plague and famine in Bakarganj—indeed, his efficiency at every post—belied the stereotype of the Bengali civil servant.[10]

Although he complained that "civilians are not allowed to speak aloud on the subject of politics," he published *The Peasantry of Bengal* in 1874, and in 1882 a critical assessment of the career of the retiring lieutenant-governor, Sir Ashley Eden. The former was his first substantial contribution to the social and economic history of India. In one way or another, he also publicized his views on the Bengal Tenancy bill, the Age of Consent bill, and the Chaukidari (village watchmen) Act.[11]

While moving from district to district he completed a three-volume history of ancient India, six Bengali novels, numerous translations of Hindu scriptures and Sanskrit poetry, school texts, and a short history of Bengali literature. He gained recognition by becoming a fellow of the Imperial Institute and the Royal Asiatic Society in Britain and by attaining the presidency of the Bangiya Sahittya Parishad, the leading literary association of Bengal.[12]

Upon retirement, Dutt returned to England to organize an "Indian party of sympathetic Englishmen" to influence the British Parliament through prominent members and to educate the British public in popular versions and accounts of Indian history and literature. In addition, he lectured in Indian history at University College, London, and wrote extensively on the history of British rule in India. He completed condensations of the *Mahābhārata* and the *Rāmāyana* in English verse. He was made a fellow of the Royal Society of Literature and served on the Royal Commission on Decentralization.[13]

In 1899 an intensive campaign was waged against the Calcutta Municipal Bill by Surendranath Banerjea and Raja Binay Krishna Deb in Calcutta. Dutt was appointed by Deb "the representative of the inhabitants of Calcutta" to oppose the bill in England. The measure, however, was passed; Indian members of the Calcutta Corporation resigned, and Dutt became pessimistic both about the progress toward self-governing institutions in India and about the value of British rule. The style of the Bengali politicians is evident: they held meetings, signed petitions, and tried to influence members of Parliament and public opinion in Britain.[14]

Late in 1899, Dutt was invited through his friend W. C. Bonnerjee, who was also spending his later years in England, to serve as president of the Indian National Congress. Dutt returned to India for the honor and delivered his presidential address in Lucknow. Shortly back in England, he cooperated with Bonnerjee and Dadabhai Naoroji in lobbying on Indian questions and forming the Indian Famine Union. Dutt debated with government officials on land revenue assessments, which he claimed were too high, and completed his *Economic History of India in the Nineteenth Century*. Finally succumbing to the offer of the Gaekwar of Baroda, he joined the Gaekwar's service as revenue minister in 1904. In 1908 he was back in England serving on the Royal

Commission on Decentralization and discussing the reforms with officials. The following year he died of a heart ailment.

As a practical complement to his interest in economic affairs, Dutt
served as president of the Industrial Conference held in conjunction
with the Congress in 1905 and 1907. He supported the Swadeshi movement, but dismissed the Extremists as men of no consequence who
would quickly fade from the scene. He supported the Morley-Minto
reforms (see chapter 3) in general and discussed them with Morley, but
opposed separate electorates for Muslims.[15]

Through his writing, Romesh Dutt set himself a number of tasks and
addressed himself to several audiences. In his prefaces he specifies these
audiences and explains how he will edify them. He saw himself per-
forming a number of link roles, providing an entrée to certain traditions which otherwise would be unavailable to these readers.

First he saw himself as a spokesman for enlightened public opinion
in India. He felt that he was interested in the prosperity of all Indians,
peasants, zamindars, urban educated, princes, etc., and that as a member of the educated and advanced group in the society, he could best
suggest what policies and programs would benefit the Indian nation.
He would have denied that he represented any regional, religious, or
class group. He may be seen in the liberal, utilitarian tradition of the
nineteenth century, but a utilitarianism with an authoritarian twist.
Dutt wanted the greatest good for the greatest number and felt the enlightened man could, would, and must speak for all. He might have to
criticize a section of the population if injustice occurred; he would still
retain his detached and impartial position. Later in life he sought to become the Indian, or one of the key Indians, in England to whom all
would turn on Indian questions.[16]

Another role he sought was that of interpreter and transmitter of the
"true history of India" and of its poetry, literature, and religious texts
to Western readers. To this audience he addressed his works on ancient India, his translations of the epics and Indian verse, and his popu-
larizations of Indian history. For those in search of information about
mysterious India, Dutt offered facile condensations, translations, history; they have a simplicity which has led some to argue that they
missed completely the essence of Indian traditions. He did no original
work on ancient India; he felt it his job to present Indian history, tra-

ditions, and literature in a clear and balanced way, rather than offering erudite scholarship.[17]

Encouraged by Bankim Chandra Chatterjee, the most famous Bengali novelist of the nineteenth century, Dutt wrote six novels in Bengali and published translations of Sanskrit religious texts in Bengali. Dutt said he wanted to portray "the glories of our past and the greatness of our national heroes" in these works.[18] "National" in this context means Hindu: the heroes in the novels are Rajputs, Marathas, Bengali Hindus, and a few North Indian Hindus. These novels were part of the widespread effort in the nineteenth century and since to glorify Hindu courage and the Hindu religion. Others who contributed to the romanticization of the Hindu past were Bankim Chatterjee, Rabindranath Tagore, Dwijendralal Roy, and B. G. Tilak. One reader described the effects:

> The historical romances of Bankim Chandra Chatterji and Ramesh Chandra Dutt glorified Hindu rebellion against Muslim rule and showed the Muslims in a correspondingly poor light. Chatterji was positively and fiercely anti-Muslim. We were eager readers of these romances and we readily absorbed their spirit.[19]

The translation of Hindu scriptures into Bengali was, Dutt said, "for my countrymen" a political and cultural rather than a religious act. As a Kayastha and as a modern man, Dutt felt some antagonism against the restrictions of caste and the privileged position of the Brahman priests. Offering Bengali versions of religious texts was one part of the reform movement at work throughout the nineteenth century.

Dutt's school texts were a third set of works for specifically Hindu readers. These included histories of India and of Bengal that were frequently reprinted. In the preface to the first edition of *A Brief History of Ancient and Modern Bengal for the Use of Schools*, he wrote in 1892:

> For a Hindu boy, the History of Bengal should not commence with the conquest of the country by Bakhiyar Khalji. He should know of the cultured Vedehas who cultivated Vedic learning and composed the Upanishads in North Behar and developed those systems of Mental Philosophy and Logic which are still admired in Europe. He should know something of the Magadhas who gave a new religion to the

human race, of Asoka who ruled over the whole of Northern India
and sent Buddhist missionaries to Syria, Greece and Egypt, and of the
University of Nalanda during the centuries immediately succeeding the
Christian Era. He should know of the Kesari and Ganga Kings of Orissa who ruled over the country for over a thousand years, and covered it with temples and edifices which still claim our admiration. And
he should know of the Pala and the Sena Kings of Bengal, the former
of whom extended their rule for a time over the whole of Northern
India. I have considered it necessary to narrate these facts of the
Hindu Period in five chapters in order that some recollections of them
may live in the minds of educated Hindus long after they have ceased
to be students.[20]

In this book, the author never addressed himself to Muslim students
or to English readers, although he spent five chapters on Muslim rule
and five more on the British period. He was aiming at the formation of
pro-Hindu attitudes in the schools. As with his Bengali translations of
Sanskrit scriptures, he was aiming at Bengali Hindus in need of guidance. They were likely to be high caste, like Dutt himself. The unanti-
cipated consequence of these writings was to contribute to anti-Muslim
bias.

Dutt wrote for the reading public of the two places where he spent
his life, Bengal and Britain. In both places he sought and achieved a literary reputation.[21] Thus, in his version of the Indian past, Dutt concentrated on the ancient Hindu period and the modern British period,
writing much more skimpily on the age of Muslim predominance.

As sources for his works on ancient India and on the literature of
Bengal, Dutt uses literary and religious texts, apparently guided by the
nineteenth-century positivist notion that literature is a mirror of the
age in which it was written.[22] His assumptions show that he has taken
prescriptions for ideal behavior in such texts to be descriptions of actual life.

Dutt sometimes mentions a belief in the "progress of the human
mind." In large part, his historiography is derived from French writers
of the Enlightenment and from British historians of the nineteenth century. Dutt had in common with most of these writers a belief in progress, a tendency to label historical periods in terms of either literary
texts or qualities of mind or both, the use of environmental or climatic

explanations of historical phenomena, and a belief that the task of the historian is to describe the conditions of the people, not to be confined to political narrative.[23]

In *A History of Civilization in Ancient India*, Dutt divided the pre-Muslim history of India into five periods: Vedic, Epic, Rationalistic, Buddhist, and Puranic.[24] When he wrote his brief but more comprehensive book the *Civilization of India* some years later, he called the Rationalistic period the "age of laws and philosophy," divided the Buddhist period into two parts, and added periods of Rajput, Afghan, Mughal, and Maratha rule.[25]

Like Rammohan Roy, Keshub Sen, Vivekananda, and Aurobindo, Romesh Dutt saw Indian history as a great rise followed by a decline. But Dutt differs from these writers in the values he gave to past periods and institutions. Dutt noted the "unique charm" of the Vedas and saw in them the "workings of a simple and manly heart."[26] He paid tribute to the mysteries of the Upanishads, but he did not have the reverence for these early religious texts and truths that was shown by the other Indians mentioned. Although Dutt's own religious beliefs are not clear, he appears to have been an agnostic, for his treatment of religion was perfunctory and concerned primarily with its social implications. Dutt preferred religions which preached equality, and so he nodded toward Buddhism, Christianity, and even Islam, while frowning on Hinduism, especially as it became more intertwined with rigid caste rules. Dutt wrote:

> Later religions are free from this weakness which has crept into Hinduism. . . . It is natural for men to seek to improve their position, and the Sudras of India, to whom Hinduism in the past and in the present has been so cruel, have struggled hard to improve their status by accepting Buddhism or Vaishnavism or Islamism or anything else which has offered them a chance. . . . Hinduism with all its noble traditions, its rich moral lessons, and its ancient wealth of philosophy and deep thought, has continuously suffered in the past by its exclusive caste-system. In the future, a catholic and all-embracing love and a brotherly recognition of equality may re-unite and save; an uncharitable exclusiveness will disunite and destroy.[27]

He never suggested that Indian religions had any special value for humanity that other religions do not have. In fact, Dutt's position was that Hinduism needed an infusion of the egalitarian ethic of other religions to improve it. He viewed Indian religions with only formal respect and occasionally with a tinge of condescension.

Since the Vedas are held in such awe and respect by Hindus, Dutt did cite them both in his history and in controversies over contemporary reform acts to show that they did not prescribe sati or a low status for women, or forbid sea voyages and the remarriage of widows. He claimed that the rules cited by the opponents of reform were later innovations unknown in the Vedic Age.[28]

Instead of the age of the Vedas and the Upanishads, Dutt thought the "Rationalistic age" (1000–320 B.C.) represented the height of Indian culture. He set a high value on the achievements in science and mathematics, philosophy and drama, that took place in this period.[29] For the more mystically inclined, this period was the end of the "wonder that was India." Dutt also praised Buddhism as a religion of "love and equality" which was accepted by a "living nation." With the decline of Buddhism, India started going downhill.[30]

There is another difference between Dutt and the advocates both of India's Upanishadic greatness and of India's mission in the modern world, for Dutt felt that significant shortcomings existed even in India's greatest eras, especially in what he called the "absence of any efforts after popular freedom." [31] He regretted that one could not rise on his own merits in ancient India and that even in their heyday Indians had shown a "lack of genius in industrial arts." [32]

In Dutt's history of ancient India, certain negative and positive values were implicit. The positive terms are strength, power, vigor, beauty, simplicity, and "healthy joyousness." The negative ones are weakness, deadness, enervation, decadence. The earlier periods, Vedic, Epic, Rationalistic, Buddhist, were characterized by the first set of terms, while the later periods, especially the era of Afghan and Mughal rule, were described with the negative words. The terms Dutt used are parameters of his own outlook. They all describe surface, almost visible characteristics. Like Vivekananda and many of his English contemporaries, Dutt used strength or power as a measure of quality. There is no special spiritual connotation here. He meant physical force, which was the manifestation of inner strength.[33]

For Dutt, the Puranic age and succeeding centuries were marked by decadence and decline. Vigor and creativity ended, new discoveries in mathematics and science and even creative experiments in art and literature were rare. Trade, sea voyages, the high status of women—all these declined. Dutt described these centuries as ones of "political decadence and the ascendancy of priests." [34] In several sections he gave a history of the development of caste and the rise of the priests who enforced the caste structure and who were responsible for imposing "barbarous rules" from the time of Manu. Dutt claimed that Manu's theory of mixed castes had been accepted by superstitious Indians for centuries and never subjected to rational criticism. He noted that

> the caste-system, which unduly exalted the powers and privileges of priests, had the inevitable result of degrading all honest trades and industries other than that of priests. We noted this in the pages of Manu himself; we note this still more prominently in the pages of Yajnavalkya. In a passage which we have referred to before, he condemns a large class of professions as impure, and classes physicians, goldsmiths, blacksmiths, weavers, dyers, armourers, and oil manufacturers with thieves and prostitutes! Thus the caste-system in its later phase has served a twofold object, as our readers will note from passages like these. It has served to *divide the nation* and create mutual ill-feeling. And it has served to *degrade the nation* in order to exalt the priests.[35]

During the centuries when priests were enslaving the people, Muslims—first Afghans, then Mughals—ruled India. In *Early Hindu Civilisation*, Dutt wrote that the Hindus spent "seven centuries of national lifelessness under Musalman rule," and in this period such Hindu shortcomings as caste, priest-domination, and loss of creativity in art and science became even more exaggerated.[36] Sometimes he discussed the Hindu nation, with the Muslims a stratum set on top, while at other times the Muslims became an integrated part of the nation. Dutt occasionally praised the Muslim rulers because, unlike the British, they sent no tribute out of India, so that there was no drain on Indian resources. Dutt mentioned the greatness of Akbar in the *Civilization of India* and also said that the self-governing institutions of the people had been left untouched under the Muslims,[37] a happier situation than the ruin of village self-government under the British.

Dutt, among others, has been criticized for depicting the village communities as egalitarian institutions, forgetting their inequalities and their ties to the caste system.[38] This is a fair criticism of his *Economic*

History, but it should be measured against Dutt's own descriptions of the priest-dominated society in his ancient history and in *The Peasantry of Bengal*. In the latter work, Dutt depicts the ruthless exploitation of peasants by zamindars in pre-British India.[39]

Later in life, Dutt began to see the zamindars as more benevolent and British rule as harsher than he had earlier thought. His affection for Hindu institutions grew as he saw the increasingly destructive effects of British rule. The onset of a new dark age of imperialism at the end of the nineteenth century made the age of the Afghan and Mughal empires look brighter. He wrote in his *Economic History*:

> And the people lived in peace in their ancient village communities, managing their own village concerns, enjoying the most complete autonomy in their village administration, and paying to the king's representatives the tax assessed on every village. These self-governing village-communities existed in India from the dawn of history to the close of the eighteenth century after Christ; they survived the fate of dynasties and empires; they escaped danger and destruction when rival chiefs or races strove for the imperial power.[40]

Dutt described at length how the interests of the rulers were identical with those of their subjects. They took no wealth out of the country, and "Indian manufactures filled the markets of Europe." [41] But Dutt's accounts of happy days in pre-British India were more anti-British than pro-Muslim.

Dutt scarcely ever forgot that the essential Indian nation was Hindu. In the *Civilization of India*, he wrote:

> The waves of foreign conquest did not weaken the Hindu nation or the Hindu rule. Each new race of invaders from the first to the fifth century after Christ settled down in India, accepted Hinduism or Buddhism, and thus merged into and strengthened the confederation of Hindu races in ancient India.[42]

The Muslim rulers, like these earlier conquerors, were simply a thin stratum at the top; beneath, the normal current of Hindu economic and religious life flowed on.

The novels deal in great part with the very period of Muslim domination which Dutt neglected in his histories.[43] The heroes of *Banabijetā* (1874) [44] are the Hindu governor of Bengal, Todar Mull; a young Bengali Hindu, Surendra Nath Chaudhuri; and a Hindu priest, Chandra

Shekar; of *Mādhabīkaṅkaṇ* (1877),[45] another young Bengali Hindu, Noren; of *Māhārāṣṭra Jīban-prabhāt* (1878),[46] the Maratha general Shivaji; and of *Rājput Jīban-Sandhyā* (1879),[47] the Rajput prince, Pratap Singh. These are the four historical novels. The main characters and heroes of a later "domestic" novel, *Sansar* (written in the 1890s and published posthumously),[48] are all Bengali Kayasthas living under a most benevolent British Raj.

The historical novels, rather than the domestic ones, were the more widely known. In these, Hindus are extolled for their martial exploits, bravery, religious motivation, and administrative skill. Here are Hindu heroes who can stand comparison, the writer and readers may have believed, with Muslim or British conquerors of India.[49]

For example, Dutt depicts Shivaji as a man motivated by religious and patriotic fervor, devoted to the goddess Bhawani and directed by her call.[50] Shivaji kills his Mughal enemies "by the grace of Bhawani," for intertwined with Shivaji's religious feeling is his patriotic and noble ambition to establish a Hindu Raj and restore Hindu freedom. The Muslims are described by one Hindu character as "enemies of our country and our religion." [51] Although the novelist mentions Akbar's wise policy of conciliation, he says that Aurangzeb is a dishonorer of the Hindu religion, deceitful, and barren of human emotion.[52] Shivaji's victories are described at length and his treachery, including lying and murdering an unarmed man to gain a triumph, are explained away as necessary means of fighting Muslims. Such methods, says Shivaji, are not to be used against fellow Hindus.

Dutt gives a much more prominent place to Shivaji's devotion to Bhawani than do other writers,[53] who mention his temple in honor of the goddess but do not give this religious feeling the centrality in Shivaji's life that Dutt does. The Mahratta devotion to Bhawani has its counterpart in the Bengali worship of Kali or Durga. It is somewhat strange that the seemingly agnostic Dutt of the histories should place such emphasis on religion in his historical novels.

Although Dutt wrote that the Indians opposed revolution and abhorred violence,[54] he himself contributed to the glorification of violence and revolution in his historical novels. It was the example of Shivaji, together with the ascetic revolutionaries of Chatterjee's *Ānandamaṭh*, upon which Bengali revolutionaries in part modeled themselves.

Dutt's belief that violence was foreign to the Indian people shows an extraordinary lack of historical and personal awareness.

In the *History of Civilization in Ancient India*, Dutt mentions Western borrowings from ancient Indian culture, especially the use of Buddhist concepts by the early Christians and the spreading of Aryan culture by the Greeks.[55] During the modern age, however, ideas flowed from the West to India.[56] It is for his numerous works on British rule in India that Romesh Dutt has gained most prominence. Even his most severe critic among his fellow Indians, Aurobindo Ghose, had some kind words for these writings:

> The best things he ever did were, in our view, his letters to Lord Curzon and his Economic History. The former fixed public opinion in India irretrievably and nobody cared even to consider Lord Curzon's answer. "That settles it" was the general feeling every ordinary reader contracted for good after reading this brilliant and telling indictment. Without the Economic History and its damning story of England's commercial and fiscal dealings with India we doubt whether the public mind would have been ready for the Boycott. In this one instance it may be said of him that he not only wrote history but created it.[57]

We must bear in mind that Dutt's writings about the recent past are propaganda as well as history. It is the combination of apparently impartial historical analysis with clearly nationalist views that have made the *Economic History* such a favorite of Indian readers.[58] Once he retired and came to England in 1897, he spent his time pouring over Blue Books, official reports and documents and accounts by travelers and civilians.[59]

Almost all these writings deal with economic matters—land revenue settlements, trade, tariffs, and industry. Dutt felt that India and England were closely interrelated in the nineteenth century and that developments in England produced effects in India.[60] This perception and his own tastes determined his decision to spend his retiring years in England lobbying and working for what he felt were the best interests of India.

Dutt's volumes on this period assessed British rule in India, its triumphs and failures.

The positive aspects of British rule which Dutt listed include the unification of the country, the bringing of order and justice and the transmission to Indians of modern trends of scientific and liberal political thought. Dutt judged British rule in India to have been beneficial insofar as the British helped to develop modern Western institutions—for example, a free press, self-governing institutions, and universities—and did not eradicate useful indigenous institutions.[61] The British made some initial errors, Dutt wrote in *The Peasantry of Bengal*, but then brought justice and a general advance in the conditions of the country. For the rule of *custom*, they substituted the more impartial and impersonal *right*.[62] About the beneficial currents of thought, Dutt said, "All that we wish to indicate is that the Hindu mind in the modern age has, under the influence of new light and progress, travelled once more in the same direction, though with feeble effort, as it did in the days of its ancient vigour." [63] Describing his native province under British rule, Dutt noted:

> The British conquest of Bengal was not merely a political revolution, but brought in a greater revolution in thought and ideas, in religion and social progress. The Hindu intellect came in contact with all that is noblest and most healthy in European history and literature, and profited by it. The Hindu mind was to some extent trained under the influence of European thoughts and ideas, and benefited by it.[64]

It should be noted that Dutt's most enthusiastic appreciations of British rule were written as a young man in the 1870s.

A major portion of Dutt's writing in the *Economic History* and his letters and papers from 1897 forward is devoted to the land revenue settlements. Years earlier, writing as a young ICS officer of 26, Dutt wrote, "Seldom in the annals of any country has hasty legislation been productive of effects so calamitous as the ill-conceived Permanent Settlement." [65] This little book is partially a diatribe against oppressive zamindars who Dutt said had rent-racked their peasants from time immemorial. But Dutt did not want to nullify the Permanent Settlement, turn out the zamindars, or make a new settlement with the ryots. He stated that he could not recommend such a revolution in the landholding system of Bengal, which had stood for long centuries and become a part and parcel of the society.[66] All that he demanded was some form of permanent restraint on the zamindars' rent demands. He was not the youthful radical whom Kristo Das Pal of the British Indian Association thought was recommending anarchy.[67]

His harsh criticism of the Permanent Settlement was blunted and became full-throated praise in the *Economic History*, but he still utilized
the same standards for evaluating the land revenue settlements. He
found the Bengal settlement beneficial in its long-range effects because,
together with the Tenancy Acts of 1859 and 1885, it brought security
to the zamindars and the ryots and shares for both in the rising prices
of food grains.[68] That both landlord and peasant shared the profits—
in what proportions he did not say—also proved the justice of the
Permanent Settlement. "Security" had to do simply with permanency.
If the revenue demand could not be raised or could only be raised in
proportion to rising prices, then it brought "security" to those on
whom it was imposed. If the demand were not permanent, then it
would bring "insecurity," the most evil state of life in which man
could live. This is Dutt's account of the one ideal land revenue settlement:

> The beneficial results of the Permanent Settlement of 1793, which lim-
> ited the State-demand from landlords, and the Rent acts of 1859 and
> 1885, which limited the landlord's demand from tenants, are obvious in
> every part of Bengal at the present day. There is an educated and influ-
> ential class of landlords, who have identified themselves with the Brit-
> ish rule, and have always given loyal help in the cause of good admin-
> istration. There is a strong and intelligent middle class, holding tenures
> of various degrees under the landlords, and forming the strongest
> element in a progressive society. And there is a resourceful peasantry,
> able to defend their rights, and able also to resist the first effects of a
> drought and a failure of crops. The rents are light; the cultivators are
> not under the thraldom of money-lenders; and British administrators
> can view with a just pride a province where their moderation has en-
> sured agricultural prosperity to a nation.[69]

His idyllic picture of Bengal in the second half of the nineteenth century is important, because it is against the prosperous and progressive
condition of his native presidency that he judged conditions in other
parts of British India where land revenue settlements were not as wisely
handled. This statement about the Punjab is typical:

> Lord Dalhousie . . . made the mistake, which has been made again and
> again by British rulers in India, of ignoring old leaders and old institu-
> tions and of trying to substitute the direct and personal rule of British
> officials. And in removing Sir Henry Lawrence from the Punjab, Lord

Dalhousie virtually uprooted his policy, swept aside the natural leaders
of the people, and brought a nation of cultivators directly under the
Government. The policy was neither wise in itself, nor has it con-
duced to good administration during the fifty years which have
elapsed since.

National institutions are the results and the outer expressions of national needs. The people of India developed Village Communities, and
lived under Polygars and Zemindars, Jaigirdars and Talukdars, Sardars
and Panchyets, because they needed them. Their social organisation
was built up according to their social requirements; they felt themselves
securer and happier under their born leaders or within their Rural Communities. It is unwise for any rulers to disturb such arrangements; it is
especially unwise for alien rulers to neglect the organised institutions
of a people.[70]

Dutt mentioned the prevalence of village communities in Madras, in
Bombay, and in North India.[71] His general argument for all these
areas was that the land revenue settlements were uncertain and excessive. He suggested that there should be an India-wide permanent settlement at a moderate assessment. It was his contention in the voluminous
writings of his last ten years, from 1899 to 1909, that excessive rates
and impermanent settlement were the major cause of famines and
agrarian disturbances in India. Only in Bengal, he claimed, where the
settlement was low and permanent and the ryots were protected did
neither of these unfortunate circumstances develop.

Another significant part of Dutt's *Economic History* was devoted to
questions of trade, industry, and tariffs. His general argument was that
policies on all these matters were made in Britain for the benefit of the
British. He presented extensive quotations and figures to show that the
British had killed indigenous industries like weaving and India's overseas export of industrial products in order to make India into an appen-
dage of the British economy, a supplier of raw materials and a market
for British manufactured goods.[72] In several respects, Dutt's argument
and ordering of data parallel Marxist analyses of imperialism, and his
data have been used by many later writers on British rule in India.[73]
But Dutt was no Marxist; he was an Indian nationalist. He was not an
opponent of capitalism or parliamentary democracy or even of feudal
princes, but an advocate of all Indian interests. He wanted nascent Indian manufacturing protected; he wanted tariffs in favor of Indian pro-
ducers, not British ones.

Yet another sphere in which indigenous institutions had been partially destroyed and no adequate new ones developed in their place was in the political system. The local village communities and the traditional landlords had been greatly weakened by the British and many areas formerly ruled by native princes had been taken under direct British administration. Dutt was remarkably indiscriminate in the native institutions he was willing to defend in his later years. Anything which had the touch of tradition, or had long been used to suit local needs, was defended. He claimed, for example, that "no part of India is better governed to-day than these States, ruled by their own princes." [74]

A theme which was hammered home relentlessly in the *Economic History* is the need for self-government in India, some way of giving "the children of the soil" a voice in how their country was to be ruled. Dutt described those who he felt should represent and help govern India as her natural, influential, educated, and moderate leaders. On the important question of how representation was to be determined, Dutt was vague because he did not have a political theory of representation. He included local zamindars and landlords, native princes, and spokesmen for "native associations," listing the Bombay Association, Poona Sarvajanik Sabha, Madras Native Association, British Indian Association, and the Congress among these.[75] He seemed to accept princes who ruled absolutely as well as the "influential," "moderate," and "educated" men in the associations noted above. He did not advocate parliamentary democracy for India, only self-government. This notion of representation was sufficiently vague to allow him to dismiss the "Extremists" of the early twentieth century as "men of no consequence" —since they were not as "moderate" or as "influential" as he and his fellow leaders of the Congress, and others in the early associations. Dutt stood for and with a generation which believed that men of position should rightfully dominate Indian politics and serve to communicate Indian opinion to officials in India and Britain.[76]

Dutt thought that India was faring even worse under the crown than she had done under the company. The drain had increased and regressive measures were being passed in close succession. He was particularly distressed by the Calcutta Municipal Act of 1899 and by the recurring famines which he felt were due to an unjust administration. And he was undoubtedly disturbed by the inability of the so-called "influential" Indians to influence the making of British policies for

India.[77] "Oligarchy" is a term which appears more and more frequently in Dutt's later writings. He thought that unwise policies and the refusal to listen to Indian opinion were undermining the confidence which he always believed Indians had had in their British rulers. His "rational optimism" and faith in British justice and inevitable progress were being shaken. Thus it is perhaps understandable that he entered the service of the Gaekwar of Baroda as Revenue Minister in 1904 in order, he thought, to put some of his ideas into practice in an area in which Indians still had some control over their own government.[78]

Romesh Dutt's conception of India's future is implicit in his view of her past and present. He wrote in his European travel journal in 1891 that the course of modern history was toward representative government and national freedom.[79] India, he felt, must progress as all nations were progressing. She must take her place among the nations of the world by utilizing foreign science, skill in mechanical arts, and medicine.[80] Dutt neither foresaw nor preached any special mission for India in the modern world. His vision of the future was an India partially built in the image of the Western countries and using their essential skills.

But, as has already been shown, Dutt wanted to continue "the old order of things" where "they are consistent with modern progress." [81] Many vital indigenous institutions had been seriously damaged or destroyed, but perhaps they could be revived. The village councils, zamindars, and native princes might still play their part in reconstructing India. From his early days, Dutt showed a sensitivity to the need for adapting Western institutions to an Indian setting. Thus he pressed the case for small industry and the development of agriculture in his *Economic History*, presaging similar arguments by Indians a few years later, and even today. Dutt described experiments in Madras and elsewhere to revive the hand-loom industry and concluded that "a civilised Government has no more sacred duty than to help these submerged classes, and revive one of the most ancient industries of India." [82]

Dutt advocated thrift, self-reliance, energy, and honesty, virtues taught by some of his Victorian contemporaries in England.[83] He advocated gradual change, since he believed that the Indian people were against revolution.[84] The acts of revolutionaries in Poona, Bengal and London beginning at the end of the nineteenth century appalled him:

The cowardly assassination of Lieutenant Ayerst and the attempted murder of Mr. Rand have aroused the just indignation of Englishmen in India and in England. The most searching inquiries are being made, and every friend of peace and order, be he Englishman or be he Indian, hopes that the perpetrators of the foul deed will be hanged amidst the just exultations of loyal Indian multitudes. The suspicion which hangs on Indian communities will thus be lifted.[85]

Dutt signed himself "Loyal Indian." Near the end of his life he was very pessimistic, still advocating slow and gradual change. He did not live long enough to understand the "new spirit" of the twentieth century in India, to which he himself unknowingly had contributed.

Some attention must be given now to his ideas about Bengal and Bengalis. For Dutt, "Bengal" usually meant the Bengali-speaking area of eastern India or the administrative area called Bengal by the British; but in the *Brief History of Ancient and Modern Bengal* for students, Dutt included Bihar, Assam, and Orissa as parts of what is often referred to as "Greater Bengal." [86]

During its pre-British history, Bengal, Dutt thought, was in the thralldom of oriental despotism. In describing the zamindari system of those days, he wrote:

in a country like Bengal where climatic and other influences have rendered the people so imbecile and incapable of resistance, every official vested with authority is likely to turn oppressive and tyrannical without evoking an active opposition from the people.[87]

The initial impact of the British caused great disruptions in the society, but the apathetic Bengalis did not rise on that occasion.

It would have ensued in the shape of a general revolution among any other people than the Bengalis, who are so tenacious to order, so persistent in their inactivity, so strong in passive resistance, that nothing ever produced or shall produce a social explosion among them.[88]

Dutt may have been influenced by Buckle's climatic explanations of historical developments and descriptions of the Bengalis by writers like Macaulay and Grant. The image we get is of weak, passive creatures who, we are also told, are "naturally so averse to actual violence and warfare." [89] He had in great part accepted and reproduced British interpretations of the Bengali and the Bengali past. With the advent of British rule, a renaissance in the world of letters was accompanied by security, order, and justice in society. Dutt was at this time in his most optimistic and pro-British state of mind. Like many British writers of the nineteenth century, he viewed the Bengali babu as a "weak and inactive creature," an urban man unacquainted with the countryside,[90] although Dutt dissociates himself and his friends from these reactionary and effete babus.

By the time he wrote his *Economic History*, Dutt had changed his assessment of the state of Bengal. It had now become the most exemplary province in British India and the standard against which to judge developments and progress in all the other provinces. And not only did Bengal have the most intelligent, resourceful, prosperous social groups, including landlords, middle class, peasantry, but she also had the best laws and the least autocratic administration. Among the native associations, Dutt mentioned the British Indian Association of Calcutta most often as deserving commendation.[91] Where Vivekananda saw the Bengalis moving outward to preach the gospel of a new age, Dutt viewed Bengal as a model for Englishmen and Indians alike of just and progressive imperial rule and a happy indigenous society. In both cases, Bengali ideologues called attention to the preeminence of their native province.

Altogether, Romesh Dutt presents a curious combination— analytical historian and passionate nationalist; extoller of martial virtues in romances but antagonist of violence in modern politics; idealizer of ancient village communities and native industry and a believer in the inevitable march of progress toward the institutional forms of the modern West. Dutt was leader of a generation labeled "denationalized" by the succeeding generation of Indian nationalists, but he was a major contributor to the ideology of Indian nationalism, particularly to its economic positions.[92]

SYED AMEER ALI, BAR-AT-LAW: MUSLIM LEADER

Ameer Ali, like Romesh Dutt, was a member of the establishment in Bengal, linking the native society and the British Raj in a number of ways. But it must be noted that although Ameer Ali lived in Calcutta and had his direct experience of India almost totally in Bengal, he did not consider himself a Bengali. In his writings he does not identify with Bengal or mention speaking or reading Bengali. He read Arabic, Persian, Urdu, and English, and spoke the latter two. He is first a Muslim, then an Indian. At the same time he is a modern man, identifying with "the men of culture who are growing up in India under western influences." [93] Ali became a spokesman for the Muslim community in Bengal and in India, and later for the worldwide Muslim community. He was taken as such a representative by the rulers of India. Ali also played an important part in two Muslim political organizations that began in Bengal, the Central National Mohammedan Association and the Muslim League; but he was like the Afghan or Mughal officials sent to Bengal, an outsider at the top with no roots in the soil.

Writing his memoirs at the end of his life, Ameer Ali dwelt on his Persian ancestry, his Syed heritage, and the train of events which led his family to India and later to Bengal. Among the dominant Sunni Muslims in India and Bengal, Ali was a Shiah, following the Mutazalite philosophical and legal school. As a member of the minority Shiah sect, Ali was marginal to the Muslim community of Bengal, in yet another way an outsider. But Ali never felt marginal to the Islamic faith or world community of Muslims.[94]

Ali grew up, he wrote, in "comfortable circumstances," son of a restless father whose ambitions in life were stillborn. Ali's older brother Syed Waris Ali was a successful government servant and at his death was much mourned by Ameer Ali as "the guardian of my youth, the dearest friend of my whole life." [95] Ali's father was a scholar of Arabic and Persian who had been writing a life of Muhammad just before his demise. The peripatetic father had been persuaded by two British officials to give his sons a Western as well as an Islamic education.[96] English came to be the one language in which Ali wrote, although he mentions speaking Urdu to Muslim audiences later in life. His aim was success in the world of Islam and in the world of English.

Two images stand out in Ali's account of his boyhood: a youthful organizer of hunts using firearms (like the rural nobility of old) and the ringleader of Muslim boys at school, raiding outnumbered Hindu boys. Although we cannot assess the accuracy of the account, it seems probable that Ali was a leader of his fellow Muslims and one willing to strike out to achieve success. No doubt he had early awareness of his membership in the Muslim community, although he also remembered that communal amity rather than enmity was more common in the nineteenth century.[97]

In his memoirs, he pays tribute to three other influences: his mother; Robert Thwaytes, principal of Hooghly College; and Syed Karamat Ali, Mutawali of the Hooghly Imambara, a Shiah religious institution. The first helped to give him manly confidence after the early death of his father; the second encouraged his Western education and moves into the world of advanced studies; the third gave him an Islamic education, faith in his religious leanings and helped to give him a "glimpse of the Mussulman gentry of the old school." Ali translated a work of the latter into English, a treatise on the origins of science.[98]

After his early Islamic and Western education, Ali studied for an M.A. at Hooghly College and then was awarded a state scholarship to go to England and sit for the bar there. Through family connections and his Western teachers, he was given introductions to the highest officials of the government of India and to high society in England. During his four early years in Britain, he lived with the family of a Mrs. Chase and was treated as "one of themselves." [99] He frequented the society of the great and powerful, "awed by the galaxy" but shortly paying tribute to the overwhelming generosity and hospitality of the English.[100] Before returning to India, he started working for a British legal firm. He was to spend many years residing in England, including the last twenty-four of his life, feeling at home, an equal, and yet different, an eminent Muslim who spoke for the Islamic community. Ali married an English woman and had his sons educated in England. In his account of his visits to England, Ali rarely mentions another Indian. He operated outside the network of Bengali Hindus abroad.

While still in England, provoked by a Christian critic of Islam and encouraged by Henry Channing, Ali wrote his first book, *A Critical Examination of the Life and Teachings of Mohammed*, published in 1873. Ali expanded this work into *The Spirit of Islam* and continued to revise it throughout his lifetime; it became a favorite of Westerners in search of an introduction to Islam and Westernized Muslims in need of a modernist version of their traditions. In the preface to the *Life of Mohammed*, Ali wrote:

> the gradual enlightenment of the human mind is shown strikingly in the silent change which is taking place in Christendom towards a more liberal conception of the grand work achieved by the Arabian prophet. . . . Maurice, Stanley, and Carlyle in England, Emerson, Parker, Chan-

ning and Draper in America . . . have testified as the result of earnest study that Islam, instead of evil names heaped upon it, merits the thanks of humanity.[101]

This short book represents Ali's completion of an unfinished dream of his father, a tribute to his teacher Syed Karamat Ali, and the beginning of his career as a Muslim apologist. The feeling of defending Islam against what he later called "Christian assailants" and of trying to guide ignorant and misled Europeans to the truth about Islam became one of the central tasks of Ali's life. Like Romesh Dutt presenting the Indian past, Ali did not pretend to original scholarship, but felt he was filling a need, writing for a general, educated audience. Ali thought it was incumbent upon him, as one accepted into professional, political, and literary circles in England, to help bring peace between Christians and Muslims.[102] The main audience he sought was composed of Europeans; next, he wanted Muslims to learn the true traditions and history of their faith; and, third, a very distant third, he wanted to enlighten non-Muslim Indians. But every one of his works was published in London, except a brief work to guide fledgling Muslim lawyers, *Student's Handbook of Mahommedan Law.*

Returning to Calcutta armed with a "wider outlook," Ali became a barrister of the Calcutta High Court. In his memoirs, he described his hardships as the only Muslim barrister surrounded by distant but occasionally helpful Europeans and by Hindus such as W. C. Bonnerjee. In this period Hindus, too, were struggling for success, but there were a few more of them, and they may have felt a comraderie for each other which was not reciprocal with Ali. But Ali succeeded. He did well as a barrister and wrote for British-edited periodicals in Calcutta (*Calcutta Observer*) and London (*Nineteenth Century*). Later, he served as officiating Presidency Magistrate of Calcutta and as judge of the Calcutta High Court from 1890 to 1904. The image he presents of himself on the magistrate's bench is that of a tolerant, sensible, and strong man whom no one could intimidate or fool. Ali also served in the Bengal and Imperial legislative councils; he had a distinguished career in the British-Indian establishment in Calcutta and felt that he had had a "blessed life." His career on the bench and at the bar gave him as full a sense of high life and low life in Bengal as did Romesh Dutt's civil service.[103]

Ali also became a scholar of Muslim law and was appointed Lecturer in Muhammadan Law at Calcutta University. He expanded his lectures into a two-volume work on Muslim law and a briefer version of the same, his *Student's Handbook*. Again, Ali felt he was filling a crucial link role between alien rulers and Indian subjects. He wrote in 1880:

> Owing to an imperfect knowledge of Mussulman jurisprudence, of Mussulman manners, customs and usages, it is not infrequent, even now, to find cases decided by the highest law courts against every principle of the Mahommedan law. It is not surprising, therefore, to learn that every miscarriage of justice adds to the long roll of indictment which the popular mind has framed against the British rule in India.[104]

To fill this knowledge vacuum, Ali offered his works on Muslim law, in which he was particularly concerned to define who the Muslims were, to give some idea of the different sects, and to specify in some detail the laws relating to succession, status, and property for each sect. He felt there would be practical consequences flowing from his volumes: judges of all the courts in India, ignorant of Muslim law and trying cases concerning Muslims, would read them and hand down fairer decisions. There would be a decrease in anti-British feeling among Muslims, and the rulers would be in closer touch with one community of their subjects. A critical concern for his fellow Muslims also filters through these books. Ali was upset that Muslims themselves did not study their own laws or train young men specifically in Muslim law. He felt that the traditions of the Muslim community should be defined and preserved. No profound work of original scholarship would be needed, but rather a codifying, simplifying process he felt suited to by virtue of his skills and experience.[105]

In addition to numerous essays published during his years on the bench, in 1899 Ali also completed a major work of history, *A Short History of the Saracens*. Drawing heavily on the last parts of Gibbon's *The Decline and Fall of the Roman Empire*, which had been a favorite since childhood, Ali declared he wanted to "enlist sympathy" and "evoke interest" in a great civilization close in time to modern Europe, but virtually unknown in the West and India. He wanted to overcome prejudices and bitterness and demonstrate the contributions of the Saracens to modern civilization. Once more Ali stated that he was filling a need. There was no brief, clear, sympathetic account of the Saracens "from earliest times to the destruction of Baghdad and the expulsion of the Moors from Spain." Ali's part was to simplify and summarize more esoteric works of scholarship and place his version before ignorant or misled Europeans and unenlightened Muslims.[106]

Pulling together different strands of his work as a writer, we can say that Ameer Ali sought to define the important religious traditions, history, and legal guidelines which would help regenerate the Muslim community in an age of European domination. He wanted to instruct Europeans who had opened an avenue for him into modern civilization and who had offered him their hospitality and an entrée into their society. He was equally concerned with aiding the Muslims, particularly in India but in other parts of the world as well, through his writing and practical works. He stressed that regeneration of the Muslim community had to come from within through hard work, growth, and thoughtfulness, although he also specified ways in which he thought the Raj could assist Indian Muslims.

To help raise the Muslim community, Ali devoted some of his energies from the late 1870s to Muslim politics. Disagreeing with Sir Syed Ahmad Khan's view that it was best to stay clear of politics, Ali felt it important that the Muslims organize and make their views known if they were not to lag even further behind the Hindus. He helped to found the National Mohammedan Association, which shortly grew into the Central National Mohammedan Association, with thirty-four branches. Although Ali often claimed that the Muslims of India (and, indeed, Muslims everywhere) constituted a homogeneous community, he learned that there were many Muslim points of view once he founded an organization.[107] In this work he was separated from prominent Muslims like Abdul Latif in Calcutta, who ridiculed Ali as a Westernized man ignorant of the religious languages of Islam, cut off from the masses, and out of touch with true religious reform.[108] Ali was also in disagreement with Sir Syed Ahmad Khan's concentration on educational work, which interested Ali but to which he gave only secondary importance. At this point, Ali needed all the confidence his Syed heritage, his comfortable childhood, and his successful career could give him. He had to face the problem of what it meant to be a Muslim and an Indian in the last quarter of the nineteenth century, defining his own version of Islamic culture and the proper politics for an Indian Muslim. Ali gathered a small group of Muslims around him that met at his house in Calcutta and went to work.[109]

The Central National Mohammedan Association, like the British Indian Association, the early Muslim League, and even the Indian Association, was first of all an organization of notables. It engaged in petitioning, advising top officials of the Muslim viewpoint whenever possible, and claimed to represent all Indian Muslims. The members were mostly non-Bengali, some from Bihar and other parts of India, and often were Shiahs like Ameer Ali. In 1882 they placed an extensive memorial before the liberal viceroy, Lord Ripon. It was obviously written by Ali, since it reads in long sections, word for word, the same as an article he published under his own name at the same time.[110] It asked for many more positions for Muslims in government services and for government assistance in providing modern education for Muslims. It mentioned the great days of Muslim rule, current discontents, and the prejudicial treatment by Hindus that often kept Muslims from advancing. Although Ali said that regeneration had to come from within, he made it clear that large-scale government help would be essential.

Like the first generation of congressmen, Ameer Ali remained a conscientious loyalist throughout his life. He was devoted to the Muslim community, but he was also devoted to "the interests of the British Empire." [111] He identified with what he called the forces of order during the Swadeshi period and wanted a firmer government hand to be applied to the troublemakers, lest the government's authority be lost. He went even further than his Hindu contemporaries, since he lavished praise upon Lord Curzon; and when the Muslim League became critical of the government, Ali resigned.[112] Wilfrid Blunt painted a picture of Ali in the 1880s as fawning before the government and letting down his countrymen.[113] It may be fair to place Ali somewhere between Blunt's harsh portrait and his self-image of resolute independence.

In his memoirs, Ali inflated his role in political events between 1880 and the end of his life. For example, Ali claimed a critical part in preventing Ripon's resignation over the revision of the Ilbert bill, and in shaping the Bengal Tenancy bill so that it more adequately guarded the ryots' interest. Later, he claimed credit for swinging Morley around to acceptance of separate electorates in the 1909 reform of the legislative councils.[114]

One feature of his politics from the 1880s through the 1920s is opposition to Muslims working with the Indian National Congress. He felt a growing antipathy toward Brahmanical Hindus and what he called their "mental pliability." [115] He argued that the reforms themselves were the most important cause in furthering communal antipathy. Western democracy, he maintained, could not simply be grafted onto the Indian body politic without rejective tendencies. He wanted political reforms to go at an even slower pace, with more weight given to the interests of Muslim groups than their educational level or percentage of the population might warrant; and he wanted full governmental authority continued. [116]

From 1908 to 1913, Ali and the Aga Khan were instrumental in setting up and running a London branch of the Muslim League. The league's founding host, the Nawab of Dacca, was an old legal client of Ali's, and the organization's loyalist, conservative cast fitted Ali's political stance in the days of Swadeshi. Ali and the Aga Khan argued skillfully in London for separate electorates, while Romesh Dutt and other congressmen, opposed but less passionately to this particular clause, lost out to the league forces allied with the viceroy, Lord Minto. [117] Ali wrote in his memoirs that he could not understand the antipathy of Surendranath Banerjea and the *Bengalee*. [118] But to congressmen, Ali was preventing Muslims from joining their organization, thus dividing the Indian political front in its approach to the monolithic facade of the "bureaucracy" or "oligarchy"—terms which congressmen were using more frequently in referring to the Raj. Ali's inability to understand congressional opposition is the counterpart to the failure of the Congress to show more sensitivity to Muslim grievances, concerns, and interests. Ali said he had always had cordial relations with Hindus; but as the Indian scene grew more politicized and feelings heightened, those who chose the side of Curzon, unquestioned loyalty to the empire, and used derogatory language toward the majority community could not expect to escape attack.

Once he had retired to England, Ali became more interested in larger Muslim causes, particularly the fate of the Khilafat and of Turkey within the crumbling Ottoman Empire. He labored to build the British Red Crescent Relief Society to aid wounded Muslims just before and during World War I, and he wrote frequently in the press about the history and significance of the Khilafat. He played a small role in the demise of the Khilafat in Turkey; in the end he mournfully reproached the Turks whom he had spent so many years defending in Britain.[119]

Ali lived on to 1928 in a European milieu, writing articles and serving on the Judicial Committee of the Privy Council. He had resigned from the Muslim League in 1913, when he said it had been taken over by "extremists," and by the end of his life was out of touch with the changes occurring within Muslim and Indian politics. In earlier days he had helped to provide religious, historical, and legal guides for a modernized Islam. This legacy lived on among Muslims within and outside India. A Marxist analyst has labeled it an ideology for a class of bourgeois Muslims.[120] Rather than pigeonholing it so facilely, it may be more useful to analyze his views of the past, suggest some of the apologetic themes, and compare his historical view with that of Romesh Dutt.

For his Western and Muslim readers, Ameer Ali transformed the conflicting sects and teachings, the complex and extensive history of Islam into intelligible accounts understandable to educated everyman. He made extensive use of Christian terms and analogies like established and dissenting church and pontiff for caliph; he also interpreted the Muslim past with concepts like socialism and democracy without undue reflection upon their possible different meaning in another historical context.[121] His general aim was to show the equivalence of Islam, and in some cases its superiority, to other great traditions and to do so using terms and values acceptable to Westerners. He wanted to gain the recognition and sympathy of foreigners and to show his fellow Muslims the glories of their past. If Westerners realized the equivalence of Islamic civilization with their own, then Muslims might gain equality of treatment and a respect that they were not receiving in Ali's time. If Muslims understood that democracy, socialism, and scientific learning were integral parts of their heritage, perhaps they would feel no inferiority toward the West as they regenerated the life of their fallen community.[122]

One approach used by Ali, especially in direct answers to Christian critics, was to go on the offensive. If his antagonists listed the barbarities of Islam—slavery, polygamy, degradation of women, intolerance of non-Muslims, etc.—Ali would respond by listing the barbarities in each category committed by Christians and then mimimize the offenses of Muslims in each category. So he claimed that slavery was against Muslim law and had been widespread in the West until the nineteenth century; polygamy was common in many civilizations and was dying out among Muslims; women had a higher position in Islamic civilization, above all in their legal rights, than in other cultures; and Muslims had always shown more tolerance toward others than Christians. He often compared Islamic theory with Christian practice.[123] He also assumed that every reader would agree with his rather puritanical values and with his assumptions that monotheism is obviously superior to polytheism, that idol worship is perforce blasphemous, that a rational rather than a mystical approach to religious experience is preferable. He dismissed Hinduism as a combination of mysticism, pantheism, and fetishism run riot; and he condemned Christian claims for Jesus as the son of God as ridiculous idol worship, further maintaining that Islam was true Christianity.[124] That he gained much sympathy from Hindu and Christian readers by including these assaults is dubious.

The grand theme of Ali's *Short History of the Saracens* and *The Spirit of Islam* is the rise of a glorious Islamic civilization and its decline. Much of his writing is devoted to charting the rise and heights, savoring the romance of conquest and the spread of earthly power, and explaining the fall. In his two major works, he is concerned with Islamic civilization in the Middle East, North Africa, and Spain; India is neglected since it is out of the main stream. It was and is useful for Western readers to see the Crusades from the other side, to understand the genuine contributions of Muslims to the transmission and extension of the heritage of antiquity, and to widen their sympathies for other peoples. But Ali goes beyond that to claim that it was the Saracens "who had spread culture, given impetus to civilisation, and established chivalry—who had, in fact, created modern Europe." [125]

Ali wrote in his memoirs that the decline of Islamic civilization was a concern of his for many years. He adhered to no one causal theory, but listed among other factors racial pride, fanaticism, tribal jealousies, the rise of mysticism leading to quietism and lethargy, patristic bondage, the attachment of extraneous elements to the one true faith, and defeats by barbarians like the Franks and the Mongols.[126] It is remarkable in light of the divisions he chronicled within Islamic civilization itself that he continued to assert in his more political writings to British officials that world Muslim solidarity had always existed. In the Indian context, he would often refer to the "one homogeneous community." [127] Throughout there is identification with the just and powerful, nostalgia for the great old days, and dismay with present weakness.

Ali wrote no major work on India comparable to his *History of the Saracens* or *The Spirit of Islam*. Although he did compose a few articles on Islamic culture in India near the end of his life, he believed that the glorious achievements of Islam had taken place outside India, and it was with those accomplishments and those Muslims that he identified. Nonetheless, it is possible to extract his views of the Indian past and present from his articles and occasional comments in his books.[128]

He confronted Hinduism with as much open-mindedness as a fundamentalist missionary and as much sensitivity as James Mill writing his history of British India. Ali felt that the spread of the Aryans through India had been a process of enslaving indigenous peoples, that Brahmanism had "deleterious effects," involving "humiliating and degrading restrictions," and that Hinduism was "divisive," "pervasive," and "conservative." He was appalled by the sexuality in Indian religious cults of the Mother Goddess and Krishna and could find no fellow feeling for idolatrous Hindus.[129]

In a paper probably written in 1912, Ali announces, "It can hardly be disputed that the real history of India commences with the entry of the Mussulmans." [130] Elsewhere he wrote in the same vein, "When the Mussulman power seated itself in Delhi a new culture arose in India which had left its mark on every institution existing nowadays in the country." [131] The Afghans and then the Mughals were bringers of order and culture to a backward, idolatrous, and divided land. His views are like those of the nineteenth-century British writers who saw the British as the new men transforming anarchy into order and beginning to educate the natives. Ali goes through the achievements of the Delhi Sultanate and the Mughal Empire, but these were not the greatest days for Islam; they were merely the high point of civilization in India. Ali mentions the development of the revenue system, cultural achievements, and the general tolerance which Muslim rulers spread over the land. He also stresses the large role which the Muslim rulers gave to Hindus in their government. Though there was tolerance and communal amity, except for the reign of Aurangzeb, Ali argues that Hindus and Muslims always constituted two "communities" or "nations." He uses these two terms interchangeably, yet maintained that he was not a separatist.[132] Those who have wanted to show Ali to be an early proponent of Pakistan have stressed his use of the word "nation" and blissfully forgotten that he never anticipated two independent and autonomous nations emerging out of British India. Ali emphasized the homogeneity of the Muslim community, but his own distaste for Sufism may have been one reason why he wrote so little on Islam in India.

The British brought further unification of the subcontinent, but Ali, like a number of European writers in the nineteenth century, felt that British India was an artificial unit, lacking the unity of Western nations. The integration process fostered by the British brought, in time, intensification of rivalries between native communities. At first the rulers assisted those who were most malleable and suitable for the lower ranks of their administration; these turned out to be mostly Hindus. British rule through the nineteenth century, Ali said, benefited "Brahmanical people" and moneylenders, predominantly Hindu.[133]

A special concern to him was the rapid decline of the Muslims since the 1820s. Ali placed most responsibility for this fall upon the shoulders of Lord William Bentinck:

> Prior to his time, the Mussulmans occupied the foremost position among the people of India. The cultivation of their law and their literature was encouraged by successive British governors, their traditions were respected, and they themselves were treated with a certain amount of consideration due to the former rulers of the land. All this changed under Lord William Bentinck's administration, and the Indian Mahommedans were relegated into the cold shade of neglect. Their institutions gradually died out, and the old race of *Moulvis* and *Muftis*, who had shed a lustre on the reigns of the Marquis of Wellesley and the Marquis of Hastings, became extinct.[134]

This passage exemplifies Ali's style of history: he believed that the ruler was the most important determinant of historical change; he projected guilt onto the British, extrapunitively, rather than placing responsibility upon the Muslims themselves for their fall; and he looked back nostalgically to the days of Muslim majesty and might. He saw the shift from Persian to English as the language of administration as the crucial turning point in the decline of the Indian Muslims, but he did realize that Muslims could learn English as well as Hindus and might flourish again under British rule. The Muslims would need help from the rulers to combat what he often referred to as the "Hindu juggernaut," the exclusive monopolization of lower administrative positions by Hindus. Here he employed a conspiratorial theory of history, again projecting guilt out onto others for Muslim shortcomings.[135]

Ali had mixed feelings about many of the changes and reforms under British rule. He criticized government monetary policy for failing to advance Indian interests; he felt that peasants and landlords were inadequately protected, especially the former; and he noted the drain. He blamed the low state of India in 1880 on shortcomings in British policy and he attacked the British and Indian "obsession with democracy," [136] He opposed nationalism as a form of atavistic tribalism and blamed the reforms of 1909 and 1919 for increasing bad feelings between the Hindu and Muslim communities. A modern constitution, Ali thought, could not be imposed on a medieval economy, using this line in his advocacy of separate communal electorates. Too rapid reforms and any weakening of the authority of the Raj would be a disaster for the people of India (meaning the Muslim community).[137] But with this catalog of criticisms, Ali remained the staunchest of loyalists; his phrase, "the necessity of British rule," [138] still lingers. He accepted the reforms of the legislative councils because they were small advances and embodied the principle of separate electorates. But in his writing on India, one feels the ever-present fear of disorder and disaster for the Muslims. British rule never brought him peace of mind.

He called upon the British officials to take action which would benefit the Muslims; the father had a responsibility to help his lagging child. He wanted "denominational universities," help for the ryots against avaricious moneylenders, and full understanding and utilization of Muslim law in Indian courts where applicable.[139] He stressed action from above; this puts him in a class with the early nationalists and authoritarian utilitarians of the nineteenth century. He placed much hope upon a just executive authority.

Ali's writings contain very little about Bengal. There is a sentence or brief opinion here and there but no particular concern for or identification with Bengal. He occasionally accepts the familiar stereotype of the Bengali babu, contrasting the "mere effervescence in Bengal" with areas inhabited by "more virile races." [140] And, although he wonders whether the Bengali character may not be changing in the Swadeshi period,[141] he himself never identifies with the people in the region in which he grew up, attained success, and spent the greater part of his life. Bengal was as marginal to Ameer Ali as it was central to Romesh Dutt. Ali had a sense of Indian and Muslim identity, but not of Bengali identity. Thus he belongs to a large section of the Muslim leadership in Bengal in the nineteenth and twentieth centuries who worked in Bengal but could not be said to be of Bengal or the Bengalis in any significant sense. The Hindu leaders of the Congress may have been as detached from the masses, but they were Bengalis, spoke Bengali, and eventually started to mobilize support lower down in the Bengali social order. Eventually, some Muslim leaders also sought wide support. The most successful of these were Bengalis, not Muslims from outside who were domiciled in Bengal.

Religion, which was of scant importance to Romesh Dutt, was vital to Ali. Religion and Muslim law were tied to the fate of Ali's community, which was, he felt, in danger of disintegration. Dutt, as a member of the majority community, was not particularly concerned with specifying who was a Hindu, although he thought it important to recall the glories of the Hindu past. Dutt is not haunted by imminent disaster. Ali, the marginal man from the minority sect of the minority religion, was often fearful about the continuity of his community.

Their views of the Indian past are antithetical. Dutt saw a golden age in early Hindu and Buddhist India, decay during the Muslim period. Ali saw barbarism in ancient India followed by a golden age during Muslim rule. Both were influenced by nineteenth-century evolutionism and hoped for greater days ahead. For Dutt, progress to an every-higher stage of humanity seemed more likely than it did to Ali. The latter doubted that there could ever be a Muslim golden age to compare with the pinnacles reached by the Saracens. There might be a European or world golden age in which Muslims would participate, but they would never again dominate, and this he lamented.

Both Dutt and Ali identified with the ruler and with the ruled. They both participated in the British Raj at fairly high levels and proclaimed their loyalty. They were respected; their advice was listened to, although not necessarily followed. They were praised for their English prose styles, although with an undertone that said, Imagine our natives doing so well. They were criticized by those with more extreme, more religious, or more nationalistic outlooks for their identification with British rule and Western ways. And they each played a variety of link roles between ruler and ruled, making important contributions to the ideologies of their era.

Part Two

The Second Generation: Swadeshi, 1905–1917

THREE
The Swadeshi Movement

ငေ§်X§5 The Swadeshi period, from 1904, inaugurates a new age in which a challenge to the legitimacy of British rule and of the dominant nationalist leadership surfaced. New spokesmen and political workers came forward, including both a fresh generation of students and men who had been marginally involved in politics earlier, who had criticized the Congress leaders for more than a decade, but had not made available an effective alternative.

The agitation was set off by the refusal of British officials, particularly the viceroy, Lord Curzon, to respond to Indian complaints regarding proposed administrative changes.[1] The failure of methods which were long considered proper for political expression brought a breakdown of respect for governmental authority. British political prototypes were called into question, setting off a search for new patterns in indigenous, Asian, and continental European sources. This quest brought with it the confusion that accompanies the rejection of established views and the construction of a new perspective.

Conflict with the Raj, or the "bureaucracy," drove Indian leaders, both old and new, to minimize their differences. They joined in meetings and demonstrations and took the first steps toward a boycott of British goods. But differences within the nationalist movement proved fundamental and could not be contained. The new nationalist leaders, the Extremists, felt themselves representative of a higher stage in Indian nationalism. They embodied nineteenth-century cultural and religious trends which were barely evident in the views and work of the earlier Moderates.[2] Some called for a return to ancient Indian ideals, widening the scope of nationalism to include all aspects of culture, and called for national revival in art, education, literature, historical research, and morality. Among the major influences on the new nationalism were the temple priest of Dakshineswar, Ramakrishna, with his disciple Swami Vivekananda, and the premier man of letters in the last quarter of the nineteenth century, Bankim Chandra Chatterjee.

Ramakrishna, though devoted to the goddess Kali, experimented with other religions and proved to his satisfaction that there were several equally viable paths to God. Using earthy wisdom and parables, Ramakrishna persuaded Westernized Bengalis that there was much value in their own Shakta and Vaishnava traditions. He taught toleration of other faiths and pride in one's own religion.[3] Although he did not engage in social reform or politics, Ramakrishna encouraged his close disciples to undertake God's work in the world through social service; and after his death in 1886, they founded the Ramakrishna Order and Mission. The most influential of these young men, Narendranath Datta, who became known as Swami Vivekananda, wandered around India as a sannyasin (mendicant holy man) and traveled to the West spreading the teachings of revitalized Hinduism. Like Keshub Sen before him, Vivekananda asserted that the West was spiritually deficient and that India had a religious message for humanity. The fundamental truth of Hinduism, according to Vivekananda, was the unity of all human and animal life, joined by the immanent Brahman within each creature. This Hinduism was the faith that could save the world; it was the most scientific and the only moral religion.[4]

The militant Hinduism taught by the mature Vivekananda differed from the tolerant faith preached by his guru. The former thought that although India lagged in material culture, she was always advanced in religion. Vivekananda wanted to preserve the "spirituality and purity of the race," [5] i.e., of the Hindus, and spread their message; but he was also envious of Western vitality, skill in coordination, self-confidence, and strength.[6] Exhorting his listeners to utilize the powers within themselves to build their country, he made remarks that were often taken in a political sense:

> We speak of many things parrot-like, but never do them; speaking and not doing has become a habit with us. What is the cause of that? Physical weakness. This sort of weak brain is not able to do anything: we must strengthen it. First of all, our young men must be strong. Re-

ligion will come afterwards. Be strong, my young friends . . . You will
be nearer to Heaven through football than through the study of the
Gita . . . You will understand the Gita better with your biceps, your
muscles, a little stronger. You will understand the mighty genius and
the mighty strength of Krishna better with a little strong blood in
you.[7]

Vivekananda criticized Bengalis for sectarianism, neglect of the
Vedas, and overattraction to foreign ideas, but he gave a special role to
young Bengal:

I have faith in my country, and especially in the youth of my country.
The youth of Bengal have the greatest of all tasks that has ever been
placed on the shoulders of young men. I have travelled for the last ten
years or so over the whole of India, and my conviction is that from
the youth of Bengal will come the power which will raise India once
more to her proper spiritual place. Ay, from the youth of Bengal, with
this immense amount of feeling and enthusiasm in the blood, will come
those heroes who will march from one corner of the earth to the
other, preaching and teaching the eternal truth of our forefathers.[8]

Just as Bengalis had moved out across India as collaborators with the
Raj and as professional men, so Vivekananda envisioned them spreading a message of renewed strength to all Indians.

The Ramakrishna Order and Mission has retained an ideology which
is militantly Hindu, yet has a certain flexibility which allows it to incorporate features of other religions. Although both the order and the
mission have remained outside politics, they have provided inspiration
for political activity. The route from the selfless, autonomous, energy-
generating sannyasin to the resourceful political worker was not a long
one.[9]

Bankim Chandra Chatterjee, the second major influence upon the
new nationalism, consciously channeled religious discussion in a political direction and helped to bring about the fusion of religion and politics which so excited many young Hindu Bengalis and so disturbed officials early in the twentieth century. His use of Bengali as a medium
of expression and his particular concern with the Bengali "jati," or
people, sharpened regional feeling. While in government service, he
wrote popular novels and essays and turned his readers' interest in the
1870s and 1880s to Bengali literature. Chatterjee wanted to link the

Western-educated few and the Bengali-educated many through their
common language.[10]

One nineteenth-century trend he encouraged was the use of historical knowledge and traditions as tools for instruction and exhortation
toward future goals. He was aware that history might be a crucial
weapon in the battle for social and political advancement in Bengal.
Certain myths and misunderstandings—for example, the weakness
and cowardice of the Bengalis—had to be criticized through a new
reconstruction of the past.[11]

In this view, Bengalis had had great achievements as well as shortcomings. Among the feats were stopping the advance of Alexander and
colonizing remote areas. But in his assessment of Bengal in the present,
Chatterjee was concerned with physical and intellectual vitality, showing the fear of inadequacy which runs through modern Indian
thought. Since the Bengalis were held especially responsible for allowing the British conquest, Bankim Chandra felt that they had to be defended as well as urged to unusual deeds.[12]

His message was spread most widely through his historical novels. In
them, he created Hindu heroes, Rajput and Bengali Hindus, who could
stand alongside Muslim and British heroes in strength and courage. In
the most politically influential of these novels, *Ānandamaṭh*, Bankim
Chandra fuses religious and patriotic symbolism as he mingles the two
significant religious traditions of Bengal, Vaishnavism and Shaktism.

The basic doctrine of Shaktism is that there is a power called
"shakti" underlying and energizing all reality. A female deity, who is
usually a consort of Shiva—Durga, Kali, Chandi, or Shakti—may
be understood to embody and express this power and may thus be wor-
shipped as the single and highest deity. This form of religion is widespread among the high castes of Bengal and among lower castes such as
kumars, or ironsmiths, coppersmiths, and saltmakers. Religious practice
involves "puja" (worship with offerings) and special observances during the year. At these festivals, and also in times of particular need,
devotees sacrifice animals and other things to the deity.[13] The concept
of shakti underlies a concept of physical strength that emerges as well
in the writings of Vivekananda, Aurobindo Ghose, and Rabindranath
Tagore.

Ānandamaṭh tells of an order of sannyasins in the 1770s who organize and take arms against their Muslim rulers. They call themselves devoted children of the Mother, who is both the divine Mother and the Motherland. Although they worship Krishna and claim to be Vaishnavas, their guiding principle is power rather than love, and they believe that violence is necessary to recover the Motherland from its depressed state.[14]

The response to *Ānandamaṭh* continued long past its immediate publication in 1880. It was read by Bengal revolutionaries decades later; and the song "Bande Mataram" (Hail to the Mother) sung in the first chapter became the anthem of Bengali Hindu nationalists.[15]

In *Ānandamaṭh*, the violence of the Hindu patriots is directed against Muslim rulers. Considering this novel and his work as a whole, Bankim Chandra is without question a Hindu nationalist who views Muslims as disruptive and often ruthless foreigners who did not merge their culture with that of the indigenous Hindus and who had nothing to contribute to Indian life.[16] But from *Ānandamaṭh* and other writings, it is clear that Chatterjee believed in a grand scheme of development for India in which Western thought and technology could be utilized within an essentially Hindu framework.[17]

Although Bankim Chandra often took a deprecating tone in his description of the Bengali babu, he thought that Bengalis could go beyond their limitations and play a crucial role in the regeneration of India.[18] He stands at the junction between the old effeminate image of the Bengali and a new image of strength and accomplishment.

To his countrymen, Bankim Chandra offered the model of a devoted order of sannyasins and Krishna as the archetype of complete spiritual and worldly fulfillment. He defended Bengali customs and presented schemes for education, scientific development, physical training, and the utilization of folk culture to instruct the masses. Through his fiction and essays, he offered a range of guides to national and personal growth.[19] The symbolism he used had a rich and continuing appeal to Hindu readers and simultaneously served to alienate the Muslims.

While Bengali ideologues were discussing India's mission and Bengal's great role, the British viceroy, Lord Curzon, had a different perspective:

He never doubted . . . that behind the achievements of his fellow countrymen in India was the invisible hand of God. . . . In such a

view of India there was no room for an Indian Intelligentsia aspiring
to lead and speak for the masses; and in so far as the Indian educated
classes claimed to be the prophets of what they themselves spoke of as
"the new Nationalism" which was stirring in the land, he simply
brushed them aside. . . . And it was more than anything else his
openly expressed assumption that it was in him, as the representative
of the race chosen by God for its loftier standards—administrative,
cultural and moral—to be His instrument in leading India along the
road to higher things, that reposed the sole right of speaking for the
Indian peoples, that earned for him the dislike of the educated
classes.[20]

Between 1899 and 1905 conflict ensued over three issues: the Calcutta
Municipal Bill, the Universities Bill, and the partition of Bengal.

Surendranath Banerjea commented on the Congress resolution regarding the first of these measures: "The Calcutta Municipal Bill was a
local measure, but it had an all-India interest as it affected the principle
of Local Self-government, in the growth and development of which all
India felt a concern." [21] It was still possible for Bengali leaders to give
local issues a national turn and assert that the cause of Bengal was the
concern of India. But the petitions and agitation fell on deaf ears and
the Calcutta Corporation was, as Banerjea wrote, "officialized." This
was a blow not only to the Moderates' belief in the power of public
opinion and their own influence, but also to their faith that steps
would be taken toward progressively greater self-government. With
the passage of the act in 1899, twenty-eight elected Indian commissioners resigned. The second measure, the Universities Bill, led to stricter
control of colleges and universities, and it too passed over Indian protest.[22]

The third enactment and the one which caused the greatest uproar
was the division of the Bengali-speaking area into the new provinces of
Bengal (with Bihar and Orissa) and Eastern Bengal and Assam. Protests
began immediately when word slipped out that this move was contem-
plated in 1904. The final decision was announced on July 20, 1905,[23]
and during the latter half of that year protest meetings were held in at
least 300 cities, towns, and villages throughout Bengal. A rough analysis indicates that more meetings were held in districts close to Calcutta and Dacca, particularly Mymensingh, Midnapur, and Khulna.[24]

After initial hesitation on the part of the older nationalists and of prominent men entering politics for the first time (Bhupendranath Basu, for example), a boycott of British goods was decided upon. The boycott spread and was fairly effective for some months, but no central organization or leadership emerged with systematic plans for political action. Opponents of the partition were the politically conscious Hindus and students throughout both parts of Bengal and some Muslims in western Bengal. The students were the most active in implementing the boycott. The movement was called the Swadeshi, or "own country," agitation because it was to encourage not only the boycotting of British goods, but also the production and use of Indian-made goods.[25]

The first days of the Swadeshi agitation were an exhilarating time. Apolitical men were swept into politics, many students joined the movement, and even a veteran like Surendranath Banerjea was moved to say,

> Swadeshism will bring the classes and the masses upon the same platform. Swadeshism is of Divine origin. The Swadeshi leaders are humble instruments in the hands of Divine Providence walking under the illumination of His Holy Spirit. . . . The spirit of self-reliance is abroad. . . . The Bengal of today—Bengal after the partition is a very different place from Bengal before the partition. . . . Bring back the ancient days of purity and self-sacrifice. Restore the Aryavarta of olden times when the Rishis sang the praises of God and did good to men.[26]

But even Banerjea, struggling to retain his central place as more radical men rushed to the stage, realized that "It is the young men who were in the forefront and who have been our martyrs in the Swadeshi cause." [27] This went with the general spirit of rebellion of the time, and with the revulsion against older leaders and political methods. For the young men, the Swadeshi agitation was both an end in itself and a preparation for later forms of political involvement. Students working in organizations shortly banned by the government were putting their education and their future careers on the line for a cause in which they believed. Some turned from the individualistic, achievement-oriented life of school and career to the more expressive and community-oriented activity of the nationalist movement. Nationalist careers, lifelong work for the movement outside the usual spheres of government service and the professions, were envisioned. The activity of the young was related to the feeling expressed by many at the time that the Swadeshi years marked a new time, a rebirth, a regeneration. The call went out for a new type of man, a more Indian type of political worker who would revitalize his country.[28]

Although many sophisticated proposals for action and new institutions were drawn up and presented to public meetings, few were implemented. One enduring group was the National Council of Education. The council owed a debt to two earlier experiments, the Dawn Society of Satish Chandra Mukherjee and Rabindranath Tagore's school, Santiniketan, both of which were developed to put Bengali youth in closer touch with their surroundings and indigenous culture. The National Council progressed beyond officially funded institutions in using Bengali as the medium of instruction and stressing technical and industrial education; there was also a concern for Indian culture and religious education.[29]

During the same period there was some important work done in the districts, especially in Bakarganj under the leadership of Aswini Kumar Dutt. He led the Swadeshi Bandhab Samiti as it founded numerous branches in the district and did such social service work as distributing food in hard times. The organization grew from Dutt's base at Barisal College, where he was proprietor and professor, and included many students. As a zamindar, Dutt could also make use of networks of ties into the countryside. But we do not know how effectively this organization reached peasants beyond its utilization of the superordinate powers that zamindars had long had over their peasants.[30]

There was also some effort to try to reach industrial workers in the Calcutta area and those lower caste groups who serviced Europeans. Aswinicoomar Banerjee and Premtosh Bose were pioneering labor organizers. Aurobindo Ghose and other popular journalists hailed the labor strikes as signs of widespread support for the movement.[31] Aurobindo talked of the Indian proletariat and Surendranath Banerjea of the union of the "classes and the masses" that had taken place as if by magic. But the strikes did not result in politically oriented unions with continuity into later periods of nationalist agitation; economic grievances were not effectively worked into the nationalist program of the day.

With the partition and the following Swadeshi agitation, Bengal became the temporary cynosure of Indian politics. The agitation marked a new high for nationalist activity. Surendranath Banerjea said to the Calcutta Congress in 1906:

> Let the Government know that when one province is injured, all the other provinces share the woe and the grief. The moral significance of such a demonstration, it would be impossible to exaggerate. . . . It will invest the public opinion of a province with the potency of the national voice of All India. It will intensify the solidarity between province and province by making them the participators in their mutual sorrows and anxieties. . . . to such an appeal made by afflicted Bengal to United India, there can be but one reply. . . .[32]

Lajput Rai wrote in *Young India* that "What was done in Bengal found its echo in the rest of the country." [33] Mohandas Gandhi, sailing home from South Africa to his native land, noted in *Hind Swaraj* that the spirit of Swadeshi started in Bengal and spread to the rest of India.[34] G. K. Gokhale pleaded the case for a united Bengal in London to Lord Morley and insisted that the revocation of the partition was one of the most important issues for Indians.[35]

POET IN POLITICS

The activities of Rabindranath Tagore, India's greatest modern writer and her most subtle and unheeded ideologue, may serve as an example of the Bengali focus of the movement, the new orientation of the period, and the difficult role of an apolitical man in politics. Born in 1861 into one of the most prominent families of nineteenth-century Calcutta, Tagore turned from concentration on the arts in his youth and early manhood to a greater concern for public affairs in the 1890s. He later described himself both as part of the mainstream of Indian culture and as an outlaw or outsider.[36] This dual perspective allowed him to participate in the national movement and to write illuminating critiques of it. During the 1890s he made attempts to have the proceedings of the Bengal Provincial Conference conducted in Bengali, and in 1898 at Dacca he himself read out his presidential speech in Bengali. He examined social and political questions writing in Bengali and with Bengal his principal frame of reference.[37]

During 1905 he took part in many partition protest meetings and in October initiated the political use of the "raktibandhan" ceremony,

symbolizing the unity of divided Bengal. Threads, symbolizing broth-
erhood, were fastened from Bengali to Bengali, and on a day of fasting,
purification, and work stoppage, Tagore led a huge procession through
the Calcutta streets singing a song he had composed for the occasion.[38]
He drew upon Bengali culture and his own work for symbols appropriate to the crisis in Bengal's life. Although he addressed meetings and
participated in organizations, his primary work was suggesting plans,
criticizing false leads, and expressing the feelings of the community.

Tagore had an image of an idyllic rural past, before European penetration, during which small units of the society undertook all the functions necessary to social welfare. For the present state of degradation
Tagore blamed British imperialism and, even more, his own ancestors.
Indian society had "lost interest in itself"; its mind had become dis-
tracted and dried up; fear and restrictiveness had become the familiar
elements of social life.

> If we had only kept ourselves acquainted with our country, that would
> have been something,—but so lazy are we, we know next to nothing
> about her. The foreigner writes our history, we translate it; the for-
> eigner discovers our grammar, we cram it! If we want to know what
> there is next door, we have to look into Hunter. We gather no facts
> first hand,—neither about men, nor commerce, nor even agriculture.
> And yet, with such crass indifference on our own part, we are not
> ashamed to prate about the duties of others towards our country.[39]

Tagore bitterly attacked the rulers. He felt that their milking of the
Indian cow for their own ends was warping the character of the
milker as well as the cow. Their morality had become debased through
service to conquest, efficiency, exploitation.[40] But Tagore held that
Bengali self-help was much more important than blaming the rulers
and sinking into self-pity. In some passages he made use of the old concept of hidden forces or shaktis within man and society which had to
be released in order for Bengalis to regain control of their own lives
and society. Tagore linked the shakti within to India's unique gifts or
essence and to the ways in which God structured the flow of modern
history.

> If there had been some centre of our *shakti*, where all could unite;
> where thinkers could contribute their ideas, and workers their efforts;
> then there the generous would find a repository for their gifts. Our ed-

ucation, our literature, our arts and crafts, and all our good works would range themselves round such centre and help to create in all its richness the commonwealth which our patriotism is in search of.

I have not the least doubt in my mind that the rebuffs which we are meeting from the outside are intended by Providence to help this centre of our *shakti* to become manifest within the nation; our petitions are being thrown back to us in order that we may turn our faces towards such centre; and the pessimism which is spreading amongst the feckless, workless critics of the government is due, not to the smart of any particular insult, or the hopelessness of any particular concession, but to the growing insistence of an inward quest for this centre.[41]

Deriding petitioning, Tagore called on Bengali political groups to rally under the leadership of one man.[42] He saw the waste of time, energy, and passion that came from intramovement conflict. He may also have been drawing on Hindu traditions of the autocratic raja and zamindar. When he put forth his plan for the Swadeshi Samaj in 1904, he suggested that the society which was to take over many of the welfare, social, political functions in Bengal should have one leader, both a concrete functionary and a symbol of the whole. He wrote,

If the community is to protect itself, it must take its stand on united strength. The best way would be to invest a strong personality with leadership and rally round him as our representative; to submit to his rule would mean no loss of self-respect, for he would be a symbol of freedom itself. . . . If we in Bengal succeed in selecting a leader of the samaj and making our social liberty bright and permanent, then the rest of India will follow.[43]

His blithe assumption that the rest of India was waiting to accept the lead of Bengal is a typical Bengali assumption of the period; there is a strong element of ethnocentricity in Bengali writing of the Swadeshi period to which even the most insightful were prone. Tagore laid out many proposals for reconstruction, trying to draw his countrymen's attention away from the actions of the British and day-to-day crises. He asked men to shift their gaze to the long-term goals and needs of Bengali society.[44]

The plan for the Swadeshi Samaj was aimed at the educated men and leaders of the society. Although Tagore may not have wished it, political and social problems were discussed from the top downward only. He himself had a predilection for thinking of leadership in so-

ciety in traditional ways, according to which the rajas initiated change
and controlled it. Tagore wanted a flow back into the countryside of
educated Calcutta men using fairs and district conferences as occasions
for making contact with the masses of Indian peasants. The educated
men were to contribute part of their income to the samaj and to help
devise ways of meeting local needs with indigenous, nongovernmental
resources. They were to be a vehicle for reclaiming the responsibility
for social welfare and transferring it from the state to the society, from
foreigners to the Bengalis.[45]

Tagore noted a widespread fear of change in Indian society among
all groups. But the peasant was the core of the problem: if rural society
could be improved, India would advance. The problem was how to
get the peasant to understand that change was needed and possible and
that even the most insignificant men in the society would have to contribute. The peasants also had shaktis within—Tagore assumed that
all individuals and groups had shaktis—and the impulse for change
would eventually have to come from within the peasant community as
well as from within the educated section of society. On his own es-
tates, Tagore addressed the peasants in their language to try to persuade them to act.[46]

The Swadeshi Samaj never took on life. Tagore was well aware that
initial enthusiasm was seldom followed by sustained achievement. The
ideas may have been imaginative and even appropriate, but Tagore was
not the leader to work at bringing the samaj to fruition. Disturbed by
divisions within the movement, upset at the primacy given politics, and
racked by personal tragedy, Tagore spent the five years from 1907 to
1911 mostly at his school, Santiniketan, and at Shelidah, his country
home.[47] Some years later, Tagore wrote to C. F. Andrews,

> I do not belong to the present age, the age of conflicting politics. Nev-
> ertheless I cannot repudiate the age which has given me birth. I suffer
> and struggle. I crave for freedom and yet am held back. I must share
> the life of the present world, though I do not believe in its cry. I sit at
> its table, and while it fills its cup with wine to slake its unnatural
> thirst, I try to listen, through the noisy carousal, to the murmur of the
> stream carrying its limpid waters to the sea.[48]

From the center of activity, Tagore moved to the periphery. He continued his own small experiments in education and village work and

commented on events in the great world, but he did not have to suffer the stings of factional strife.

DIVISIONS IN THE MOVEMENT

Amidst the exaltation of the first Swadeshi years, differences were submerged in order to present a united front of Bengalis against the Raj. By 1906, however, cleavages began to show. These were not temporary lines of division but fundamental conflicts of generation, of views about the ends and means of nationalist action, and of political power. A majority of the politically conscious Muslims were separated from the antipartition agitation. Three years or so after the beginning of the agitation, some young Bengalis turned to violent resistance, particularly political murders and robberies, and this cut them off from many of those involved in the Swadeshi movement who would not countenance violence.[49]

The most celebrated split was between the Moderates and the Extremists, divided along ideological lines and shortly struggling for control of the Congress. The Extremists, who were a loosely organized group, challenged the authority of the British to rule India. They wanted to protest strongly against the basis of this rule and to set up parallel institutions outside the scope of the British Raj. The Extremists were also more concerned with the fate and development of Indian culture than the older, often more Anglicized Moderates. One aspect of the Extremist challenge was a critique of the Moderates' politics, values, cultural positions, and even their personal habits and behavior. In Bipin Pal's assessment of Surendranath Banerjea, we may discern Pal's conceptions of negative and positive nationalist identity:

By no means an unaccommodating person, Surendra Nath has never learnt the secret of converting a private surrender to a public victory. He is not a far-seeing statesman either—he does not see all the possibilities of a situation long before they become manifest. He is not even an idealist, who can be oblivious of all practical consequences in his quest for the ideal. He is not a hero who can bravely face the direst personal losses at the call of duty. He is not even a Nationalist in the true sense of the term, for he never learnt anything of his country, its ancient literature and special culture, neither as a youth when he went to school among Anglo-Indians and Eurasians to the Deveton College, nor in later life; and thus, both by training and heredity, he has been like so many of his contemporaries far too much denationalised to make a true and ideal patriot.[50]

Years earlier, Pal's journalistic and political colleague Aurobindo Ghose maintained that the timid methods of the Mehta-Banerjea Congress showed its members to be less than men, particularly when compared to French and Irish revolutionaries who had been purified by blood and fire.[51]

The Congress, in Bengal and nationally, was an organization within which a dominant faction fought off the challenges of competing factions. Some, like Lajpat Raj and Motilal Ghose of the *Amrita Bazar Patrika*, moved between the main factions without tying themselves irrevocably to either side. Since the 1880s the *Patrika* had been shooting barbs into the sensitive skin of Surendranath Banerjea and it argued in 1904:

> In the first place, the Congress has no constitution and is consequently nothing but a three-day ceremony; whereas its work should be steadily continued throughout the year and the masses made to take an interest in the movement which should be made much less costly.[52]

Once Bipin Pal and Aurobindo Ghose joined in producing the daily and weekly paper *Bande Mataram* in 1906, the attacks grew more intense. Pal wanted to break up what he called the "old lawyer rings" of the Congress and plant new seeds of democracy from which would flower a new leadership.[53]

The challenge was stated, but it was still necessary for the Extremists to organize and act on their belligerent words. The New Party, as the Extremists called themselves, had plans for a democratic and representative organization running from the province to the district and village levels. Such an organization, however, never existed except on paper, although some groups called "National Volunteers" appeared.[54] By 1906, Gokhale wrote, Calcutta had become a

> regular pandemonium—Surendranath's inexcusable excesses, the *Patrika*'s vindictive pursuit of Surendranath, the fierce quarrel between Surendranath and Bipin Chandra Pal and the latter's unscrupulous ambition to play at all costs the role of a new leader, the Anglo-Indian ferocity let loose against Indians, Mohamedan ill-will stirred up against Hindus . . .[55]

Gokhale stressed the base motivations of the Moderates' enemy Pal; with such perceptions it is explicable why the collisions of Moderates and Extremists at national and provincial Congress sessions in 1907 were marked by mutual lack of capacity for understanding or for compromise.

The Extremists did compromise at the 1906 Calcutta Congress; but the following December at the Midnapur District Conference, and then at the Surat Congress, differences proved unbridgeable. At Midnapur, the Moderates had to call in the local police so that they could run the meeting as they desired.[56] The showdown came at Surat. The Moderates put up Rash Behari Ghose, a wealthy Bengali barrister, as their candidate for president and pushed his selection through the reception committee. The presidency had in the past been decided on by a coterie of Moderates, but at Surat the Extremists challenged this method as autocratic and demanded a role in preparing resolutions for the Subjects Committee.

The Extremists, led by Tilak and Aurobindo Ghose and supported principally by delegates from Bengal, Maharashtra, the Punjab, and the Central Provinces, protested the selection of Rash Behari Ghose and the meeting was suspended. The following day efforts at an orderly meeting failed, disorder ensued, shoes flew, hired club-wielders entered. The Moderates and Extremists then met separately, the former calling their meeting a "convention" and laying down rules for participants. The Moderates drew up a new constitution and an oath confining members to political action by constitutional means only.[57] From 1908 to 1914, the Moderates met, with declining attendance and enthusiasm, in what one of their number called a "rump Congress." [58]

The New Party was hampered by the imprisonment of many of its important leaders and the departure of others from the political field. Bipin Pal, disturbed by the violence and hatred engendered by the movement and differing with colleagues on *Bande Mataram*, left Bengal for England in August 1908. He returned in 1911 more moderate and idiosyncratic in his ways and unable to work effectively with an organized party during the remaining twenty years of his life.[59] Aurobindo Ghose was imprisoned in 1908 for a year while awaiting and on trial, and in the same year, Tilak was sentenced to a long term of imprisonment for sedition.[60] In December 1908, the Indian Criminal Law Amendment Act was passed; this allowed the government to cast its net widely, sweeping up nonviolent Extremists and a few Moderates as well as young revolutionaries.

After Surat some efforts were made to reconcile the Congress factions. Aurobindo Ghose met Surendranath Banerjea at the Bengal Provincial Conference at Hooghly and also at Sylhet in 1909, but Ghose was not willing to abide by the new Congress constitution.[61] Ghose shortly left for seclusion and religious activity in Pondicherry, but the internecine warfare within the nationalist movement continued. The *Nayak* maintained in 1911 that

> Their deliberations are nowadays held *in camera* in the rooms of the Indian Association. One no longer sees the faces of men like Sures Chandra, editor of *Basumati*, Sakharam, editor of *Hitavadi*, Upendra Nath Sen, Asvini Kumar Dutta, Syam Sundar Chakravarti, Hemendra Prasad Ghosh, Chitta Ranjan Das and A. Rasul in their meetings and conferences.[62]

Of even greater long-range consequence than the temporary split and long ineffectualness of the Congress was the absence of any appreciable Muslim representation in the nationalist ranks. In 1904, Lord Curzon toured eastern Bengal explaining to Muslim leaders how they would benefit from the proposed partition. One important convert was the Nawab of Dacca, Khwaja Salimulla, a recognized leader of Bengal Muslims until his death in 1915.[63] Salimulla and other Muslim notables joined in the Simla deputation to the new viceroy, Lord Minto, and then combined to form the Muslim League in 1906. The league's main object was the protection of Muslim interests, and a London branch was soon opened by Ameer Ali and the Aga Khan.[64]

Some Muslims from western Bengal, including Guznavi Rasul, Abdul Gafur, Liaquat Hussain, Abul Kasem, and Dedar Bux, supported the Swadeshi movement.[65] Even though Surendranath Banerjea and others called for Muslim support, most politically active Muslims and even the remnants of the Fara'idi movement (composed of poor, rural Muslims) accepted the partition and opposed Swadeshi.[66] Antagonisms engendered by the boycott campaign, antizamindar feeling among Muslim peasants in eastern Bengal, where the zamindars and moneylenders were mostly Hindus, and incitement by Maulvis led to a number of communal disturbances in a few districts of Eastern Bengal and Assam during 1907.[67]

The lack of Muslim participation in the Swadeshi agitation became a great concern to Tagore, Pal, and a few Hindu spokesmen from 1907. In 1908 Tagore wrote,

> When our speakers failed in Mymensingh and other areas to win the heart of the Mussalman peasantry, they felt very indignant. They never thought for a moment that we have never given proof of our real interest in the welfare of the Mussalmans or of the common people of our country. We cannot, therefore, blame them if they are rather suspicious of our professions of goodwill. A brother does, of course, suffer for the sake of another brother, but if somebody just turns up from nowhere and introduces himself as brother, he is not very likely to be straight away shown into his share of the inheritance.[68]

Tagore's realization of the communal gap and its significance was not shared by many Hindu Bengali leaders. At the Bengal Provincial Conference in 1908, Tagore called for Hindus to support special concessions to the Muslims in order to bring about a healthy relationship between the communities.[69] Such an effort was not made until C. R. Das's Bengal Pact in 1924. In the meanwhile, the fusion of Hinduism and nationalist politics was making the recruitment of Muslims to the common nationalist cause increasingly difficult.

GOVERNMENT RESPONSES: REPRESSION, REFORM, REALIGNMENT

In the complex interaction between the government (of India and of Bengal) and the nationalist groups, officials, especially in the Home Department, saw law and order as one of their primary functions. During these years the efforts of the CID burgeoned and many political leaders were under constant surveillance. Thus the government, soon armed with special powers and seeking to extend them, determined who was capable of engaging in politics. Surendranath Banerjea notes wistfully in his memoirs that in the 1870s political men worked freely without being watched, while in the new century, officials were fearful and the European population of Calcutta was often on the verge of mass hysteria. The threat of revolution and anarchy arose periodically, along with memories of rebellion half a century earlier; and as long as the viceroy was close to Calcutta's Europeans, he had to act strongly against any breaks in the wall of order.[70]

Lord Minto argued that "government by the strong hand is what appeals to the majority of the different populations of this country." [71] He believed, as did many later officials, that if the small band of troublemakers was suppressed and concessions were made to those calling for reform, then all would be quiet. Before the outbreak of political murder and robbery, the main moves of the government were directed against those harsh critics of British rule whom they called "seditionists." Several leaders of the Extremists, especially Tilak, suffered from both the special measures and new uses of the old regulations.[72]

With the rise of the Extremists and then the revolutionaries, the Moderates and the government were pushed together by circumstances outside their own making, and in time the Moderates began to look more like loyalists. Minto wrote to Morley after meeting Surendranath Banerjea:

> It was simply marvellous, with the troubles and anxieties of a few months ago still fresh in one's memory, to see the "King of Bengal" sitting on my sofa with his Mahommedan opponents, asking for my assistance to moderate the evil passions of the Bengali, and inveighing against the extravagances of Bepin Chandra Pal.[73]

Under the pressure of agitation, the Morley-Minto reforms were written into law as the Government of India Act of 1909. But the advance was limited. In a memorandum to Morley, Minto insisted that

> The Government of India must remain autocractic; the sovereignty must be vest in British hands and cannot be delegated to any kind of representative assembly. No such assembly could claim to speak on behalf of the Indian people so long as the uneducated masses, forming ninety percent of the adult male population, are absolutely incapable of understanding what 'representative government' means and of taking any effective part in any system of election. . . . There is all the difference in the world between the arbitrary autocracy of the Asiatic despotism and the constitutional autocracy which binds itself to govern by rule, which admits and invites to its councils representatives of all the interests which are capable of being represented, and which merely reserves to itself, in the form of a narrow majority, the predominant and absolute power which it can only abdicate at the risk of bringing back the chaos to which our rule put an end.[74]

Minto maintained that the reforms were not a capitulation to the agitators, although he did admit that one goal of the reforms was to help rally the Moderates.[75] The Moderates pressed for the reforms by lobbying in Calcutta and London, as did the newly organized Muslim League. The Muslim Leaguers wanted separate electorates and reserved seats because, as the Aga Khan wrote, the Congress had chosen Muslim yes-men to represent Madras and Bombay in the Imperial Legislative Council, and Muslim hopes had been "dashed again and again" by the Congress.[76] R. C. Dutt and other congressmen argued against separate electorates as divisive. In the end, Minto and the league won their point. Morley and the congressmen were more concerned with the advances toward representative government, which although small, were welcomed by Surendranath Banerjea and the Congress.[77]

The imperial and provincial legislative councils were expanded and Indian members were added to Morley's and Minto's councils. For all their criticism of the Bengalis (especially Minto's), several Bengalis were considered for these posts, including R. C. Dutt and Sir Asutosh Mookerjee. Finally, two Bengalis were chosen: K. G. Gupta, ICS, for Morley's council; and Lord Sinha, advocate-general of the government of India and a leading barrister, for Minto's council.[78] Pleased though the Moderates were at the advance, they were critical of the regulations following the reforms, of separate electorates, and of official control that would be maintained even with a slight majority of nonofficials in the Bengal council. But however hamstrung they were, the Moderates accepted, as always, the British and Indian government groundrules and cooperated.[79]

To the Extremists, the reforms were petty advances not worth the consideration of serious nationalist leaders. Aurobindo Ghose wrote in the *Karmayogin:*

> The mountains have again been in labour, and the mouse they have produced this time is enormous in size and worthy of the august mountains that produced him, but not the less ridiculous for all that. What is it that this much-trumpeted scheme gives to a people which is not inferior in education, or intellectual calibre to the Turk, the Persian and the Chinese who already enjoy or are in sight of full self-government? There are four elements which have always to be considered in a change of this kind, first the nature of the electorate, second, the

composition of the body itself, thirdly, the freedom of election, fourthly, the scope, functions and powers of the assemblies. There is not one of these points in which the people have really gained and there is hardly one of them in which they are not worse off than under the old system.[80]

In the elections for the reformed Bengal Legislative Council, the Moderates did fairly well contesting the general seats. Although they worked under the reformed constitution, they wished to gain greater powers, such as full provincial autonomy. The Extremists remained outside the gate.

Under the new team of Lord Hardinge and Lord Crewe, replacements for Lord Minto and Lord Morley respectively, just one year after Minto's departure the partition of Bengal was annulled and provincial boundaries were realigned. Bengal proper, containing most of the Bengali-speaking districts in eastern India, was constituted as a province with a governor like Bombay and Madras. At the same time, the capital of British India was shifted to Delhi. The announcement, rumored for some time, brought forth a tumult of joy and anger. Some alliances of previous years were reversed: the Moderates and the *Bengalee* warmly praised the government; the Muslims of Bengal felt that they had been betrayed after being the "favorite wife" of Lieutenant-Governor Bamfylde Fuller of Eastern Bengal and Assam; the European press of Calcutta criticized the government. The *Bengalee*, defending the government, suggested the editor of the *Statesman* be hauled in for sedition, and the *Statesman* attacked the government for not consulting public opinion.[81]

For the Moderates of Bengal, the nullification of the partition was the cherished goal of many years of petitioning and an action which they said vindicated their political methods. Some of them wrote an open letter to the public which was printed in many papers. It read in part:

> There may be differences of opinion regarding the removal of the capital to Delhi, but it must not be forgotten that it is a most necessary adjunct to the establishment of provincial autonomy in Bengal. It affords as a result, a good opportunity for the realization of our high political ambitions. In particular, every patriotic and loyal citizen will realise that this removal of the capital conduces to the upholding of the dignity of the country, for, in the distant past, it was Delhi which was

the seat of Hindu and Moslem empires. The most glorious memories of us Hindus and Moslems are associated with the old historic city of Delhi. It is desirable in every way that those ancient glories of Delhi should be revived under British rule.[82]

The letter ended with the hope that the announcement would bring forth the loyalty and gratitude of all Bengalis. The *Hitavadi* and *Sanjivani*, two important Bengali newspapers, said it was a great day for Bengal and for the Bengali people, and the *Nayak* printed its comment in purple.

The strongest critics of the moves were the loyalist Hindus, the European community in Calcutta, and the Muslims. Mr. W. A. J. Archbold wrote in a life of Lord Carmichael, the first governor of reunited Bengal,

> The Europeans of Calcutta felt that they were being sacrificed; and the Indian landowners were fearful that the value of their property would suffer. As a witty Indian told his fellow Bengalis: 'You have been crying for the moon, and they have given it to you; they have at the same time taken away the sun.' [83]

The *Englishman* and the *Statesman*, organs of the European community, and the *Hindoo Patriot*, an organ of loyalist Hindus in the British Indian Association, assailed the government and particularly the viceroy and were joined in their criticism by Lord Curzon and the journalist Lovat Fraser.[84]

The Europeans and the Indian landed and business interests thought they would lose economically by the transfer. They saw as well that their political influence would be diminished if the imperial government were no longer stationed for at least six months of the year in Calcutta. After the first rapturous moment, some of the Moderates and of the Indian press came to agree with this point of view and regretted the transfer.[85]

The other group most unhappy about the two actions, especially the nullification of the partition, was the Bengali Muslim press. The *Moslem Hitaishi* tempered its criticism with loyalist restraint:

> The news that our most respected King-Emperor has placed the two Bengals under the rule of one Governor has caused delight to us, for we have no right to object to any arrangement which Government may make for good government. Our sole object is to live happily and

peacefully under the protection of the Government. The Partition of Bengal was advantageous to the Musalmans of Eastern Bengal in all ways. This is why we rejoiced at the Partition and prayed to the Government to uphold it. However that may be, the present arrangement of placing the two Bengals under one Governor has satisfied the Musalmans of Bengal; but their prayer to the Government is this that the advantages which the Partition gained for the Musalmans of East Bengal in District Boards, Local Boards and Municipalities and in the public service and the field of education, may be maintained. In short, it is the earnest desire of all Musalmans in Bengal that a system of separate representation, like that for election of members to the Legislative Councils may be introduced regarding election to District Boards, Local Boards and Municipalities also. Besides this, it is desirable that Government should see to the distribution of posts in the public service in a district amongst Hindus and Musalmans according to their respective numerical strength.[86]

Some more severe Muslim comments were published in the Calcutta-based *Comrade*, edited by Mohammed Ali, a non-Bengali Muslim with an Oxford degree:

As for the Musalmans of East Bengal, they must derive what cold comfort they can from the well-known lines:—

> Laugh, and the world laughs with you.
> Weep, and you weep alone.

After all they are only "loyal and contented" and as a reward of their loyalty and contentment they have been given a generous helping of the humble pie.[87]

In the same issue of *Comrade:*

Except in Bengal, where it touches certain vested interests too closely, the transfer of the Government seat to Delhi has been received with considerable satisfaction in every other part of the country. Calcutta had made it possible for the Bengali to loom beyond all proportions in Indian affairs, and it is no fault of the Indian Government if it viewed public questions affecting the whole of the country sometimes in a false perspective and consequently blundered. In Delhi, while perpetuating a great Imperial tradition and finding an appropriate capital for a great Empire, the Government will find the necessary detachment for the impartial conduct of Indian affairs. The Anglo-Indian press in Calcutta is up in arms against the change. The non-official community in this city is as a class very powerful and the Anglo-Indian press is ever ready to dance to its tune.[88]

As the *Comrade* observed, many non-Bengali and non-Calcutta groups and interests were pleased with the transfer. As one high civil servant pointed out in his memoirs, they had long been jealous of Calcutta's influence on the affairs of the empire and were glad to see it reduced.[89]

The shift of the capital did mark a turning point in the history of Bengal's role in Indian history. It was only with the coming of the Europeans and the establishment of the British Raj that the Bengalis and Bengal were placed at the center of a vast empire. The possibility for the conversion of parochial issues into Indian ones gave the leaders of nonofficial Calcutta and Bengal a prominence in Indian affairs that was in part a product of geographic circumstance. There were, of course, other factors, such as the rapid development of Western education, the press, and the professions in Bengal, but these were also related to the importance the British gave to the area by settling their imperial government there. The adaptability of Bengalis in taking to a new culture and to changes in administration was involved as well. When the governmental seat changed, the special place of Bengal was seriously impaired. Moreover, in their inability to sustain the Swadeshi agitation or to build an effective, on-going organization, the Bengali politicians had failed as national leaders, a fact that also was to have important consequences for the history of Bengal in the Indian nationalist movement.

But there were several positive results of the Swadeshi period. It marked a much more developed stage of agitational politics than could be seen in previous Bengali nationalist activity. For some, verbally at least, it meant the end of the legitimacy of the Raj and the realization that only Indian self-government would foster their rights and interests. There was, too, the growth of both the Bengali and the English-language press, spreading news of the movement to most of the important district towns of Bengal and, in turn, reporting the agitation going on in outlying districts. The press of the time was filled with Swadeshi poems and songs heralding an emotional release and expressiveness which became a feature of nationalism in Bengal. The cry "Bande Mataram" and the adoption of this song from Chatterjee's novel symbolized the confluence of cultural currents and political activities and the mood of defiance which characterized the Swadeshi years.

Although most Muslims and ordinary Bengali villagers remained outside the nationalist movement, the Swadeshi period did see a further move toward the creation of a genuine nationalist political party, even though its activities were limited. More realistic proposals for party-building were put forward, even if they were not implemented. The idea that nationalist politics involved devoted work and the possible sacrifice of one's career spread among the younger men in the colleges. Probably many more Bengalis were made aware of contemporary political developments, if only by a brief public meeting in their towns or villages, than at any earlier time under British rule. To more fully explore this period, the career and personality of the Extremist Aurobindo Ghose are analyzed in the next chapter.

FOUR
Aurobindo Ghose: Secrets of the Self and Revolution

Aurobindo Ghose, Extremist leader and secret revolutionary, participated in Bengali and nationalist politics for less than four years, but his writings and ideas then and at other times in his life made a sharp impression on many political workers in Bengal. During this brief and exciting period, he also became one of the Indian politicians most feared by the Home Department of the government of India, and its constant surveillance and treatment of him may be taken as a case study of its new policy of repression.[1]

In 1910, in the midst of intense political activity, Aurobindo suddenly left the public stage to become a yogin and guru. His shift to the religious life has increased the difficulties for critical biographers of his career. Many of those who have gathered information about Aurobindo Ghose (or Sri Aurobindo, as he was called later in his life) have been disciples. Almost without exception, they have given readers the life of a saint, who they assume was an avatar. The human characteristics and personal drama have been lost in the process.[2] To this difficulty has been added another: Aurobindo was secretive about his personal life and feelings. He wrote and spoke of himself in the third person, lengthening the distance between himself and his actions. Aurobindo and his disciple-biographers wrote about his political career years after it had taken place and read back the holy man into the earlier stages of his career, viewing the political activities as preparatory to the religious and ascetic stage.[3]

PREPARATION AND EDUCATION, 1872–1892

Aurobindo's father, Dr. Krishnadhan Ghose, came from a Kayastha family associated with the village of Konnagar in Hooghly District, near Calcutta. After training in Edinburgh, Dr. Ghose became a civil surgeon and was posted to Bhagalpur, Rangpur, and Khulna during his career in the government service. He married Swarnalata, the daughter of Rajnarayan Basu, a prominent Brahmo Samaj leader and an important figure in the cultural life of Calcutta.[4] Basu participated in the Hindu revival of the later nineteenth century and helped to found the Hindu Mela festival.[5] His daughter Swarnalata has been said to have suffered from "hysteria" and fits of violence and depression which made life for her husband and children extremely difficult.[6] It is unfortunate that more specific examples of the behavior of Swarnalata have not been recorded. The term "hysteria" seems to imply that she went into melodramatic fits which brought her much attention. Although it often appears that a hysterical person is weak because of such fits, it is possible that they function as a means of getting power over others. It seems justifiable to suggest that Aurobindo's lifelong obsession with mother figures dates from his childhood. In his writing, especially his writing about himself but even in his writing about the clash of cultures in modern India, there is a melodramatic quality that may stem from the scenes of childhood.[7]

Aurobindo was the third of five children, having two older brothers, Binoybhushan and Monomohan, a younger sister, Sarojini, and a younger brother, Barindra Kumar. He was born in 1872 and spent the first seven years of his life shuttling between his family's home in Khulna, his maternal grandfather's home in Deogarh, and the Loretto Convent School in Darjeeling.[8] Aurobindo's father is said to have become an atheist after a brief period of interest in the Brahmo Samaj. He was firmly attached to Anglicized personal habits and beliefs. He decided to give his children a completely English education and sent them to English private schools during their early years. In 1879 he took the family to England, where he left three of the young boys in the care of English families to obtain a Western education. They remained there alone for some thirteen years, the only contact with their parents through the mail.[9] Aurobindo frequently had the company of his brothers, but, according to his own account, made few friendships in England, and those few inconsequential. Writing of his early years at the school in Darjeeling, Aurobindo described a dream in which he was enveloped in darkness, or "tamas" in the philosophical terminology he adopted in his later writing. The life of the Ghose brothers was so difficult and unusual for children of a high-caste, fairly well-to-do family that perhaps Aurobindo could only see a life of darkness before him.[10]

Aurobindo's father was caught between two national identities and tried to resolve this problem for his sons by encapsulating them in an English environment. But the father and his sons remained in a bipolar dilemma. The father implicitly or explicitly laid down certain ideals for his sons, but even these had a bipolar quality. They were to succeed in English schools and institutions as adjudged by English standards. When it came to career choices, however, their Indianness came into play. Aurobindo was to try for the Indian Civil Service, not the English civil service. Monomohan did teach English literature and write poetry in English, in India. In part, both father and sons were trapped without a country with which they could fully identify. The Indian nation, as an independent entity at least, was just in the process of creation. They had to try to make good in the English world, the world of the rulers and, as Aurobindo and many other Indians came to believe, of the oppressors of India. Identification with the oppressor had tragic potential for many Indians; grasping the English rose, they might be pierced by the thorns.

The loneliness of the Ghose brothers in England came during the crucial period of adolescence. At this time one usually forms important and sometimes lasting ties to one's peers, but Aurobindo, by his own admission, did not.[11] This may have hampered the formation of relationships with others throughout his life and may partially account for his tendency to retreat into himself at times of stress.

Aurobindo lived in Manchester from 1879 to 1884, in London from September 1884 to July 1890, at Cambridge from 1890 to 1892. He spent his last months in London before returning to India at the end of 1892. While in Manchester, he was tutored by the Reverend William H. Drewett, with whose family he was staying, and his two older brothers attended the Manchester Grammar School. Aurobindo displayed a high aptitude for classical studies and was admitted to St. Paul's School in London and later to Cambridge University mainly on the basis of his abilities and achievements in languages and literatures.[12] In his own account of himself as a youth, he wrote:

> In those days I was not particular about telling the truth and I was a great coward. Nobody could have imagined that later on I could face the gallows or carry on a revolutionary movement . . .[13]

A more prosaic and neglected account appeared amid Home Department files concerning the seditionist and conspirator Aurobindo, written by Mr. A. Wood, ICS, who had attended St. Paul's School with the Ghose brothers in the 1880s:

> Aravinda Acroyd Ghose attended St. Paul's School as a day-boy from about 1884 to 1890. He joined with a brother M. M. 5 years older, but apparently grounded with him and not so bright, so that Aravinda soon left him behind and reached the top of the school very rapidly, on the classical side. Unlike his elder brother, he knew no Indian language: he mispronounced oriental names in the same ways as an Englishman, but talked English with an Indian accent. Though Aravinda seems to have dropped his 'Acroyd' since, both brothers in their school-days used to attend prayers and were understood to be Christians, though where or how they lived or who looked after them, I think none of us knew or cared. We only noticed that Aravinda especially grew more and more dirty and unkempt and looked more and more unhealthy and neglected. Neither of them played any games or made any friends that I ever saw, except that some boys used to patronize Aravinda a little because he was so childish. That continued, his characteristic—and 'Baby Ghose' his nickname—all his school-days. At Greek and Latin he was brilliant, but no use at anything else, and seemed to have no ideas in his head.[14]

Mr. Wood went on to detail how Monomohan began to write "revolutionary and erotic lyrics in English" and grew wilder and shabbier as he grew older. He found it hard to believe that "Baby Ghose" had become a revolutionary leader and that his older brother was uninvolved. Mr. Wood's account shows the loneliness and poverty in which the Ghose brothers lived in England, when their father's remittances were irregular and infrequent. Aurobindo wrote poetry and read a great deal. For all his academic achievements and prizes for classical studies, he was still an outsider. As Mr. Wood pointed out, he did not engage in games or make friendships and so become one of the crowd either at St. Paul's or at Cambridge.[15] It should be noted that similar themes run through the lives of Aurobindo and his older brother Monomohan. Both went through periods of rebellion and both had to try to find some compromise between their English training and their Indian nationality. Both wrote English poetry but turned more to Indian themes. In their youth Monomohan was the more rebellious; in his mature years he found his niche as a professor of English literature in India. Aurobindo came to rebellion in his mature years and it became a more dominant theme in his life.

The extent to which Aurobindo was "denationalized" by these English years has been overstressed. He lived in an English environment, but his main social contacts were with his brothers, who were older and had lived longer in India. Dr. Ghose wrote to his sons and sent clippings from the *Bengalee* describing English injustices in India. At Cambridge, Aurobindo joined the Indian Majlis, an organization of Indian students, and he said he made nationalist speeches to this group.[16] A check of Aurobindo's records as an ICS candidate reveal that in the final examination he received 298 marks out of a possible 400 in Bengali, 167 out of 500 in Sanskrit, and high marks in the history and geography of India.[17] Mitra says that Aurobindo tried to learn Bengali and Sanskrit on his own and read many volumes in the Sacred Books of the East series.[18]

Some biographers of Aurobindo claim that his father endured some disappointments during his career in the medical service, and that his embitterment compounded that of his sons. It appears that the fruits of Aurobindo's education were a thorough knowledge of several Western languages, an elegant English prose style, and an extreme hostility to the rulers of India. Before he left England, Aurobindo, probably at his father's urging and with the encouragement of his brothers, took the ICS examination. He scored high on the academic and linguistic portions but was not passed because he did not appear for the riding test.[19] Mr. A. Wood claimed in his note on Aurobindo in 1908 that it was said that Aurobindo had an unspecified physical defect which was one of the reasons he was failed. But a search of the relevant files showed that although he was at first failed in the medical examination, he did subsequently pass it.[20] Aurobindo said years later that certain "revolutionary" speeches he had made at the Indian Majlis probably led to his disqualification, but a consideration of such speeches is nowhere to be found in the government files.[21]

In the Judicial and Public Proceedings there are several letters by Aurobindo to British officials, including one to the Earl of Kimberley, then Secretary of State for India, in which Aurobindo pleaded for a second chance at the riding test.[22] After this appeal was granted and he failed to appear again, he sent a request to receive the £150 usually given to probationers for expenses during the testing and preparatory period. The files contained as well a letter from one Jas. S. Cotton to Sir Arthur Macpherson, an official in the relevant department, begging that Aurobindo be given a third chance at the riding test:

> As you may know, Mr. Ghose was disqualified for failing to pass his examination in riding, or perhaps I should say, for failing to keep the appointment made for him by the examiner, after he had previously shown similar want of punctuality and disregard for the requirements of the examiner. His excuse (such as it is) is that want of money prevented him for [from?] taking the needful lessons in riding, and that, at the last, anxiety and moral cowardice made him lose his head.— He tells me that he did turn up at Woolwich for the examination, half an hour late.[23]

On the surface at least, it seems that Aurobindo was eager to join the ICS at that time and that it was a very real possibility for him. He suggested in retrospect that God did not mean him to join the ICS because He had other important work for him to do.[24] This explanation, however, seems to be completely ahistorical. Aurobindo had worked hard to develop intellectual skills and linguistic capabilities but had never participated in games or any active form of physical exertion. Rather than openly show his incompetence, he was conveniently late for the test. It seems to have been the fear of failure rather than God's call or nationalist speeches that kept him out of the ICS.

There is also a high probability that Aurobindo had considerable ambivalence about joining the ICS. By the time he began training for the examination, he was receiving the Indian press clippings sent by his father. He was in touch with other Indian students at Cambridge and probably had begun to shape out his nationalist opinions. He may have found it hard at that point in his life to deal with what one might call the double message of father to son: do well by English standards, but also be an Indian man.

EDUCATIONAL WORK AND BARODA YEARS, 1892–1906

The same Mr. Cotton who had written to the government on Aurobindo's behalf arranged a meeting with the Gaekwar of Baroda.[25] Aurobindo was offered and accepted a position in the service of the Gaekwar. Thus after thirteen years in England separated from family and country, Aurobindo returned to India. For the next fourteen years, the state of Baroda in Western India served as his home and base of operations.

He soon published one series of articles on the state of Indian politics and another on Bankim Chandra Chatterjee, with the aid of an Indian acquaintance from Cambridge, K. G. Deshpande.[26] The articles on Indian politics, entitled "New Lamps for Old," were published in the *Indu-Prakash*, a Bombay weekly, from mid-1893 to early 1894. The Chatterjee series was published from July 16 to August 27, 1894. Both contributions were printed without the author's name.[27] These articles show the continuity of Aurobindo's political opinions from his early twenties through the intense political phase of his life. The pieces on Bankim Chandra give cultural opinions, which shifted considerably through time.

The political opinions were couched in a pugnacious and provocative style. In arrogant tones, the author gave examples from ancient and modern European history to show the narrowness of other political commentators and the limitations of the Moderates' adherence to British models for political organization and ideology. Aurobindo asked why the Indians should copy the British when they were really more like the French and the Athenians.[28] Although Aurobindo had had considerable training in English literature, his concentration on classical studies had turned him more to classical and continental European history and literature. All his political writing is filled with references to Greek and Roman history and also to French history. He helped to widen the range of organizational and ideological possibilities for his generation of Indian nationalists.

The "new men," or representatives of the new middle classes, as they described themselves, seemed to Aurobindo to represent a narrow

sliver of Indian society, with a mendicant political policy as well as a
limited historical perspective.[29] Still under the influence of his Western
education, Aurobindo was more prepared to borrow from Western experience than he was later in life, when he found ancient Indian models more congenial. He always displayed an antipathy for British institutions. He attacked the legalistic constraints upon Indian political
activity, attributing them to the prevalence of lawyers in politics. He
was among the first Indian writers to call for connection to the masses.
Here he was borrowing words more from the political vocabulary of
continental Europe than from England. Noting and playing up the
slightest signs of turbulence, he described the reactions of an Indian
peasantry which he had never seen: the "fierce pain of hunger and op-
pression cuts to the bone." [30] In his image of society, he saw a deca-
dent nobility, narrow-minded burgesses on the English model, and a
torpid but potentially powerful proletariat which, he thought, represented "our sole chance." [31] By "our" he probably meant the politically conscious group within Indian society. He wanted a leadership
group more radical than the Moderates, but as yet he could point to
no group or individual as an example. Thus he looked to the field of
letters and picked the Bengali novelist Bankim Chandra Chatterjee as a
heroic model.

Aurobindo portrayed Bankim Chandra as a demigod, a gigantic figure
astride the mid-nineteenth century, the central figure of the Indian
renaissance. While he derided Anglo-Indian babus, the servile imitators
of the haughty, greedy, rude, and ambitious British bureaucrats, Aurobindo held up Bankim Chandra as the one Indian hero who could
stand comparison with the great leaders and literary men of Europe.[32]
This is another example of the colonial "need for the conviction of
cultural equivalence." [33] In this phase of life, Aurobindo was still
under the influence of the thought and standards of the West and even
referred to the "hideous grotesques of old Hindu art." [34] He was
searching for men as well as works of art and literature that would
bear comparison with Western examples.

For all his harsh criticism of the Moderates and the contemporary
generation of political leaders, Aurobindo was not ready to offer any
thoughtful alternative or to plunge into political organizing himself.
The years at Baroda have most often been viewed by his biographers as

a period of "Indianization" or renationalization to recover from the English years of "denationalization." There seems no doubt that Aurobindo did spend much of his time working at Bengali and Sanskrit. A young Bengali who helped Aurobindo with his Bengali in this period described his appearance:

> [His] footwear was a pair of nagra sandals of the primitive type; his dhoti half-tucked at the back of the waist, was coarse-spun Ahmedabad-mill khadi with an ill-looking border; a coarse banian covering the trunk; thin, long hair, parted half-way on the head, hanging down to the neck; . . . eyes soft and dreamy; complexion a shade dark . . . a living fount of English, French, Latin, Hebrew, Greek . . .[35]

Trained in classical studies, Aurobindo was able to turn to the study of Indian classics and progress rapidly. He read extensively in Sanskrit literature and philosophy and, in the course of time, adopted ancient Indian philosophy and values, as he interpreted them, for his own. What Aurobindo's biographers seem to have overstressed is the discontinuity with his previous education. He had already begun to study Bengali and Sanskrit and to read Indian philosophy in England, and the training in Western intellectual disciplines undoubtedly facilitated his Indian studies in Baroda. His work on Shakespeare and Homer prepared the ground, one might well argue, for his researches on Kalidasa and the *Bhagavad Gītā*.

At Baroda, Aurobindo was employed as an English professor at the college in the state's capital and also handled some of the Gaekwar's correspondence. But he also led a kind of secret religious and political life. He made contact with political workers in Maharashtra who formed one wing of the Extremist or nationalist party and so came in touch with Indian politics in a concrete way.[36] He traveled to Bengal to visit his family and also to marry, but he does not seem to have thought of living and working in Bengal until the early 1900s.[37] He met some revolutionary workers from the Bombay Presidency, where such activity had begun in the 1890s and where the first anarchist acts were committed. He had held up the examples of Irish, American, Italian, and French revolutionaries in his first published political writings as men purified by blood and fire.[38] In his political ideology two general strategies always seem to be considered: the line of mass movement and the path of secretly plotted violent revolution. When he surfaced at the end of his Baroda period, he was to work at both these strategies; but in the Baroda years he was slowly feeling his way and working toward an elaborate and viable alternative to the political models of the Moderates.

Aurobindo's preparations at Baroda may be divided into two parts that eventually run together: the spiritual and the political. At Baroda and in other parts of western India, Aurobindo participated in seances, searched for a guru, and began to practice yoga. In his memoirs, Aurobindo wrote that he was told by Ramakrishna and Vivekananda in one of the seances to make a temple and worship the Mother as strength.[39] He was visited by Sister Nivedita, a disciple of Vivekananda [40] who was later to become one of Aurobindo's political collaborators in Calcutta.[41]

It is not clear just when Aurobindo began his practice of yoga, but it was undertaken to gain strength and self-control.[42] Although one might see this as a new chapter in his life, culminating in his withdrawal into a religious vocation in 1910, it is also possible to see it as a further step in developing and expanding his inner resources. During his youth in England, he had been forced by circumstances to draw heavily on his inner resources and intellect. He made his principal contacts with his environment by utilizing these carefully developed abilities to gain academic prizes and advancement at St. Paul's School and Cambridge. In an Indian setting, not as cut off by circumstances from social and political contacts, he was making an effort in a new way to control and to use his inner talents and drives to win victories in an often hostile (and English-dominated) environment. It is not so surprising that one thrown back on himself for thirteen years should have continued the habit of long periods of withdrawal and "inner work" to be later expended in the world of activity. With such careful preparations, one might hypothesize, went fears of premature and uncontrolled personal exposure. Putting one's self on the line was potentially threatening to one who as a youth had been ridiculed and demeaned in a foreign setting with which he was not altogether able to cope. In the Baroda period and afterwards, we can see in the pattern of life Aurobindo chose elaborate and secret preparations and then, in the field of politics, careful and controlled exposures to the outside world. There were, of course, good reasons for this, since he was engaged in yoga and revolution, but it is interesting that he chose to involve himself in fields that necessitated withdrawal and secrecy.

In his memoirs, which are partially in the form of answers to questions of his disciples and were meant to correct false impressions of his life, Aurobindo placed the stress on spiritual "sadhana" (discipline) in the Baroda that some had described. He said in part:

> Sri Aurobindo had some connection with a member of the governing body of the Naga Sannyasis who gave him a *mantra* of Kali (or rather *stotra*) and conducted certain *kriyas* and a Vedic *yagna*, but all this was for political success in his mission and not for Yoga.[43]

The priorities are clear: in the later years at Baroda and the first two or three years in Calcutta (perhaps 1900 to 1908 or 1909), Aurobindo placed politics before religion, although he often couched his political writing and speeches in religious phraseology.[44]

During the Baroda years, he began slowly to emerge onto the political scene. He sent emissaries to Bengal and was in touch with developments in Maharashtra, for he met Tilak and several revolutionary workers from that part of India.[45] He turned to his native region as the logical ground for his political work. In his articles in the *Indu Prakash*, Aurobindo had described the position of Bengal:

> In politics, the Bengali has always led and still leads. But the Congress in Bengal is dying of consumption; annually its proportions sink into greater insignificance; its leaders, the Bonnerji's and Banerji's and Lalmohan Ghoses, have climbed into the rarefied atmosphere of the Legislative Council and lost all hold on the imagination of the young men. The desire for a nobler and more inspiring patriotism is growing more intense; and in the rise of an indigenous Trade Party we see the handwriting on the wall. This is an omen of good hope for the future; for what Bengal thinks tomorrow, India will be thinking tomorrow week . . . let Bengal only be true to her own soul, and there is no province in which she may not climb to greatness.[46]

Bengal had the capacity to lead India if she had the right leaders, and Aurobindo identified himself with Bengal as one of the men who could lead her forward.

In the missions to Bengal, Aurobindo employed a young Bengali who served in the Baroda military service, Jatin Banerjee, as well as his younger brother, Barindra Kumar Ghose. Banerjee went to Bengal in

1903 and began to make contacts with the societies of young men that had been formed for both political and apolitical reasons since the later years of the nineteenth century. Aurobindo himself is said to have visited Bengal and given an oath to P. Mitra, one of the earliest of the revolutionary organizers, as a Maharashtrian had given him a revolutionary oath in 1901. By 1904 and 1905, centers for later revolutionary work are said to have been set up in Khulna, Rangpur, Dacca, and Midnapur.[47] In addition to this secret political work, Aurobindo attended the 1902 session of the Congress in Ahmadabad and the 1904 Congress in Bombay. Sisirkumar Mitra maintains that at this time, Aurobindo laid plans for the eventual capture of the Congress organization by a more extreme political group.[48]

While still in Baroda, Aurobindo wrote a short pamphlet called *Bhawani Mandir* (Temple of Goddess Bhawani). Years later, Aurobindo said that he wrote it at the urging of his brother Barin rather than from any motivation of his own.[49] Most of his biographers treat it with full seriousness, but it is possible that it was a facade for very different aims. In any case, the pamphlet was secretly published and circulated. It was an assessment of the Indian situation and a plan for the revival of India using religious concepts. It has been connected to Chatterjee's *Ānandamaṭh* and to the tradition of Tantric religious practice and philosophy.[50]

The world in *Bhawani Mandir* is described as being created anew in each epoch and energized by a different aspect of the female principle. "In the present age, the Mother is manifested as the Mother of Strength. She is pure Shakti." [51]

> The deeper we look, the more we shall be convinced that the one thing wanting, which we must strive to acquire before all others, is strength—strength physical, strength mental, strength moral, but above all strength spiritual which is the one inexhaustible and imperishable source of all the others.[52]

The view of the world as shakti is linked to the Indian nation:

> What is our mother-country? It is not a piece of earth, nor a figure of speech, nor a fiction of the mind. It is a mighty Shakti, composed of the Shaktis of all the millions of units that make up the nation, just as Bhawani Mahisha Mardini sprang into being from the Shakti of all the millions of gods assembled in one mass of force and welded into unity.

The Shakti we call India, Bhawani Bharati, is the living unity of the Shaktis of three hundred million people; but she is inactive, imprisoned in the magic circle of tamas, the self-indulgent inertia and ignorance of her sons. To get rid of tamas we have but to wake the Brahma within.[53]

The terms and concepts used by Aurobindo in this pamphlet and especially in this passage are drawn in large measure from the *Mārkāṇḍeya Purāna*, which was a Brahamanical text with Tantric influences.[54] The other influence obviously seems to be Bankim Chandra's *Ānandamaṭh*, where there is a mingling of Shakta and Vaishnava traditions. Here and in his later writing, Aurobindo showed much more of an affinity for Shaktism over Vaishnavism and for devotion to the Mother Goddess than did Bankim Chandra. The political sannyasins of *Bhawani Mandir* are to build a temple to the Mother as Shakti (see p. 80) and to work for the regeneration of India. They are to put aside all personal gratifications while striving to achieve a greater end. Their work is divided into practical tasks to be carried out in conjunction with the "people," "the Middle Class," and "the Wealthy Classes." [55]

In this treatise, the religious and the political, according to modern Western categories, are fused. Aurobindo has set the dilemmas of the nationalist in a religious setting so that the deterioration of the world in the Tantras becomes the deterioration of India. Kees W. Bolle, in relating Aurobindo to the Tantric tradition, has noted that in *Bhawani Mandir*, as in the Tantras, the urge for emancipation and the urge for power go together. Aurobindo, demonstrating what Bolle calls "the urge to incorporate everything," has syncretized religious elements and national messianism. Aurobindo gives fallen India a mission to "aryanise the world." [56] In designing a world historical mission for India, he has followed in the tradition of Keshub Sen and Vivekananda. In the early twentieth century not only Aurobindo, but also Tagore and Bipin Pal were all sketching out a world role for India, providing different ideological frameworks and practical proposals for their countrymen.

In *Bhawani Mandir* the British are not present and are not held responsible for the fall of India. Rather, Indians abandoned Shakti and therefore were abandoned by her.[57] Aurobindo is trying to arouse the necessary emotions of pride, pity, hope, and devotion to the Mother as

Shakti and as he does so, he separates the Arya shaktis from the mleccha (foreign) shaktis. It would seem from both internal evidence and wider information about Aurobindo's thought that he either completely ignored the Muslims or would include them with the mleccha shaktis.[58] In doing this, he was following the implicit or explicit anti-Muslim line of the Hindu nationalists and religious ideologues of the later nineteenth century. As British officials realized, and pointed out in memoranda they exchanged with each other, by encouraging nationalism in a religious direction men like Aurobindo were exploiting the religious sentiments of many Hindus but alienating the Muslims.[59]

The passages quoted from *Bhawani Mandir* and the pamphlet as a whole may appear wild, abstract, and irrelevant to practical politics. But the assessment of fallen India, the evaluation of responsibility for the fall, the division of Indian society into three large classes, and some of the directions for revival are quite similar to the views Aurobindo couched in secular terms in "New Lamps for Old." He may have erected a religious facade to make his pamphlet more innocuous to the censors, but it is not so far out of line with his later writings.

It is possible to interpret the conflict described in *Bhawani Mandir* as one going on within Aurobindo. Perhaps he felt inside himself the battle between the Arya shaktis and the mleccha shaktis. From his first political articles and certainly from the later years at Baroda, it is clear that Aurobindo wanted to purge the foreign elements from within himself and from his country. He saw his individual conflicts writ large in English-Indian relations.

The Baroda period, then, might be seen as a training period. He learned a good deal about Indian culture and studied Bengali and Sanskrit; he chose lieutenants to help him in his political work; he made contact with both political and spiritual advisers in western India; and he made trips to Bengal and to Congress sessions that helped him to understand Indian politics more concretely. During the same years, Aurobindo began to write about Sanskrit literature, to do some translations, and to write his own poetry.[60]

After the partition of Bengal and the start of the Swadeshi movement, Aurobindo decided that the moment was right and emerged onto the political stage in Bengal. He felt that partition was a great blessing in disguise, for it awakened many Bengalis to political life who had previously been ignorant or uninterested. Unlike Rash Behari Ghose or Gurudas Banerjee, who had felt that politics was not their proper sphere of activity, Aurobindo had displayed nationalist passion in his early twenties; but he had waited for what he considered the opportune moment, when he could help achieve the goals in which he believed. As the Swadeshi movement brought in the young and the apolitical, it captured middle-aged men like Aurobindo and Tagore, who decided that the time had come for active participation.

POLITICAL CAREER IN CALCUTTA, 1906–1910

In a speech on August 22, 1907, to the students and teachers of the Bengal National College, Aurobindo said: "the experience I am going to undergo was long foreseen as inevitable in the discharge of the mission that I have taken up from my childhood, and I am approaching it without regret." [61] The mission Aurobindo was imagining at this point was his role in Indian politics. He later conceived of an even more difficult mission of raising the consciousness of mankind. His sense of mission may be linked to his lonely and unusual adolescence, which may have led him to believe that he was specially and even divinely chosen. The shifts in his activity followed long periods of preparation and, one might suppose, fantasy of greatness.

Now Aurobindo had to establish contacts for himself in Calcutta and in Bengal, the home of his family and his birthplace but a region in which he had spent little time since the age of seven. In March 1906, on leave from his position in Baroda, he had attended the Barisal Conference and toured east Bengal, and in July 1906 he left Baroda permanently.[62] His brother Barin and several others, including Bhupendranath Datta, younger brother of Swami Vivekananda and lifelong revolutionary, started the Extremist paper *Jugantar* (New Era), for which Aurobindo seems to have served in a supervisory capacity. Mitra mentions conflicts on the staff involving Barin that Aurobindo settled against Barin's position.[63] In doing this, Aurobindo was fulfilling one important role of traditional Bengali political leaders: he was moving rather autocratically to settle internal disputes. It was in such a supervisory capacity, as well as in the role of theoretician, that Aurobindo was to do much of his political work. He often left concrete plans and actions to his brother or other subordinates.

One contact that Aurobindo made in Bengal was with Subodh Mallik, one of the important financial backers of the National Council of Education and of the paper *Bande Mataram*. Aurobindo accepted the position of first principal of the Bengal National College,[64] which gave him a legitimate position in Calcutta and brought him to public attention. He received a small salary; it appears that after he gave up his post in Baroda he did not have much money, and he lived a rather simple life in Calcutta. Aurobindo was forced to resign his principalship while under trial in the Alipore bomb case (see below) in 1908.[65]

From 1906 to 1908, Aurobindo wrote a great number of articles on the political issues of the day and gave several speeches of a political nature.[66] The most coherent and organized statement of Aurobindo's political ideas in this period can be found in *The Doctrine of Passive Resistance*, which appeared as a series of articles in *Bande Mataram* from April 9 to April 23, 1907. The final article was seized by the police before it could be published. The significant themes in Aurobindo's writing during this period were the Indian past, the present Indian situation, the rise of Indian nationalism and the nature of the Indian nation, the Bengali role, the priority of politics, the methods and rationales of the struggle, ideals for the nationalist worker, and the destiny of nation, party, and self.

Following the ideas set forth in *Bhawani Mandir*, Aurobindo stated in many articles that India was a unique culture and civilization. In "Spirituality and Nationalism" he wrote:

A great light is drawing on the East, a light whose first heralding glimpses are already seen on the horizon; a new day is about to break, so glorious that even the last of the *avatars* cannot be sufficient to explain it, although without him [i.e., Ramakrishna] it would not have come. The perfect expression of Hindu spirituality was the signal for the resurgence of the East. . . . The East alone has some knowledge of the truth, the East alone can teach the West, the East alone can save mankind. Through all these ages Asia has been seeking for a light within, and whenever she has been blessed with a glimpse of what she seeks, a great religion has been born, Buddhism, Confucianism, Christianity, Mahomedanism with all their countless sects. But the grand workshop of spiritual experiment, the laboratory of the soul has been India, where thousands of great spirits have been born in every generation. . . . Of all these souls Sri Ramakrishna was the last and greatest. . . . What Christianity failed to do, what Mahomedanism strove to accomplish in times as yet unripe, what Buddhism half accomplished for a brief period and among a limited number of men, Hinduism as summed up in the life of Sri Ramakrishna has to attempt for all the world. This is the reason of India's resurgence, this is why God has breathed life into her once more. . . . The movement of which the first outbreak was political, will end in a spiritual consummation.[67]

This passage links Aurobindo to the Bengali religious leaders and ideologues of the later nineteenth century as well as to the other spokesmen of the Swadeshi movement. Rather than stressing the mixing and combining of traditions, as did Tagore, Aurobindo stressed the religious aspects. Aurobindo saw the political phase as a prelude, a necessary first step, to the spiritual stage to follow. As God had chosen Asia, and especially India, to be the source of religious leadership and religious ideals, so also God was behind the Indian nationalist movement, which was divinely inspired. Aurobindo was trying to bring together religion and politics by his stress on the divine nature of not only Indian nationalism and the message of his own party, but finally his own thought. More and more frequently, he employed concepts and terms from Indian religion in his writing.[68] In the Calcutta period he asserted the priority of politics, but by 1910 he had reversed his priorities and decided that spiritual and moral regeneration would have to precede political advance.

In this period, he viewed nationalism as a religion. The Almighty, he said, was the leader of the national march forward.[69] He conceived of the nation itself in several different ways:

a nation cannot be made,—it is an organism which grows under the stress of a principle of life within. . . . A nation is indeed the outward expression of a community of sentiment, whether it be the sentiment of a common blood or the sentiment of a common religion or the sentiment of a common interest or any or all of these sentiments combined.[70]

In *Bhawani Mandir* he had stressed the combined shaktis of the 300 million Indians who composed the nation. Here he stressed the organic nature of the nation through which the religious-*cum*-nationalistic lifeblood pulsed. He was implicitly seeking to refute the British writers who said India had never been a nation and was only now becoming something like one because of the British-run political and administrative framework. Aurobindo maintained that the common sentiment which all Indians were gradually coming to feel would have to be linked with political independence.

> To be content with the relations of master and dependent or superior and subordinate would be a mean and pitiful aspiration unworthy of manhood; to strive for anything less than a strong and glorious freedom would be to insult the greatness of our past and the magnificent possibilities of our future.[71]

Aurobindo's contemporary, Rabindranath Tagore, stressed that national reconstruction should be the first task and need not follow political independence; but Aurobindo in his political phase insisted that independence from Britain had to come first. Only after such a separation could men turn their energies without fear of reprisal to the work of village redevelopment, national art and literature, and the restructuring of the educational system. Aurobindo offered rationales from Indian religious texts, most often the *Bhagavad Gītā*. Turning from the lofty rhetoric of India's spiritual mission in the modern world, Aurobindo argued that Indians were not saints and that loving other races—especially one's foreign rulers—was against Nature.[72] India was faced with national death and emasculation, or what one might call the white peril.[73] At such times, men should not laboriously debate the proper means to be employed in political action, because all methods were permissible. He stated:

> The school of politics which we advocate is not based upon abstractions, formulas and dogmas, but on practical necessities and the teaching of political experience, commonsense and the world's history. . . . We recognize no political object except the divinity in our Motherland, no present object of political endeavour except liberty, and no method of action as political good or evil except as it truly helps or hinders our progress towards national emancipation.[74]

Aurobindo listed three kinds of resistance: armed revolt, aggressive resistance short of armed revolt, and defensive resistance, whether passive or active.[75]

> [T]he circumstances of the country and the nature of the despotism from which it seeks to escape must determine what form of resistance is best justified and most likely to be effective at the time or finally successful.[76]

Since the Indian people were unarmed and not prepared in any way for an armed struggle,

> The present circumstances in India seem to point to passive resistance as our most natural and suitable weapon. We would not for a moment be understood to base this conclusion upon any condemnation of other methods as in all circumstances criminal and unjustifiable.[77]

The main feature of passive resistance was to be total boycott of British-run administrative, economic, educational, and judicial institutions. The concomitant of boycott was to be self-help, or Swadeshi. At the same time Indians were to try to bring the British-controlled system to a halt, they were also to build an indigenous system, more suited to Indian conditions. Aurobindo was not offering anything new in this program. Tagore, Bipin Pal, Subodh Mallick, and others had been advocating these same ideas for several years; Aurobindo was simply restating them in an orderly fashion.[78]

At the same time, however, Aurobindo was offering a slightly disguised but visible rationale for the use of violence that could scarcely escape any reader of *The Doctrine of Passive Resistance*. He wrote:

> Under certain circumstances a civil struggle becomes in reality a battle and the morality of war is different from the morality of peace. To shrink from bloodshed and violence under such circumstances is a weakness deserving as severe a rebuke as Sri Krishna addressed to Arjuna when he shrank from the colossal civil slaughter on the field of Kurukshetra.[79]

He was ready to answer those Englishmen or Indians who offered what he called "the cant of the oppressor":

> It is the common habit of established Governments and especially those which are themselves oppressors, to brand all violent methods in subject peoples and communities as criminal and wicked. When you have disarmed your slaves and legalised the infliction of bonds, stripes and death on any one of them, man, woman or child, who may dare to speak or to act against you, it is natural and convenient to try to lay a moral as well as a legal ban on any attempt to answer violence by violence. . . . But no nation yet has listened to the cant of the oppressor when itself put to the test, and the general conscience of humanity approves the refusal.[80]

In presenting his case for the justifiable use of violence, Aurobindo offered backing from the *Bhagavad Gītā*, from comparative historical experiences of many peoples, and from "the general conscience of humanity." [81] The Indian tradition as well as Western, or simply human, traditions were mentioned in support of his arguments. Although he felt Indians had an unusual penchant for enduring suffering which made passive resistance particularly appealing to them, they were no strangers to the use of violence should circumstances demand it. In his vision of the use of violence as an important and necessary aspect of the Indian experience, Aurobindo was reading this experience differently from Tagore, Bipin Pal, and the whole school of Indian Moderates, as well as the Gandhians of a decade and a half later. [82] But Aurobindo would have answered that all these men were subject to the "cant of the oppressor," and thus were misunderstanding Indian history. Although there has been much mixing and blurring of lines in Bengali religious traditions, it can be maintained that willingness to use violence when necessary is more in accord with the Shakta than with the Vaishnava tradition. Thus Aurobindo was closest to the Shakta tradition, although he held up the Krishna cult as one of India's greatest achievements. In selecting those aspects of Krishna's teaching that were important, however, he chose the *Bhagavad Gītā*, rather than the more peaceful *Bhāgavata Purāṇa*, and interpreted the *Gītā* in a particularly literal way. [83]

In analyzing the contemporary Indian situation, Aurobindo blurred the dividing lines between the definitions of aggressive and passive resistance which he had set down at the beginning of *The Doctrine of Passive Resistance*. In the last article, which was partly an answer to a call by Tagore for love, understanding, and self-help, Aurobindo wrote:

> The morality of the Kshatriya justifies violence in times of war, and boycott is a war. . . . Aggression is unjust only when unprovoked; violence, unrighteous when used wantonly or for unrighteous ends. . . . The sword of the warrior is as necessary to the fulfilment of justice and righteousness as the holiness of the saint. . . . To maintain justice and prevent the strong from despoiling, and the weak from being oppressed, is the function for which the Kshatriya was created. "Therefore" says Sri Krishna in the *Mahabharata*, "God created battle and armour, the sword, the bow and the dagger." [84]

Aurobindo could not have offered a much more direct rationale for the use of violence. With Rabindranath, he saw that many were implicated in the use of violence by a few Bengalis, including the rulers of India. He disagreed with Rabindranath, however, on the appropriateness of aggressive resistance in the Swadeshi period. Rabindranath felt that the use of arms was not in keeping with Indian traditions and would be an ineffective political shortcut. Aurobindo saw armed resistance as perfectly compatible with those Indian traditions which were meaningful to him.[85] Both men intermingled religion and politics. It becomes obvious that Indian religious traditions can be used to sanction a variety of viewpoints.

Although Aurobindo supported the boycott and the national education movement, he felt by 1907 that "the Boycott is not yet effective except spasmodically and in patches." [86]

> [F]or the want of a central authority to work for the necessary conditions, to support by its ubiquitous presence the weak and irresolute and to coerce the refractory, it has not been properly carried out. For the same reason national education languishes . . . it requires also an iron endurance, tenacity, doggedness, far above anything that is needed for the more usual military revolt or sanguinary revolution. . . . Boycott has been admitted as permissible in principle to all parts of India though the recommendation to extend it in practice as an integral part of the national policy was not pressed. It only remained to develop the central authority which will execute the national policy and evolve with time into a popular Government.[87]

Like Rabindranath, Aurobindo saw that the Bengalis were adept at formulating plans but had not developed the ability to organize or to carry them out effectively. In the passage above, Aurobindo spells out the norms which he thought should guide nationalist activity: a strong central organization on the political level, tenacity, capacity for and individual self-denial, suffering, and sacrifice. In specifying these general guides, he was following the prescriptions of Vivekananda and other religious ideologues of the late nineteenth century. The religious currents of the nineteenth-century Bengal flowed rather directly into the nationalist movement in several ways. For instance the ideals of conduct for Brahmo Samaj preachers and for members of the Ramakrishna Mission were being taken over as role models for the political or nationalist worker.

Though Aurobindo could easily rise to heights of generality and speak of India's mission or the role of Asia in regenerating the world, his primary concern was Bengal. In a speech to an audience in Bombay on January 19, 1908, after the Surat Congress, Aurobindo described the place of Bengal:

> Nationalism is immortal; Nationalism cannot die; because it is no human thing, it is God who is working in Bengal. . . . Let me tell you what it is that has happened in Bengal. . . . You know very well what you yourselves used to say of the Bengali. . . . If anybody had told you that Bengal would come forward as the saviour of India, how many of you would have believed it? . . . What has made the Bengali so different from his old self? One thing has happened in Bengal and it is this that Bengal is learning to believe. Bengal was once drunk with the wine of European civilization . . . Bengal became atheistic. . . . But still in Bengal there was an element of strength. Whatever the Bengali believed, if he believed at all, . . . there was one thing about the Bengali, that he lived what he believed.[88]

He was concerned to show the moral and religious superiority of the Bengali, but he wanted even more passionately to demonstrate equality of strength which would help to bring independence from the rulers who not only oppressed his country but also derided its inhabitants. Especially for the ridiculed Bengali, a special role in turning out the foreigner was essential. Aurobindo felt called upon to answer British characterizations of the Bengali, and thus he responded to the *Times:*

> For sometime past its columns have been disgraced by the most foul suggestions and insinuations against Indian character, especially against the character of the Bengalees who have perhaps been showing a more unconquerable determination to bring its pretences to the ground than their countrymen in other parts of the country. . . . Utterly confuted in its favourite theory of moral incapacity as an inherent failing of the Bengalee character, by the self-devotion of our workers who have demonstrated to a certainty the moral superiority of the National movement in Bengal to the alien bureaucracy that rules over the country, the *Times* has now laid desecrating hands upon the sanctity of our inner life. Frustrated in its lying criticism of our men, it has now turned to a shameless and brutal attack on our women.[89]

The *Times* article indicated that some widows in Dacca allowed themselves to be abducted rather than commit suttee or endure the hardships of traditional Indian widowhood. Aurobindo answered with a spirited defense of Indian women, marriage, and treatment of widows, and verged on defending suttee, a custom which British officials and liberal Indians had worked so hard to abolish in the nineteenth century.

Aurobindo and some of his contemporaries spoke more directly and bluntly in their articles and speeches than had been usual for the early nationalists. Aurobindo openly expressed his hatred and aggressive feelings. After the call of Surendranath Banerjea and the Moderates for order, restraint, and conciliatory tones at all times, the Swadeshi period and the writings of the Extremists show an outpouring of passion. Many songs and poems arousing and celebrating the new enthusiasm were written. The cry of "Bande Mataram" was the most common call of defiance; in some parts of Bengal, the British forbade it.[90] The era of careful petitions and conciliatory words was fast drawing to a close.

When Aurobindo returned to Bengal, according to both his own memoirs and his biographers, he had planned for himself a threefold program of action. First, he would help to educate the public through his writings; second, he would work with other Extremists to capture the Congress organization from the Moderates; and third, he would secretly help prepare for violent insurrection.[91] When he came to Calcutta in 1906, he joined with Bipin Pal and others in founding *Bande Mataram* and collaborated more indirectly with Barin in editing the even more revolutionary paper *Jugantar*. Both papers lasted less than two years, but they had some impact on Indian readers and succeeded in bringing down the repressive hand of the Home Department. To the government, particularly to the Home Department, which was concerned with law and order, Aurobindo was an editor of "seditious papers" and a "dangerous character." They were worried about his influence on "impressionable youths" with whom he was popular by 1907.[92] Whatever his failures in political action, Aurobindo, together with Barin, Bipin Pal, and Bhupendranath Datta, coeditor of *Jugantar*, helped to increase political consciousness among literate Bengalis— especially the young men—during the early Swadeshi years.

At the same time, Aurobindo joined the political Extremists in the Congress and tried to capture control of that organization. He had been a spectator at Congress sessions in 1902 and 1904, and in 1906, while visiting Bengal, he happened to attend the conference at Barisal which led to the arrest of Surendranath Banerjea and a few other Congress leaders.[93] The split in the Congress camp was becoming wider with each passing year and was publicly obvious by 1906.[94] Aurobindo joined a movement already under way, but he and Bipin Pal soon became leaders of the Extremist party in Bengal. Aurobindo claimed that he tried to organize the Extremists into a more tightly knit, more coherent party before the Calcutta Congress of 1906.[95] Both Aurobindo and his biographers recount a meeting held prior to the Congress session:

> He called a meeting of the forward group of young men in the Congress and they decided to organise themselves openly as a new political party joining hands with the corresponding group in Maharashtra under the proclaimed leadership of Tilak and to join battle with the Moderate party which was done at the Calcutta session.[96]

In *The Doctrine of Passive Resistance*, Aurobindo described the organizational plans of the New Party:

> It was for this object [i.e., setting up a central authority of the nationalist movement] that the New Party determined not to be satisfied with any further evasion of the constitution question, though they did not press for the adoption of their own particular scheme. It is for this object that a Central National Committee has been formed; that Conferences are being held in various districts and sub-divisions and committees created; that the Provincial Conferences are expected to appoint a Provincial Committee for all Bengal.[97]

It is clear from Congress histories that the Extremists did organize a caucus-type group within the Congress and press for the adoption of their program both at the 1906 and 1907 sessions of the Congress and at provincial sessions from 1906 to at least 1909.[98] What is not satisfactorily analyzed in any account is the extent to which the Extremists developed the beginnings of a mass party organization in these years. The leaders, including Tilak and Aurobindo, had been complaining for years that the Congress was a narrowly based party and needed mass support. This was a central theme in Aurobindo's early article, "New Lamps for Old," and was a continuing theme during his Calcutta period. It does not seem that Aurobindo either gave much of his time to the details of organizing or sent men into the districts, towns, or villages to do such work. Volunteer groups formed in many districts which often did Swadeshi work and spread the message of the Swadeshi leaders in Calcutta.[99] Some of these groups were aiming at revolutionary action, but some also worked for passive resistance, boycott, and Swadeshi. Although their success seems to have been limited, they did bring into politics many young men who were to have lengthy careers in the nationalist movement.[100] To a great extent, however, the Extremists, like the Moderates, remained a small and elitist party. Aurobindo was more adept at small-scale, clandestine organization than at large-scale mass organization. He would have preferred success at the latter, but like other Swadeshi leaders, he was denied it.[101]

During 1907, Aurobindo was a prominent Extremist spokesman and leader at the Midnapur District Conference and at the Surat Congress in December. At these meetings both the Nationalists and the Extremists failed to put through their programs or to gain control of the sessions. They left the meetings amid considerable uproar.[102] Both parties saw the Surat session as a showdown meeting and sent large numbers of delegates. In his account Aurobindo gave himself a considerably larger role than any other contemporary observer ascribed to him. As usual, he portrayed himself as manipulating things from behind the scenes.[103]

> History very seldom records the things that were decisive but took place behind the veil; it records the shown front of the curtain. Very few people know that it was I (without consulting Tilak) who gave the order that led to the breaking of the Congress and was responsible for the refusal to join the new-fangled Moderate Convention which were the two decisive happenings at Surat.[104]

After the Nationalists left the opening meeting of the Congress, the two parties met separately, with Aurobindo presiding over the meeting of the Extremists. Although he believed that it was important for the Congress to show a united front to the British, he and his colleagues would not agree to the new loyalty oath (demanding nonviolence) or to the constitution devised by the Moderates.[105]

After the fiasco at the Surat Congress, Aurobindo left the public eye to obtain some spiritual help. With the assistance of a Maharashtrian yogin, Aurobindo arranged to meet Vishnu Bhasker Lele at Baroda. Aurobindo had been practicing yoga for about three years, but he still wanted assistance from a guru in his sadhana.[106] In his memoirs, Aurobindo described his instruction at the hands of Lele:

> The results were remarkable. Many visions of scenes and figures I used
> to see. I felt an electric power around my head. My powers of writing
> were nearly dried up; they revived with a great vigour. I could write
> prose and poetry with a flow. That flow has never ceased since then.
> If I have not written afterwards it is because I had something else to
> do. But the moment I want to write it is there. Thirdly, great health. I
> grew stout and strong, the skin became smooth and fair and there was
> a flow of sweetness in the saliva. I used to feel a certain aura around the
> head.[107]

After this encounter Aurobindo claimed that his mind was blank before writing and speaking, but then a message "from a new status of
mind" came to him and the words flowed easily.[108] He gave a few
speeches on his way back to Calcutta and from this time felt more
strongly that he was an instrument of God.

During this same period Aurobindo was also working with his
brother Barin and others to prepare for "universal unrest" and "national insurrection." [109] Before he came to Calcutta, his goal was a central organization extending all over Bengal and eventually throughout
India that would secretly prepare for armed resistance in case the mass
Swadeshi and swaraj movements failed.[110] He tried to establish such an
organization and met with others in a central committee, but it never
seems to have gotten off the ground.[111] A small group was formed
with Barin and other young men as the organizers and actual working
revolutionaries. Aurobindo served as theoretician and probably helped
to make important decisions. The government, in a Home Department
report, described his role:

> Lieutenant-Governor . . . has no doubt . . . that he is the master-mind
> at the back of the whole extremist campaign in Bengal. He is not only
> a fluent and impressive writer, but an organizer of great ability and in-
> genuity; and it is probably to him more than to anyone else that it is
> due the extraordinary mingling of religion with politics which has im-
> parted such a dangerous character to recent developments . . . he is
> hopelessly irreconcilable.[112]

The intelligence officials probably overestimated Aurobindo's organizing abilities, for the only specific result of his revolutionary career was
the abortive Alipore bomb plot. This was a scheme of Barin's to train
revolutionaries and equip them with arms and bombs; the plotters were
working at a garden house in Maniktola when the police raided.[113]

They linked these trainees to a number of murders which had recently occurred and arrested several dozen Bengalis, including Barin and Aurobindo. In the previous year Aurobindo had been arrested for sedition but released because of insufficient evidence. In May 1908, however, Aurobindo was seized at his home at 48 Grey Street, Calcutta, in the early hours of the morning. He wrote an account of the arrest and the subsequent year in jail in a short Bengali work entitled *Kārākāhinī* which is a major source for the following discussion.[114] The arrest marked the temporary curtailment of Aurobindo's political work and a further stage in his spiritual activity.

After consulting all the available sources, including Home Department files, histories of the Bengal revolutionary movement, and memoirs and biographies of Aurobindo, I think it is evident that Aurobindo never directly participated in revolutionary acts. As with the editorship of *Bande Mataram*, he was careful never to endanger himself. Barin, for example, was much more exposed and was convicted in the Alipore bomb case, while Aurobindo was acquitted and released with the aid of his lawyer Chittaranjan Das, one of the leading figures of the Calcutta bar and a member of the Extremist party in the Congress. The government argued that Aurobindo was in close contact with the plotters and used a letter from him to Barin referring to the distribution throughout the country of "sweets," which they held referred to bombs. The letter was later disallowed as evidence.[115] Barin, along with six others, was sentenced to imprisonment in the Andamans and remained there for almost fifteen years.[116] Under the stresses of imprisonment he confessed, and with the weight of direct evidence against him, he was forced to suffer the consequences of his actions.

The account of Aurobindo's year in jail is one of the most personal of his writings. It was written immediately after his release, and it seems reasonable to assume that it approximates Aurobindo's state of mind and feelings while in prison. One striking feature of the account is the melodramatic way in which Aurobindo described the arrest and the conditions of his imprisonment, writing of his great "sufferings" and "sacrifices." He was "tortured by British opinions" of the Indians.[117] Rather than demonstrating the dauntless courage he felt Indians should have, he seems to have shown more continuity with the fears and anxieties of his youth. Rather than showing selflessness and passion for the cause of his country and the welfare of others, he recounted a very personal and constant concern for his bath, his room, his bowels, his comfort, his food, and for special luxuries.[118]

There is a strange quality to *Kārākāhinī*, for Aurobindo alternated descriptions of depression and of religious joy. He claimed that while he was in prison, God protected him; at one point he described himself in the lap of the World-Mother, cared for like a child.[119] He called the prison both an ashram (religious hermitage) and a torture-home.[120] It was a scene both of inhuman and cruel treatment and of ecstatic moments in which he saw the divine in all things and heard the voice of Vivekananda.[121]

In another interesting passage, Aurobindo claimed that the revolutionary prisoners looked like young supermen, their strength and courage visible.[122] They were the equals of their British captors, while the regular prisoners looked like puny and inferior men.[123] For all his advocacy of democracy and the raising of the masses, Aurobindo showed a lack of consideration for ordinary men and a concern that he be accorded the special treatment due him as a political leader and a high-caste Bengali. A similar concern for caste status is displayed in Barin Ghose's *The Tale of My Exile*. Barin was describing the process of learning rope-making in prison:

> None could best Upen on that day! Such a natural gift of workmanship as his was considered by all as a rarity! However, he was a little mortified when he found that I did as a matter of fact have the longest rope. He said, "You must have worked then secretly at home," as if I, a scion of the House of the *Ghoses*, was no better than a *dom* [rope-maker, sweeper, etc., by caste]. The insinuation set fire to all the blood in my veins! But we were in the Blessed Land of Prison and I could only gnash my teeth and pocket the insult! [124]

Aurobindo and his brother both felt that they had by right, or had earned, a high place in the society of their Bengal. To Aurobindo this place was the result of birth, training, political role, martyrdom by imprisonment, and especially the fact that he was chosen by God for glorious and important work. While in prison, he said he learned from an inner voice that he was to have a worldwide purpose.[125] His visions and communications with God were the good that came out of the evil of imprisonment and were the basis for his claim that a new man, a new Aurobindo emerged from the Alipore Ashram in May 1909.[126]

When Aurobindo came out of prison, he faced a changed situation. He was in agreement with Home Department officials that the movement for Swadeshi and swaraj was passing.[127] Some leaders had been deported, others had left the movement, and only the Moderate group of Surendranath Banerjea and the beginnings of a small revolutionary movement were left on the scene. But perhaps more importantly, the fairly wide public support for Swadeshi among significant segments of the Hindu population that had contributed to the effectiveness of the boycott during its first year had fallen off. Calls for the revocation of partition still appeared in the press, but these were the only remaining sparks of the protest.

Still, Aurobindo set to work after his release. He founded two papers, *Karmayogin* and *Dharma*, and wrote many articles during his last years in politics.[128] He attributed both his release and his renewed activity to divine power:

> I attribute my escape to no human agency, but first of all to the protection of the Mother of us all who has never been absent from me, but always held me in her arms and shielded me from grief and disaster.[129]

He said he had received an "adesh," or command, in prison:

> I have given you a work, and it is to help to uplift this nation . . . I give you the *adesh* to go forth and do my work . . . I am giving them [the Indian people] freedom for the service of the world.[130]

The government was determined not to make him a martyr. One official insisted, "let the moribund agitation die in peace" and held that "many of the older politicians consider him to be deranged." [131] But the government was wary of his impact on the young men and students:

> No one can doubt what Aurobindo's aims are [i.e., use of violence and independence] or how his ambiguous phrases are interpreted by the students and young men who crowd to hear him. It may be admitted that he carries little weight with elderly men, but it is not they who furnish the agents for outrage and dacoity.[132]

A constant debate continued behind the scenes in the Home Department as to whether to deport or arrest Aurobindo for sedition. He undoubtedly knew that he was under constant surveillance, and he seems to have cut down on his communications with revolutionaries during his last year in Calcutta.

Aurobindo attended the Bengal Provincial Conference at Hooghly and also met privately with Surendranath Banerjea to try to work out a rapprochement with the Moderates and so unite the Congress against the British.[133] But the refusal of Aurobindo and the Extremists to subscribe to the new Congress constitution and oath, coupled with the unwillingness of the Moderates to relax their terms, made an agreement impossible.[134] Aurobindo saw a need for organized action rather than speeches or ineffectual resolutions, but he was not capable of directing such activity. His words inspired some, but the movement needed more than talk. Some young men, seeing the failure of the mass effort, were turning to secret plots of murder and robbery for political ends.

PHILOSOPHICAL AND RELIGIOUS WORK, 1910–1950

As he witnessed the failing movement and the ineffectiveness of his own political work from May 1909 to February 1910, Aurobindo turned to yoga, and retired more into silence and isolation. In his account of his life, he noted a number of occasions when "he drew back into silence" or "took refuge in silence." [135] Sometimes these temporary retreats followed failures of others to respond to what he had done or written. From 1907 or early 1908, when he met Lele, he spent more time practicing yoga and, as he wrote, "I kept all that went on in me to myself." [136]

An important concomitant of this pattern of behavior during the last year in Calcutta was a change in his ideology from the advocacy of the priority of politics to a stress on the moral and religious preconditions for political activity and the achievement of political goals. He wrote an essay in the *Karmayogin* entitled "The Strength of Stillness" in praise of the quiet and power of the yogin.[137] Aurobindo was shifting from a political to a cultural position. He was also shedding the role of political ideologue and revolutionary and putting on the garb of the guru.

Then, seemingly with great suddenness, Aurobindo disappeared from Calcutta and politics at the end of February 1910 and did not reappear until April in the French territory of Pondicherry. He had first gone to French-held Chandernagore near Calcutta and then traveled secretly by steamer to Pondicherry. This is Aurobindo's own account of the reason for his withdrawal:

> Sri Aurobindo one night at the *Karmayogin* office received information of the Government's intention to search the office and arrest him. While considering what should be his attitude, he received a sudden command from above to go to Chandernagore in French India. He obeyed the command at once, for it was now his rule to move only as he was moved by the divine guidance and never to resist and depart from it; he did not stay to consult with anyone, but in ten minutes was at the river *ghat* and in a boat plying on the Ganges; in a few hours he was at Chandernagore where he went into secret residence. . . . At Chandernagore he plunged entirely into solitary meditation and ceased all other activity. Then there came to him a call to proceed to Pondicherry.[138]

By some standards, Aurobindo's flight might be adjudged an act of cowardice. Under the pressure of possible police action against him, he left political involvement and fled. But, if we grant that he may well have felt that he heard a call inside himself that he identified as divine, and if we place his action in an Indian context, then it may be viewed as a culturally legitimate solution to a personal dilemma. It has been common in India for men in many walks of life to experience a sudden leap of faith and to retire to a meditative life. At any rate, the political phase of Aurobindo's life had ended, and he resisted all entreaties to return and again take up a position of political leadership.[139]

Aurobindo stayed with a few disciples in Pondicherry, living in poor circumstances for the first years there. In 1914 he agreed to collaborate with Paul and Mira Richard, a French couple, in writing and publishing a journal called *Arya*. The journal continued for about six years, and a good deal of each issue was written by Aurobindo. After a four-year silence, words and ideas poured forth in a great torrent, and out of his *Arya* articles several massive volumes were collected.[140]

Through these years a small religious community began to develop around Aurobindo. After a few years, Mira Richard became his disciple and some years later he elevated her to a position nearly equal to his own. She gradually took over all the practical details of running the burgeoning ashram. She also came to be called the Mother by Aurobindo and his disciples, and he wrote of her:

> There is one divine Force which acts in the universe and in the individual and is also beyond the individual and the universe. The Mother stands for all these, but she is working here in the body to bring down something not yet expressed in this material world so as to transform life here—it is so that you should regard her as the Divine Shakti working here for that purpose. She is that in the body, but in her whole consciousness she is also identified with all the other aspects of the Divine.[141]

In 1901 Aurobindo had married Mrinalini Bose in a house belonging to the Hatkhola Dutt family. Aurobindo was 29 and his bride was 14 at the time.[142] Aurobindo lived with his wife on and off during the next nine years and wrote a series of letters to her explaining that he had been marked out by God for special work.[143] In one letter, dated December 6, 1907, Aurobindo wrote:

> This suffering is your inevitable lot, since you have married me. At intervals there is bound to be separation, because, unlike ordinary Bengalis, I am unable to make the happiness of the relatives and of the family the main aim of my life. In these circumstances, what is my Dharma is also your Dharma; unless you consider the success of my mission as your happiness, there is no way out.[144]

It does not seem that Aurobindo formed a satisfactory relationship with his wife; Mrinalini died in 1918 en route to Pondicherry from Calcutta. He did form a much more lasting relationship with Mira Richard, the Mother, and some time after her permanent return to the ashram in 1920, she moved into quarters adjacent to Aurobindo's and lived there for the rest of his life. In his public writing, at least, he idealized her as the Mother of Gods and the concrete manifestation of vast forces at work in the universe, maintaining that she had been sent by God to him and the ashram.[145] One might suggest that after the violent and disruptive relationship with his own mother that relationships with mother figures assumed continuing significance for him. Instead of carrying out a more normal relationship as a husband to a Bengali girl, he devoted himself to abstractions of the Mother Goddess and the politically linked concept of the Motherland. Later, when a strong, intellectual woman came into his life and devoted herself to him, he began to see her as a manifestation of the abstractions of which he had written. So the relationship to the Mother may have served as a substitute for the marriage tie, and even more, the solution to his problems with female figures. Goddesses play a predominant role in Bengali culture, and Aurobindo's concern with mother figures was to some extent part of his sharing in a common culture; but he went beyond the ordinary in seizing upon a French woman, bringing her into a permanent role in his life, and trying to persuade his countrymen and disciples that she was the equal consort of an avatar, i.e. himself, and the Mother of Gods.

In Pondicherry, Aurobindo devoted himself to yoga, writing, and the training of his disciples. He felt that he had tremendous power, and that he could shape the workings of the world by his soul-force.[146] He carried out what Mircea Eliade has called "ritual interiorization" of the cosmic process.[147] He believed that he and the Mother were determining the course of world forces by their yoga. Rather than arguing that he was seeking solitary salvation, he said he was doing a wider work.[148]

After long searching, he had found an adult role psychologically and culturally satisfying to him. In none of these did he expose himself to the scorn either of his countrymen or their foreign rulers. The secret, behind-the-scenes work that he preferred was now his life. His only contacts were with his immediate disciples, some others who wrote to him, and those who responded to his writings.

Aurobindo's views in the *Arya* period and during the remainder of his life became increasingly spiritualized and abstract. In writing of Indian culture, he emphasized its more spiritual essence compared to other civilizations. The Vedic and Upanishadic age in particular seemed to him mankind's first period of greatness.[149] Calling for inner freedom, Aurobindo pointed to a new age which men should work toward. One means of reaching the pinnacle of human destiny which lay ahead was yoga and the gathering of men's inner forces.[150] Although he called himself a "spiritual anarchist," Aurobindo wrote a good deal about world affairs. What he wanted was a confederation of all men and all social units which would pass beyond the limiting bounds of individuals and nations.[151]

Whatever the importance of his later philosophical and political writing, he had forsaken the field of ordinary political action forever. He was watched by the CID for years and was often asked by Indian nationalists to return to political work. But Aurobindo had found a sat-

isfying place and believed that his was the highest course that any man
could follow. To the Home Department, it must have been a happy
moment when they realized that the man whom they had considered
so dangerous had left the political field of his own volition and become
simply another, although a renowned, Indian holy man. Aurobindo's
writings and his ashram have had some influence in India, but he left
the concrete work of organizing and revitalizing his native land to
others.

FIVE
The Organization of the Revolutionaries

Once the mass agitation efforts were foundering and the divisions within the nationalist camp were manifest, some young men together with a few older leaders turned to violence to catalyze sentiment in favor of national independence. In the nationalist period, the use of violence for political ends was important in only a few areas of the subcontinent, namely Bombay, Bengal, Punjab, and later the United Provinces. The leaders and most of the participants were from a few social groups and castes to whom violence was a culturally acceptable means of political action.

The first outbreaks were in the Bombay Presidency, and this was the arena for the nationalist use of violence until the Bengali movement got under way in the first decade of the twentieth century.[1] The Bengal revolutionaries were active from 1907 to 1915 and later in the early 1920s and 1930s. The timing of these stretches of revolutionary action was linked to the rhythm of the nationalist movement as a whole, to events outside India, such as the two world wars, and to the effectiveness of government campaigns of repression.

The illusion that the Indian and Bengali past was nonviolent has been nurtured by the British notion that there were "non-martial races," including the Bengalis, and by a misunderstanding of the place of Mahatma Gandhi in Indian history.[2] The political life of pre-British India was permeated by violence; local rajas and zamindars had private armies that were used in carrying out judicial, administrative, and police functions. First the Mughals and then the British gradually curtailed their military strength, but we hear of bands of lathials, or club-wielders, still at work in the nineteenth century.[3] Further, there was a long-standing association of violence with Shaktism in Bengal.

In ascribing meekness and cowardice to the Bengalis, British writers and others who have shared their attitude have ignored continuities of religion, social structure, political organization, and values from the pre-British period to modern times. Bengalis did not suddenly give up their language and culture, or their social and political forms. The older culture was reshaped under changed circumstances, but not forsaken. The predilection for Shaktism and the awareness that many Bengali political leaders of earlier times had used violence for political ends remained with many nineteenth- and twentieth-century Bengalis. In the writings of many leading literary figures of the nineteenth century, historical situations in which violence was used were recounted and idealized.[4] A further element was the growing awareness of revolutionary movements in other parts of the world, which became more important in India as some of the politically conscious became disillusioned with British models of political activity. Thus Naren Bhattacharya, whose career is to be examined in detail, studied what he and his friends envisioned as "the whole revolutionary history of the world."[5] The knowledge that others had thought the use of violence legitimate under certain circumstances supported the feeling of these young men that the use of violence was within Indian traditions as they understood them.

A CASE STUDY OF NARENDRANATH BHATTACHARYA

Narendranath Bhattacharya, later known as M. N. Roy, was in his youth a devoted revolutionary and lieutenant to a famous Bengali revolutionary leader, Jatin Mukherjee.[6] A description of the career of Roy is useful and appropriate for several reasons. First, Roy is one of the few revolutionary Bengalis about whom interesting data is available. Second, Roy followed a pattern that was often repeated among Bengali political workers during the twentieth century: from terrorist and insurrectionary activity to communism and then to open Congress work. Third, both the data collected about Roy and some of his own writings give graphic pictures of two important features of Bengali revolutionary politics: the "dal" or faction and the "dada" or leader of such a group.

Narendranath Bhattacharya was born in Arbelia in 24-Parganas, Bengal, in 1887. He was the fifth child and third son of Dinabandhu

Bhattacharya. Dinabandhu was in the main branch of a family of officiating priests for the village of Kheput in Midnapur district. Dinabandhu left Kheput in search of employment and found it as a Sanskrit teacher first in a junior high school in Arbelia and later in a school in Kodalia, a village near Calcutta. Dinabandhu's first wife, Kodhonkumari, died in 1868, and in 1872 he married Basanta Kumari of Kodalia, by whom he had 7 children, a son Sushil, a daughter Sarojini, then 2 sons Narendranath and Phonibusan, 2 daughters, Mohanaya and Jaydurga, and finally a son Lalit.[7]

Naren went to school in Arbelia until 1898, when the family moved to Kodalia. In "The Dissolution of a Priestly Family," written just before his death in 1954, Naren describes his memories of the annual visits to Kheput, where his father, as head priest of the village, would officiate at certain ceremonies in honor of the goddess Durga. Naren's essay recounts two village myths about how the Shakti temple came to be built in Kheput and how a particular line of Brahmans came to be responsible for officiating at ceremonies in her honor. Dinabandhu apparently continued to return to the village annually until his death in 1905, but after that the goddess and the village languished without the presence of a head priest. When Naren, now the famous political leader and ideologue M. N. Roy, visited Kheput in 1938, the village elders asked him to return once a year to propitiate the goddess. But Roy was an atheist and fierce priest-hater, and steadfastly refused the discarded mantle of his father.[8]

Dinabandhu is said to have moved to Kodalia in 1898 in order to take over some property of his second wife's family. In Kodalia, Naren attended school, studying Sanskrit, English, and Bengali. Here he discovered politics and the possibilities of revolution. Naren's best friend of those days and a confidant later in life as well was Hari Kumar Chakravarty. Professor Robert North's notes from a 1958 interview with Mr. Chakravarty describe the young Naren:

Mr. Chakravarty's mother and Roy's mother were the closest of friends, talked together, ate together, sewed together, and Chakravarty and Roy were the best of friends from small boyhood. . . . As a boy, Roy was very religious. In 1905, at the time of the Bengal partition, Chakravarty organized a meeting in the school compound . . . and Chakravarty prevailed upon Roy to conduct the meeting. The two of them, and two other boys were arrested and this was the start of Roy's political career. Released, the boys determined to read every book they could find on revolutions . . . the whole revolutionary history of the world including the American revolution. Gradually, they gathered a considerable library and attracted a group of young men, who gathered, read, and discussed—a kind of debating society. . . . The group also read other kinds of literature, seeking broad culture, and they studied various religions of the world. Particularly they were influenced by the Bengali cult of Sanwasi [? This word is obviously incorrect. It might refer to Shakti or Sarasvati, or it might be sannyasi, which could mean a free and disciplined man.] The cult of Shree Chaitanya, of Ramakrishna and Vivekananda, and the cult of love. . . . The group tried to achieve a rebirth of the early 19th century Bengali unitarianism of Raj Ram Mohan Roy. . . . From boyhood, Roy had a thirst for knowledge. He used to say as a young man that knowledge is freedom, that the urge for freedom is inherent in every man, that freedom must be achieved through knowledge.[9]

Chakravarty also mentions Roy's attachment to the cult of the Mother Goddess. Ellen Roy (Roy's widow) told North of Roy's claim that members of his group had devotee relationships with older women.[10]

The lengthy list of influences mentioned by Hari Kumar Chakravarty shows how difficult it would be to demonstrate that any one religious, intellectual, or political current was decisive in shaping these young men. One example of the actions that were inspired by religious reform teachings was discussed by North and Chakravarty:

I asked Chakravarty if he could corroborate a story Ellen (Roy) heard from Roy re: the group volunteering to carry corpses of plague victims to the burning ground. . . . Yes, Chakravarty said, the group, most of them Brahmins, used to carry corpses to the burning ground irrespective of caste—as protest against the concepts of caste.[11]

The date and context of these activities are unclear, but such service, partly out of devotion and partly as a form of protest against certain kinds of authorities, was common in the period.[12]

During the last years of the nineteenth century and the first few years of the twentieth, a few men in Maharashtra and in Bengal began to plot revolutionary violence against the British Raj. The Chapekar brothers had assassinated a British official in Poona, and P. Mitra and Barindra Kumar Ghose were seeking to channel the activities of restless young men along revolutionary lines. In Bengal, "samitis," or societies, were formed, sometimes secretly, to practice physical culture and to inculcate Hindu doctrines. They can be related to the Hindu revival and to the attempt by Indian youths to demonstrate their physical manliness, which they felt the English had called into question.[13]

In 1905 Naren's father died and he and his brothers came to Calcutta to make their own way. Naren had finished his course at the local school about this time. At various times during the next ten years, he lived with one or another of his nonpolitical brothers or moved in with one of several revolutionary comrades.[14] According to Sibnarayan Ray, in 1907 Naren "was a student of the Bengal Technical Institute and had passed the Entrance Examination from the newly founded National College." [15] There is no other information about Roy's education and it is doubtful that he attended many classes in Calcutta.

The first recorded "action" (the name given by participants to political dacoity, or robbery) in which Roy took part was at Chingripota, a railroad station near Kodalia. Phanindra Kumar Chakravarty, a compatriot of Roy's in Jatin Mukherjee's group, described the action:

> Naren took up the idea; he himself, Sailen Bose, and Nipen Bose happened to be great pals of the Station Master with whom they were quite free in regard to their political sentiments. Naren took the Station Master into confidence, and the latter agreed to hand over the key of the safe to the dacoits on the condition that the dacoits were to *pretend* to use force, but were not actually to do so. On the appointed day, these three men accompanied by some more men from Calcutta, turned up at the station. At the last moment the Station Master's heart failed him, and he refused to hand the keys over. Naren and his men then proceeded to use real force. They locked the Station Master and his wife in a room and started looting the safe. The station people, hearing the row, turned up and assaulted the dacoits. In the fight some of the station people were wounded or injured, and then they all ran away and Naren and his party carried about six hundred rupees in cash away.[16]

Although we do not learn much about the structure of the revolutionary group or its leadership from the account, the reaction of the "public" should be noted. It seemed to them that dacoits were dacoits and robbery was robbery. Patriotic motives were not written on the foreheads of the group. Especially after political assassinations began, it was difficult to raise money from the public, and robbery seemed the only alternative source.[17]

Naren was arrested, as is noted in a Home Department political file: "The station-master complained at once and Narendra was put in his trial but discharged by the Deputy Magistrate of Sealdah . . . at the time of his arrest a most seditious manuscript was found on his person and a book on modern warfare." [18] Before 1930, Roy was arrested numerous times, but either escaped while on bail or was released. The literature mentioned probably included *Bartaman Rananiti* (or *The Modern Art of War*), written by either Abinash Chandra Battacharyi or Barin Ghose, which was circulating among Bengali revolutionaries at the end of 1907.[19] Two types of literature were circulated by the revolutionaries: theoretical and religious tracts, like the *Bhagavad Gītā* or *Bhawani Mandir*, and practical manuals—how to make bombs or conduct warfare. The former, as Professor Richard Park has suggested, were often in English, and were for the more educated among the revolutionaries, while the latter were more likely to be in Bengali.[20]

During his Calcutta years—1905 to 1915—Naren went from job to job, house to house, living on the edge of respectable society. He even tried to start a restaurant that could serve as a rendezvous for revolutionaries. One of his residences was in a boarding house run by the Anushilan Samiti in Calcutta. The Calcutta Samiti operated in the open until the government cracked down and dissolved it and the other samitis in 1909 after the CID uncovered revolutionary plotting.[21]

Naren was next involved in a much larger revolutionary conspiracy, the Howrah gang case, which was brought before the public in 1910 and 1911. Quite a few revolutionary groups were implicated in this case. Naren was among those arrested, but the case against him was weak. Although the Home Department noted both the earlier case and the fact that he carried with him copies of inflammatory literature, including issues of Aurobindo's *Karmayogin* and another paper called *Dharma*, he had to be released.[22]

It was apparently just after the Howrah gang case that Naren left Calcutta in the guise of a sannyasin and went to Banaras and other parts of North India. He was shadowed by the police and soon returned to Calcutta. Whether he had religious motivations in going or was simply trying to stay out of sight is not clear.[23]

A number of informants have told me that Roy was initiated by a Vaishnava guru during this period, but the evidence for this is too sketchy, and several different gurus have been suggested as the man in question.[24] An important relationship was formed at this time with the revolutionary leader Jatin Mukherjee which lasted until Naren left India in 1915.

Jatin Mukherjee, who is known in the annals of Bengali revolutionary history as "Bagha Jatin" or "Jatin-Bagh"—Jatin the Tiger—came from Kustea subdivision in Nadia District, according to Home Department records. Jatin-da, as his followers called him (from "dada," elder brother, a term used for political leaders), was for some time a shorthand typist in the Bengal Secretariat. It was said that Jatin worked actively "for the circulation of *Jugantar*" in his home district. Jatin seems to have kept his job in the Bengal Secretariat even after becoming involved in revolutionary work. Only with the Howrah gang case did he become well known to the CID.[25]

Phanindra Chakravarty mentions in his confession that he had met Jatin in Darjeeling some years before when Jatin was giving instruction to youths in athletics and the *Gītā*.[26]

It is not clear when Naren met Jatin Mukherjee. Naren wrote in 1949,

> Once I overheard a few sentences of a conversation. I still belonged to the entourage of another Dada, and heard him rebuking a Chela presumably of wavering loyalty. The latter had been visiting some other Dada. Ultimately, in exasperation, the rebuked apostate rejoined mildly: "Dada, why do you want me not to see him, when he has never asked me to join his party; he has no party." I was curious to know who was that strange sort of Dada, and buttonholed the rebuked Gurubhai after he was dismissed by the extremely annoyed Dada. The next day I was taken to the unusual Dada who did not play the game of "Cheledhara," and was caught for good.[27]

"Chela" is a term referring to a disciple of a revolutionary leader; "Gurubhai" means a coreligionist, a follower of the same spiritual guide; "cheledhara" means one who snares "cheles" (children) or "chelas" (disciples), i.e., a kidnapper. It was a mark of Roy's attachment to his dada that many years later, an older, more secular, and often cynical man, he could still write,

> All the Dadas practiced magnetism; only Jatin Mukherjee possessed it. Therefore he was a puzzle and a despair to the rivals engaged in the game of "cheladhara." He never cast out his nets; yet he was loved by all, even the followers of the other Dadas.[28]

The political system referred to above probably dates back many centuries in Bengal.[29] The basic unit of action is the "dal," organized around a single dada and often bearing his name. On a second level there are somewhat unstable alliances of dals, where the heads of single factions might act as followers of one superior leader or as equals trying to attain common goals. As in the segmentary political system of the Nuer described by Evans-Pritchard, there could be either fission (of the larger alliances or of a single dal) or fusion of two or more dals into a larger alliance or party.[30] Single factions, at the lower level, were localized, while alliances could extend over a fairly wide territory.

The dals as well as the alliances of dals were conflict groupings with the primary aim of opposing the British Raj and working for Indian independence. Although allied dals cooperated in the utilization of men, weapons, and money, there were also conflicts between dals. The dal as a unit of political organization in Bengal villages and rural areas has been described by a nineteenth-century ICS officer, Robert Carstairs, and also by a contemporary anthropologist.[31]

The revolutionaries' political organization shows several kinds of relationships. In addition to his primary function as a political leader, the dada seems to hold something of the neoparental authority which the older brother would exercise in a Bengali family.[32] All evidence indicates that the dada was older than his followers. The relationship also seems to reflect an important religious concept: the guru-shishya relationship, where the disciple is to give his complete loyalty, devotion, and respect to his teacher. Idealization of the guru, particularly among the esoteric but numerous religious cults of Bengal, may be seen in the following quotation taken from the text of one such cult by Sir John Woodroffe:

Guru is Brahma. Guru is Viṣṇu. Guru is Deva Maheśvara himself.
Guru is the place of pilgrimage. Guru is the sacrifice. Guru is charity
(that is, the religious merit acquired by means of charity). Guru is devotion and austerities. Guru is fire. Guru is Sūrya. The entire Universe
is Guru.[33]

Followers call the dada their preceptor, and dadas often engaged in
teaching practical skills, ideology, and political strategy to their followers.

In theory, the disciple or follower of a dada was completely devoted
and loyal. For example, the Sedition Committee *Report* quotes from
the initiation oath of the Dacca Anushilan Samiti: "I will carry out the
orders of the authorities without saying a word. I will never conceal
anything from the leader and will never speak anything but the truth
to him." [34] In one standard history of the revolutionary movement in
Bengal, N. K. Guha mentions that one is to follow exactly the com-
mands of the leader. Guha also presents a long description of how a
leader persuaded a would-be member to join his dal, using the argument that to serve the country is to serve God.[35] Thus the dada presented himself, as a guru might have done, as the intermediary or representative of God to ordinary men. Also, it must be noted that a
number of tracts were distributed, read, and explained to give a religious rationale for worldly acts—e.g., Aurobindo's *Bhawani Mandir*
and the *Bhagavad Gītā*, which was interpreted in an activist, literal
way as sanctioning all acts for a righteous cause, including murder.[36]

The acts to be performed by the disciples were most often violent
—robbery and murder—and were often only vaguely related to the
goals of India's independence. Guha gives a long account of how the
first political dacoity was permitted by the Dacca Anushilan Samiti's
dada, P. Mitra. The disciples complained that they had given up all for
the cause and for their dada, and they were slowly starving. P. Mitra
did not like the idea of dacoity, but finally decided that it was necessary under the circumstances. According to Guha, once the first dacoity was committed, the floodgates opened and every dal was out
doing one.[37]

Nirad C. Chaudhuri has suggested that there was a tradition among
well-to-do Bengali families of private murder for revenge. He claims
that the means used by the revolutionaries grew out of this tradition

and resemble those for which zamindars in earlier, more anarchic times
had hired retainers or kept private armies.[38] There was a hostile response from the public, both rural and urban, to the earlier acts of the
revolutionaries, which were seen by all but their perpetrators as criminal actions.[39] Later commentators, including Bipin Pal and Lord Ronaldshay, viewed these acts as guided by idealistic ends but performed
by evil and perverted means.[40]

Roy mentions that his dada differed from the other dadas in that:

1. Jatin-da never set out nets to snare disciples, and yet they came.
2. He was loved by all, including disciples of other dadas.
3. He had no air of condescending superiority.
4. "In what he said, there was no hint (a usual trick of the trade
   of Dadaism) of an extensively ramified secret organisation accu-
   mulating vast quantities of arms and money for the Day of Liberation."
5. He gave advice; "he never issued orders."
6. He opposed premature and indiscriminate violence.
7. He was the first revolutionary to die fighting.
8. "He was kind and truthful as well as bold and uncompromis-
   ing."
9. He was not a great, but a good man.

Roy had become a "radical humanist" by the time he wrote his reminiscences of Jatin-da. At the end of the article, Jatin-da too became a
humanist:

> Like all modern educated men of his time, he tended to accept the re-
> formed religion preached by Swami Vivekananda—a God who
> would stand the test of reason, and a religion which served a progres-
> sive social and human purpose. He believed himself to be a Karma-
> yogi, trying to be at any rate, and recommended the ideal to all of us.
> Detached from the unnecessary mystic preoccupations, Karmayogi
> means a humanist. He who believes that the self-realisation can be at-
> tained through human action, must logically also believe in man's
> creativeness—that man is the maker of his destiny. That is also the
> essence of Humanism. Jatinda was a Humanist—perhaps the first in
> modern India.[41]

To generalize about dadas and their disciples it would be necessary
to get comparable data for other dals, including more statements from

leaders and followers. At this point such data is only available in anecdotal form. However, a number of further points can be dealt with here: the relationships between dals, the internal differentiation of dals, and an evaluation of the dal as a form of political organization. Most of these points will be discussed in the context of a history of Naren Bhattacharya and Jatin Mukherjee's dal from about 1912 to 1915.

Although dals were the usual basic unit of revolutionary political organization, they were too small and too localized to carry out larger "actions." Some groupings were composed of a large number of branches with a more or less central headquarters and leader. These included the Dacca Anushilan Samiti and the Jugantar Party after 1912 and 1913. It is not always clear what the relationship was between branches and center in these organizations. Often larger parties or revolutionary forces were formed by the alliance of dals. The Jugantar party was organized originally in this way.[42]

The members of many dals in Bengal—no one has ever tried even to guess their number—were recruited from a small stratum of the society, and the figures given by caste, age, and occupation in the Sedition Committee *Report* for "persons convicted in Bengal of revolutionary crimes or killed in commission of such crimes during the years 1907–17" are probably proportionately correct. The tables given in the *Report* are listed below.[43]

AGE

10–15	16–20	21–25	26–30	31–35	36–45	over 45	not recorded
2	48	76	29	10	9	1	11

CASTE

Brahman	Kayastha	Baidya	Rajput	Tanti	Mahishya	Subarnabanik
65	87	13	1	1	3	1

Vaishya	Karmakar	Kaibarta	Barui	Saha	Mudri	Sudra	Uriya
1	1	3	1	2	1	1	1

Europeans and Eurasians (in arms traffic)
4

PROFESSION OR OCCUPATION

students	teachers	landowners	persons of no occupation	trade and commerce
68	16	19	24	23
clerks, persons in government service	newspapers and presses	cultivators	opium smugglers	not recorded
20	5	1	1	2

It is obvious that almost 90 percent of the revolutionaries came from among the high castes of Bengal, Brahman, Vaidya, and Kayastha, and that most were between 16 and 30 years old. These high castes formed only about 5.6 percent of the total population of Bengal, but contributed a very high percentage of those attending schools and colleges and those counted as literate.[44]

The figures for occupation or profession must be taken more warily. It is not at all clear what the different categories mean; for example, who is a landowner? Was Jatin Mukherjee counted as a government servant? It does make sense, however, that at least 45 percent of the convicted revolutionaries were students or teachers. The schools and colleges and the towns and cities in which they were located were probably, as the Rowlatt Committee argued in its report, fertile recruiting grounds for revolutionaries.[45] Young men probably learned of a revolutionary group by word of mouth and were invited to meet the dada or other leading members. Persuasion and promises followed, with visions painted of a romantic and exciting life devoted to the service of the country. The different dals had their "adda," or rendezvous spots, where they would talk politics and throw out suggestions for future actions. Phanindra Chakravarty mentions that the adda of Jatin Mukherjee's dal shifted from place to place, as did the living quarters of the members. Once the members and their adda became known to the police, they had to keep on the move.[46]

The training of dals varied from group to group. Phanindra Chakravarty mentioned that Jatin-da instructed his followers in athletics and in the *Gītā*. Members practiced "lathi" or club play and also target shooting whenever they could obtain pistols and ammunition. Guha and Nirad C. Chaudhuri also describe the military drilling that some of these groups practiced.[47]

The Sedition Committee *Report,* which has been taken as an accurate record by almost all later writers on the revolutionaries, systematically excludes certain kinds of information. Particularly, it eliminates information appearing in Home Department records that was used by the Committee in compiling its account of the rivalry and antagonisms between revolutionary dals and competition for resources of men and weapons. To build a more fearsome picture of the danger of the revolutionaries to the British Raj and to inspire more severe legislation for their control, the Rowlatt Committee did not mention that revolutionaries often argued and opposed each other, sometimes refused to make alliances, and even came to the brink of violence against each other.

This point can be illustrated by the accounts of the distribution of Mauser pistols in 1914, an event considered important by the Sedition Committee:

> The theft of pistols from Rodda and Co., a firm of gunmakers in Calcutta, was an event of the greatest importance in the development of revolutionary crime in Bengal. . . . The 10 missing cases contained 50 Mauser pistols and 46,000 rounds of Mauser ammunition for the same. . . . The authorities have reliable information to show that 44 of these pistols were almost at once distributed to 9 different revolutionary groups in Bengal, and it is certain that the pistols so distributed were used in 54 cases of dacoity and murder subsequent to August 1914. It may indeed safely be said that few, if any, revolutionary outrages have taken place in Bengal since August 1914 in which Mauser pistols stolen from Rodda and Co. have not been used.[48]

Later in the Sedition Committee *Report,* the names of some of the groups which used Mauser pistols are mentioned:

> The persons in whose possession the Mausers were found must also be noted. These included members of the Madaripur party, Jatin Mukharji of Western Bengal, of the Chandernagore group of Bepin Ganguli's party, and of the Mymensingh, Barisal, North Bengal and Dacca parties. That arms were interchanged between the several groups is shown by various statements.[49]

The last quotation comes from a section of the Sedition Committee *Report* headed "Co-operation of Groups"; and, indeed, there was such cooperation. But some of the bitterness engendered by the distribution of pistols is evident in this passage from the confession of Phanindra

Chakravarty. The predicament he mentions is the need of money to send an agent abroad to make contact with the Germans.

> Whilst we were in this predicament we suddenly came into possession of 28 Mauser pistols, and some 20 or 22 thousand rounds of ammunition out of *Rodda's* theft. I am not sure how exactly they came into our possession, but I will tell you what I heard then. Of course you know that *Bepin Ganguli* had committed the theft of the arms. Bepin lodged the arms with a *Marwari* in the first place. The former had just been able to dispose of about 22 of the pistols when the *Marwari* became restive and demanded the removal of the remainder from his house. The *Marwari* handed him 28 pistols and a part of the ammunition. Noren made them over to me, and I kept them in my house in Mir Jaffer's Lane. . . . Soon after the arms came into our possession, Bepin Ganguli came to my house and demanded his pistols. I refused to make them over. He was so angry about it that he actually threatened to shoot some of us with the revolvers he had. I defied him to do so, and there was much soreness on both sides over the matter for some time. We refused to part with the arms because we had the idea of using them in committing dacoities for the purpose of raising money to send people out of India.[50]

Several sections later, Chakravarty mentions that, "The disagreement existing between Ganguli and us was smoothed over by Dada by taking charge of all the arms. The taking charge of the arms was nominal only, and did not involve transfers. He merely said he was responsible for the custody and use of the arms; and we bowed to his decision." [51] The Sedition Committee described the cooperation but not the controversies over the arms. The settling of the dispute by Jatin Mukherjee and the acquiescence to his decision by Bepin Ganguli, the leader of another dal, should also be underscored. Dadas might deal with each other as equals—either rivals or friends—or some dadas or one particular dada might gain priority or prominence in an alliance made to carry out a larger action.

GERMAN CONSPIRACY

The more extensive action that several dadas and dals cooperated with Jatin Mukherjee to carry out was the famous German conspiracy of 1914–1915. The origins of the Jugantar Party of which Jatin Mukherjee was the leader are described in a valuable history of the Bengal revolutionaries by Gopal Halder:

Jugantar, the suppressed weekly had served as rallying point for the Aurobinda-Barindra group of Calcutta, and the title stuck to others of diffeent groups who came later to be connected with the close or distant work of the paper, like Abinash Bhattacharya, Dababrata Basu etc. So in 1910, the members of these different groups ("Bagha Jatin" or Jatindranath Mukherji was then their leader) who were being tried together in the Howrah Conspiracy Case were designated by the prosecution, presumably to strengthen its case, as members collectively of the 'Jugantar Party' (as distinct from those of the Anushilan Samiti by which were meant the members of the *Dacca* Anushilan only and its branches). The authorities gave a name perhaps to a thing which came into existence, though these groups never merged, and the Jugantar, unlike the Anushilan, never meant anything more than a federation of revolutionary groups. What the Jugantar thus lacked in centralised leadership it made up for by a certain flexibility of mind and method and by probably the intellectual quality of its cadre.[52]

The Jugantar Party does not seem to have been formed until late 1914 or early 1915. It meant an alliance between groups for the largest revolutionary "action" yet planned. The groups involved were mentioned in Phanindra Chakravarty's confession:

> I have mentioned to you before the men who were actually working in this cause at this time. They were mainly (1) Bepin Ganguli's party, (2) Noren Chowdhery's party, (3) our own (this is Dādā's party). The Dacca or Moti Lal Roy's party was out of this as Moti Lal refused to take part in our original deliberations. The Faudpar or Puran Das's party was so completely merged into our own that we two were practically one.[53]

The members of the groups in the conspiracy met to plan an armed revolt to seize control of eastern India. In the action described below, Jatin Mukherjee lost his life and the dal disintegrated, but the loose federation of groups, the Jugantar Party, continued in operation for several decades under other leaders.

One aspect of revolutionary activity which has not yet been mentioned is the network of overseas connections. In the two decades preceding 1915, many revolutionaries had traveled in England and in Europe trying to gain support and assistance for their efforts. Naren Bhattacharya, in the years following the failure of the German conspiracy, became one of the most famous overseas revolutionaries, propagandists, and organizers.[54]

It was from several Indians who had been abroad that Jatin Mukherjee and his followers learned that the Germans, who were then at war with the British, were willing to supply Indian revolutionaries with arms, money, and military instruction. Several steps were necessary to set the plan into operation:

1. Funds had to be raised to send agents abroad to make direct contact.
2. The agents then had to determine with the Germans just when arms and money were to be sent and in what quantities.
3. The plans for a general uprising had to be made more specific and timed to coincide with the arrival of the supplies.
4. An alliance of several groups had to be made to gather sufficient manpower to begin the uprising and detailed assignments agreed upon by participants.[55]

The operations were set in motion by two daring dacoities at Garden Reach and Beliaghata during February 1915. The Sedition Committee called these the "taxi-cab dacoities and murders." A CID man, Nirod Haldar, who came upon Jatin Mukherjee and his men while he was searching for Naren, was shot at Jatin's order.[56] And during one of the dacoities, a taxi driver who was not a revolutionary but had simply been used as a driver was shot so that he could not talk. As was usually the case, Indians on both sides rather than Englishmen lost their lives at the hands of the revolutionaries, although a few English officials were murdered. N. K. Guha mentions in his history of the revolutionaries that men who were working directly against the revolutionaries were killed, and that a few others were murdered as a warning to the public to acquiesce in their violent deeds and not to inform or cooperate with the officials.[57] It is not at all certain that Naren killed anyone during these revolutionary days, but he was an intrepid and poised revolutionary and probably would not have hesitated to kill if necessary.

There is not too much known specifically about the internal differentiation and specialization of the dal. But there are a number of references to "departments" within the dal, namely the "finance department," the "violence department," and the "foreign department." It is also well known that certain men were sent to Europe to learn how to make explosives. We do not know whether they were called members of the "research department." The "financial minister" was probably responsible for keeping records and for the protection of the dal's money.[58]

N. K. Guha writes that the leaders of the dals never actually took part in actions and in fact constantly moved from place to place to avoid endangering themselves. It is probably true that dadas did refrain from taking unnecessary chances and that the theoreticians of the revolutionaries, like Aurobindo Ghose, never participated in any action.[59] But in the larger plots where field direction was needed and the whole dal was involved, the commanders were probably present.

Naren was described as a trusted lieutenant of Jatin Mukherjee. He was especially favored by his dada because during 1915 he made two trips to Batavia to meet with the German Consul there and arrange the arms shipments. On his first voyage, Naren, traveling under the name "C. Martin," persuaded the German officials to send the *S. S. Maverick* with 30,000 rifles, 400 pounds of ammunition for each, and two lakhs of rupees to Rai Mangal in the Sundarbans. The revolutionaries used a firm called "Harry and Sons" in Calcutta as a front, and the Germans, via "Martin," wired Rs. 43,000 to the firm, of which the revolutionaries actually received Rs. 33,000.[60]

The rest of the plan may be quoted from the Sedition Committee *Report*, which seems to be based on Phanindra Chakravarty's confession, since all the details are the same.

> They decided to divide the arms into three parts, to be sent respectively to—
>
> (1) Hatia, for the Eastern Bengal districts, to be worked by the members of the Barisal party.
> (2) Calcutta.
> (3) Balasore.
>
> They considered that they were numerically strong enough to deal with the troops in Bengal, but they feared reinforcements from outside. With this idea in view, they decided to hold up the three main railways into Bengal by blowing up the principal bridges. . . . Naren Chaudhuri and Phanindra Chakravarti were told to go to Hatia where a force was to collect, first to obtain control of the Eastern Bengal districts, and then to march on to Calcutta. The Calcutta party, under Naren Bhattacharji and Bepin Ganguli, were first to take possession of all the arms and arsenals around Calcutta, then to take Fort William,

and afterwards to sack the town of Calcutta. The German officers arriving in the *Maverick* were to stay in Eastern Bengal and raise and train armies.[61]

One more detail should be added from Phanindra Chakravarty's confession. He describes how the revolutionary army was to grow:

> We had expectations of about 50,000 joining in the first rising. They were to join us from all parts of Bengal. We had counted upon 5,000 men in Calcutta itself to start the rebellion and we had every hope of nearly 20,000 youths, mainly students, joining hands with us immediately afterwards.[62]

The *Maverick* was delayed; the revolutionaries then heard that another ship with far fewer supplies was being sent. Frustrated and worried, they sent Naren and Phanindra Chakravarty to Batavia in August 1915 to see what was going on. They found that the British had uncovered the plot. The police were searching for Jatin Mukherjee and some of his dal in connection with the Garden Reach and Beliaghata dacoities, and he and a few of his men were tracked to Balasore, where they were hiding. During the resulting gun battle, Jatin Mukherjee and another revolutionary were killed.[63] Eventually many of the other conspirators were captured, including Phanindra Chakravarty, who was held first by the French in Shanghai and then turned over to the British officials. The British transferred him to Singapore, where he learned of Jatin-da's death. He was terribly confused and upset. It was only some nine months later that he was able (and willing) to give an accurate confession.[64]

Naren Bhattacharya escaped the British and traveled first to Japan and then to the United States. He met some of the Indian nationalists and revolutionaries in exile during his American tour, and he attended meetings and studied in New York. While in California, Naren took the name Manabendra Nath Roy or M. N. Roy. He was arrested in New York as a member of a revolutionary conspiracy and fled while on bail to Mexico; there he met Mexican leaders and a cosmopolitan, international set of radicals, including the American radicals Mike Gold and Carleton Beals.[65] In Mexico, Roy wrote several pamphlets in Spanish, an open letter to President Woodrow Wilson in English, and a lengthy book in Spanish entitled *La India, su pasado, su presente y su porvenir.*[66] Much later in life, Roy wrote his memoirs, covering the years 1915 to 1923, beginning with his journey across the Pacific to the United States. From these writings, a few points may be suggested about Naren's outlook and personal style. The caution must be added that these observations are made about him at the end of his revolutionary career and just before his communist career was to begin. The *Memoirs* were written near the end of his life, and his view of his own young manhood is seen through the prism of later values and conceptions of the world.

Roy wrote about this period as one of transition from narrow or "cultural nationalism" to international communism. Although he liked to think of himself as a heretic, Roy held fervently to each new faith that he adopted until disillusionment set in.[67] Several passages like the following show him looking back and looking ahead.

> I was tormented by a psychological conflict between an emotion (loyalty to old comrades) and an intelligent choice of a new ideal. I could not forget the injunction of the only man I ever obeyed almost blindly. Before leaving India for the second time, I personally escorted Jatinda to the hiding place where he later on fought and died. In reply to the thoughtless pledge of a romantic youth—"I will not again return without arms"—the affection of the older man appealed: "Come back soon, with or without arms." The appeal was an order for me. He was our Dādā, but the Commander-in-Chief also.
>
> Jatinda's heroic death had absolved me from the moral obligation to obey his order. Already in the autumn of 1915 while passing through Manila, I had received the shocking news. But then, my reaction was purely emotional: Jatinda's death must be avenged. Only a year had passed since then. But in the meantime I had come to realise that I admired Jatinda because he personified, perhaps without himself knowing it, the best of mankind. The corollary to that realisation was that Jatinda's death would be avenged if I worked for the ideal of establishing a social order in which the best of man could be manifest.[68]

The older Roy saw the young Naren Bhattacharya as a romantic, idealistic, ignorant of social theory and the world of letters, a rather stiff and silly puritan and teetotaler. He thought his earlier faith in India's mission to be constrictive and immature as he passed first into his communist and then into his humanist phase. He describes in the *Memoirs* how he learned to overcome his awkwardness in society and among women, and how he moved from the puritanical world of his

youth to the cosmopolitan society of the Third Communist International in its early years, the world Roy called "a community of free
human beings." It is difficult to obtain independent confirmation of
Roy's transition from puritanism to liberation (in his terms); but
Carleton Beals has told me that Roy was loath to taste alcohol in
Mexico, and he thinks he handed Roy his first glass of wine. It is also
known that Jatin Mukherjee preferred his men not to marry, and it
was in California, not India, that Roy met and married his first wife,
Evelyn Trent. Though he was aware of his social awkwardness during
this period, he was also conscious that he was a tough and battle-hard-
ened revolutionary.[69]

Roy's writings in 1916–1917, mostly in Spanish (and probably
done with the assistance of an anonymous native Spanish writer) present a black-and-white view of India and her past. The pamphlets and
letters are frankly written as political propaganda to counteract views
of India which Roy said were completely incorrect. But his lengthy
book, *La India,* is a little more scholarly and factual, although it gives
essentially the same vision of India's glorious past and her bondage
under British rule.

Pre-British India, according to Roy, was a thriving nation with all
its young men at schools and universities and with commerce and industry growing apace. Although the Mughal emperors were despots,
they were more benevolent than their contemporaries in Europe. And
India was the land of great cultural achievements with writers greater
than Tagore.[70] With the British came the end of that happy and boun-
teous age. The British came to power by trickery and deceit, and
under their rule the country fell from its previous state. By Roy's time,
it had become a land of famines and uneducated men, a land whose
commerce and agriculture benefited only the men of another nation.
India, said Roy, was a land of beggars. He mentioned the drain of resources from India and claimed that there had been no benefits from
British rule. Even the railways were not constructed to benefit India,
but only to suit British military convenience. Roy asserted that the reforms granted to give the beginnings of self-government were a sham
and that the men elected were toadies of the rulers, not representatives
of the people.[71]

Roy went to some lengths to defend the nationalists and revolutionaries, especially in his letter to President Woodrow Wilson. He compared the Indian revolutionaries to the American revolutionaries of the eighteenth century and equated German assistance to the Indians with French assistance to the Americans during their war for independence. "Liberty," wrote Roy, "is the innate right of every human being." [72] If Wilson supported "the noble ideal of liberating the Belgians, the Serbs, the Poles, the Slavs, the Bohemians, the Magyars," why should he not also support the liberation of Indians from the British yoke? [73] Roy even listed the betrayals of despotic Indian princes by the British as a mark of Britain's bad faith; it is as if all that is Indian is good, all that is British is evil. All his writings are larded with quotations from Western writers. Roy seemed to feel that Western readers would accept Western authorities on Indian questions.

The Roy of these writings has a very simple view of politics, society, and history. It is still a long step from these earliest works with their rationalization of nationalist revolution and anarchism to the Marxist analysis of India that Roy was to write a few years later. India, to Roy, still had a mission. Part of this global historical role was stated in the title of one section in his letter to Wilson: "The freedom of India will be a great step toward world peace." [74]

Despite the efforts of Naren and many young men, the British were able to crush the revolutionaries, at least momentarily, and they were continually able to prevent outbreaks of violence from enveloping large sections of the country. This can be explained in large part by the weaknesses existing within the revolutionary movement.

The dada organizational system that was widespread in Bengal contained several inherent deficiencies. Although devotion and loyalty to the leader of the *dal* were valuable in sustaining the group, the death of the dada would bring disintegration to his immediate faction. Thus Phanindra Chakravarty broke down and confessed after Jatin-da's death. Naren Bhattacharya went his own way, since his promises and loyalty were bound up with the person of the leader and death ended these obligations. The looser alliance of groups, called Jugantar, did continue, with Jadu Gopal Mukherjee as the new leader of the party. Phanindra Chakravarty's confession also indicated another problem for the revolutionaries connected with loyalty. Although Jatin Mukherjee's death might have ended Phanindra's connection to the revolution-

ary movement, he did not have to offer a full confession which implicated dozens of revolutionaries still in the field.

Moreover, if the loyalty of members is to a small group headed by a
charismatic leader, how is a larger revolutionary movement to be
built? Larger units were undoubtedly constructed, but it is evident
that considerable rivalry and antagonism hampered the movement.
Gopal Halder describes the debilitating rivalry of the Anushilan and
Jugantar groups over a long period of time.[75] As was indicated earlier
the revolutionary workers in Bengal were drawn from a small spec-
trum of the population. They were almost all high-caste Hindus and
excluded, for the most part, low-caste Hindus and Muslims. We can
only speculate as to whether they might have secured wider popular
support if they drew their membership from a more representative
cross-section of the population. The Hindu symbolism, rites of initiation drawn from Hindu sects and Hindu beliefs, and especially the
conception of the Mother Goddess and the Motherland fused as an object of devotion and a cause generating action, must have prevented
any kind of Muslim support. Most nationalists, even sophisticated and
Westernized ones, were quite oblivious to the Hindu character of their
nationalist symbols, heroes, and beliefs.

The revolutionaries often acted on impulse and emotion without
proper plans or precautions and had only short-term goals. The link
between specific acts of violence and the independence of India was at
best a hazy one. Perhaps it is in the nature of revolutionary activity
not to have well-formulated conceptions of past or future. They lived
in their present plots and "actions."

The connections between the revolutionaries and public movements
like Swadeshi and Noncooperation have never been completely or systematically spelled out. It is clear that the revolutionaries participated
in these public works and that some public leaders often counted on
the support of the revolutionaries.

It may be further observed that the Bengal revolutionaries were very
Bengali. Naren told the Germans who were about to send the *Maverick* to Karachi that it was no place to make a revolution. Bengal was
the center of real "actions" and wide support for revolution.[76] Bengali
revolutionaries drew upon their own symbols and beliefs in rationaliz-
ing revolution. There were similarities and sympathies with revolution-

aries elsewhere in India, but few direct connections. The Bengalis did send out some revolutionary "colonists," especially to Bihar and Orissa, to show these lesser folk how to do revolutionary work, and Rash Behari Bose went to the Punjab and the United Provinces to help lead revolutionary activity there. But for the most part, Bengal was the center of activity and the model from which other Indians and other areas might learn. At least, that is what her revolutionary sons thought.[77]

At the beginning of the revolutionary period, a number of important Swadeshi leaders offered assessments of the revolutionary movement. In the spring of 1908, after several murders and revolutionary "actions" had taken place, Tagore felt called upon to make his position known. He wrote two essays on the situation at the time, entitled "Path o patheya" (The way and the means) and "Samasya" (The problem).[78] While other figures like Surendranath Banerjea were proclaiming that these murders and robberies were the work of a few deranged men, Tagore felt that matters were much more complicated and that all Bengalis had to take responsibility for these acts. He noted that, previously, violence of words combined with a lack of commensurate action had made the Bengali an object of ridicule. But even beyond this ridicule, all Indians felt humiliated and alienated from their rulers. The British had used their power indiscriminately and were insensitive to native opinion. They did not allow the Indians to be human. Tagore pictured India as a prison house in which it was often hard to hear more than the clanking of chains.[79] He said that in France before the French Revolution the people had paid for the luxuries of a few, but in India the situation was much worse and more humiliating because India was paying for the luxuries of a whole nation of foreigners.[80] Thus Tagore was placing a good share of the blame for the violent acts on the ruling power and the whole European community in India.

Tagore then turned his attention to the perpetrators of the acts themselves and asked whether the acts were for the good of the country and whether they went against the basic values of Indian civilization. He characterized the revolutionary acts in the same way that he described many other political activities in the Swadeshi period: they were all attempts at short-cuts. "Just because I am in a hurry," wrote Tagore, "the road does not shorten." In the variety of expressions that an artist has at his command, Tagore described the revolutionaries and all exclusively political nationalists as sudden sparks, storms, people who wanted to fly instead of walk, and people taking a drink who might fall into the unfortunate situation of making the alcohol an end in itself.[81] Their actions, these sudden spurts of energy, were not equal to the tasks confronting India. They were no substitute for the creative process and the sustained arduous work that was needed. Tagore's point was not that their action was an evil to be condemned without reflection, but that it was not the best way to achieve the goals on which all might agree.

One of the main thrusts of Tagore's argument against the revolutionaries and political nationalists was that their actions were not in keeping with the spirit of Indian culture. He thought that India was a unique experiment in the mixing of cultures; cultural forces or shaktis were at work during long epochs. Harmonizing these forces was a slow and difficult process and required mutual tolerance and understanding. Sudden and sometimes violent actions would not substantially contribute to the real task at hand.[82]

The antagonism of the Moderates and the searching critique of Tagore had little impact on the revolutionaries. The government of India and of Bengal succeeded in temporarily halting the movement during the First World War. Many young men were imprisoned and the repression was effective. But by the early 1920s, many of the prisoners were released. Though a majority worked in the mass movement to see whether it would be effective in achieving their goals, they soon began plotting, organization, and violent action.[83]

THE IMPACT OF WORLD WAR I AND POLITICAL SHIFTS

Other politically active men reacted differently to the outbreak and progress of the war. The Moderates in the Indian Association and Congress supported the British war effort, participated in the Bengal Legislative Council and attended sessions of the rump Congress.[84] The loyalist attitude of the Muslim notables was shaken by the revocation of partition and by growing pro-Turkish, pan-Islamic feeling. At its 1912 session, the Muslim League shifted its major aim to "a form of self-government suitable to India." [85] This change in program opened the way for a Congress-League agreement which was achieved in the Lucknow Pact of 1916. By this scheme for political advance, the Congress agreed to the principle of separate electorates and reserved seats for the Muslims. Bengal's Muslims were to receive 40 percent of the nonofficial seats in the legislature.[86] A. K. Fazlul Huq, a rising star in the Muslim firmament, and other league leaders signed the pact, but its provisions were criticized by some Bengali Muslim leaders. The defectors left the Bengal Muslim League, worked through the Central National Mohammedan Association, and then formed their own organization, the Indian Moslem Association. They thought Bengali Muslims were entitled to the percentage of seats coincident with their 52.6 percent of the Bengali population.[87]

The Nawab of Dacca, a leading Muslim spokesman in Bengal, had died in 1915. In his last years he gave Fazlul Huq a lift along the road to political prominence. Huq, from a family of vakils in Barisal, was an honor-winning student and vakil in Calcutta, professor at Raychandra College, editor of the Bengali magazine *Balak*, and protégé of the Nawab from the partition period. Huq, with the Nawab's help, held a government post from 1906 to 1912 and then was returned to the Dacca Muslim seat in the Bengal Legislative Council unopposed in 1912. From 1913 to 1916 he served as secretary of the Bengal Presidency Muslim League, well launched on a political career that was to span more than fifty years. In the combination of family status, achievement, and fortunate connections, he resembled the Hindu establishment men involved in the Congress. Huq was an emotional, eloquent, ambitious Bengali who could never be called an outsider in Bengal, as Ameer Ali or the Dacca Nawab were.[88]

Besides new life on the Muslim side, Indian politics was revived through the efforts of Tilak, recently emerged from prison, and Annie Besant, newly turned to politics. They organized the Home Rule movement in different parts of the country and moved to capture the Congress from the lingering Moderates.[89] B. Chakravarty, Jitendralal Bannerjee, and a group around C. R. Das supported Mrs. Besant in Bengal, but Surendranath Banerjea waited outside to watch and see. Several years before his death in 1915, G. K. Gokhale had written of Bengal:

> the conduct of the Bengal Moderates is hastening disintegration. They have no leader on our side. Surendra Nath is an orator, but without energy and backbone, and cannot keep in hand the unruly pack whom

he professes to lead. . . . the whole feeling in Bengal is towards Extrem-
ism.[90]

By the end of World War I, a concerted challenge was mounted to
Banerjea's bastion in the Indian Association and Bengal Congress, led
by C. R. Das, lawyer and Extremist.

During the years 1904–1917, Bengal loomed large on the national
scene as the focal point of the Swadeshi agitation; but as that movement
was not very successful, and as the capital had been transferred to
Delhi, Bengal seemed to have become just another area of India by the
post–World War I period. There was a serious failure of leadership
in both the Extremist and the Moderate parties in Bengal in these
years, for neither provided sustained national leadership. Surendranath
Banerjea confined himself too much to the affairs of Bengal and insisted that the only goal of the Swadeshi agitation was the nullification
of the partition of Bengal. This was not a suitable aim around which to
arouse national support. Although Bengal was the cynosure during the
Swadeshi years, none of the spokesmen for Swadeshi remained on the
scene long enough or demonstrated enough ability to be a national
leader or to reach the goals the Extremists set forth. Surendranath Banerjea was the only Moderate who enjoyed widespread prominence,
but as Gokhale said, he could not keep his own followers in line, let
alone bring about unity with the Extremists in Bengal. The activities
of the revolutionaries in Bengal had been crushed by 1917, by either
prison, exile, or death.

The Bengalis had proven resourceful in trying out the strategies of
passive resistance and conspiratorial revolution. But they proved better
at words and sporadic actions than at sustained work and organization.
Too often they confined themselves to Bengali issues. The Muslims and
the vast majority of Bengalis were still outside nationalist politics. New
leadership, commitment, and organizing skills were needed to bring
new thousands into the movement for swaraj.

Part Three

The Third Generation: Bengal and Gandhi, 1918–1940

SIX

The Gandhian Age and the Rise of Chittaranjan Das

ᴄᴇᴋᴋᴊᴏ Mahatma Gandhi's rise to the top of the Indian National Congress at the end of World War I marks several important changes in its organization and program. During this time, there was also a shift in the regional balance of its leadership from Bengali and Maharashtrian dominance to a more even distribution, with men from Gujarat and North India playing a larger role than previously. At the same time, the Gandhi-led Congress began to tap new sources of support throughout British India.[1]

The regional shift resulted in tensions and antagonisms which continue into the present. In order to explore the role of Bengalis in the national movement, one focus here is upon Gandhi's relationship with Bengal's political leaders and ideologues: who supported Gandhi and who opposed him at different moments. Leadership of a complex movement must be considered as having both negative and positive functions for the individuals and groups participating. Indian traditions, especially in their regional variations, may be drawn upon to support a number of different nationalist ideologies and strategies.[2]

Political and economic conditions after the First World War were propitious for renewed efforts by Indian nationalists. Wilson's doctrine of self-determination for subject peoples added to Secretary of State for India Edwin Montagu's statement about "the progressive realisation of responsible government in India" raised hopes in the subcontinent.[3] News of the turmoil in Ireland and the Russian Revolution circulated in India, and Bengali political workers felt an affinity for the nationalists and revolutionaries in both countries.[4]

The war had brought rapid industrial development in the Calcutta area and other parts of Bengal that were beginning to modernize. The release of soldiers and the financial slump of 1920 put pressure on provincial and imperial resources; analysts noted an omnipresent middle-class unemployment in Calcutta.[5] The metropolis was also the scene of serious communal rioting in 1918, with Marwaris the chief victims and Muslims the most active rioters. These riots were signs of underlying frustration, but they also mark the growing politicization of the Bengali Muslims.[6] The Marwaris, a Rajasthani caste heavily involved in business activity and active participants in the economic growth of Calcutta, became important financial supporters of Gandhi. But they continued to be the object of suspicion and hostility among native Bengalis who felt the Marwaris were taking over their city.[7]

Gandhi, among others, had been critical of the reforms Montagu offered, but he maintained a positive attitude toward them into 1919. He worked for a softening of the self-government resolution introduced by C. R. Das of Bengal at the Amritsar Congress of 1919.[8] Yet during these same years, Gandhi became the leader of the national resistance to the repressive Rowlatt bills, which were passed over the concerted efforts of the Indian members of the Imperial Legislative Council. In March 1919, many Indians took the Satyagraha vow, and civil disobedience followed National Satyagraha Day in April. Violence soon broke out in Delhi, Calcutta, Bombay, Ahmadabad, and Amritsar, whereupon Gandhi temporarily suspended civil disobedience.[9] Throughout this brief campaign of civil disobedience, he was opposed by the Moderate wing. The Moderates shortly left the Congress and joined the National Liberal Federation. By the end of 1919 the separation was complete.[10]

During the campaign, disturbances in the Punjab had been followed by a massacre at Jallianwala Bagh, a significant turning point in Indian-British relations. It led to increased bitterness on the part of Indian nationalists, it turned congressmen in a more Extremist direction, it vitiated the 1919 reforms, and it led to a further weakening of the legitimacy of the Raj. Gandhi, C. R. Das, Motilal Nehru, Abbas Tyabji, and M. R. Jayakar served on the Congress inquiry committee, with Gandhi most responsible for the report.[11] Gandhi came to know Das and the elder Nehru, later rivals for Congress leadership. Jayakar has recounted how the inquiry committee was often persuaded by Gandhi's incisive arguments:

> Gandhi often stood alone against all this fusillade of argument; the process went on occasionally for a day or two; Gandhi struggling with his weak voice, but with stern logic, and clear arguments, which cut like a sharp rapier through our knotted reasoning. . . . I can recall more than one occasion when Das rose from such interviews, at the end of the day, thumping the table with a characteristic remark, "Damn it all, Gandhi, you are right and we are wrong." [12]

From these sessions, Gandhi, Motilal Nehru, and Das brought away mutual respect which lasted through even the most bitter disagreements of 1922–1925.[13]

Throughout World War I, Indian Muslim feeling against the British had been rising because the war had placed Turkey and Britain on opposite sides. Agitation for lenient treatment of Turkey and the Khilaf continued with the end of hostilities. Some time in the fall of 1919, Gandhi joined with Muslim leaders and groups in their agitation on this issue,[14] a move which brought much wider national support during the Noncooperation Movement of 1920–1921.

C. R. DAS AND THE CONGRESS IN BENGAL

In these same years, a number of other men who had not previously been in the front rank of Congress leadership were beginning to play a larger role in its policy-making and organization. Among these was C. R. Das, who had been a legal defender for the Extremists during the Swadeshi period. He participated in Bengali politics and became widely known in India through his legal work in the decade from 1907 to 1917. With his 1917 presidential address to the Bengal Provincial Congress, he began to take a more active part in politics, and within three years he was recognized as the foremost Bengali nationalist spokesman. In the next five years, from 1920 to 1925, he led the reorganization of the Congress in Bengal. He systematically structured it down to the district level and instituted direct elections for the Bengal Provincial Congress Committee. He enlisted a cadre of able lieutenants who were destined to play a dominant role in the Bengal Congress for several decades, and brought many young men and ex-revolutionaries into the Congress organization. He made important efforts toward Hindu-Muslim cooperation in Bengal. In the years 1922 to 1925 he became the president of the Swaraj Party, which successfully challenged Gandhi's control of the Congress organization and his policy toward the legislative councils.

Das was born in 1870 in Vikrampur, Dacca District, into a Vaidya family which had become associated with the Brahmo Samaj.[15] He came from a family of lawyers and attended Presidency College. His lifelong interest in literature and particularly Bengali poetry was awakened during these years, and as a student he argued that Bengali should have a larger part in the curriculum of Calcutta University. As a youth and then as a student in Calcutta, Das was brought in touch with the nationalist movement in the decade that the Congress was founded. He served as secretary of Surendranath Banerjea's Student Association, and also heard Bipin Pal, who later became a political ally. In 1890 Das went to London to prepare for the ICS, but failed the examination twice.[16]

With his father's encouragement, Das joined the Inner Temple and was called to the bar in 1893. Later in the same year, he was sworn in as an advocate of the Calcutta High Court. During his years in London, Das took an active interest in politics; he made several speeches calling for Indian reform in the election campaign of 1892. Although he came from a family with several generations of experience in law, Das had to struggle for years in mofussil courts to pay off large debts of his father. It is clear that he was a shrewd, hard-working lawyer with considerable oratorical ability.[17]

With his return from England, Das began to publish books of Bengali verse.[18] Like several other well-known Brahmo Samaj members of the late nineteenth century, Das yearned for a more emotional and expressive faith. All these men moved toward the Vaishnavism of Bengal.[19] Das's attachment to the faith he shaped out for himself and to Bengali cultural traditions is revealed in his later political speeches.

He came to prominence during the Swadeshi period. At the 1906 Bengal Provincial Conference in Barisal, Das drafted the main resolution on the new nationalist line of self-reliance. But more than his participation in these activities and his association with the Extremists, Das became well known through his work as legal defense counsel for

Bipin Pal, Aurobindo Ghose, Barindra Kumar Ghose, and Ullaskar Dutta.[20] In defending these men, Das wove together his careful arguments on small legal points with an intensity of feeling about the righteousness of his case and the nationalist cause that was persuasive in court. He lost many months' fees, but he greatly increased his legal and political reputation by these activities.

In the following decade, Das undertook several other political cases, including the Dacca conspiracy case of 1910, the Delhi conspiracy case in 1914, the Alipore trunk murder case of 1918, and the Kutubdia Detenu case. During these years, too, Das was one of the lawyers in the Dumraon case involving a complex inheritance suit, and the high fees that he earned from this and his other nonpolitical cases made him one of the wealthiest barristers in India and enabled him to make large contributions to charities and later to political causes.[21] The lavish patron in Hindu society is accorded increments of social rank for his good works, and this is but one more way in which Das came to public attention.

On April 23, 1917, C. R. Das gave the presidential address at the Bengal Provincial Conference meeting at Bhowanipore. He was proposed for this honor by Surendrenath Banerjea.[22]

The address to Bengalis in Bengali has been translated as "Bengal and the Bengalees" and "The Culture of Bengal." [23] In the opening passages, Das recalled the former greatness of Bengal and the names and achievements of the great Bengalis. He maintained that the Bengali—Hindu, Muslim, or Christian—was "a distinct type, a distinct character, and a distinct law of his own." [24] Then Das went on to wax emotional about this unique human creature:

> In this world of men, the Bengalee has a place of his own—a claim, a culture and a duty. We understood that the Bengalee, if he means to realise himself, will have to be a true Bengalee. In the wonderful variety of God's infinite creation the Bengalee represents a distinctive type; nay more, it is the life and soul of that type. And with the dawn of this consciousness in our souls, the Mother radiant in her glory, revealed her infinite, her universal beauty before us.[25]

Das further linked his concern for the full development of the Bengali language with the revival of the Bengali people and with the unfortunate chasm between the small English-speaking minority and the ne-

glected Bengali-speaking majority. Das quoted Bankim Chandra Chatterjee at length and joined Bankim Chandra and the leaders of the
Swadeshi movement in calling for a national movement tied to the regional culture and language which would bring together the high-
caste Westernized Bengalis with the lower Hindu castes and the Muslims.[26] He detailed plans for agricultural programs, displaying a rural
nostalgia and distrust of industrialism worthy of Gandhi. Das talked of
the fusion of religion and politics, but demonstrated an awareness that
much of Bengal's population was Muslim.[27]

A theme set forth by Das in this speech and repeated thereafter was
the need for egalitarianism in Indian life. In the 1917 speech he said
that God was in all men:

> In our oppressed and down-trodden fellow-brethren let us recognize
> the image of Narayana: before that sacred and awful image, let us
> abandon all false pride of birth and breed and let us bend our heads in
> reverence and true humility. These seething millions of your land—
> be they Christians or Mahomedans or Chandals—they are your
> brothers; embrace them as such, co-operate with them and only then
> will your labours be crowned with success.[28]

In putting forth a feeling of kinship with all his fellow countrymen,
Das used a religious framework that drew upon his Brahmo and Vaishnava background. And although he eventually built a political organization that reached out to more Bengalis than had any previous provincial political group, systematically including men elected from
every district, he never acted on his egalitarian ethic in the striking
ways that his contemporary Mahatma Gandhi did.

During the later months of 1917, Das spoke at a number of Muslim
and Hindu-Muslim meetings both in Calcutta and in the mofussil.[29]
Like other leading members of the Nationalist or Extremist Party who
had lived through the widening Hindu-Muslim division that had come
in the wake of the Swadeshi movement, Das was determined to press
for improvements in communal relations. Indeed, Das not only argued
that such progress in communal harmony was essential for Bengal and
for India; he also placed his leadership and reputation on the line and
went farther than any Hindu politician to secure Muslim support in the
immediate postwar period in India.

At a Home Rule meeting in Barisal in October 1917, Das praised the
development of Muslim political consciousness:

there came to be a sort of estrangement between the two nationalities at the time of the Swadeshi movement. They [the Muslims] kept away from that movement and even fought with their might and main against it. Now, gentlemen, I told you I am not sorry for that. I do not remember how I felt it then but now I see that the very attitude which the Mahomedans had taken, that very opposition was the result of their national awakening. We used to deprecate the work of the late Nabob Salimulla in those days because he had organised the Mahomedan opposition to the Swadeshi movement in Bengal. I do not do that now because whatever the form of that activity might have been, Nabob Salimulla succeeded in organising the Mahomedans. The spirit of nationality spoke amongst the Mahomedans at that time. . . . What is the result to-day? I went to Dacca and the Mahomedans invited me to an informal conference. When I went there what did I find? Not that estrangement but an intense anxiety on their part to side with the Hindus, to combine with the Hindus, to fight shoulder to shoulder with the Hindus for working out the real salvation of Bengal. If the Swadeshi Movement was the first step in our national self-consciousness so far as Hindus are concerned, I say it was equally the first step of Mahomedan self-consciousness. Its appearance was against the nation, but its reality was in our favor.[30]

Das argued both on this occasion and throughout his active political career that the interests of the two major communities of Bengal were identical in the long run.[31]

Another issue to which Das often returned in his speeches of 1917 and 1918 had a strongly regional cast. Das propounded a familiar Extremist Party position that government repression caused the revolutionary movement to develop and that only extensive concessions leading to self-government would end the revolutionaries' quest. At the special Bombay session of the Congress in August and early September 1918, Das attacked the "shameless government." [32] He not only defended revolutionaries in court and sympathized with their ideals, but he also understood the fact that a successful national leader in Bengal had to take a strong and consistent position on this issue and call for release of prisoners at every turn.

Das, Motilal Ghose, Bipin Pal, Fazlul Huq, and Byomkes Chakravarty joined the Home Rule agitation and split with Surendranath Banerjea, who refused to lead his party into the Home Rule League.[33] Banerjea, in the usual Moderate tradition, was willing to join protests against undue suppression by the government but was wary of mass protests. The differences on the Home Rule League spilled over into the question of the Congress president for the 1917 session in Calcutta. The two groups in the Reception Committee compromised on the issue of Congress president, and there was some reshuffling in the composition of the committee before the Congress session, but this was more temporary face-saving than resolution of fundamental differences.[34]

The two main factions in the Bengal Congress differed on the reforms and on how much power should be put into Indian hands how soon. Das and Byomkes Chakravarty wanted full responsible government, while Banerjea held to the more restrained demands agreed to in the Lucknow Pact.[35] The other main question was the simple one of political power—who was to control the Congress in Bengal. Although Das had said in his presidential address to the 1917 Bengal Provincial Conference that his only claim to political leadership was by virtue of "deep and passionate love," [36] he led the thrust by the challenging party for control of the Bengal Provincial Congress Committee. First, Das, Byomkes Chakravarty, and Fazlul Huq led an unsuccessful fight to capture control of the Indian Association and through it, the Bengal Provincial Congress in early 1918.[37] After this avenue failed, they questioned the legitimacy of Banerjea's and Calcutta's hold on the Provincial Congress. The challengers held an All-Bengal Political Conference and then captured a majority in the Bengal Provincial Congress Committee (BPCC) when the Moderates failed to attend a crucial meeting. Once in power, the Das group cut the representation of the Indian Association in the BPCC, and therefore the power to send hand-picked men to the National Congress sessions.[38]

Das supported Gandhi's call for a nationwide hartal (general strike) and Satyagraha against the newly enacted Rowlatt Acts. After the massacre in Amritsar, Das joined Gandhi, Motilal Nehru, and others on the Congress Punjab Enquiry Commission. Das's victory on the provincial level, his active participation in the work of the Home Rule League in Bengal and in the Congress sessions of 1917–1919 led him to national leadership. At the Amritsar Congress in 1919, Das argued that the reforms were inadequate, but as a political pragmatist he did not disavow utilization of the councils for their own purposes. But Das and other Congress leaders who took a flexible line were overtaken by the Gandhi whirlwind which captured control of the Congress platform in the following year.[39]

NONCOOPERATION

Although Mahatma Gandhi had at first cooperated with the government of India, he moved away from this position with the introduction of the Rowlatt bills and the massacre at Jallianwala Bagh. By the early months of 1920, Gandhi had moved full circle to become a staunch Noncooperator and an opponent of the reformed legislative councils.[40] Throughout 1920 he embarked on a tour of the country in order to convert others to his new view and swing the Congress position into line with his own. Indian Muslims had been distraught during and after World War I about possible efforts by the Allied Powers to restrict or dismantle the Khilafat, or leadership of the Islamic community, in the wake of Turkey's defeats. Gandhi decided to make this issue one of those around which he would organize Noncooperation. During 1920, he added the call for swaraj to the grievances about the Punjab brutalities and the Khilafat issue as those around which his nationwide campaign would be conducted. Although "swaraj" meant independence to some congressmen, Gandhi gave it a vaguer meaning and opposed resolutions calling for self-government at the annual Congress sessions until the end of the 1920s.[41] By his energetic work through 1920, Gandhi was able to win many converts to his side and to isolate waverers and opponents. M. R. Jayakar has described Gandhi's campaign:

> What happened to Das in Bengal was emblematic of the transformation which took place in several other Provinces. In each Province, there were, in those days, one or two leading men who would have liked to oppose the advance of the new ideas, but they were all isolated. One group did not know what was passing in the mind of a similar group in another Province. Gandhi was becoming popular too rapidly to allow these groups to meet together and consider a common course of action. His whirlwind campaign none could withstand. . . . In this welter of ideas, some of the thoughtful leaders of Bengal saw the great danger of letting an outsider like Gandhi have an unhampered hold over the youth of their Province. Das saw this danger, perhaps more clearly than any other leader. It is certain that, for a long time, his virile mind rebelled against the puerilities of the new doctrines, but their sacrifice and renunciation appealed to him. He was then at the height of his glory, both as a lawyer and as a public leader. . . . He soon saw that it was a glorious opportunity to lead and direct the young men of his Province in seeming accord with the new doctrine, but with freedom later to modify it to suit his conception of a

popular movement. After some hesitation, he placed himself at the crest of this wave.[42]

The Noncooperation program as finally worked out included boycotts of government schools and colleges and of government legislative bodies, and the renunciation of titles and distinctions conferred by the government.[43]

By the time of the special Calcutta Congress in September 1920, Gandhi was able to carry a majority of the Subjects Committee with him on his resolution that progressive nonviolent Noncooperation be undertaken until the Punjab and Khilafat wrongs were righted and swaraj established. Bipin Pal introduced a resolution calling for a mission to England which would attempt to persuade the British government to grant immediate autonomy while at the same time the country considered Gandhi's program. Jinnah, Baptista, and Jayakar from Bombay, Satyamurti, Malaviya, and Das all supported Pal's resolution, but it was defeated.[44] Although he had to override some strong opposition from Bombay and Bengal, the two earliest strongholds of the Congress organization, Gandhi gained his first triumph in Calcutta.

At the regular Congress session held in Nagpur at the end of December 1920, Gandhi gained a more complete victory. Congress leaders came to Nagpur prepared to regain the Congress leadership from Gandhi and revise the program passed in Calcutta. Their failure has been pictured by Jayakar:

> Das had brought a contingent of 250 delegates from East Bengal and Assam to undo what had been done at Calcutta in favour of Non-cooperation. Maharashtra's opposition was not less intense nor less organised. . . . Stalwarts like Pal, Malaviya, Jinnah, Khaparde, Das and Lajpatrai appeared to be overpowered. . . . though the acceptance of the Non-co-operation Resolution at Nagpur was an event by itself, its vital feature was that the Resolution was moved by Das and seconded by Lajpatrai.[45]

It should be pointed out that in 1918 and 1919, Das was more critical of the Montagu-Chelmsford reforms than was Gandhi, who insisted on thanking Montagu for the reforms at the 1919 Amritsar Congress. Das was a shrewd and pragmatic politician, and his partial conversion to the Gandhian program for the duration of 1921 may be seen as a decision to work with the majority in the Congress.[46]

A contemporary writer friendly to Das noted the significance of his changeover to the majority position in the Congress:

> Throughout 1920 Bengal was pre-eminently in the grip of the moderates and the despair of the non-co-operators. Though the Special Congress held at Calcutta passed the non-co-operation resolution there was still a great volume of moderate opinion which could not be easily moved. But suddenly the atmosphere was changed. Mr. C. R. Das, the leading lawyer of Bengal, announced a sudden renouncement of all his earthly possessions, including his princely practice at the Bar, and came out Gandhi-like, along with his wife and children, to lead the new movement. Since that galvanising resuscitation Bengal has once more been steadily leading in the progressive march of the Indian Nation towards the coveted goal of Swaraj.[47]

Das acquiesced to Gandhi's majority in 1920 and became the leader of the Noncooperation movement in Bengal during the following year.

From the Nagpur Congress, Gandhi became what Jawaharlal Nehru called the "permanent superpresident of the Congress," and the younger Nehru described Gandhi as "consciously humble" but also "imperious." [48] Gandhi's asceticism began to take hold of the Congress, and foreign clothes and finery, drinking, and lax moral habits of all kinds fell into disfavor. Motilal Nehru and C. R. Das, both wealthy barristers known for their high living and sensual proclivities, turned to more spartan ways in the Gandhian age.[49]

Among the changes instituted by Gandhi were the reorganization of the Congress structure into linguistic regions; [50] an attempt to make sessions more representative by having delegates elected at a ratio of 1 for 50,000 Indians; the introduction of a four-anna dues' requirement for membership; and the development of systematic district Congress committees.[51] In Bengal the number of these committees grew from 4 in 1918 to 16 in 1919 and to 29 in 1921 under the new constitution. The changes already begun by Das in Bengal were in line with the kind of changes in organization that Gandhi wanted for the whole of India. During these same years the percentage of Bengali AICC delegates who were from Calcutta dropped severely. In 1921, 21 of 25 AICC delegates representing Bengal were from Calcutta; in 1922, 27 of 48; and in 1923, 25 of 48.[52] Although C. R. Das lived in Calcutta, he was a native of Dacca District in eastern Bengal. He helped to bring many more mofussil, paticularly East Bengali ones, into the Congress organization. In doing this, he had to combat what one East Bengali congressman called the "Calcutta coterie."[53]

A major innovation of the Nagpur Constitution was the establishment of a working committee of the Congress as a year-round executive committee of the AICC. Gandhi suggested its proper role and functions:

> The Working Committee is to the Congress what a Cabinet is to Parliament. Its decisions must command respect . . . its members must be those who command the greatest respect of the All-India Congress Committee and the nation. It dare not take any hasty decisions, and it must be a homogeneous body. It cannot have two policies or two or three parties within itself. Its decisions have largely to be unanimous. When a member cannot pull on with the rest, he can resign, but he may not obstruct or affect the deliberations of the Committee by an open discussion of its deliberations in the Press . . . It can be dismissed by the All-India Congress Committee by a vote of no-confidence.[54]

Gandhi's view that the Working Committee had to be homogeneous and come to unanimous decisions was the seed of later conflicts. Gandhi insisted that the officeholders in the Congress adhere to much stricter disciplinary regulations than rank-and-file members. Lawyers who had long played such a dominant role in the Congress began to lose some of their hold, but many non-practicing lawyers like Gandhi, Jawaharlal Nehru, and Rajendra Prasad continued to lead the Congress.[55]

As Gopal Krishna suggests, "Gandhiji was something of a genius in collecting money."[56] With Gandhi as the central figure, the Congress forged an alliance with some Indian business, commercial and financial interests which has lasted into the post-independence period. One conquest that Gandhi made in the early 1920s was of Ghanshyamdas Birla, a member of the Marwari community, who took Gandhi as a kind of spiritual adviser and offered him many large financial contributions for his constructive work in the long years before independence.[57] Birla had become involved in Indian politics by 1921 and by 1924 was growing close to Gandhi. Gandhi wrote him on October 1, 1927:

> My thirst for money is simply unquenchable. I need at least Rs. 2,00,000/—for Khadi, Untouchability and Education. Then there is the Ashram expenditure. No work remains unfinished for want of

funds, but God gives after severe trials. This also satisfies me. You can give me as much as you like for whatever you have faith in.[58]

And Birla replied, "Whenever you find any particular kind of work impeded for lack of funds, you have only to write to me." [59]

Another achievement of the early 1920s and the first Noncooperation movement was the assembling of a cadre of able leaders in the major regions. These included men who had already played a significant role in nationalist politics as well as comparative novices recruited into the movement by Gandhi. Among the older and experienced men were Motilal Nehru, Lajpat Rai, C. R. Das, N. C. Kelkar, the Ali brothers, Moulana Mohammad and Moulana Shaukat Ali, and the Patel brothers, Vithalbhai and his younger brother Vallabhbhai.[60] Among the younger men were Jawaharlal Nehru, Rajendra Prasad and Subhas Bose. Some of these men and a number of others grew closer to Gandhi over the years and were called the "High Command."

Among the groups in the Bengal Congress were the Bengal Gandhians, whose loyalties were more to Gandhi than to any regional leaders in Bengal. Shyam Sunder Chakravarty often served as leader and spokesman for this group and edited its paper the *Servant*. Other Gandhians included Prafulla C. Ghosh, Suresh Banerjee, and Nripendra Chandra Banerji.[61]

To understand how the Gandhians were recruited, we may consider the career of Nripendra Chandra Banerji. He had known Rajendra Prasad while both lived in the Eden Hindu Hostel and attended Presidency College in the early years of the twentieth century. J. M. Sen Gupta, later crucial in the development of Banerji's political career, was one year senior to Banerji at Presidency College, and Banerji mentions the "old boy" ties among graduates linking him to Sen Gupta.[62]

For years Banerji was a college teacher and a fringe participant in nationalist politics. In 1921 an important change occurred in Banerji's life when C. R. Das persuaded him to become a political worker.[63] Sen Gupta headed the Chittagong District Congress Committee and Nripendra Banerji became his second-in-command. Banerji started the Saraswata Ashram to do constructive work and carry out the Gandhian program. When Gandhi came to the area, the Mahatma stayed with Sen Gupta and was guided in his tour by Banerji.[64]

It is also interesting to note that though Banerji called Gandhi his guru, stated that Gandhi never made an error, did Gandhian work, and generally supported Gandhian ideals for most of his mature life, he felt that he could not call himself a 100 percent Gandhian. Throughout his life, Banerji retained doubts about nonviolence; he could not always control his thoughts and words, and occasionally called for violence.[65] He remarked that it was hard for a Bengali Shakta to follow Gandhi.[66] Banerji liked Gandhi's ideas about decentralization and the rural life. In one political tract, he wrote, "The thought of a *Swaraj* for India, which means, not only political *Swaraj*, but also local and regional *Swaraj*, appeals to me intensely." [67] His antipathy to Western culture and the Western-educated in India brought him closer to Gandhi than some of his Bengali contemporaries, but his ambivalence on nonviolence made him a suspicious character to some of the more orthodox Gandhians in Bengal.[68]

Another set of smaller units that fused, at least partially, into the Bengal Provincial Congress Committee was the revolutionary movement in Bengal.[69] A Home Department political report describes the return of many revolutionaries to political life in 1920:

> During 1920, consequent on the Royal amnesty of December 1919, all the old Bengal revolutionists, who were confined or detained under Regulation III of 1818 or the Defence of India Act were, as an act of clemency, released and those who were evading arrest were allowed to resume their normal mode of life. The great majority of these persons naturally continued to hold extreme views and, in consequence, took considerable interest in politics, and unfortunately many of them reverted to revolutionary conspiracy. It took these irreconcilables some time to bring any definite revolutionary organisation into being and by the time they had succeeded, Mr. Gandhi had captured the Congress in December 1920 at Nagpur with the programme of non-violent non-cooperation.[70]

The revolutionaries, especially those in the Jugantar organization, were persuaded by C. R. Das to work openly in the mass movement at least for the duration of 1921. At a secret meeting at the time of the Bengal Provincial Conference, they agreed to work in the Noncooperation movement for a year.[71] Their penetration of the Congress organization in Bengal began at this point and was a feature of Bengal politics in the following decades.

Changes also took place in the Bengal Congress organization at the district level. In Midnapur, for example, the Moderate leaders were replaced by men who lined up with C. R. Das. Later, orthodox Gandhians were turned out when tensions rose between the Swarajists led by Das and the No-Changers' faction led by Gandhi.[72] The Midnapur Congress organized the Bengal Volunteer Corps during the Noncooperation period, and in Midnapur the groups of volunteers were soon infiltrated by revolutionaries. These volunteer groups did much of the hard work in the Noncooperation effort in addition to serving as recruiting grounds for the revolutionaries.[73]

With the rapid development of the district Congress Committees and the systematization of the Congress at the national and regional levels, the play of political groups or factions between the three levels became more complex. The national and regional organizations became more closely interlocked. Political ties were formed that sometimes went above or outside the formal procedures of the AICC, the Working Committee, and the provincial Congress committees. The Working Committee and AICC would henceforth become involved in regional disputes and, similarly, provincial Congress committees might step in to resolve problems in district committees.[74]

Elections for the newly reformed legislative councils were held at the end of 1920 and these bodies began to meet from the beginning of 1921. Before that time, Gandhi, the Congress, and their allies had successfully seized the initiative, and the first Noncooperation campaign became the focus of public attention.[75]

Exhilarated, perhaps, by the ease with which he gained supporters in 1920, Gandhi promised that if his program were put into action properly, swaraj would be obtained within one year. Jayakar has suggested that Gandhi was overconfident in making such a rash promise to his countrymen.[76] With the sense that much had to be done in a short time, the Noncooperators were galvanized into action. The work included the collection of money for the Tilak Swaraj Fund and the organization of national education and nongovernment courts. The Khilafat agitation was pressed forward simultaneously and a call went out for communal unity.[77]

Although C. R. Das led the Noncooperation campaign in Bengal through 1921, the Bengali efforts were keynoted by Gandhi, who vis-

ited Bengal during late 1920 and early 1921. Gandhi spoke not only to
groups of students urging them to learn to spin and to speak Hindu-
stani, but also to gatherings of Marwaris, where he collected funds and
asked for support.[78] In a message "To Young Bengal" published in
Young India in January 1921, Gandhi wrote:

> I have just read an acount of your response to the nation's call. It does
> credit to you and to Bengal. I had expected no less. I certainly expect
> still more. Bengal has great intelligence. It has a greater heart, it has
> more than its share of the spiritual heritage for which our country is
> specially noted. You have more imagination, more faith and more emo-
> tion than the rest of India. You have falsified the calumny of coward-
> ice on more occasions than one. There is, therefore, no reason why
> Bengal should not lead now as it has done before now.[79]

Until his arrest late in 1921, Das worked to make the movement a success in Bengal. In some of his speeches to students asking them to leave
their schools, he spoke in terms reminiscent of Aurobindo Ghose and
Bipin Pal in the Swadeshi years. Das, although he leaned to Vaishnavism and Brahmoism in his personal faith, spread what he was soon to
label "The Call of the Motherland":

> God has not given me power to express in language the happiness that
> you have given me by coming out of your Colleges. I feel it in my
> heart of hearts that, those of you who have come out, are greater than
> any of us here, and I humbly bow to you—to the manifestation of
> strength that you have displayed to-day. I want you to realise that,—
> to realise the strength in you. It is not yours—it is not human, it is
> the will—the divine will of the country and the God of our being. It
> is the will of *Deshamabrika* that has been manifested through you.
> What, she is, I do not know, but she is the Goddess of our Nation. I
> now can say with head erect—blessed be thy waters, Mother Bengal,
> blessed be thy trees. . . . I promise before you all, to-day, that, within
> fifteen days or utmost a month, we shall have a College—a National
> College established, of which there is no equal here, and where you
> will get your national education, where you will learn to love your
> country and appreciate freedom. . . . Mr. Achjutaram of Bangabashi
> College said that he hailed from Andhra and they learnt all their na-
> tional lessons at the feet of Bengal. When they saw that Bengal had
> not been doing anything they were getting disheartened. Now that
> Bengal was coming to herself again, he would be able to tell his fel-
> low-countrymen in Andhra that things were all right in Bengal.[80]

Some of the same feelings and emotions, long dammed up, had cascaded out during the Swadeshi period about fifteen years earlier. But Noncooperation was a national and not a regional effort. The leadership consisted of Gandhi and a corps of leaders in which Das was the only Bengali of national stature. Das put forth a view in the quote above that was to be common in the writings of other Bengalis in this period and thereafter: Bengal was once the leader in Indian nationalism, then lagged, and is now trying to recover a preeminence and position of initiative that, for all of Gandhi's praise, is becoming a thing of the past. In the earlier stages of the nationalist movement, Bengali leaders went out to spread the word and make converts; now a national leader from Gujarat had come to Bengal to begin a new phase of the national struggle.

During the year of Noncooperation, many young men and women as well as older and more experienced Bengalis were brought into the movement. As in the Swadeshi period, a concentrated effort was made to have students take an active role in the movement. Subhas Bose wrote,

> Students responded to the appeal in large numbers and the response was the greatest in Bengal. . . . It was these student-workers who carried the message of the Congress to all corners of the country, who collected funds, enlisted members, held meetings and demonstrations, preached temperance, established arbitration-boards, taught spinning and weaving and encouraged the revival of home industries.[81]

There was a good deal of resistance to bringing the students out of their schools and colleges, even by men who had some sympathy for the nationalist cause. Sir Asutosh Mookerjee, vice-chancellor of Calcutta University, opposed the educational boycott, as did Rabindranath Tagore, who had a good deal more feeling for the nationalist cause than Sir Asutosh.[82]

As in other spheres of the movement, it is exceedingly difficult to tell how effective this boycott was. A great deal more detailed investigation would be necessary to assess the results. It is clear that some men gave up their legal practices temporarily during the height of the movement.

One feature of the Noncooperation period which did carry into later years was the development of small ashrams, or communities, where education, spinning, and other elements of what was soon to be called the Gandhian "constructive program" were centered. The best known of these was the Abhay Ashram founded by Suresh Banerjee and Prafulla Ghosh in East Bengal.[83]

The Indian National Congress made public its sympathy with trade unionism at Nagpur in 1920. An important aspect of the postwar period generally and of the Noncooperation years in particular was the growth of trade unions and the large number of strikes. One government report listed 106 strikes affecting 170,000 employees in Bengal in the last six months of 1920.[84] Vera Anstey mentions in her survey, *The Economic Development of India*, that "The Bengal Committee on Industrial Unrest of 1921 analyzed the facts and features of 137 strikes. It reported that in many cases the immediate causes were noneconomic." [85] Some were due to politically organized hartals, attempts to close down all activity in the Calcutta area. C. R. Das and other leading congressmen took an active part in labor disputes and the organization of industrial workers.

During November, as Noncooperation spread and there were calls for even bolder steps against the government, C. R. Das was named the "dictator" of the movement in Bengal. He was to be in firm charge of Khilafat and Congress volunteers. He would thus be in a better position to deal with irresponsible activities unapproved by the national and regional leadership of the Noncooperation movement. At this time it was announced that the Prince of Wales was to visit India. The Noncooperators were determined to close down Calcutta when he appeared. Fearing serious disturbances, the government finally moved, declaring the volunteer groups and public meetings illegal. Several Noncooperators were arrested, including C. R. Das's wife, Basanti Devi, and his son. The arrest of Mrs. Das and other women brought cries of outrage and numerous volunteers seeking arrest. The government shortly released Mrs. Das, but soon her husband and many of the leading Noncooperators of Bengal were arrested. Das, then the president-elect of the Indian National Congress, spent most of December and part of early 1922 in the Alipore Jail in Calcutta.[86]

Once Das was arrested, the leader of the Gandhian faction in the

Bengal Congress, Shyam Sunder Chakravarty, wired to the Mahatma, "Kindly wire opinion if places of imprisoned All-India Congress Committee members may be treated vacancies and filled up." Gandhi replied on December 16, 1921, "Vacancies should be filled up." [87] The Gandhians filled up the vacated posts of the faction loyal to Das, and Das and his men were obliged to spend a good part of the following year regaining control of the Bengal Provincial Congress organization.[88] The Gandhians had the support of Marwari merchants in Calcutta, who feared that Das's movement might threaten their property interests.[89] The rift began to widen as the year ended with swaraj not yet in sight. Das was angry at Gandhi because negotiations under way with the government broke down over certain demands put forth by the Mahatma.

In the last weeks of December 1921, negotiations were started by a conference group headed by Pandit M. Malaviya, which included P. C. Roy, Fazlul Huq, G. D. Birla, A. Chaudhury, and M. R. Jayakar. It attempted to bring the government and the Congress together. Das and Gandhi were among the bargainers for the Congress, with Gandhi having a de facto veto power.[90] Malaviya led a deputation to the viceroy and contacts were established with Das and Gandhi. The group offered to hold a round table meeting to discuss constitutional changes if the Congress called off its planned December 24 hartal. Das wanted to accept the offer, primarily because it included the release of almost all political prisoners, but Gandhi held out for further concessions. The offer was withdrawn. Das argued that the Congress must show some results by the end of 1921 since Gandhi had promised swaraj in one year, and the proposed conference would be a sign that the Congress was on its way toward its goal. Some time later, still angered by Gandhi's rejection of the offer, Das stated, addressing Gandhi and the country:

> I myself led people to prison. I started the movement in Bengal. I sent my son first to jail. My son was followed by my wife, and then I went to prison, because I knew there was electricity there. I knew that the spirit of resistance that manifested itself was mighty and the proudest Government did bend to it. You bungled it, and mismanaged it. Now you turn round and ask people to spin and do the work of the Charka

alone. The proudest Government did bend to you. The terms came to me and I forwarded them to the Headquarters, because at that time I was in jail. If I had not been in jail, I would have forced the country to accept them. After they had been accepted, you would have seen a different state of things.[91]

At the annual Congress held in Ahmadabad at the end of December 1921, Gandhi read Das's presidential address, since Das was in jail. In the incomplete speech, entitled "The Call of the Motherland," Das defended Noncooperation and presented a critique of the Montagu-Chelmsford reforms.

At the end of 1921 preparations were made for civil disobedience and the application of Satyagraha by the Congress. In the same way that Das was made Congress "dictator" in Bengal, Gandhi was made Satyagraha "dictator" for the Congress. Gandhi had been shaken by the outbreak of violence in Bombay upon the visit of the Prince of Wales to that city in late 1921, but he was still determined to press the movement forward as 1922 began.[92] During early February 1922, however, there was more violence at Chauri Chaura in the United Provinces. A mob burned a police station, killing some 22 policemen. Gandhi was horrified and at a special session of the Congress Working Committee called in Gujarat, he announced that he was calling off the planned Satyagraha campaign until the country and the participants could insure that there would be no violence.[93] Although Gandhi gained majority support in the Working Committee and at a subsequent AICC meeting, many congressmen were stunned and angered by his decision. Among these were C. R. Das and Motilal Nehru, who thought that isolated acts of violence must not be allowed to prevent the Congress and the movement from going forward.[94]

In the AICC a censure motion against Gandhi was defeated, but he felt the lack of full support. Gandhi maintained that the people did not yet understand nonviolence and were not ready for the movement to continue.[95] While Das, Motilal Nehru, and others despaired of Gandhi's course, the Mahatma turned to his "constructive program," desiring it to be the Congress' focus for the present.[96] The government, which had been waiting for Gandhi's support to wane, seized this moment of growing disagreement to arrest Gandhi and after a brief trial he was sentenced to six years in prison.[97]

CRITICISM OF GANDHI

At this point it seems appropriate to consider some of the criticism of Gandhi's Noncooperation efforts by Bengali leaders and to assess the results of the campaign up to 1921. The Bengal Moderates, who had held control of the provincial Congress organization from the 1880s to 1918, had formed the National Liberal Federation and stood for election to the reformed legislative councils in 1920. Although some of them sat in the Bengal Legislative Council, even in its comfortable chambers they were haunted by the popular movement going on outside. Surendranath Banerjea, who was writing his memoirs, *A Nation in Making*, during this period, was disturbed by the din of what he called anarchy and revolution brought on by Noncooperation. He decried the "frenzy for incarceration and fame" that had engulfed Bengal. The purity and greatness of the past were gone, wrote Banerjea, now that leaders who talked in the name of the country represented only themselves. The new men pressed forward by "force and fraud." [98]

Another prominent Bengali leader of former years who broke with the Congress during 1921 was Bipin Chandra Pal. When Gandhi first put forth his program of Noncooperation in 1920, Pal gave it grudging support in a series of lectures reprinted under the title *Non-Co-operation*.[99] Pal said that Bengal had been the first to adopt Noncooperation in the Swadeshi years, while the rest of India held back. Calling himself an Extremist, Pal asserted that Bengal should support Noncooperation or some better form of passive resistance. Since he was not altogether happy with Gandhi's stages, Pal argued for "constitutional non-co-operation" and said that he was against bringing on anarchy or disorder.[100]

Pal put forth his own program of Noncooperation and included noncooperation within the legislative councils, a suggestion to which Gandhi was opposed. Following his line of previous years, Pal attacked the reforms as a sham, but he thought that the council chambers should not be given up to the Moderates.[101] He feared that Bengal would reject Gandhi's program and was relieved when the Bengal Provincial Congress Committee backed Gandhi. Pal said this vote "has after all saved the face of Bengal." [102] He insisted that Bengal had been first to put forth such a program and that Bengal's "superior spirit" would not have allowed events like those in the Punjab. He would not accept Gandhi's program without changing it. It is not altogether clear whether Pal was moved by personal or regional animosity, but he did note Bengal's failures in Swadeshi and national education during these lectures. Occasionally, there is a hint of bitterness about the declining place of Bengal within the national movement.[103]

Perhaps an even more respected, revered voice was that of Rabindranath Tagore. He spoke out critically against Gandhi and Noncooperation from 1921. Tagore and Gandhi had broad areas of agreement in their views of life: both advocated inner swaraj as necessary before external swaraj could be won; both stressed the need for suffering and constructive work; both had an image of harmonious, self-sufficient village life which should be recaptured in the future; and both felt that love and truth were fundamentally related.[104] Tagore admired Gandhi's fight for awakening the rural masses to self-help and political consciousness and Tagore is even said to have given Gandhi the name "Mahatma." [105]

Tagore, however, was very disturbed by some aspects of the Noncooperation movement and expressed his anxiety in private correspondence and in two powerful essays, "The Call of Truth" (1921) and "The Cult of the Charkha" (1925). From the same long-range and moral perspective he had taken when he evaluated Swadeshi and the revolutionary movement, Tagore thought that Indians were again looking for some easy way to freedom: "I am afraid of a blind faith on a very large scale in Charkha in the country which is so liable to succumb to the lure of short-cuts when pointed out by a personality about whose moral earnestness they can have no doubt." [106]

What Tagore found most distasteful was the blind obedience to a new guru and the unquestioning faith in his message. The poet wrote in 1921:

Today, in the atmosphere of the country, there is a spirit of persecution, which is not that of armed force, but something still more alarming, because it is invisible . . . I found, further, that those who had their doubts as to the present activities, if they happened to whisper them out, however cautiously, however guardedly, felt some admonishing hand clutching them within . . . The sight that met my eye was, on the one hand, people immensely busy; on the other intensely afraid. What I heard on every side was, that reason and culture as well, must be closured. It was only necessary to cling to an unquestioning obedience. Obedience to whom? To some *mantra*, some unreasoned creed! [107]

During the times Tagore was describing, Surendranath Banerjea and Bipin Pal were hooted down at public meetings and some incidents of intolerance by Noncooperators were reported. It would not be fair to call Tagore's view regional, although he might have been able to find more supporters for his assessment among Calcutta intellectuals than elsewhere. Jayakar quoted Tagore's warnings about Gandhian intolerance with approbation and held that Bengal and Maharashtra were moved by similar high ideals.[108]

As during the Swadeshi agitation, Tagore felt in 1921 that the national movement was too negative, too narrow, and too constricting in its ideals and its practices. Tagore objected to the single ideal of spinning for everyone, and so he wrote of Gandhi,

> his call came to one narrow field alone. To one and all he simply says: "Spin and weave, spin and weave." Is this the call: "Let all seekers after Truth come from all sides?" Is this the call of the New Age to new creation? When nature called to the bee to take refuge in the narrow life of the hive, millions of bees responded to it for the sake of efficiency, and accepted the loss of sex in consequence. But this sacrifice by the way of self-atrophy led to the opposite of freedom. Any country, the people of which can agree to become neuters for the sake of some temptation, or command, carries within itself its own prison house. . . . The Charkha in its proper place can do no harm, but will rather do much good. But where, by reason of failure to acknowledge the differences in man's temperament, it is in the wrong place, there thread can only be spun at the cost of a great deal of the mind itself. Mind is no less valuable than cotton thread.[109]

Tagore saw progress through unity and synthesis and had, as Gandhi shrewdly noted, "a horror of everything negative." [110] Tagore wanted to, retain the gains of Western education—science, medicine, technology—and lay the ground for the meeting of all cultures on a basis of mutual exchange. He feared that Gandhism, particularly in practice, would end in India's turning in upon herself and bringing about her own destruction.

Gandhi let many criticisms of his goals and methods pass by, but he felt called upon to answer Tagore's "The Call of Truth." The response, entitled "The Great Sentinel," was published in *Young India* in October 1921. Gandhi maintained that the spinning wheel had only been accepted by some after due reflection and said he called upon all to spin because, "When a house is on fire, *all* the inmates go out, and each takes up a bucket to quench the fire." He continued:

> When all about me are dying for want of food, the only occupation permissible to me is to feed the hungry. It is my conviction that India is a house on fire because its manhood is being daily scorched; it is dying of hunger because it has no work to buy food with. . . . Hunger is the argument that is driving India to the spinning wheel. The call of the spinning wheel is the noblest of all. Because it is the call of love. And love is Swaraj. . . . We must think of millions who are today less than animals, who are almost in a dying state. The spinning wheel is the reviving draught for the millions of our countrymen and country-women.[111]

Gandhi pressed his argument that home spinning would be the economic salvation of India's masses. He implicitly condemned the poet for living off others and ignoring the economic questions facing India in his concern for cultural ideals. Each conceived of the other too narrowly: Gandhi ignored Tagore's long-standing concern with village revival as well as with cultural issues; and Tagore construed Gandhi's constructive program as only spinning.

Other critiques offered of Gandhi were usually political assessments more concerned with the results obtained than with fundamental moral issues. For example, in his account of the nationalist movement written in the 1930s, Subhas Bose mentioned C. R. Das's private estimation of Gandhi, dating from the Noncooperation period:

> I am reminded of what the Deshabandhu [C. R. Das] used frequently to say about the virtues and failings of Mahatma Gandhi's leadership. According to him, the Mahatma opens a campaign in a brilliant fashion; he works it up with unerring skill; he moves from success to success til he reaches the zenith of his campaign—but after that he loses his nerve and begins to falter.[112]

How widespread the feeling was that Noncooperation had failed in its main object is difficult to say. One indicator that Indians were ready for an alternative strategy is the success that the Swaraj Party was eventually able to gain in the years 1923 to 1925. Many government officials and Europeans evidently felt that the movement had been unsuccessful, although somewhat threatening at its height. One such assessment was offered by L. S. S. O'Malley:

> On the whole the non-co-operation movement failed to get a hold over Bengal in 1920. Mr. Gandhi's followers abstained from taking part in the elections to the legislature, but few pleaders were altruistic enough to give up their practice. One man gave up his title; a few honorary magistrates and subordinate police officers resigned; but the people generally were indifferent to the movement. . . . About 50,000 students were diverted to so-called "national schools," ill-staffed and ill-equipped. Disillusion soon came to those who had listened to the non-co-operators, when the national colleges glibly promised by them failed to materialize. . . . The boycott of foreign goods was a failure. The people had had experience of the futility of such a boycott during the agitation following the Partition of Bengal, and spectacular bonfires of foreign cloth were rare.[113]

O'Malley's view of the practical results was probably accurate. Even Gandhi became disturbed at the lack of progress of his program in Bengal, and especially by the internal conflicts within the Bengal Congress. In the course of an interview with Bengal delegates to the 1921 Congress session, Gandhi commented, "I have not seen so much bitterness amongst ourselves as I have seen in Bengal," [114] and he decried the lack of leadership and the shortage of khaddar-wearing Bengalis. In answer to a question about the lack of volunteers for the Noncooperation movement, Gandhi said, "If, then, there are not enough volunteers in Bengal, I should think she should be swept into the Bay of Bengal and make room for better men and women." [115] In March 1922, a correspondent in *Young India* pointed out that khaddar was making virtually no progress in Calcutta. Gandhi responded that if such progress was not made, "the battle of Satyagraha cannot be won" and swaraj could not be obtained.[116] It appears that Gandhi was not satisfied with the support he was getting in Bengal, although he did not blame Das publicly for this failure.

After the withdrawal of the Satyagraha campaigns, the Congress appointed a Civil Disobedience Inquiry Committee which included Hakim Ajmal Khan, Motilal Nehru, C. Rajagopalachari, and Vithal-

bhai Patel among its members.[117] The report of the committee admitted that the school and legal boycotts did not work. On the question
of participation in the reform councils, the committee was split. Although it was stated that the councils were used against the movement
and the members were held up as representatives of the people, only
Khan, Nehru, and Patel came out for changing this part of the
Gandhian program.[118]

SEVEN
The Swaraj Party

⟨⟨⟨⟩⟩⟩ The abrupt curtailment of the Satyagraha plans set congressmen to discussing new possibilities for political action. Some had never been too happy with the Gandhian program. This group included Das and his supporters in Bengal, Lajpat Rai from the Punjab, Motilal Nehru from the United Provinces, M. R. Jayakar, Vithalbhai Patel, the so-called Tilak group in Bombay, and some leaders from South India. It was these men, and more than 100 others, who moved to form the Swaraj Party during the second half of 1922.[1]

While Das was in prison earlier in 1922, he had sent his wife Basanti Devi to give the presidential address at the Bengal Provincial Conference in Chittagong and to send up a trial balloon for Noncooperation within the legislative councils.[2] After his release and following upon the report of the Congress Civil Disobedience Inquiry Committee, Das made a public statement on changing the Congress program:

> The Reformed Councils are really a mask which the bureaucracy has put on. I conceive it to be our clear duty to tear this mask from off their face. To end these Councils is the only effective boycott. A question has been asked as to whether it is possible. I think it is possible if non-co-operators get the majority, and I believe that having regard to the present circumstances of the country they are likely to get the majority. . . . The question is also, supposing we are in a majority, what are we to do? We should begin our operations by a formal demand of the particular way in which we desire to mend the councils. If our demands are accepted we have obtained a real foundation of Swaraj. If our demand is not recognized we must non-co-operate with the bureaucracy by obstructing everything, every work of the council. We must disallow the entire budget. We must move the adjournment of the House on every possible occasion. In fact we must so proceed

that the Council will refuse to do any work until our demands are satisfied.[3]

This statement embodies the strategy and rationale which Das was to use during the remaining years of his life. He tried to convince those who had supported Gandhi's Noncooperation program that the Swarajist line simply extended the strategy of Noncooperation. But Gandhi and his more devoted supporters viewed the Swarajist strategy as opposed to their Noncooperation and constructive programs and suspected that possible cooperators wore Swarajist masks. Once in the councils such men would eventually work with the government on piecemeal bits of legislation and, at the same time, neglect the Gandhian constructive program. These fears of the Gandhians were not unfounded.

During 1922, while the Swaraj Party was in the process of formation, Das and his supporters in Bengal participated actively in flood-relief work in northern Bengal and Das presided over the first All-India Trade Union Congress.[4] These activities helped build support for the Congress in Bengal, particularly for the Das faction. At the trade-union congress, Das made his first call for "swaraj for the 98 percent" and tried to identify the Congress with the best interests of the masses of Indians. He was aware that the Congress had been dominated by high-caste Hindus, while Muslims and lower-caste Hindus had always remained a small minority. How he would concretely help the down-trodden and excluded 98 percent is not clear, but his speeches struck a responsive chord among members of the Third Communist International, whatever effects it may have had on the trade unionists. Several of Das's lieutenants, including Subhas Bose, followed his example by devoting some of their energies to labor organizing.[5] The Congress was extending its constituencies from the High Court bar to the factories.

From the fall of 1922, Swarajist congressmen sought supporters in their challenge to the confirmed Gandhians. Even though Das was the Congress president in 1922–1923, he was not able to persuade the majority of congressmen to accept the Swarajist program. The Gandhian foes of Das were led by C. Rajagopalachari, who successfully piloted an anti–council entry resolution through the Subjects Committee to a vote of 203 to 87. The details of the division of votes show that of 40 Bengali representatives, 25 supported the Gandhians and 15 were with Das and the Swarajists.[6] Thus even in his own province, Das did not have the support he needed to widen the Congress program.

At the end of the 1922–1923 Congress, Das resigned as president. He felt he could better gather majority support for his proposal if he was not the official leader of an organization which had defeated it. The Swaraj Party was founded on December 31, 1922, and its manifesto was signed in January 1923. It was both the minority, challenging faction within the Congress and an organization running candidates for legislatures outside the purview of the Congress. From the end of 1922, the Swarajists were called the "Pro-Changers," while the Gandhians were labeled the "No-Changers" or "Whole-Hoggers," terms which had to do with the attitude of party or faction towards the Gandhian program.

In order to challenge the Gandhians and confront the government in the legislatures, Das and his colleagues had to build a party organization which was strong in the provinces as well as nationally. Since they had the task of campaigning for legislative seats during 1923, they undoubtedly had to pay less attention to Gandhi's constructive program. At the same time they had to continue work for a majority within the Congress and prevent their own elimination from all Congress executive posts, which was Gandhi's desire.[7]

As president of the All-India Swaraj Party, Das had a number of important functions to perform. Working closely with Motilal Nehru, who was virtually his copresident, Das had to settle intraparty disputes like the one that arose between the Patel and Jayakar groups in Bombay.[8] In the Congress, Das, with able support from Motilal Nehru, Vithalbhai Patel, and others, had to present the Swarajist position and maneuver with the Gandhians at meetings of the AICC and other bodies. To win support throughout the country in the elections and in the Congress, Das made some speaking tours of areas outside Bengal, most notably an extensive series of engagements in Madras in 1923.[9]

Simultaneously, Das had to strengthen and solidify his hold on the Bengal Congress, link the Bengal Congress and the Swaraj Party in Bengal, and prepare and carry through an election campaign for seats in the Bengal Legislative Council. Dealing with all of these charges would have been impossible had not Das had a rare gift for recruiting and selecting able, intelligent, and committed lieutenants and supporters. The most important of these men were to play a vital part in the politics of Bengal for almost forty years. They included J. M. Sen Gupta, B. N. Sasmal, Kiran Sankar Roy, Anil Baran Ray, Protap Chandra Guha Roy, Subhas Bose, Satya Ranjan Bakshi, Maulana Akram Khan, and a group later called the "Big Five": Tulsi Goswami, Nalini Ranjan Sarker, Dr. Bidhan Chandra Roy, Nirmal C. Chunder, and Sarat Chandra Bose. Most of these men were in their twenties and thirties. They were Western-educated and several, including Chunder, Goswami, Sen Gupta, and the brothers Sarat and Subhas Bose, had attended Presidency College in Calcutta. Sarat Bose, Sen Gupta, and Nirmal Chunder all had lucrative legal practices. Dr. B. C. Roy, who was at first an independent affiliated with the Swaraj Party, had received his medical education in London and Edinburgh and had established a fine practice in Calcutta and connections to Calcutta University. Guha Roy was a journalist and medical practitioner, while Nalini Sarker was a self-made businessman who had made a considerable fortune with the Hindustan Cooperative Insurance Company and other enterprises.[10]

M. R. Jayakar has described Das's relationship to his followers and his ability to raise money:

> His followers always evinced a commendable regard and reverence for him, and he trusted them implicitly—an admirable feature wanting in some other 'patriots' who rose to a similar civic distinction in other parts of India. He had a great capacity for begging and had such rich followers in Bengal that, on one occasion, in the course of a few hours, he could obtain no less than Rs. 150,000, to finance a paper which he then intended to bring out.[11]

It is unimportant whether Das raised Rs. 150,000 in one day, but it is significant that he did bring some wealthy backers into the Congress and was successful in supporting the Swaraj Party and Congress activities in Bengal. He was adept at delegating responsibilities to his lieutenants and coordinating their work. Chunder served as treasurer of the Bengal Provincial Congress Committee (BPCC) from 1921 to 1925. Tulsi Goswami was treasurer of the All-India Swaraj Party, following in the footsteps of his wealthy ancestors, who were zamindars and rajas of Serampore.[12] Sen Gupta became secretary of the Swaraj Party and deputy leader to Das of the Swaraj Party in the Bengal Legislative Council. Sarat-babu's younger brother Subhas Bose helped to organize demonstrations, worked on *Forward*, was active in the youth movement, and in 1923 became Chief Executive Officer of the newly revamped Calcutta Corporation. Anil Baran Ray served as secretary of the BPCC, Kiran Sankar Roy as an important party functionary and member of the Bengal Legislative Council from Dacca, and B. N. Sasmal as a member of the Swaraj Party executive. Beneath this top level of party leaders, there were shrewd, tough, and hard-working men such as Satya Ranjan Bakshi, who was responsible for seeing that *Forward* was properly published. Under the guidance of the Swaraj Party leaders, *Forward* became a leading nationalist newspaper from its inception in 1923.[13]

It has been mentioned that some Bengal revolutionaries began to move into the Congress organization. Their organization was spread out in the districts of Bengal and they helped to build a party that was not merely a Calcutta affair, but had some roots in every district. According to a government intelligence report of 1924, the revolutionaries aimed at control of the Bengal Congress, and had made certain agreements with Das. This report also details how Das secured support from them for the Swaraj Party:

> Mr. C. R. Das was released from jail in August 1922 and about this time the proposal to non-co-operate within the Councils was first seriously mooted. But this policy was not at first supported by the Jugantar Party. Among the Bengal representatives on the All-India Congress Committee, elected about November 1922, were four important members of this Party, namely Amarendra Chattarji (ex-absconder), Upen Banerji (ex-convict) Bepin Ganguly (ex-convict) and Satyen Mitter (ex-detenu). Similarly, on the Bengal Provincial Congress Committee, elected at the same time, the Jugantar were, out of a total of sixty, represented by Satyen Mitter, Bepin Ganguly, Bhupati Mazumdar (ex-State prisoner), Gopen Ray (ex-convict) and Amarendra Chattarji, while Monoranjan Gupta (ex-State prisoner) was one of the Assistant Secretaries. On the Executive Council of this Committee were Gopen Ray, Amarendra Chattarji and Bepin Ganguly. Most of these individuals at the time of their election appear to have held anti-council entry views but that they had no decided opinion on the subject and merely desired to serve their own ends, is apparent from the fact that Mr. C. R. Das gained them over to his side before or at the Gaya Congress in

Christmas week, 1922. How Mr. C. R. Das gained their support was, at that time, a mystery, for it was known that his policy had little chance of success at the Congress at Gaya, but information subsequently received indicates that at this period he entered into a definite pact with these revolutionists. In April 1923, the 24-Parganas police learnt that the Swarajya Party . . . had agreed to cooperate with revolutionists as long as the latter abstained from overt acts and that as soon as revolutionary methods were adopted the Swarajya Party would stand aside and would not interfere.[14]

There seems to be no doubt that there were some men with a revolutionary past and hopes in the organization of the Bengal Congress and Swaraj Party. Das, Subhas Bose, and others were probably aware of these revolutionary goals. But without some independent confirmation, it does seem hard to believe all the details in the report about elaborate plots and arms smuggling, especially about Das's and Subhas Bose's support for these schemes.[15]

Using such information, as well as stories of immediate threats to law and safety in Bengal, the Government cracked down on the revolutionary groups during the fall of 1923 and early 1924. They arrested revolutionaries outside and inside the Congress, as well as such Swaraj Party leaders as Subhas Bose and Anil Baran Roy. Das insisted until his dying day that Bose and some of the other Swarajists arrested were innocent and for this reason they were held without charges under the extraordinary powers and statutes of the government.[16]

BENGAL PACT

From 1921, communal relations in India were deteriorating, and several serious riots occurred.[17] There were efforts at reconciliation and a number of important Muslims, including the Ali brothers and Maulana Azad, continued to participate in the high councils of the Congress. As early as 1917, and perhaps much earlier privately, Das had realized that to be an effective leader in Bengal he would need Muslim support. When he ran the Noncooperation campaign in Bengal in 1921, he had had this support. Seeking increased backing for the Swaraj Party in 1923, he worked out a provisional agreement with several Muslim leaders in Bengal, which was subsequently called the Bengal Pact. Its aims and provisions have been sympathetically summarized by Maulana Azad:

In Bengal, Muslims were the majority community, but for various reasons they were educationally and politically backward. Even though they numbered over 50 percent of the population, they held hardly 30 percent of the posts under the Government. Mr. C. R. Das was a great realist and immediately saw that the problem was an economic one. He realized that till the Musalmans were given the necessary assurances for their economic future, they could not be expected to join the Congress whole-heartedly. He therefore made a declaration which impressed not only Bengal but the whole of India. He announced that when Congress secured the reins of power in Bengal, it would reserve 60 per cent of all new appointments for the Musalmans till such time as they achieved proper representation according to population. He went even further in respect of the Calcutta Corporation and offered to reserve 80 per cent of the new appointments on similar terms. He pointed out that so long as the Musalmans were not properly represented in public life and in the services, there could be no true democracy in Bengal.[18]

Das was accused in 1923–1924 of trying to buy Muslim support.[19] There was a great deal of opposition to this pact in the Bengal Congress and among Hindu Bengalis generally, but after some difficulties Das was able to secure backing for it.

An analysis of the membership of the Bengal Provincial Congress Committee for 1924–1925 shows that Muslims comprised only 13 percent of the total.[20] In the Bengal Legislative Council, however, Muslim Swarajists constituted more than 50 percent of the Swarajists in that body, and on several crucial votes even some Muslim members who were not Swarajists supported Das and his party. From statements made in the council chamber and from descriptions of Das in the memoirs of several Muslim leaders, it can be argued that he succeeded in gaining the trust and support of many Muslims in Bengal and in other provinces as well.[21]

From 1921 there were differences between the Das faction in the Bengal Congress and the more devoted Gandhians. This factional split was formalized and widened once the Swaraj Party was founded and the Das group became committed to a program which Gandhi opposed. Through the years 1922 to 1925, there were always some congressmen in Bengal who were opposed to or lukewarm toward Das. But from the middle of 1923, when many Gandhians resigned from the Bengal Provincial Congress Committee, until Das's death he maintained his supremacy in the Bengal Congress.[22] In July 1924, some Bengal Gandhians formed their own organization, the Bengal Non-co-operation League. The writer of the report on the 1924 Bengal Provincial Conference for the *Indian Quarterly Register* maintained that "The conference showed that Bengal was 90 per cent Swarajist." [23]

An analysis of the names of members of the Bengal Provincial Congress Committee for 1924–1925 shows that of 229 members, 159 or 69.4 percent were definitely or likely from high castes, 11 or 4.8 percent were quite likely low-caste Hindus, and 31 or 13.5 percent were Muslims. If those of indefinite Hindu caste are included with the high-caste group, then figures rise to 186 or 81.2 percent, but if they are included with the low-caste members, this group increases to 38 or 16.5 percent. It is obvious that, by and large, the Congress in Bengal was still dominated by members from the high-caste Hindu population, who constituted only 5.6 percent of the total population of Bengal according to the 1921 census.[24] Some incomplete figures for the Bengal Moderates at the 1907 Surat Congress show that out of 82, 72 or 87.8 percent were definitely and likely high-caste Hindus; 4 or 4.87 percent were low-caste Hindus and the same number were Muslims.[25] The comparison is based on fragmentary evidence, but no other quantitative evidence has been produced.

In 1923 Bengal Swaraj Party and the Bengal Provincial Congress Committees were partially distinct organizations. The Congress was linked to Gandhian activities as well as the Swarajist program, and the Swaraj Party was particularly concerned with electoral and legislative politics. Congressmen were also involved in other organizations, such as trade union organizations, the Bengal Youngmen's Association, the Calcutta Khilafat Committee, and the Bengal Provincial Hindu Sabha.[26] There was also a Brahman Sabha in Bengal, and Das led a civil disobedience campaign, usually called the Tarakeswar Satyagraha, in direct opposition to the Brahman Sabha. The Tarakeswar Satyagraha was a movement to replace the religious head or Mohunt of a temple in the Calcutta area and involved acrimonious religious and political charges. A temporary solution to the affair was achieved in 1924, but the agreement broke down. Das would rather have steered clear of the whole matter.[27]

Throughout 1923 and 1924 the Swarajists in the Congress strove for acceptance of council entry as an integral and valid part of the Congress program. By May 1923, Jayakar, a Swarajist, claimed that the Swarajists were gaining, although a good deal of hostility still existed.[28]

A special session of the Congress in Calcutta in September 1923 aimed at solution of differences. Maulana Azad, who presided at Calcutta, said that he had tried to bring the two parties together.[29] Although Azad wrote that he was successful, the compromises at Calcutta and then at Cocananda were only temporary. The struggle continued, and when Gandhi emerged from prison in the following year, the Gandhians aimed at excluding the Swarajists from all executive positions in the Congress organization. At the Cocananda Congress in December 1923, the Bengal Pact was brought before the annual Congress session as a possible national pact. On the Bengal Pact, Das had been fighting a multisided defensive struggle. Some nationalist papers, the *Servant, Ananda Bazar Patrika*, and *Basumati* among them, had attacked the pact, while Das and his party answered in *Forward*.[30] Das spoke at Cocananda in defense of the Bengal Pact and for consideration of the Indian National Pact:

> The Bengal Provincial Congress Committee has approved of a particular draft not finally but as a suggestion and they have placed that suggestion for the consideration of the Indian National Congress. . . . The resolution says that the opinion of the whole country should be taken upon it not only upon the Bengal Pact, but everything that would be placed before the Committee. . . . Many of you are under the impression having regard to the few speeches that have already been made that you are asked to accept the Bengal Pact, that it is a wicked Pact, that it created division between the Hindus and Mussalmans. . . . Why is this resentment against Bengal? What has Bengal done? . . . The Bengal Provincial Congress Committee has made its suggestion. It may be right or it may be utterly wrong. . . . Is Bengal debarred from making that suggestion? . . . You may delete the Bengal National Pact from the resolution. But I assure you, you cannot delete Bengal from the Indian National Congress or from the history of India! Bengal demands the right of having her suggestion considered. . . . You cannot delete Bengal. . . . She is an integral part of the Constitution of the Indian National Congress. And she is intimately associated with the history of all political agitation from the commencement of this Congress down to the present day.[31]

The Congress did not choose to make the Bengal Pact a national one and Das was unable to push his attempt at communal accord from the provincial to the national level within the Congress. Some Bengali

leaders felt that Bengal was being isolated from the mainstream of nationalist work and that proposals from Bengal and Bengali leaders, per-
ticularly if not supported openly and strongly by Gandhi, would receive limited consideration. An understanding of the changing role of
Bengal in the nationalist movement is half-submerged and half-appar-
ent in Bengalis' speeches and writings of this period. Somehow Bengal
was out of step and the Congress was not giving Bengali spokesmen
what they felt was a proper hearing.

After Gandhi emerged from prison in May 1924, he held meetings
with Das and Motilal Nehru to try to come to an agreement with the
Swarajists, but, at least as far as Gandhi was concerned, no satisfactory
settlement was achieved. Soon thereafter, the Bengal Provincial Conference was held at Serajgunge. Resolutions were passed supporting the
Bengal Pact, the strategy of council entry, the Tarakeshwar movement, and Gandhi's nonviolent Noncooperation program.[32] The resolution that was to cause the most furor was the one concerning
Gopinath Saha, a revolutionary who had murdered an innocent person
while attempting to assassinate an official. He had been captured and
was later executed. The resolution passed at Serajgunge read:

> This Conference, whilst denouncing (or dissociating itself from) vio-
> lence and adhering to the principle of non-violence, appreciates Gopi-
> nath Saha's ideal of self-sacrifice, misguided though that is in respect of
> the country's best interest, and expresses its respect for his great self-
> sacrifice.[33]

Das voted for this resolution, and soon a storm of criticism arose from
officials, nonofficial Europeans, and Gandhian congressmen directed at
Das and his party in Bengal. This resolution was read by Gandhi and
the Europeans as indirect support of violence.

From June 27, 1924, the AICC met at Ahmadabad to consider a
number of issues. Gandhi issued a statement on "Congress Organisation" which included this passage:

> the executive organisation of the Congress must not contain titled
> persons, Government school-masters, practising lawyers and members
> of Legislative bodies and persons who use foreign cloth. Such persons
> can become Congressmen, but cannot and should not become members
> of the executive organisations. They can become delegates and influ-
> ence Congress resolutions, but once the Congress policy is fixed, those

who do not believe in that policy should, in my opinion, stand out of the executive bodies. The All-India Congress Committee and all local executive committees are such bodies and they should contain only those members who whole-heartedly believe in and are prepared to carry out the policy.[34]

This position was presented as a resolution at the AICC meeting and was a direct challenge to the Swarajists, for, if agreed to, it would deprive the Swarajists of their places in the AICC, the provincial Congress committees, and other offices like Das's presidency of the BPCC. After the resolution was introduced, Motilal Nehru, speaking for the Swarajists, said that they supported the constructive program and added that

the Congress belongs as much to us as to the opposite party. We will not, if we can help it, allow its constitution to be changed at the caprice of a narrow majority whenever it may think necessary to crush the minority. The demand that the Swarajists should go out of the executive is an unreasonable demand and it is only due to our self-respect that we must resist it. We declare that the resolution under discussion is an unconstitutional contrivance and we go away today only to return with a majority.[35]

With this declaration, the Swarajists and their sympathizers walked out of the meeting and the Gandhians had the floor to themselves. A number of those remaining said that the penalty clause against members of legislative bodies should not be passed because it would ruin the Congress. Gandhi remained firm, however, and an amendment to delete the penalty clause was defeated by 67 to 37. But seeing that as many as 37 of his own party were openly willing to oppose him on this issue, Gandhi backed down and the penalty clause was withdrawn.[36] The Swarajists returned and the meeting continued.

Gandhi had published his own Gopinath Saha Resolution before the AICC had gathered. The Gandhian resolution was undoubtedly more forthright in its condemnation of violence than the one passed at Serajgunge.[37] But Das insisted that the Serajgunge version be passed. The writer for the *Indian Quarterly Register* summarized his speech:

In moving the amendment Mr. Das said that there was hardly any difference between the original motion as proposed by M. Gandhi and his amendment. . . . If there was no difference why did he forward the amendment? The reason was simple. The question before the meeting was not one of "No-changers" *versus* "Pro-changers." It was not a party question. He brought forward the amendment because he had been deliberately and wilfully misrepresented for the Serajgunge resolution, which was also misreported. Had it not been for the vulgar threat of Regulation III of '18 directed against him and others who were responsible for the Serajgunge resolution, he would not have brought forward an amendment. . . . If only as a manly answer to the bluff, they should accept his amendment. The heart of Bengal was agitated over the mischievous agitation set afoot. If they had any sympathy for the sentiment of Bengal, they should all unanimously vote for the resolution.[38]

Following Das, Dr. Paranjpye from Maharashtra rose to support Das and said that his region, like Bengal, did not strictly adhere to the Gandhian faith in nonviolence under all circumstances. It is not clear whether Das wanted to have his position interpreted in this manner. The support that Maharashtra gave to the Swaraj Party and to Das in this moment indicates that there was considerable opposition to Gandhi in the two areas which had been dominant in the national movement during its first thirty years.[39]

When a vote was taken on Das's amendment, it lost by 70 to 78. Gandhi's motion was then carried.[40] But Gandhi broke down at the final session of the AICC meeting, feeling that he was losing his strength in the Congress. After the gathering had disbanded Gandhi wrote an article in *Young India* entitled "Defeated and Humbled." He wrote, in part,

> I had a bare majority always for the four resolutions but it must be regarded by me as a minority. The House was fairly evenly divided. The Gopinath Saha resolution clinched the issue. The speeches, the result, and the scenes I witnessed afterwards—all was a perfect eye-opener. I undoubtedly regard the voting as a triumph for Mr. Das although he was apparently defeated by eight votes. That he could find 70 supporters out of 148 who voted had a deep significance for me. It lighted the darkness though very dimly as yet.[41]

Although Das had maintained that the Serajgunge resolution and Gandhi's resolution were essentially the same, Gandhi certainly did not agree:

> Mr. Das sees no difference between my resolution and his. I can only say it is self-deception. Those who spoke in support of his proposition

did not mince matters. They had room for political murder in their philosophy and, after all, is it not the common philosophy, the majority of the so-called civilised peoples believe in and act upon? On due occasions they hold that for a disorganised and oppressed people political assassination is the only remedy. That it is a false philosophy, that it has failed to make the world better to live in, is only too true. I merely state that if Mr. Das and his supporters have erred they have the bulk of 'civilised' opinion on their side. The foreign masters of India have no better record to show. . . . In my opinion the amendment was in breach of the Congress creed or the policy of non-violence.[42]

In the same articles in *Young India*, Gandhi suggested that he might retire from the Congress. At other times through 1924, he insisted that if unity were not achieved in the Congress, he would carry out his threat. The Swarajists had been elected in considerable numbers to the central legislature and to several provincial legislative councils, including the one in Bengal. Their effective party organization in the legislatures probably helped their campaign in the Congress. By the end of the year Gandhi and Das made a compromise called the "Calcutta Pact" which would allow both Gandhians and Swarajists to work from the Congress organization in their own ways. Das reiterated his support for Gandhi's program and Gandhi told his supporters not to challenge the Swarajists.[43] The Swarajists had momentarily achieved the parity they sought in the Congress and the strategy of council entry was employed by the Congress again in the 1930s after passage of the Government of India Act of 1935, which provided for provincial autonomy and a federal system at the center.

DYARCHY AND THE BENGAL LEGISLATIVE COUNCIL

After the 1917 visit by Edwin Montagu, the Secretary of State for India, the reforms proposed by him and by others both inside and outside the government were finally worked out. They were enacted by the British Parliament as the Government of India Act of 1919. One main feature of these reforms was "the trend toward federalism." Certain functions were specified as provincial ones, and the provinces were to have their own budgets. The act provided as well for ministers, to be chosen from among the elected Indian members, who were to be in charge of the "transferred departments" under the scheme of dyarchy.[44]

The electorate and the size of the Bengal Legislative Council were increased considerably under the 1919 act. The electorate was about 1,000,000 in 1920, slightly more for the 1923 election, and more than 1,100,000 in 1926. Only a fraction of these eligible voters actually voted, but the number voting increased once the Swarajists entered the lists in 1923 and again in 1926.[45] The Legislative Council was composed of 140 members, of whom 114 were elected and 26 were officials or nominated members. Generally following the provisions of the Lucknow Pact, the Muslims were represented out of proportion to numbers and wealth in 6 provinces, while they were underrepresented in Bengal and the Punjab. According to the Lucknow Pact, the Bengali Muslims were to have 40 percent of the elected seats, while non-Muslims were to have 60 percent. In the Bengal Council formed under the 1919 act, the elected Muslims numbered 39, elected Hindus 57, so the percentage was slightly over 40 percent. The balance of the seats was held by Europeans, Anglo-Indians, commercial bodies, and nominated members for the Indian Christians, the depressed classes, labor, 2 unspecified nominees, and not more than 20 officials.[46]

Even with the withdrawal of the Congress candidates and the rather low turnout in the 1920 election, British officials, including Lord Ronaldshay, then Governor of Bengal, and the Moderates led by Surendranath Banerjea entertained high hopes for the accomplishments that might be possible through the reformed council. It was with these hopes that Surendranath Banerjea became minister in charge of the Local Self-Government, Public Health, and Medical departments. Mr. P. C. Mitter, also a Moderate but with considerable independence of mind, served as minister in charge of the Education and Registration departments, and Nawab Saiyid Nawab Ali Chaudhuri, the third minister, headed the Public Works, Agriculture and Industries, and Excise departments. These three men served continuously from January 1921 until January 1924.[47] The first council, serving from early 1921 to the end of 1923, had worked relatively smoothly but was enveloped in unreality.[48] All members were aware that much attention was focused on the Noncooperators and some expressed sympathy with its goals. Some council time was given to discussions of events involving the Noncooperators, including the Chandpur affair, the Calcutta hartal, and the general issue of law and order.[49]

What many elected councillors and officials seemed to fear was the possibility of widespread disorder and revolution. They thought that Gandhi was, in effect, a revolutionary in sheep's clothing. These fears had haunted the Moderates and the government in Bengal since the beginning of the Swadeshi agitation. With the growth of the revolutionary movement and of exaggerated beliefs as to its size and potential, the fear of revolt was always with these men who wanted gradual change.[50]

Even their fear of anarchy, however, did not prevent the elected councillors from opposing many of the laws put through by the government of Bengal to cope with demonstrations, disorder, and revolutionaries; 50 councillors, all Indians and almost all elected members, voted to withdraw some of the repressive laws, including the Criminal Law Amendment Act of 1908 as amended in 1920 and the Seditious Meetings Act of 1911. They were opposed by 36 who supported these laws and numbered among them ministers, officials, and European nonofficials. The opponents of these laws argued that the government's repressive apparatus was helping the Noncooperation movement and that ordinary laws rather than these special repressive measures could be used to deal with the situation.[51]

Although no group or party within the council had a strong organization inside or outside the chamber, there was a de facto alliance between several groups which dominated the council. This alliance, which supported the ministers, included officials, nonofficial Europeans, Anglo-Indians, and a large majority of the Muslim members. The Hindu members were often divided, with several supporting the ministers and some others, loosely organized, comprising the opposition. As Ajoy Dutt, a member of the first council under the 1919 act, has pointed out, "The control exercisable by the Council over the Ministers is however very nominal in practice." [52] Even when a majority could be gathered on a particular vote to oppose the government and the ministers, this negative vote meant little. It did not put the ministers or the government out of office; that is, the ministers were not dependent on maintaining a majority in the council, as in Great Britain. The governor had certain powers which he could use to change most council actions, but there were some constitutional ways in which the council could paralyze the ministers. The cooperators in the first council did call for increased powers for the elected members. They argued that control over finances was essential if the reforms were to have any appreciable significance.

The discussion of the Calcutta Municipal Bill during the first council brought to the surface considerable opposition to one provision of the measure and an interesting controversy about who truly represented the Bengali Muslims. The bill was piloted through the Bengal Council by Surendranath Banerjea. The provision that drew so much heat concerned the number of Muslim members and the method of electing them to the new corporation. Banerjea preferred joint electorates and the reservation of about 13 seats for Muslims. The Hindu liberals generally supported Banerjea. Most Muslim members called for separate electorates for the Muslim seats and a larger number of reserved places. During the debate in the late months of 1921, Syed Nasam Ali, speaking for the Bengal Provincial Moslem League which he said represented the Muslims, claimed that in order for there to be Muslim representatives to the corporation in reality rather than in name only, there would have to be separate electorates. Dr. A. Suhrawardy disputed Syed Nasam Ali's view and challenged the latter to stand for election in a Calcutta ward against a Khilafatist candidate. The debate was filled with acrimony, several Muslims claiming that they were the best or most "representative" spokesmen.[53] The majority of Muslim councillors clearly wanted separate electorates, and eventually Banerjea backed down in the interests of having this important measure passed.[54]

The debates on the Calcutta Municipal Bill and on another bill concerned with Dacca and Calcutta Universities make clear several points about the Muslims and the council. First, the Muslim members were not organized into any kind of tight party, and there were considerable differences between them. The common factor of religion did not in itself unite them. Second, although they were all concerned with speaking for Muslim interests, they had different perceptions of what these interests were. At one point in the debate on the number of seats Muslims were to have in the Calcutta Corporation, Fazlul Huq said,

> The Muhammadan community is certainly not backward. Unfortunately, the Muhammadans are disorganized. They have not learnt to organize themselves according to the Western method. The moment

they can organize themselves you will find that they are ready for a good fight and a fight against anybody.[55]

There were signs of communal as well as subregional tensions in statements from several councillors objecting to a measure to cut the funds for Dacca University. Khwaja Mohammad Azam, a representative from Dacca, said, in part:

Eastern Bengal supplies the bulk of Bengal income and we do not grudge that the bulk of its expenditure is swallowed by West Bengal, and I cannot understand why West Bengal people should grudge us a pittance which has been long overdue and should have been given to us years back. I cannot also understand the jealousy of Calcutta University men for Dacca.[56]

After a number of Hindu members as well rose to oppose the cut, Fazlul Huq issued a warning:

My own feeling has been that ever since Lord Hardinge announced that there would be this university in Dacca city—this long-promised, long-deferred, long-wished-for university—Dacca—has been a sort of eyesore to the intellectual savants who control the destinies of the Calcutta University. I do not wish to go into this matter, but I wish to give this warning to my friends of Western Bengal, who rise up on every occasion, when funds are provided for Dacca, to try and take away from this provision—"Hands off," I say. If you raise this question in Council, you will cause a cleavage between the two sections of the province, which will be disastrous to the work of the administration. It is not merely on behalf of the Muhammadans of East Bengal but on behalf of the people of East Bengal in general, that I appeal to my friends to drop all opposition to this grant which the Minister wants for the Dacca University.[57]

There was also considerable disagreement between Muslim councillors on the issue of women's suffrage. The more Westernized supported the extension of the franchise to women, while a majority, perhaps two-thirds of the Muslim members, felt that such a move was potentially destructive.[58] The Muslim conservatives were joined by a good number of Hindu conservatives, mainly from among the representatives of the landowners. There were other lines of cleavage in the council and in Bengal than the Hindu-Muslim divide.

The first council, 1921 to 1923, passed a number of measures, the most important of which was the Calcutta Municipal Act of March

1923. Surendranath Banerjea, gratified that the bill had been passed after almost two years of work, suggested that it serve as "a model for the rest of India." [59] Although Bengal was no longer as prominent as it had been in the nationalist movement, Banerjea was a product of the days when Bengal and Bengalis were in the forefront.

The budgets that were set proved to be a bitter pill for the liberals to swallow. Bengal's financial condition was very poor and had not been helped by the Meston Award, a division of tax revenues between the central and provincial governments. That Bengal had suffered unfairly by the terms of the Meston Award and that all efforts should be made to redress this grievance were about the only views that all politically active Bengalis and all government officials agreed upon.[60] Only small sums were available for the transferred or "nation-building" departments. The financial pressure was such that the cooperators' plans for improvements, inter alia in education and health, were very limited, and their implementation was slow. The elected councillors, for the most part, blamed the government for this state of affairs. Lord Lytton, who became governor of Bengal in 1923, placed the blame on "a sudden depression due to world causes for which the Government of Bengal had no responsibility." [61] Whatever the causes, the large strides forward that had been expected were not made. This probably was an important factor in the defeat that the liberals suffered at the polls at the end of 1923.[62]

Writing earlier in that year, Governor Lytton mentioned what he felt to be some of the advances made under the Montagu-Chelmsford reforms:

> I have indicated that in my opinion the Reforms in their present stage are on the whole working well. There is, however, a practically universal demand among Indian politicians for their further extension at any early date. The non-co-operators . . . are jealous of the opportunities afforded to the Legislative Council of influencing Government policy, and there is a growing opinion, especially in Bengal, in favour of entering the Councils. . . . Those who are inside the Councils are showing an increasing interest in the business of Government and a growing sense of responsibility. Some of them are, of course, merely destructive critics, but the majority are . . . studying the procedure of the Council in a humble spirit and with genuine interest; but their attitude is very largely influenced by the desire to justify themselves in the eyes of the non-co-operators outside. They are anxious to show

that they have accomplished more in the interest of their country by coming into the Council than by remaining outside.[63]

The aims and methods of the Swarajists who entered the elections at the end of 1923 were not yet clear to Lytton, and he was naïve in believing that he could persuade them to cooperate on his terms under the reforms as they stood.

In late 1923, Swarajist candidates ran for seats in the central assembly and in provincial chambers. A passage in the Bengali government's report on the reforms summarizes their successes:

By 1923, the Swarajist party had arisen with improved organisation, a definite political programme, substantial party funds and a declared policy of contesting on behalf of the party as many seats in the Council as possible. The party discipline was also good, and not more than one Swarajist candidate was put forward in any constituency. Consequently in 1923 and 1926 the Swarajists gained a large number of seats and were able to form a powerful party in the Council.

There was no other well organised party in the general constituencies. In most cases candidates fought each for himself with little regard for party. The Muhammadan non-Swarajist candidates, although loosely arranged in groups, were entirely disunited during the general election, and subjected to no sort of party discipline.[64]

The Swarajists in some cases also made alliances with independents who ran with Swarajist support. One such candidate was Dr. B. C. Roy, who defeated Surendranath Banerjea in the 24-Parganas Municipal North constituency.[65]

The Swarajists entered the council "as a compact and strictly disciplined party numbering 47 under the leadership of Mr. C. R. Das." [66] The policy and an important alliance of the Swarajists have been sketched by the government of Bengal:

They had further the general support of the Independent Nationalist party led by Mr. B. Chakrabarti, which by March, 1924, consisted of 19 members. The Swarajists were themselves unwilling to take office. They concentrated their efforts on making the survival of a Ministry drawn from any other source impossible and on hampering all the normal activities of Government.[67]

Although Lytton was aware of the Swarajist program, he nevertheless asked Das first whether he wished to become a minister and help choose the other ministers. Lytton and Das argued, the governor of

Bengal maintaining that the Swarajist policy "had had a most mischievous effect in India." [68] Das held to his views and refused office.
Lytton gave his impression of Das:

> I formed the impression that he was a man more influenced by senti-
> ment than argument, whom it would be impossible to convince. He
> did not strike me as a leader of men or a man with any strong person-
> ality. I should certainly have found it very difficult to work with him,
> as once he had made up his mind on any question where he had been
> swayed by sentiment, he would have been quite immovable.[69]

Lytton then approached other individuals and groups in an effort to
find the best and most widely supported men who would agree to become ministers.[70] There were serious difficulties with the other groups
in the council as he describes in his memoirs:

> The Mohammedan Moderates were divided into groups composed of
> the personal followers of three or four prominent individuals with lit-
> tle liking for each other. In addition, there were 17 elected Europeans
> who would support any Ministry formed from the Moderates and
> there would be 26 nominated or *ex-officio* members whom I had not
> yet appointed. . . . There was no personality whom all the members of
> the Moderate Party—if Party it could be called—accepted as
> leader. Neither the 11 Hindus nor the 18 Mohammedans, even, had a
> leader of their own, and almost every member of the 29 wanted to be-
> come a Minister himself! [71]

As a result of his extensive interviews, Lytton was finally able to form
a "ministry" of Messrs. S. N. Mallik, A. K. Fazlul Huq, and Mr. A. K.
Ghuznavi. Shortly thereafter, Mallik was unseated on an election peti-
tion.[72] This left the two Muslim ministers each with a personal following and the backing of the Europeans, the officials, and some of the
other Moderates. The ministers' supporters constituted about half the
house, but it was an unstable situation and the ministry proved to be
short-lived.

As Lytton and the other government officials realized, the Swarajists
were the best organized and disciplined party in the council. More
than one-third of their solid party members in the council were Muslims, and several other Muslims listed in the Fazlul Huq group often
voted with them as well.[73] Although serious efforts were made to split
the Muslim Swarajists from their Hindu colleagues during the council

session, Swarajist solidarity was maintained until the end of 1925. In accordance with the Bengal Pact, the Swarajists had agreed to give Muslims 60 percent of all government posts once self-government or complete provincial autonomy had been attained. The opponents of the Swarajists put up a motion calling for immediate implementation of the agreement. They thought that in this vote all Muslims would join together on one side and all Hindus on the other.[74] Not only did the Muslim Swarajists vote with the Hindu Swarajists to table the motion, but Major Hassan Suhrawardy, deputy president of the council, and Mr. Hussein Shaheed Suhrawardy, a Muslim member of the independent nationalist group, both spoke up to defend C. R. Das's good faith and to advocate following the terms of the pact to the letter. Das's motion to table passed by 66 to 48, and the effort to split the Swarajists was defeated.[75] Das had gained considerable Muslim support for his party at the ballot box and in the council, and many believed in his determination to create better communal relations in Bengal. Maulvi Abdur Rashid Khan had been appointed secretary of the Swaraj Council Party,[76] and the percentage of Muslims in the BPCC had risen. Once the Swarajists gained control of it many Muslims were given positions in the Calcutta Corporation.[77]

The independents, or Nationalists as they called themselves, numbered between 12 and 19 members. Byomkes Chakravarty, who had once worked with the Congress, was their spokesman. Their most outspoken Muslim member was Hussein Shaheed Suhrawardy, a barrister who was in his early thirties in 1924 and was destined to play an important part in Bengali politics into the 1950s. Suhrawardy was born in Midnapur in 1893 and attended the Calcutta Madrasah, St. Xavier's College, and Oxford University, where he gained honors in jurisprudence. He trained for the bar at Gray's Inn, and after his return to India entered politics. In 1920 he was elected to the council from a Muslim constituency in Burdwan and in 1923 he was returned by the Calcutta South Muslim constituency. When the Swarajists entered the Calcutta Corporation under the recently passed Calcutta Municipal Act, C. R. Das was elected mayor and Suhrawardy deputy mayor. Although he was not a congressman, Suhrawardy supported the Khilafat movement and explained the rationale for the 1921 Noncooperation campaign in the Bengal Legislative Council.[78] Suhrawardy was a frequent speaker in the council and sometimes engaged in arguments with other Muslim councillors, ministers, and officials. At one point during a debate in early 1923, Surendranath Banerjea said of Suhrawardy, "He is dissatisfied with Government—that he always is." [79]

The Nationalists also included Kumar Shib Shekhareswar Ray, representative of the Rajshahi Landholders. The Nationalists were not averse to taking office, and the Kumar Shib became president of the council when H. E. A. Cotton retired.

Besides the Swarajists and Nationalists, there were a number of other groups of liberals, loyalists, and Muslims as well as a few elected members not affiliated with any group. The liberals, including Babu Jatindra Nath Basu, P. C. Mitter, and S. C. Mukherji, were the few remaining descendants of the Bengal Moderates who once played such an important part in the Bengal Legislative Council. These men usually voted with the government and ministers, but P. C. Mitter was of independent mind. Although he served as a minister from 1921 to 1924 and again in 1927, he voted with the Swarajists against the introduction of the Bengal Criminal Amendment Bill in January 1925. [80]

Loyalists are identified here as those elected members, both Hindu and Muslim, who voted on the government side on all important divisions which have been checked. Among the Hindus, these included a few landholders; in the Muslim loyalist party were some prominent Muslims like Nawab Saiyid Nawab Ali Chaudhuri and Khwaja Nazimuddin. Several loyalists, including Nawab Ali Chaudhuri, Maulvi Musharruf Hossain, and Raja Manmatha Nath Roy Chaudhuri, served as ministers for varying periods of time in the years 1921 to 1927. [81] Khwaja Nazimuddin, who was to make his mark in Bengali and national politics, was a scion of the family of the Nawab of Dacca and was born in 1894. He attended the Mohammadan Anglo-Oriental College in Aligarh and Trinity Hall, Cambridge. In 1922 Nazimuddin became chairman of the Dacca Municipality and the following year was elected to the Legislative Council from a Bakarganj Muslim constituency and also became a member of the executive council of Dacca University. [82]

The Europeans and Anglo-Indians and a few nominated nonofficial members should also be included as loyalists. They almost always sided and voted with the ministers and the government, although they occasionally differed on budgetary and financial issues. Finally, there was a small group of Muslims who may be called followers of Fazlul Huq. They were solidly with the government while Huq was a minister in 1924, but when Huq was forced to leave office and became embittered, this group sided with the Swarajists on a crucial vote on the ministerial question in 1925.

It should be noted that the divisions into parties and groups cut across community lines. The Muslims as well as the Hindus were members of different groups which often included members of the other community. The Swarajists had quite a few Muslim members, and through this period of worsening communal relations in other parts of India, Hindu-Muslim solidarity in this party was an impressive achievement. Although there were Muslim organizations, such as the district anjumans and the Bengal Provincial Muslim League, none of these seems to have developed a particularly strong, provincewide organization in the early 1920s.[83] The only party with such an organization was the Swarajist Party, which was able to dominate the Bengal Provincial Congress Committee and district Congress committees.

In their campaign to obstruct the reforms and frustrate the work of the Bengal Legislative Council, the Swarajists chose two major fronts on which to challenge the government and the ministers. The first and more important of these was the issue of the ministers' salaries and the second was the budget, especially grants for the transferred departments. A motion by the Muslim Swarajist Maulvi Mohammad Nurul Huq Chaudhury in March 1924 to reduce the ministers' salaries to Rs. 1 for the coming year was passed by 63 votes to 62, with the Nationalists joining the Swarajists.[84] There was a joyful demonstration in the galleries, which were packed by the Nationalists, when the vote was announced. The Swarajists, in effect, prevented any ministers from serving with majority support in the council from early 1924 to 1927, since ministers did not want to serve after such a rebuke from the council.

The two ministers whose salaries had been ignominiously reduced to Rs. 1 each, Messrs. Fazlul Huq and A. K. Ghuznavi, agreed to serve under these conditions until another vote could be taken in the chamber. Charges flew back and forth in the following months about attempts to buy votes and bribe members; *Forward* published a letter purportedly written by Fazlul Huq on the eve of the crucial August vote, in which Huq offered to buy a member's vote.[85] Huq denied on the floor of the council that he had written the letter and Das insisted that he could prove that the signature was Huq's.[86] The government of Bengal had had to get a court order and change the rules of the council in order to have a second vote taken during 1924 on the ministers' salaries. A number of non-Swarajists objected to this procedure and also to the fact that the ministers had continued to serve from March to August, even though a majority had clearly shown that they would not support these two ministers. Explaining this position, the Liberal P. C. Mitter said,

> In my opinion this vote is demanded for the retention of two Ministers who have flouted this House and have flouted public opinion by retaining their office against the constitution. As a constitutionalist I take a far more serious view of the situation than even Mr. C. R. Das. I believe with the fervour of a religious faith that the future of India lies in evolution, and if evolution has to be properly worked it must be on constitutional lines. I must therefore oppose anyone who goes against the constitution even should that person be my personal friend.[87]

Even before the vote was taken, Fazlul Huq, who had spent most of his time during the preceding months canvassing for votes rather than running the transferred departments in his charge,[88] expressed his disgust by saying, "As regards the point at issue I do not want to say anything except that so far as diarchy is concerned, I wish with all my heart that it comes to an end to-day." [89] When the division was made, it showed that the Swarajists and their supporters had 68 votes and the government and the ministers, 66. The following day the governor prorogued the council until further notice and it did not meet again until 1925.

Early the following year, Lytton and his government tried a different tack in trying to outmaneuver the Swarajists. They held meetings with the leaders of the different parties in the council and tried to separate the issue of having any ministers from the question of approving the salaries of two or three specific men as ministers. The government moved in the council to have ministers' salaries included in the budget and two Swarajist attempts to defeat this provision were not passed. Most of the Nationalist members abstained from voting, and the small Muslim group with Fazlul Huq supported the government.[90]

Lytton then chose Nawab Saiyid Nawab Ali Chaudhuri and Raja Manmatha Nath Roy Chaudhuri as the two ministers, and in March 1925, motions for the salaries of the two were put before the council. Kumar Shib Shekhareswar Ray, a landholder himself, said he had nothing against the two big zamindars who had been chosen as ministers, but that he, speaking for the Nationalists, had no confidence in the ministry.[91] Then, unexpectedly, Fazlul Huq rose to deliver a blow against the government. He said he was not a Swarajist, but he was against the two ministers and had found dyarchy to be an unworkable system. In the course of his speech, Huq said,

> I have been in office for eight months, not when there was nothing but a calm sea when any naviagator might navigate, but I have had to face the most stormy sea; and I challenge any one to contradict me if I lay a claim without any undue vanity that you could not find two men more devoted, or who could put up a more gallant fight in face of strenuous opposition in the Council, than Mr. Ghuznavi and my humble self. We tried and we have failed; and out of experience has grown this belief that so long as the present conditions last, you may have any number of Ministers you like, but nothing like constructive work will come out of that Ministry.[92]

In terms similarly melodramatic, Mr. Villiers, a European councillor, said that the fate of India was hanging in the balance and proceeded to attack Fazlul Huq:

> And all Mr. Fazl-ul Huq's verbiage still leaves me wondering what consituted the 30 pieces of silver which has induced Mr. Fazl-ul Huq to change his mind in the past 24 hours, and betray his conscience and his country.[93]

Speaking in spite of a serious illness, C. R. Das rose to defend Fazlul Huq and to summarize the Swarajists position. He argued that Huq's position was a logical one. Ministers without responsibility, power, and funds were a sham. If a workable system were offered with these three attributes, then the Swarajists would cooperate. Questioned about what would follow if the ministers were defeated and if more meaningful reforms not put forward, Das answered in his usual pragmatic way that he would have to see how circumstances developed.[94] On the vote that followed on March 25, the Swarajists and their supporters gathered 69 votes and the government and ministers, 63. The Nationalists, Fazlul Huq's group, and some unattached independents voted with the

Swarajists; and Huq's small group cast the deciding votes in a close division of the council. From March 26, 1925 until early 1927, the governor took over the transferred departments.

Each year there was an acrimonious debate about the budget, since the Swarajists and many other elected members felt that full control of finances was necessary before transferred subjects or responsible government could have any meaning at all. Das, speaking for the Swarajists, suggested that the government of Bengal float bonds for long-term loans which would be used to help the masses. This proposal does not seem to have been seriously considered, and it is not clear in what spirit Das offered it to the council and to the public.

Another subject that was often raised in debate and brought bitter controversy in its wake was what the Swarajists called political repression and the government called control of crime, anarchy, and potential revolution. In 1924 some important Swarajists, including two councillors, Anil Baran Ray and Satyendra Chandra Mitra, and the chief executive officer of the Calcutta Corporation, Subhas Bose, were arrested. Many other political workers were also arrested, often held indefinitely and without specific charges. They were supported by the Nationalists and by liberals who objected to the limitations on political activity. At the beginning of 1925, the governor called a session of the council to consider the Bengal Criminal Amendment Bill, under which the government would have increased powers to suppress "terrorist crime." Introducing the bill for the government, Sir Hugh Stephenson said, in part,

> In the Government statement the Serajgang resolution praising Gopi Nath Shaha is referred to as the starting point of a new impetus to the conspiracy; our information is that for one reason or another pressure was thereafter brought to bear on the leaders not altogether successfully, to postpone overt acts and strengthen their organisation and, a matter of very great importance, our information shows that one important section of the conspiracy were relieved of the necessity of obtaining funds for their operations and support of absconders through the old channels of dacoities and obtained their funds from elsewhere.[95]

The implication was scarcely hidden that the Swarajists were closely involved in the revolutionary plotting, and a rumor was about that

Calcutta Corporation funds or the private funds of important Swarajists were being turned over to the revolutionaries.

The Swarajists answered that 62 of their political workers had been
among those arrested. They denied any connection with terrorist
schemes. The council voted 66 to 56 not to allow the government to
introduce the bill, and the governor was forced to enact it under powers given him by the Government of India Act of 1919.[96] In December
1925, the council voted 55 to 35 to repeal the Bengal Criminal Amendment Act, but this was simply an act of defiance by the councillors
and did not change the position of the government.[97] By their persistent questioning of officials about the treatment of prisoners, the Swarajists probably served as a partial check on prison officials and relieved
their own frustrations against the government. The government raised
the specter of imminent revolution in the debates and mentioned the
plotting of the communist M. N. Roy.[98] Anil Baran Ray, who was then
still in the council, answered Stephenson:

> Sir, the Hon'ble Sir Hugh Stephenson has spoken to us about the Bol-
> shevik bogey, and the Indians, the majority of our people, I may assure
> you, are afraid of Bolshevism, but, Sir, Bolsheviks are far away from us
> and their menace is not real, but the menace of the police is very near
> us.[99]

During the same period in which the Swarajists were elected in considerable numbers to the Bengal Legislative Council, they also captured
control of the Calcutta Corporation. Under the reformed procedures of
the Calcutta Municipal Act of 1923, 48 councillors were elected by
general non-Muslim constituencies, 15 by Muslim constituencies, 10 by
commercial associations, 2 by the port commissioners, 5 by the councillors themselves, and 10 were appointed by the government of Bengal.[100] The Swarajists gained a majority in the corporation and then
elected C. R. Das Mayor and Subhas Bose Chief Executive Officer.
The Swarajists were roundly criticized by men like Surendranath Banerjea and by the government of Bengal for using the corporation for
their own political ends.[101] But the Bengali government's report on the
reforms mentioned some positive features of Swarajist control as well:

> The difficult period of transition from a wide official control to the
> complete control of elected representatives has passed without disaster,
> and there is no apparent demand for a return to the former constitu-

tion. Mr. Das and Mr. Sen Gupta both presided over meetings with fairness and dignity. Councillors in general show no lack of interest in civic affairs and give up much time to attendance at Corporation and committee meetings. There is great keenness on medical and public health work, and the zeal for free primary education is shown by the large number of new schools which have been started during the last few years.[102]

The government of Bengal retained control over any large financial transactions of the corporation, and the appointments of the chief executive officer and a number of other important corporation officers remained subject to government approval.[103] Although Banerjea was correct in noting the Swarajists' lack of municipal experience, they did show an eagerness to learn and to improve the quality of life in Calcutta during the early years of their participation in the corporation.[104]

THE LAST DAYS OF C. R. DAS

After the council's final defeat of the motion to grant salaries for two ministers, C. R. Das agreed to meet the Governor of Bengal secretly to see if some *modus vivendi* could be arranged.[105] This conference was followed by Das's public declaration a few days later of his antipathy to the use of political violence. He said, in part,

> I have made it clear and I do it once again that I am opposed on principle to political assassination and violence in any shape or form. It is absolutely abhorrent to me and to my party. I consider it an obstacle to our political progress. It is also opposed to our religious teachings. As a question of practical politics I feel certain that if violence is to take root in the political life of our country it will be the end of our dream of Swaraj for all time to come. . . .
>
> I have also made it clear and I again make it clear that I am equally opposed to and equally abhor any form of repression by the Government. Repression will never stop political assassination. It will only encourage and give life to it. . . . We are determined to secure Swaraj and the political equality of India on terms of equality and honourable partnership in the Empire.[106]

In retrospect, it seems remarkable that some European contemporaries of Das and some historians writing today have described this as an extraordinary and new statement of Das's views.[107] This manifesto, Das's reply to a statement of Secretary of State Lord Birkenhead, and his speech to the Faridpore meeting of the Bengal Provincial Conference in

May 1925 essentially restated the public position on the use of violence and repression that he had taken continuously since 1917. Lord Birkenhead, speaking in the House of Lords, welcomed Das's manifesto and called for Das to help eradicate the revolutionary movement. Das replied:

> Why is it that the Government makes no efforts in the way of removing those deep-rooted causes of political and economic discontent, without which mere repression can never succeed in curing the disease affecting the body politic in this country, and of which the activities sought to be suppressed by repressions are but symptoms? . . . The Government should recognize that, however mistaken the revolutionaries may be, however wrong and futile their methods, and however criminal and reprehensible their acts, the guiding principle of their lives is sacrifice for the attainment of political and economic freedom for their country. The moment they feel that at any rate the foundation of our freedom is laid by the Government I venture to assert that the revolutionary movement will be a thing of the past.[108]

Das's objections to the use of violence were based both on religious views and on his assessment of its impracticality. Although he doubtless had contact with them, he should probably be put in a group with Rabindranath Tagore and Bipin Pal and other Vaishnava-leaning Brahmos, who were fundamentally less sympathetic to the revolutionaries than the many Shaktas in Bengal.

At the same time, Das said to the Bengal Provincial Conference in May 1925 that "Repression is a process in the consolidation of arbitrary powers—and I condemn the violence of the Government—for repression is the most violent form of violence—just as I condemn violence as a method of winning political liberty." [109] His belief that violence would not bring swaraj and his view that the revolutionary movement was brought to life by government repression had been stated many times earlier in his career.

In his reply to Lord Birkenhead and again at Faridpore, Das spelled out the terms on which he was willing to cooperate with the government, reiterating his own views of many years and the Swarajist Party program. Das and the Swarajists would be willing to cooperate with the government if granted real responsibility and control of the operation of Bengal and the other governments in India. Going as far as he could toward conciliation at Faridpore, Das said, in part:

In the first place, the Government should divest itself of its wide dis-
cretionary powers of constraint, and follow it up by proclaiming a
general amnesty of all political prisoners. In the next place, the Government should guarantee to us the fullest recognition of our right to
the establishment of Swaraj within the commonwealth, in the near future and that in the meantime till Swaraj comes a sure and sufficient
foundation of such Swaraj should be laid at once. What is a sufficient
foundation is and must necessarily be a matter of negotiation and
settlement—settlement not only between the Government and the
people as a whole, but also between the different communities not excluding the European and Anglo-Indian communities, as I said in my
presidential address at Gaya.[110]

From a careful reading of Das's statements in 1925 and from Gandhi's
comments on them, it is clear that Das and Gandhi, at least, did not
think that Das was making a new departure. What Das wanted was a
change of heart and policy on the part of the government that he had
brought to a standstill through obstruction in the councils. Gandhi's
Noncooperation movement had turned to constructive work rather
than to civil disobedience and the revolutionaries had been brought to
a halt by the effective use of repression by the government of Bengal.
But the Swarajists had been effective in achieving their aims in the
Bengal and central legislatures; so Das felt that the government should
make concessions. If concessions along the lines he suggested were not
forthcoming, Das threatened that new national civil disobedience was
in the offing and that this might include nonpayment of taxes.[111]

After the Faridpore speech, Das, in failing health, went to Pabna
and then to Darjeeling for a rest. Before leaving Calcutta, he put his
own large home in trust for the nation and divested himself of many of
his worldly goods. Ravaged by fever, he lost some of his fire and ag-
gressiveness and became gentler and more concerned with religion in
his last month. While in Darjeeling, Das was visited by Gandhi, with
whom he had maintained warm relations even through political strife.
No concessions were announced by the government, but Das was
hopeful that some big step forward lay close ahead. On June 16, he
died quite suddenly.[112] His body was returned to Calcutta by train,
and about half a million mourners led by Gandhi accompanied it to
the cremation site. Gandhi spoke at the condolence meeting:

Deshbandhu was one of the greatest of men. I have had the privilege of knowing him intimately for the last six years and when I parted from him only a few days ago at Darjeeling, I said to a friend that the closer I came to him, the more I came to love him. I saw during my brief stay at Darjeeling that no thought but that of the welfare of India occupied him. He dreamed and thought and talked of freedom of India and of nothing else. . . . He was fearless. . . . His love for the young men of Bengal was boundless and even his adversaries admitted, there was no other man who could take his place in Bengal. His heart knew no difference between Hindus and Mussalmans and I should like to tell Englishmen, too, that he bore no ill-will to them.[113]

Many tributes were paid to Das, including one by the President of the Bengal Legislative Council, H. E. A. Cotton, who said of Das, "To me in his flowing robes he always conveyed the picture of a great Roman senator, and I used to sit and watch with admiration the consummate skill with which he led his party."[114] Many years later Chaudhri Muhammad Ali, a Muslim leader and prime minister of Pakistan in 1955, wrote in his memoirs, "C. R. Das's death in the summer of 1925 removed the one Hindu leader who inspired unreserved confidence among Muslims; never again was Hindu leadership to rise to his height."[115]

Many assessments have been made of the work and character of C. R. Das. Some, like the governor of Bengal, the Earl of Lytton, and the historian J. H. Broomfield, following and detailing Lytton's view, have pictured Das as a weak man, an opportunist, and as one led rather than leading.[116] Das's biographers have shown him marching from triumph to triumph and have underplayed the conflicts and hostilities on the Bengal and Indian political scene in the early 1920s. M. R. Jayakar, a fellow Swarajist, recalled Das as the boss of a political machine with autocratic tendencies and at the same time as an emotional man. Das was, he wrote, a magnificent talker, a lover of music and poetry, and a man with a thorough knowledge of Hindu culture.[117] As a mature man, he was a fascinating combination of the emotional and the practical, the Vaishnava and the worldly lawyer, the Swarajists' passionate ideologue and successful money-raiser.

There seems to be little doubt that the pacts and alliances that Das made from 1921 to 1925 were fragile creations based more on his personal tact and ability than on party strength or impersonal forces. Within three years, the All-India Swaraj Party, the Bengal Provincial Congress Committee, and communal relationships in Bengal were to be torn by divisions. No one can say that these conflicts would not have arisen in any case; but, equally, one cannot say that Das would not have continued to contain them had he lived and regained his health.

Even before his death, the Bengal government and a Muslim executive councillor were trying to disrupt communal harmony on which Swarajist power rested. Broomfield has described this policy:

> From 1924 to 1926 the Government of Bengal used its powers to en-sure that there was no such [i.e., communal] compromise in its prov-ince. Sir Abdur Rahim, a communalist to the core, called the pace, and he was aided and abetted by the British officials. It was a short-sighted and irresponsible policy that led Bengal into grave trouble in 1926.[118]

Against this rising tide and alliance of Muslim officials and the govern-ment of Bengal, it is possible that the efforts of any man or party would have failed. Nonetheless, Das had the one essential element that no other Hindu in Bengal ever fully gained: the trust of many Muslims in Bengal and throughout India. He encountered numerous difficulties from Hindus more narrow-minded than himself, but with both Hindu and Muslim support, Das might have helped prevent the rapid deterio-ration of communal ties.

The European Association of Calcutta in 1924 argued that the Swa-rajists and leaders like Das represented a narrow social and political oli-garchy. John Langford James, Secretary of the European Association, issued a statement in June 1924, which read in part:

> The Reforms Scheme is a political experiment. . . . The first and most obvious criticism is that any form of democracy naturally presupposes that there should be an electorate of the people. The electorate for the Provincial Councils is 2% of the population; for the National Assem-bly 35%. The people whom the Councils and Assembly represent are an infinitesimal part of the people, who alone could demand democ-racy; they do not in any sense represent the people; they are a small intelligentsia whose interests are in many respects opposed to those of the vast masses of agriculturalists and labourers who form the main bulk of the peoples of this country. The obvious goal of this intelli-gentsia is an indigenous oligarchy to replace what they delight to call the bureaucracy. . . . there is no such thing as an Indian Nation. . . .

The Swarajist oligarchy have so far succeeded in their attempts, but can Europeans in this country possibly sit idle and permit these attempts to go unchallenged? [119]

Mr. James was continuing an old argument of officials and nonofficial Europeans who insisted that the Indians were only motivated by self-interest and sought to gain power for their own benefit. A further corollary of their argument was that the foreigners in India understood and wanted the good of all and should therefore speak for the Indians and make political decisions. This is the root from which Broomfield has developed his thesis. The heroes in such a treatment are the British officials and liberal and loyalist Indians willing to work within the British-dominated system and who do not push militantly for more far-reaching goals or speedier access to these goals. It is an historical argument with a distinctive ideological slant.

A serious question is that of the political line adopted by the Swarajists. Their successful prevention of the working of dyarchy may have been good short-term tactics, but it does not seem based upon any coherent principles other than the goal of political freedom for India. With Das's death, a simmering factionalism broke out in more virulent form. The party was split within two years into the Responsivists and the noncooperative groups. There was no logical way of slowly escalating tactics within the councils. Work within the councils had to be carefully coordinated with mass pressure outside the councils, but such activity, suggested by Das in his Faridpore speech, was not forthcoming.

By the period described in this chapter, 1917 to 1925, the Bengali nationalists had become only one regional group among many in the national movement. They had lost their early preeminence, particularly since the coming of Gandhi. Some articulate Bengalis found this new position difficult, and the problem of coping with a changed position relative to other regions and to leaders from other regions may have contributed to the asperity in many critiques of Gandhi, including those of Bipin Pal, Tagore, and the Marxist M. N. Roy. These men and the Swarajists in Bengal were more sympathetic, on the whole, to the personal and political drives behind revolutionary activity. Few could equal Gandhi in his principled adherence to nonviolence. A Bengali Gandhian such as Nripendra Chandra Banerji and the Vaishnava C. R. Das were closer physically and culturally than Gandhi to the revolutionaries in Bengal and could never condemn them without reservation. This was one issue which divided Gandhi and many Bengalis.

A second issue might be called moral and aesthetic. Bengali leaders and writers following Tagore had a richer and more varied view of freedom and the good life than they believed Gandhi and rigid Gandhians had. The ideals Gandhi set, although in some ways appealing, were in many ways frightening. Many Bengalis were more sensitive to literature, art, and other cultural activity than Gandhi. Tagore, doubtless speaking for others then and since, did not like the whiteness or the tyrannical strand in Gandhism. As Tagore wrote, "The white colour [that is, of the Sabarmati Ashram] is a colour of intolerance. Gandhi has adopted it, it will have its consequences." [120]

EIGHT
Subhas Bose and Nationalist Politics, 1925–1938

ᏧᏫᏣᏓᏍᏯᏫᏍᏯ The division between the Swarajists and the Gandhian No-Changers in the 1920s was succeeded by the tensions between the right and left wings of the Congress during the 1930s. The broad rubrics of left and right covered several conflicting groups, and the two wings would best be described as flexible alliances. The left, which always remained fragmented, was composed of the Congress Socialists, who crystallized into a formal group in 1934; the communists, who had to follow the turns and twists of the Third Communist International (Comintern); the followers of M. N. Roy (Royists); and a number of unattached socialist-inclined leaders, such as Jawaharlal Nehru and Subhas Bose. There were also mass organizations, principally labor unions and Kisan Sabhas, or peasant leagues, that often had political leaders at their head. Spurred by worsening economic conditions, Congress Socialists, communists, Gandhians, and others entered the urban and rural labor field, beginning a competition for support which continues today.[1]

Socialist and communist ideas had a strong and early impact on political workers in Bengal, and numerous leftist groups concentrated their organizing efforts in Calcutta and other industrial centers. Some small leftist groups started in the 1920s, and by the mid-1930s there was a host of small parties and secret coteries at work in Bengal. The attraction of socialist ideas was felt by congressmen and ex-revolutionaries who tried to formulate an ideology combining leftist ideas and nationalism.[2]

In the Bengal Congress, a struggle for supremacy ensued after the death of C. R. Das. A group headed by Subhas and Sarat Bose gained an uneasy and unstable control in the late 1920s. Gradually, however, some of Das's other recruits began to ally themselves with Gandhi and the High Command. To simplify this account, all those Bengali leaders who established close ties with Gandhi and the central Congress leadership during the period will be called Bengal's Gandhians, although the term has often been reserved for the narrower group who were wholly devoted to Gandhi's constructive program and ideology. The broader definition thus includes allies like Dr. B. C. Roy, J. M. Sen Gupta, and Nalini Ranjan Sarker, as well as the orthodox Gandhians like P. C. Ghosh, Suresh Banerjee, and Nripendra Chandra Banerji.[3]

THE EARLY CAREER OF SUBHAS CHANDRA BOSE

One of the main actors in all the different dramas of Bengal and Congress politics through these years was Subhas Chandra Bose. He was a convert to socialist ideas and a hero of students and aspiring leftists; his group became the major faction in Bengali politics to resist Gandhian control of the regional Congress organization. Subhas Bose became a representative of Bengal and of the left in a conflict within the Congress which ended in defeat for the left and victory for the Gandhian High Command at the end of the 1930s.

Although he never gained Muslim support, as had his mentor, C. R. Das, Bose was disturbed by the growing communal divisions, and once the Government of India Act of 1935 went into operation his group sought an alliance with Fazlul Huq's party. Such an arrangement was finally worked out in the early 1940s by Bose's elder brother Sarat Bose and other party leaders. The Progressive Coalition formed the ministry of Bengal from late 1941 to mid-1943 and represented one effort toward Hindu-Muslim cooperation.

Finally, Bose was the *bête noire* of the European officials in the government of Bengal (and the government of India as well). It was thought that Bose was in league with revolutionaries. Officials believed, perhaps correctly, that a leader without scruples about the use of violence who had mass and revolutionary support was much more dangerous than Gandhi or a Gandhian. So Bose was under constant surveillance, and officials were happier when he was not actively on the scene.[4]

Before descending into the maelstrom of factional strife and party politics in the period from C. R. Das's death to 1940, I propose to sketch the early career of the times' foremost protagonist. A few significant themes of Bose's political and psychological life are these:

1. Identification with the young and with youth movements.
2. A tendency to rebel against many kinds of authorities, while also displaying a desire for authority, discipline, and order. Bose continued to try to be both a "good boy" and chief "mischief maker"—two important elements in his youthful self-imagery.[5]
3. Frequent use of the imagery of self-immolation common in Indian religion and nationalism, although he also expressed a desire to "remain in history." [6]
4. A strong identification with both Bengali and familial traditions in religion, social organization, and politics, combined with modern Western ideas about science, technology, and organization.
5. Occasional expression of a desire for a religious withdrawal but more frequent expression of a need for activism and selfless work in the world. In prison, inactivity led to illness, and upon release and recovery he became hyperactive.
6. Throughout his youth and early manhood, a desire for a guru to show him the way, first in religion and then in politics. He had difficulty moving from discipleship to leadership after the death of C. R. Das, his chosen guru.
7. From his early manhood, use of the language of struggle and battle, and considerable interest in the military. This theme continued into his later life when he became General-Officer-Commanding of the Calcutta Congress in 1928 and still later commanding general of the Indian National Army during World War II.

Subhas Chandra Bose was born in 1897, the ninth child and sixth son of Janakinath and Probhabati Bose. He was descended from two fairly prominent Kayastha families, on his mother's side the Hatkhola Dattas and on his father's side the Boses of Mahinagar.[7] During his adult years, Bose expressed pride in being a gentleman.[8] He demanded the privileges due to him by virtue of his "rank and station in life" while in prison,[9] and together with his older brother Sarat wanted to help bring improvements to the family's ancestral village of Kodalia near Calcutta.[10] Subhas also wanted to extend the Kayastha marriage circle in order to make their subcaste less provincial.[11] These small incidents, taken with Bose's prominent display of his family genealogies in an autobiography written when he was nearly forty, all point to the closeness he felt to his family and caste traditions and his sense of his own high status in Bengali society.

During Subhas Bose's early years, his family resided in Cuttack in the present state of Orissa. His father was a prominent lawyer and participated in civic affairs. Young Subhas attended a missionary school where he learned English well, and then joined the Ravenshaw Collegiate School in 1909.[12] He was always an excellent student and stood near or at the top of his class throughout his educational career.

Equally important for his development was the education, principally religious, that he obtained outside of school. The two crucial religious educators in Subhas' early life seem to have been his mother, a strict and devoted Shakta, and Beni Madhab Das, a teacher at the Ravenshaw Collegiate School.[13] Subhas' letters to his mother in these years concerned devotion to female dieties, usually Durga or Kali, and his growing appreciation of the lives of Ramakrishna and Vivekananda. Although Beni Madhab Das was a Brahmo, he served as a general instructor for Subhas in Hinduism and directed him to the Upanishads and the Epics.[14]

In these adolescent years in Cuttack, Subhas learned about Shaktism, Vaishnavism, a little about the Tantras, and came to believe in the efficacy and importance of prayer and the way of devotion. He wrote to his mother that he wanted wisdom and character more than bookish knowledge. Subhas began to meditate and to practice yoga and continued these activities throughout his life, especially when he was in prison.[15] At the same time Subhas also picked up the activist side of Vivekananda's teaching and the idea of expressing religious feelings through service to the poor, the sick, and the illiterate. He worked with cholera-stricken villagers and with untouchables, and taught a night class for adults and children while still in his teens.[16]

After standing second in the matriculation examination for Calcutta University in 1913, Subhas Bose entered Presidency College. His family's base was still in Cuttack, but they later purchased a house in Calcutta, and the family gradually came to be identified with Calcutta rather than with Cuttack.[17] At Presidency College, Bose studied philosophy, paying little attention to his studies and focusing most of his energy on his religious interests.[18] During his first year at college, Bose and a friend left on a pilgrimage to find a guru in North India. Without leaving word where they were going, they traveled to Hrishikesh, Hardwar, Brindaban, Banaras and Gaya, but never found the spiritual teacher they sought.[19] The journey may be seen as a religious quest and also as an expression of feelings of rebellion against his parents. He had come to feel "more at home when away from home," [20] and his long trip to North India was a signal to his parents that he wished to travel on his own without abiding by their authority, although at the same time he wished to be a good boy and to do well by the standards of accomplishment of his day.

While at Presidency College, Subhas made one close friendship that was to endure throughout his life. This was with Dilip Kumar Roy, a man who has put the biographers of Subhas Bose in his debt by writing an insightful memoir, *The Subhash I Knew*. Describing the Subhas Bose of Presidency College days, Dilip recalled his energy, laughter, his capacity for leadership without condescension, and his aristocratic generosity. Dilip also mentions that Subhas was stiff with women and naïve about sex until later in life.[21] That Subhas was so naïve seems open to question, but it does seem clear that he was awkward with women and troubled by his sexual desires. In order to deal with these desires, Subhas tried to follow the course suggested by Ramakrishna. One was to think of every woman as one's mother and not as a sexually desirable or attractive creature.[22] This led Bose to the idealization of women, to the identification of the ordinary women in his life with the Mother Goddess, and to an arduous effort to suppress all sexual desires. Since Bankim Chandra Chatterjee had identified the Mother Goddess with the nation, young men like Subhas Bose so identified their own mother or the mother figures in their lives.[23] Two further points about Subhas's relations with women may be added here. First, no direct statement of his indicates that he was or determined to be a brahmacharya (in student stage of life or celibate). Although some of his followers claimed that he privately vowed not to marry until India was free, it appears that these supporters imagined this declaration as implicit in the fact that Subhas did not marry while in India. The transformation of Subhas Bose into a mystic, a sadhu, and a brahmacharya seems part of the effort by some of his followers and friends to make him over into even more of a religious man than he actually was.[24] In an interview in early 1965, the widow of C. R. Das, Basanti Devi, who had been close to Subhas from 1921, said that Subhas had never indicated that he would not marry. She and her husband had teased Subhas about getting married during the Noncooperation period. It is more likely that Subhas simply concentrated all his energies on national work and did not think to get married.[25] His dependence on his family for economic support, even when a grown man, may also have had something to do with his single state. Second, all the prominent friendships he formed with women until he was at least into his middle thirties were with older, married women, including Mrs. Dharmavir, Mrs. Naomi Vetter, and Mrs. Kitty Kurti.[26] Bose finally did marry Miss Emilie Schenkl when he was in his forties. She had assisted him in the preparaton of several of his books in the 1930s and they were married when he returned to Europe during the Second World War.

A major event in the life of Subhas Bose and one which brought him considerable attention in Bengal took place while he was a student at Presidency College in 1916. This was the Oaten Affair. A number of students at the college beat up a professor, E. F. Oaten, who it is alleged, had insulted India and "manhandled" Indian students at Presidency College.[27] It has never been clear whether Bose was one of those who actually hit Oaten or whether he "masterminded" the attack, as some have alleged.[28] In his autobiography, Bose says that he was an eyewitness.[29] Whatever Bose's actual role in the affair, he openly admitted his participation. After testimony in the case was heard, it was decided, inter alia, that Bose was to be expelled from Presidency College. The punishment was harsher than Bose had expected. He had written to his friend Hemanta Sarkar before the hearings that, "I am well-known as a 'good student' . . . the vast majority of the public feel that I am innocent, Ashu Babu knows of me personally and the evidence of the orderly against me is much too weak. So, there is every possibility of my being found innocent and let off." [30] Long after the event, Bose's friend Dilip Roy wrote that the affair made Bose a hero and a marked man.[31] Writing later, Bose gave the incident a crucial significance in his own development:

Little did I then realise the inner significance of the tragic events of
1916. My Principal had expelled me, but he had made my future career. I had established a precedent for myself from which I could not
easily depart in future. I had stood up with courage and composure in
a crisis and fulfilled my duty. I had developed self-confidence as well as
initiative, which was to stand me in good stead in future. I had a fore-
taste of leadership—though in a very restricted sphere—and of the
martyrdom that it involves. In short, I had acquired character and
could face the future with equanimity.[32]

Although it may well be that this was the most important event in
Bose's late adolescence, it does appear that writing twenty years after
the event, he was playing down the fears he probably had about his future career and was making a smoother connection with his future nationalist career than existed. This was another instance in which one
who had been "a good student" thought that this reputation would
make the punishment for his "mischief" lighter. In contrast to his
sneaking away in search of a guru, this rebellion had an element of nationalism in it. It was directed against one who was felt to be a cold,
harsh representative of the British educational system in India. A year
later, Bose, with the assistance of Sir Asutosh Mookerjee, was permitted to join Scottish Church College to finish his college education.[33]
Two elements of later rebellions are foreshadowed here. Bose wanted
to achieve within the system and yet to rebel against it. The ambivalence he had about the educational system of British India he later
showed toward Western culture in general, the ICS, and the Congress.

During 1917 to 1919, Subhas Bose attended Scottish Church College
and gained his B.A. with honors in philosophy, standing second in the
first class. He then joined the postgraduate class, reading psychology.[34]
At this time, Subhas and some other students petitioned the government to obtain a University Military Training Corps.[35] Although he
said he had unfortunately neglected sports as a youth, Bose eagerly
sought military training both in India and later when he was at Cambridge.[36] This marks a lifelong fascination with the military and the
theme of strength and weakness. Bose accepted the British assessment of
the physically weak condition of Indians and Bengalis, but he insisted
that it was due completely to lack of proper training. Thus he seized
the opportunity for military training and later called upon others to do
likewise. Bose believed that military and technological skills and proper
methods of organization were the most important lessons that Indians

could learn from Europeans.[37] The worship of the goddess Kali as power and his admiration for the military might of India's European conquerors seemed to flow together into a single channel. Although he believed that Indians had a spiritual message for humanity and had gone further than Europeans in developing their inner resources, he was concerned about meeting Westerners on their own terms. Bose did not believe, like Gandhi, that inner strength should be emphasized almost to the exclusion of the physical capabilities of man. His quest for military training and his aim to meet the British equally in a military context started with this rudimentary course during his World War I student days.

Hardly had Bose settled into his postgraduate studies when his father urged him to go to England and prepare for the Indian Civil Service examination. He expressed doubts about going to England in a letter to Hemanta Sarkar:

> I am facing a most serious problem. Yesterday the family made an offer to send me to England. . . . My primary desire is to obtain a university degree in England; otherwise I cannot make headway in the educational line. If I now refuse to study for the Civil Service, the offer to send me to England will be put into cold storage for the time being (and for all time). . . . On the other hand, a great danger will arise if I manage to pass the Civil Service examination. That will mean giving up my goal in life.[38]

He decided to take his family's offer and he sailed for England to prepare for the examination at Cambridge, where he studied history and politics, became a leader of the Bengali students in England, and learned about English life and people at first hand.[39] Some seventeen years later, Bose wrote:

> During the six terms that I was in Cambridge the relations between British and Indian students were on the whole quite cordial, but in few cases did they ripen into real friendship. I say this not from my personal experience alone but from general observation as well. . . . The war undoubtedly had its effect. One could detect in the average Britisher a feeling of superiority beneath a veneer of bon-homie which was not agreeable to others. On our side, after the post-war events in India and particularly the tragedy at Amritsar, we could not but be sensitive (perhaps ultra-sensitive) with regard to our self-respect and national honour. . . . We were politically more conscious and more sensitive than we had been before.[40]

Here Bose touches upon a major social and psychological problem for himself and for many other Indians who lived under British rule, the question of inferiority and superiority. Dilip Roy has written that Bose had malevolent feelings toward the British when in college.

How Subhash used to curve his firm lips in strong contempt whenever he inflected the word *sahib* in a tone in which one pronounces vermin. And youth is a prolific season when seeds of contempt and rancour once sown multiply like mushrooms.[41]

And again in a letter of Bose's from Cambridge to Hemanta Sarkar in 1919:

Whether one wills it or not, the climate of this country makes people energetic. The activity you see here is most heartening. Everyman is conscious of the value of time and there is a method in all that goes on. Nothing makes me happier than to be served by the whites and to watch them clean my shoes. Students here have a status—and the way the professors treat them is different. One can see here how man should treat his fellow man. They have many faults—but in many matters you have to respect them for their virtues.[42]

Bose appears to have had a deep-seated ambivalence toward the British, compounded of admiration, envy, and hatred. Although Bose did not make any close English friends, he did maintain respect for certain Englishmen as individuals. He disliked the English people as a general category for what he believed that they were doing and had done to Indians, but he was sensitive enough to appreciate individuals for themselves when circumstances permitted. Bose studied hard in England and spent a good deal of time with other Indians, including Dilip Roy and Mr. and Mrs. Dharmavir. The Indians in England, like the British in India, made little communities among themselves which served as a shield against a potentially hostile native population.

Bose's high need for achievement, particularly by British standards, led him to work hard for the ICS examination, and he finished fourth.[43] Then, after a good deal of self-searching and exchange of letters with his family and with C. R. Das, he decided to resign from the ICS and take up "national service," that is, to join the national movement in some suitable capacity.[44] He had wanted to gain respect from the British by excelling in an examination prescribed by them for their elite service in India, but he then expressed his personal and nationalist an-

tipathy to them by resigning. Following the paradigm suggested before, Bose was again the good student and the rebel.

Bose corresponded about his desire to resign with his older brother
Sarat, rather than writing directly to his father. He had a warm relationship with Sarat and often used the latter as a buffer in dealing with
his parents. Sarat wanted him to take up the ICS career for which he
had qualified, but Subhas was a strong-willed young man and he chose
to chart his own course.[45] The ICS decision was a rebellion both
against the British and against his own parents.

In Bose's last year in Cambridge, C. R. Das became a central figure
in his life. Das had become the leader in the national movement in Bengal in the years when Bose was finishing college and heading for England. In 1921, Das had given up his legal practice, and this sacrifice
served as a model for Bose.

> If C. R. Das at his age can give up everything and face the uncertain-
> ties of life—I am sure a young man like myself, who has no worldly
> cares to trouble him, is much more capable of doing so. If I give up
> the service, I shall not be in want of work to keep my hands full.
> Teaching, social service, cooperative credit work, journalism, village
> organization work, these are so many things to keep thousands of ener-
> getic young men busy. Personally, I should like teaching and journal-
> ism at present. The National College and the new paper Swaraj will af-
> ford plenty of scope for my activity. . . . A life of sacrifice to start
> with, plain living and high thinking, whole-hearted devotion to the
> country's cause—all these are highly enchanting to my imagination
> and inclination. Further, the very principle of serving under an alien
> bureaucracy is intensely repugnant to me. The path of Arabindo
> Ghosh is to me more noble, more inspiring, more lofty, more unselfish,
> though more thorny than the path of Ramesh Dutt.[46]

From Cambridge, Bose wrote two letters to C. R. Das asking the latter
if he had a place for him in the national movement. These letters contain numerous suggestions by Bose for improving and expanding nationalist activities. Although we do not have the answer that Das sent,
Bose does mention in a later letter to his parents that Das had described
the possibilities of a nationalist career.[47]

Rejecting the advice of his parents, Bose returned to India later in
1921. En route he stopped off in Bombay to see Mahatma Gandhi. He
later wrote that he found the Mahatma's program and strategy fuzzy,[48]

but this evaluation was probably the fruit of later reflection. Upon returning to Calcutta, Bose met with Das and was shortly given a number of fairly important assignments in the Noncooperation campaign in Bengal, particularly for one so young. Bose worked in the National Education College, and he helped to organize the hartals against the Prince of Wales' visit. A little more than two years later he became an advisory editor of *Forward* and chief executive officer of the Calcutta Corporation.[49]

More significant than the actual assignments was the fact that Bose felt that he had found in Das the guru he had been searching for. Bose was moved by the warmth, charm, religious fervor, and nationalist passion of Das and took Das as his model of a leader when he himself was called upon to lead. Bose wrote that Das was tied to the masses of Indians by bonds of love and devoted himself to them as had Swami Vivekananda.[50] He also grew close to Basanti Devi, Das's wife, and some have suggested that he was closer to her at this period of his life than to his own mother. Bose called Das his guru throughout his life even though Das died only five years after the relationship began, showing how complete and intense this tie of guru to pupil or leader to follower can be. In effect, Das was Bose's teacher, leader, and guide. Mr. and Mrs. Das together became to a certain extent his chosen substitute parents.[51] Bose remained in intimate touch with his real family and was especially close to Sarat throughout his life, but he had only one guru.

For three years after leaving Cambridge, Bose threw himself wholeheartedly into "national service." He received much praise for his work on the hartal, in directing flood relief in northern Bengal in 1922, and in the Calcutta Corporation.[52] He had always expressed some admiration for the revolutionaries of Bengal, and rumors passed about that he was in league with them. The government of Bengal arrested him along with many others suspected of collusion with the revolutionaries at the end of 1923, basing its evidence on that of its informers within the movement.[53] Bose spent the next three years in prison, most of it under arduous physical conditions in Mandalay Jail. To deal with what they thought to be a severe threat to their rule, the governments of India and Bengal put into effect what the nationalists called "lawless laws." These were laws and regulations made, the government said, to deal with abnormal conditions.[54] Bose and all the others held under these regulations never knew when or if they would be released, and their attempts to have the charges specified were usually futile.

The prison experience of those thousands of Indian nationalists who often willingly and sometimes unwillingly went to jail from the late nineteenth century until independence has not been systematically analyzed. Men like Subhas Bose, Jawaharlal Nehru, Barindra Kumar Ghose, Mahatma Gandhi, and many others spent a good part of their lives in prison. The experience of incarceration offered opportunities for degeneration, boredom, growth, reflection, and scholarship. It seems possible to examine the functions and dysfunctions of imprisonment for the individuals and groups held during the nationalist movement. Some tried to continue their work and to further political activity outside prison. Others used the opportunity to develop and reinforce political contacts and to recruit new members, particularly to a different ideological persuasion. Many took the period of confinement as a time for thought, writing, research, and meditation. A few studied prison conditions and the life and motivations of the ordinary, nonpolitical prisoners. The prison experience of Subhas Bose should be examined with these possibilities in mind.

Bose's health usually deteriorated during periods of captivity, although he usually recovered upon release. But even with the loss of weight and disturbing symptoms that accompanied imprisonment, Bose tried to read, write, and continue his political work. In Mandalay Jail he worked to continue and complete what he described as his "sadly neglected" education.[55] Surendra Mohan Ghose, imprisoned along with Bose in Burma, said that Bose concentrated especially on Indian history and philosophy.[56] Bose felt his "colossal ignorance of Bengali literature." [57] He wrote home for books on Indian philosophy, Tantric texts in particular, and for works of Bengali and European literature. At the same time, Subhas wrote a number of essays, took notes on his reading, sketched plans for longer pieces on nationalism, prison life, and municipal problems.[58]

Among the topics Bose reflected upon in prison was his view of the Bengalis, although a number of comments that we consider here were made earlier or later than his imprisonment. Bose's view on Bengal, her past, present, and future, are intermingled with perceptions about India as a whole. But in the 1920s, particularly, he showed a special interest in Bengal. Writing about Bengal before the British conquest, Bose described the glories of ancient Gaur and of the cultural center at Navadvipa. Bengal was a region in which several cultural traditions mingled, including Vedic culture, Tantrism, Vaishnavism, and Nyaya logic. Bengal had created a unique synthesis, he believed, but he was aware of the ravages and vagaries of time. Bose also mentioned the natural beauty of Bengal and the physical vigor of its inhabitants in past ages. Bengali literature in the past had been a common bond connecting high castes and low.[59]

Although he is nowhere specific on the matter, it appears that he believed the decline of Bengal from its ancient heights had begun with the coming of the British. In one of his fragmentary writings of 1925, he said,

> Hundred and fifty years ago it was the Bengalees who betrayed the country to their foreign enemies. The Bengalees of the twentieth century certainly owe it to themselves to atone for that great sin. It will be the duty of Bengal's men and women to revive the lost glory of India. How best to accomplish that end is Bengal's greatest problem. . . . Bengal may be lagging behind in other spheres of life but I am firmly convinced that in the fight for Swaraj she goes far ahead of others. . . . Although Mahatma Gandhi, who is the sponsor of the national movement, happens to be a non-Bengalee, still no other province can claim national activities on such a tremendous scale as Bengal.[60]

With the entry of the British into India, the Bengalis had committed the grievous sin of collaboration and had further declined into ridiculousness and weakness. Accepting the British stereotype of the babu, Bose berated his fellow Bengalis for becoming physically weak, for lapsing into pettiness, and for tearing selfishly at each other rather than uniting and rebuilding.[61] Even Bengali literature, commented Bose after reading some works of Dinesh Chandra Sen on modern Bengali writing, had become enmeshed in "Feringi" or Anglicized Bengali:

> Present-day Bengali is somewhat Feringi Bengali . . . and because of this factor this literature has remained confined within the confines of a few English-educated Bengalis. Among the common people this literature has not been widely circulated. . . . The literature seems to be unreal; it has not been able to establish an intimate relationship with

the heart of the society. . . . This kind of intimate relationship . . .
should be reestablished. Stories of happiness and miseries in society,
and of ambitions and ideals—even the merits and demerits of its accepted customs—should again be reflected in its literature. And only
then will the literature become a living one. From this kind of literature, everybody irrespective of caste will derive aesthetic pleasure
and delight . . . themes of the modern age should be circulated among
the common people.[62]

The revival of a purer Bengali literature and its spread to a wider circle of readers was part of the program which Bose laid out for Bengali
readers and listeners.

Some of his proposals for the revitalization of Bengal were addressed
to students and contained an assessment of contemporary student life.
Bose seemed especially concerned to illustrate the shortcomings of the
so-called good boy, by which he meant those who only did well in ex-
aminations, won scholarships and medals, and then obtained high positions on the basis of their academic achievements. Such students
should, he said, "be called misguided, worthless, invalids." [63] He continued,

> Those who are considered good boys in the society are in fact nothing
> but eunuchs. Neither in this world nor in any other has any great
> work been achieved or will any great work be done by these people.
> These boys somehow or other reduce their burden of sin and they fol-
> low the track of the most orthodox people like a herd of sheep.
> Throughout their most prosaic life there is no taste of anything new
> or novel, there is no outburst of full-hearted laughter, there is no in-
> spired self-sacrifice . . . the Bengali will never become manly unless
> the so-called good boys are totally uprooted . . . and unless a new race
> is born in India. One has to love new things, one has to grow mad for
> the unknown, one has to express himself in the free wind and under
> the open sky by breaking through all the barriers of life and by razing
> them to the ground.[64]

In opposition he set up a countermodel of the robust, socially concerned, adventurous young man, giving as inspiring examples one P. R.
De, who had walked alone through the hills from Calcutta to Rangoon
on foot, Lord Robert Clive, Sir Francis Drake, Shivaji, and Tennyson's
Ulysses. "We have altogether given up the practice of *lathi* play and
gymnastics in fear of the police or for the sake of gentility." [65] Perhaps

in reaction to his own unathletic youth and to the continued derision by the British of the effete Bengalis, Bose stressed the physical and masculine side of human development. At an earlier time in his life, he had written to his mother that the strength to change Bengal was in its mothers.[66] After the death of C. R. Das, Bose wrote to Das's widow that she, as a kind of fulfillment of the female power energizing the world, would have to lead the Bengalis.[67] But in most of his writing and speaking, Bose laid his emphasis on the tough, determined, courageous male ideal. He was, in effect, accepting the terms for cultural and individual achievement laid down by the Bengalis' British tormentors.

Moreover, for all his disparagement of the good-boy mentality prevailing in Bengal and with his sense of the divisions among Bengalis themselves, he still thought of Bengal as the premier province in India. He realized that Gandhi and his followers were leading the national movement, but he still gave Bengal first place in the struggle for swaraj. He also maintained, in answer to charges that he was a Bolshevik agent, that his interests and work were completely in Bengal. An official in the Home Department acknowledged that "we did not regard him as an international anarchist, but as interested mainly if not entirely in the revolutionary national movement in India." [68] During the earlier part of his political career and up to the time he served as Congress president in 1938, Bose rarely roamed to other parts of India except for Congress meetings and an occasional speech. He tried to develop a political base and build the Congress political organization within his own region. He was perhaps more concerned with Bengal's needs and fate than with those of India.

While in prison during this period, Bose put down some thoughts on religion. He wrote a rough draft of an essay entitled the "Failure of Buddhism" and compared Christianity, Vaishnavism, and Islam. Although his claim that he was exposed to a variety of religions in his youth, including Christianity, many forms of Hinduism, and Islam,[69] may have been historically accurate, his religious feelings seem to have been aroused primarily by the predominant sects of Hindus found in Bengal, the Vaishnavas and the Shaktas; and his links to other faiths were through their similarities to Hinduism. Thus Christianity was a devotional faith stressing the principle of love, as did Vaishnavism.

Bose was struck by the fact that believers in Christianity and Islam had built empires and converted large numbers to their faiths, and he devised a plan for spreading Hinduism to Africa as one part of making India a great nation once again.[70] Religion and politics, for Bose, were often closely related, especially through devotional and patriotic songs, which he wrote down in his prison notebooks. These included songs and poems of Rabindranath Tagore, D. L. Roy, Kazi Nazrul Islam, and older religious lyrics both Vaishnava and Shakta.[71] These songs as sung, transcribed, and reflected upon represent the quiet, meditative side of his personality.[72]

In most of his writings and even in the fragment from his prison notebooks on good-boy types, Subhas Bose obviously preferred an activist philosophy, religion, and view of the world. He criticized those who "ran away from the world" and was harsh on Aurobindo Ghose and his retreat, although he admired Ghose greatly as a political leader.[73] He was upset by the decision of Anil Baran Ray, a Bengali Congress leader, to follow Aurobindo to Pondicherry and tried to get Ray to return.[74] He wrote that he himself had run away as a youth, but he would never run away again. Writing to Dilip Roy in 1925, Bose commented:

> the active side of a man might get atrophied if he remained cut off for too long from the tides of life and society. This need not, indeed, apply to a handful of authentic seekers of uncommon genius, but the common run, the majority, ought, I think, to take to action in a spirit of service as the main plank of their sadhana. For a variety of reasons our nation has been sliding pauselessly down to the zero line in the sphere of action; so what we badly need today is a double dose of the activist serum, rajas.[75]

For a man used to activity and advocating energetic and goal-directed work, the long years in prison must have been terribly galling. There were few ways in which he could express his passion for action while still imprisoned. One method was to keep in touch with his political and social concerns through letters. He did this as best he could through his brother Sarat. Bose gave opinions and advice on political questions and municipal affairs within the limitations imposed by the government censor who read all his letters. After some deliberation and urging from outside, Bose, while still imprisoned, stood for election to the Bengal Legislative Council in 1926 from a North Calcutta non-Muhammadan consituency and was elected.[76] He led a hunger strike in Mandalay Jail during 1926 directed toward obtaining greater allowances from the prison officials for the conduct of religious activities inside the prison.[77]

The event which struck Bose the hardest while he was imprisoned was the death of C. R. Das in 1925. Bose was heartbroken personally at losing his leader and guru whom he had found only after long years of searching. And he felt that the consequences for Bengal and for India would be incalculably high. In Mandalay Jail, Bose sat down and composed a long tribute to his mentor and wrote letters to Das's widow, Basanti Devi, asking her to take up the political mantle of her fallen husband.[78] He described her as a goddess and the mother of Bengal. Even after she had declined the call to political leadership, Bose, shortly after leaving prison, asked her,

> Please give some thought to the duties and tasks awaiting me. When I see you, my first question will be about this. I hope you know how highly I value your opinion. I do not wish to take up any work now without consulting you.[79]

This letter has overtones connecting it to the letters to C. R. Das from Cambridge in 1921 when Bose asked Das to assign him some work in the national movement. Bose found it hard to make the transition to leadership, even though he felt especially chosen by Das to take up the work and the leadership role left by him. While in prison, Bose had decried the factionalism rampant in Bengal. After his release he thought that the Congress in Bengal was languishing and blamed particularly J. M. Sen Gupta and Kiran Sankar Roy. What was needed, he believed, was one strong man to settle factional differences and make one unified national party in Bengal.[80] After leaving prison, Bose stayed outside the factional conflicts momentarily while he began to get reacclimatized. He tried to work with all parties, but given the factionalism already rampant in Bengali Congress politics and the fact that his older brother, a personal and political confidant, was involved, Bose could not and did not remain outside Congress conflicts.[81]

POLITICAL GROUPS IN BENGAL

The simple dichotomy between Gandhians and the Bose faction, although a relatively accurate description of the situation at a high level of abstraction, does not do justice to the richness and complexity of Bengali politics from the late 1920s to the 1940s. Although the Gandhian High Command was the dominant faction at the center of the Congress organization and the Boses were most often the dominant faction in the Bengal Congress, Bengali politics was a tangled web of shifting alliances. Bengal was known for its factional politics; after the death of C. R. Das, no individual or single group was able to control all the factions.[82] A serious and humorous commentary on the factional situation and on the motivation of the political actors in Bengal was offered near the end of this period in *Forward*. A columnist calling himself "Wayfarer" began a piece entitled "In Lighter Vein" in this way:

> I was enquiring of a Congress friend of mine about the number of parties or groups within the Congress in Bengal and about their ideological differences. My friend mentioned Full-Khadi, Half-Khadi, King's Own, Royists, C.S.P., and C.P., indicated the particular characteristics of each and lastly mentioned the C.O.P. Having been unfamiliar with the term "C.O.P.," I looked askance at my friend. My friend explained that C.O.P. was an abbreviation for "Congress Opportunist Party," which had been the majority party in the Congress for the last 52 years. Explaining the present object and programme of the C.O.P., my friend said that this party had absolute faith in the creed of attainment of Swaraj by peaceful and legitimate means. But the party's interpretation of the words "peaceful" and "legitimate" was quite different from their ordinary meanings. "Peaceful means" implied entry into the Legislatures and the Calcutta Corporation at any cost and "legitimate means" implied securing seats in the different committees of the Legislatures and the Corporation by means fair or foul. The Programme of the party was as simple as it could be, namely, to pay visits to Jhowtola at 7 A.M., to "Ranjani" at 8 A.M. to Wellington Street at 9 A.M., and to Woodburn Park or Elgin Road at 10 A.M. It is no wonder that a party with such a noble and patriotic objective has the largest number of adherents and is gaining strength day by day.[83]

Even before the death of C. R. Das there had been some jostling between his followers for official and Swarajist posts. For example, there was a contest for Chief Executive Officer of the Calcutta Corporation, when disgruntled Calcutta residents put up Subhas Bose against the older leader from Midnapur, B. N. Sasmal. Hemendra Nath Das Gupta, a Congress worker at the time and biographer of C. R. Das and Subhas Bose, claims that the backers of Bose did not want a mofussil resident like Sasmal becoming chief executive officer of their city government.[84] This tension between city and countryside was to appear again as one of several factors dividing the Bengal Congress.

Upon the death of C. R. Das, J. M. Sen Gupta, a barrister from Chittagong, was backed by Mahatma Gandhi for the so-called "Triple Crown" that had been worn by Das: mayor of Calcutta, president of the Bengal Provincial Congress Committee, and leader of the Swaraj Party in the Bengal Legislative Council.[85] But even before the crown had been firmly fixed on Sen Gupta's head, those who felt he did not deserve it began to make their feelings known in public or in private.[86] Sen Gupta had returned to his legal practice before the boycott of law courts ended, and some argued that for this reason he should not be president of the BPCC.[87] But there was no immediate opposition to Sen Gupta.

At about this time, two groups within the Congress began to exert their influence. The first was called Karmisangha (Workers' Society), and was formed from among released political prisoners in the Calcutta area. This group chose Amarendra Chattopadhyay Chatterjee as its president and Suresh Das as secretary.[88] The second group was a rather loose, temporary coalition that was a group more in name than in fact: Dr. B. C. Roy, Tulsi Goswami, Nalini Ranjan Sarker, Sarat Bose, and Nirmal Chunder Chunder. They all had wealth and connections in Calcutta; Priyanath Gupta in his *Statesman* column "Indian Comment" had labeled them the "Big Five." They served on the Board of Directors of *Forward* and as trustees of the Deshbandhu Village Reconstruction Fund.[89] By early 1928, within the three years after Das's death, both these groups supported Subhas Bose and eventually succeeded in making him president of the Bengal Provincial Congress, thus cutting back Sen Gupta's political support in Bengal.[90]

The divisive rivalry with Sen Gupta was still submerged; Sen Gupta served as president of the Bengal Provincial Conference in 1928. At a meeting held at Basirhat in early April, Bose moved a resolution calling for complete independence for India. The conference, following the lead of their provincial Congress president, passed the resolution.[91] The conference also passed a resolution introduced by Gandhian Satis Chandra Das Gupta calling for people to use the spinning wheel to revive the country.[92] While the conference also passed a resolution calling for communal harmony, it was apparent that most of the Muslim members of the Congress and of the Swaraj Party had left these organizations and that the Bengal Pact was dead.

In the same year, Bose became a candidate for mayor of Calcutta. Sen Gupta withdrew his own candidacy and started to help Bose. But B. K. Basu of the Liberal Party was elected mayor, and some recriminations against different groups began to circulate in the Bengal Congress.[93] It seems, however, that at this point Sen Gupta was satisfied with his position in the Bengal Legislative Council and left Congress business to Bose and to Kiran Sankar Roy, who was then secretary of the BPCC.

Both Bose and Sen Gupta, as well as dozens of eminent leaders from all over India, met at the All-Parties Conference held in Calcutta in early December 1928. They were all brought together by common opposition to the Indian Statutory or Simon Commission formed to consider constitutional advances for India, but they were unable to agree to a joint positive plan for constitutional advance.[94] The proposal offered by the Congress was the Nehru Report, the result of the deliberations of a committee headed by Motilal Nehru, Congress president in 1928. The Muslim League, with Mohammad Ali Jinnah as a chief spokesman, presented fourteen points on which the league wanted agreement before it could go forward in step with the other parties present.[95] The Nehru Report called for joint electorates with reservation of seats and Jinnah, still in a conciliatory mood, pressed other Muslim leaders to accept this provision if other demands of the Muslims were met. But the Congress and Hindu leaders at the All-Parties Convention would not agree to reserve one-third of the Central Legislature seats for Muslims, nor to other points in their program.[96] It was evident from discussions at the Bengal Muslim All-Parties Conference held at the end of December 1928 that many spokesmen for Bengali Muslims would not take less than the percentage of seats due to them in the Bengal Legislative Council by their numerical weight in the population of Bengal.[97] Some historians have seen the meetings and failures during December 1928 as a crucial turning point in Hindu-Muslim and Congress-League relations in India.[98]

At the Calcutta Congress held in December 1928 after the All-Parties Convention, Bose came to national attention by pressing for adoption of an independence resolution passed by the Bengal Provincial Conference.[99] Bose was opposed by a phalanx of older Congress leaders, including Mahatma Gandhi and Motilal Nehru. The Nehru Report recommended dominion status for India, and this was as far as Gandhi and the elder Nehru were prepared to go at this moment. Bose had strong support from most of the Bengali delegation and from some of the younger congressmen, but it was not sufficient to override the opposition. Bose maintained that Britain and India had nothing in common and that India should forsake the Commonwealth and become the leader of Asia.[100] Jawaharlal Nehru made a speech supporting Bose's position, and then Gandhi spoke.

> Replying to the debate, Mahatma Gandhi said that his remarks were principally addressed to young Bengal and if they considered for one moment that a mere Gujrati could not understand young Bengal, then I say that Young Bengal would commit a most serious blunder.[101]

Gandhi argued that calling for independence at this point was merely to mouth a hollow phrase. As he had done in 1920, Gandhi said, "If you will help me and follow the programme honestly and intelligently, I promise that Swaraj will come within one year." [102] Bose's amendment lost, 973 to 1,350 votes. About two-thirds of the Bengali delegates supported Bose's view.[103] Bose was on his way to becoming a spokesman for what he believed were the young and radical forces in the Congress.

In describing another aspect of that Congress, Nirad C. Chaudhuri has written:

> The first expression of Bose's militarism was seen at the session of the Indian National Congress in Calcutta in 1928. For it Bose organized a volunteer corps in uniform, its officers being even provided, so far as I remember, with steel-chain epaulettes. Bose designated himself as its General-Officer-Commanding, G.O.C. for short, and his uniform was made by a firm of British tailors in Calcutta, Harman's. A telegram addressed to him as G.O.C. was delivered to the British general in Fort

William, and this was the subject of a good deal of malicious comment in the Anglo-Indian Press. Mahatma Gandhi, being a sincere pacifist vowed to non-violence, did not like the strutting, clicking of boots, and saluting, and he afterwards described the Calcutta session of the Congress as a Bertram Mills circus, which caused great indignation among the Bengalis.[104]

Although Bose continued to work within the Congress and cooperated with Gandhi and the other leaders until 1940, he seemed marked as a troublemaker within the organization. Unlike his mentor, C. R. Das, Bose was not a peer of Gandhi and Motilal Nehru in age or political experience. For all his public remarks about his feelings for Bose, Gandhi never had the same respect and affection for Bose that he had had for C. R. Das. In addition to an ideological gulf which widened over the years, there was a generation gap which Gandhi successfully bridged in his relationship to Jawaharlal Nehru but never with Subhas Bose. And for his part, Bose did not harbor what Gandhians felt was the proper respect for the Mahatma of the nationalist movement.[105]

In March 1929, Bose served as president of the Bengal Provincial Conference at Rangpur and extolled his native province in the address:

> Bengal has a message of her own to deliver to the world. That message is the sum total of life and history of Bengal as a whole, and as she tried in the past to make that message heard, was doing it even now. She would continue to do so in future. That message was ingrained in the character of Bengal. . . .[106]

Giving an abundance of examples of this point, Bose went on to attribute to Swami Vivekananda and C. R. Das crucial roles in the development of modern Bengal.

> In the work of man-making, Swami Vivekananda did not confine his attention to any particular sect but embraced the Society as a whole. His fiery words—'Let a new India emerge through the plough of the cultivators, through the baskets of the fishermen, cobblers, and methars, through the workshop and from the huts and bazaars'—are still ringing in every Bengalee home. This Socialism did not derive its birth from the books of Karl Marx. It has its origin in the thought and culture of India. The gospel of democracy that was preached by Swami Vivekananda has manifested itself fully in the writings and achievements of Deshabandhu Das who said that Narayan lives amongst those who till the land and prepare our bread by the sweat of their brow,

those who in the midst of grinding poverty have kept the torch of our civilisation, culture and religion burning.

The first step towards nation-building is the creation of true men and the second step is organisation. Vivekananda and others tried to make men while Deshabandhu tried to create political organisation and he created such an organisation that extorted the admiration even of the Britishers.[107]

Although he had begun to emerge on the national political scene, Bose still had firm roots in Bengal and a strong concern for the common man.

The 1929 provincial conference passed a resolution calling for closer ties between the Congress and "the peasants' and labourers' organisation." [108] Following C. R. Das's example, Bose began to take an active part in trade-union work and served as president of the All-India Trade Union Congress in 1929.[109] He was much in demand as a speaker at meetings of youth and student organizations. Bose and Nehru were heroes for nationalist youths.

Unfortunately for Bose and the Bengal Congress, however, the year 1929 was marked by serious factional struggles and the emergence of conflict with Sen Gupta, both within the Bengal Congress and in a Bengali election dispute that came before the national organization at the end of the year.[110] The rivalry between these two men and the various groups that supported each was to continue until the death of Sen Gupta in 1932 and Bose's temporary exit from the Bengali scene, which began in that same year. Several explanations have been offered for the Bose–Sen Gupta competition: that Bose was a Calcutta Kayastha and Sen Gupta an upstart from the mofussil, an East Bengali or "bañal"; that Sen Gupta believed in nonviolence and had Gandhi's support and that Bose did not; and that the important revolutionary groups in the Bengal Congress lined up on different sides for their own reasons.[111] All these factors undoubtedly had a place in the conflict, but one informant has suggested that it was fundamentally a clash of personalities and a struggle for power.[112]

At the end of the year there was a controversy over Bengal's members in the All-India Congress Committee. Dr. B. C. Roy tried to work out a compromise, but Bose and his followers stormed out of the meeting. Bose made a public statement challenging the authority of the

Working Committee of the Congress. Later he returned and clarified
his statement satisfactorily, but Sen Gupta rejected the compromise offered by Dr. Roy.[113] The Working Committee finally made a settlement in the dispute deciding who should be the Bengal members of the
AICC. In the aftermath, Gandhi named the Congress Working Committee members for 1930; Sen Gupta was selected, while Subhas Bose
was not. There was an attempt to have Bose added to the committee,
but Gandhi wanted those representing what he called the "minority"
left off.[114] The support at the center of the Congress organization
which Sen Gupta enjoyed probably helped him with some groups in
Bengal, but it hampered him with many others to whom he simply became a spokesman for Gandhi in Bengal. Piqued at his treatment by
the national Congress and wishing to express his political opposition to
the majority, Bose formed the Congress Democratic Party, but it disintegrated while Bose was imprisoned during 1930.[115]

As has been mentioned, in 1930 Bose was elected mayor of Calcutta,
and in his acceptance speech he recalled the municipal aims of C. R.
Das and his own long-standing civic concern. As a disciple of Das,
Bose said, "I have tried to follow the torch that he held aloft for the
nation with all the reckless abandon of which a sentimental Bengali is
capable." [116] Bose put forth a program for education, medical care, and
aid to the poor as well as plans for establishing improved transportation
and administration. He stated:

> if I may put his [Das's] policy and programme in modern language,
> I would say that we have here in this policy and programme a syn-
> thesis of what Modern Europe calls socialism and fascism. We have
> here the justice, the equality, the love which is the basis of socialism,
> and combined with that we have the efficiency and the discipline of
> fascism as it stands in Europe to-day.[117]

From this point in his career, Bose began talking of this synthesis,
which was to be tailored to meet Indian conditions and traditions. He
was one of the few Indian leaders who expressed admiration for fascism
and he was to encounter both Hitler and Mussolini on their home
grounds. However, Bose's estimate of the blessings of fascism was tempered by his encounters in Europe during the 1930s.

From 1923 on, Bose took a special interest in the welfare of his native Calcutta. He visited other cities both in India and Europe to seek

out models for civic improvement.[118] One observer who was close to the Bose family has suggested that Bose's involvement with the corporation was not a successful experience:

> When Subhas Bose came back to the Calcutta Corporation after his release from detention, he became more and more a prisoner in the hands of the hard-boiled and worldly middle-class of Calcutta, to whom civic welfare meant the welfare of their class. Still, Bose could never shed his infatuation for this Delilah. He showed his man-of-action's bias in preferring practical power in the Corporation to ideological power in the Congress Working Committee, and until he left India to find salutary release from it, the Calcutta Corporation remained a millstone around his neck.[119]

The corporation, nonetheless, was one of the few places in which the Congress retained some power and patronage.[120] With the resignation of congressmen from the legislatures, together with the Swarajist antipathy to holding office in the Das era and the later refusal of the Congress to form a coalition ministry in 1937, the Congress had effectively handed over whatever power and patronage could be gained through the Bengal Legislative Council to other political groups.

After failing to gain the concessions they wished from the government and refusing to attend the First Round Table Conference, the Congress undertook a campaign of civil disobedience in 1930. Because of the split between the forces behind Sen Gupta and those marshalled behind Bose, these two led different organizations into the fray.[121] Both men and many others were arrested and spent about half of 1930 in prison. The Bengali Congress leaders claimed that they were beaten in prison and from 1930, Sen Gupta's health began to deteriorate.[122]

Also in 1930, there was a revival of revolutionary activity in Bengal, marked by one of the few large-scale operations of the whole revolutionary movement. Since 1923 repression by the government of Bengal had stopped the revolutionaries temporarily. In prison, a split developed between the younger men and the more experienced revolutionaries, the former calling themselves the Revolt or Advance Group.[123] Some of the revolutionaries held a secret meeting at the time of the 1928 Calcutta Congress and the following year made plans for uprisings in Chittagong, Mymensingh, and Barisal.[124] They were successful in mounting an uprising only in Chittagong. With many revolutionary dals cooperating, the Chittagong Armory Raid began on April 18, 1930. Taking the officials and European community by surprise, the revolutionaries captured and destroyed the armory, the communications center, and other buildings. They seized arms to carry on the fight. They received some popular support and much silent acquiescence from the district's inhabitants. Through several errors, however, a large group was killed by government forces and the rest fled to the forests, from which they carried on guerrilla warfare for several years. The leader of the uprising was Surja Sen; he eluded his pursuers for almost four years and was finally captured in 1933, tried, and hung in 1934.[125]

Other changes had taken place in the revolutionary movement. Most of the religious trappings had been dropped. A more secular pattern of organization was adopted, and women were recruited into the movement. Furthermore, many revolutionaries were turning socialist, and gaining a wider social and international perspective.[126]

Between 1930 and 1934, some Bengal revolutionary groups continued acts of political assassination and robbery. The Chittagong effort, which included proclamation of a free government in the local area, was the only partially successful attempt to create a larger uprising in hopes of setting off large-scale revolution. By crushing the Chittagong groups and cracking down on those groups attempting assassinations, the government of Bengal had again brought the movement to a halt by 1934.[127] From this time many of the revolutionaries turned to the Congress and to the small leftist parties that were beginning to form in Bengal. Secret terrorism was for the most part left behind, and a future of more open political work in the Congress and the left-wing parties lay ahead.

In 1931 Gandhi and Irwin agreed to a political rapprochement between the Congress and the Government of India. Gandhi decided to attend the Second Round Table Conference in London later that year, and the civil disobedience campaign was placed in abeyance. Sen Gupta was given the difficult task of defending the Gandhi-Irwin Pact in Bengal.[128] Bose criticized its terms and Gandhi's wish to be the sole Congress representative in London.[129] The governments of India and Bengal were determined not to release those Bengali prisoners whom they considered revolutionaries or in league with the revolutionaries.

Though Gandhi succeeded at this time and later in obtaining the release of those held for civil disobedience, he could not gain the release of other political prisoners; in Bengal it was charged that he did not try but bargained only for those who worked within the bounds of his strategy. Whether this was true or not, the charge helped increase the unpopularity of Gandhi and those allied with him in Bengal.[130]

In London, from September to December 1931 Gandhi served as Congress spokesman and claimed to represent all the Indian people. Dozens of other Indians speaking for other groups and interests denied Gandhi's claim. This question was never resolved, and Gandhi did not obtain the concessions from the government for immediate steps toward independence that the Congress wanted.[131] With Gandhi's return to India after his failure in London, the Congress began civil disobedience again and hundreds of congressmen, including Gandhi, Sen Gupta, Bose, and Jawaharlal Nehru, were arrested. In August 1932 the government announced the Communal Award, which split the caste Hindus and the untouchables into separate electorates. In protest, Gandhi undertook his famous fast while imprisoned that September. An agreement, the Poona Pact, was reached by the government, Gandhi, and the Congress with the representatives of the untouchables.[132] It provided for joint electorates of caste Hindus and untouchables, with a large number of reserved seats for the latter. According to this agreement, 30 of the 78 seats for non-Muslims in the proposed Bengal Legislative Assembly were to be reserved for the untouchables or "scheduled castes" of Bengal. The Assembly was to have a total of 250 members. When the provisions of the Poona Pact became known in Bengal, there was considerable dissatisfaction among Bengali caste Hindus, and they organized the Congress Nationalist Party to defend the rights and interests of caste Hindus in their province.[133] Although the Congress Nationalists never became a great force, they and the Hindu Mahasabha furthered the polarization of communal groups in India.

In 1933, Mahatma Gandhi suspended civil disobedience and undertook one of his several withdrawals from the Congress organization. During the same year, Bose, in poor health after another period of imprisonment, left India under government supervision to seek medical treatment in Europe. He was to spend the greater part of the following five years in exile in Europe.

One politician who worked closely with Subhas Bose has suggested that Bose had significant support among the revolutionaries and ex-revolutionaries who had moved into the Congress organization in the 1920s and 1930s.[134] Satya Ranjan Bakshi has maintained that Bose had strong support of this kind in East Bengal and in Nadia, 24-Parganas, and Midnapur. A historian of Midnapur has written that C. R. Das and later Subhas Bose had widespread support in that district and that congressmen and revolutionaries worked side by side, with the Bengal Volunteers serving as an organizational meeting ground.[135] Such relationships undoubtedly changed through time, and the connection between the Bengal Congress and the Midnapur DCC was weakened when B. N. Sasmal left the Congress and ran as a Nationalist candidate against the Congress in a 1934 election. After the death of Sasmal that same year, political organization was in disarray in the district until 1937, when Bose came in to help reorganize the district Congress Committee.[136]

Youth groups and trade unions gave Bose additional popular support and he spent a good deal of his time speaking to such groups and encouraging them in their work. Bose's support for agitation by youth groups and trade unions was a crucial factor, Satya Ranjan Bakshi has argued, in the division that took place in the Big Five from the late 1920s. Dr. B. C. Roy was associated with the administration of Calcutta University and Nalini Ranjan Sarker was a leader of the Bengal National Chamber of Commerce; they came to oppose Bose for his encouragement of disruptive political activity by students and workers.[137]

Although some leftist groups criticized Bose for his authoritarian control of the Bengal Provincial Congress at the end of the 1930s,[138] other sources indicate that Bose never built a strong or united party organization in Bengal and that this was one of his serious failures. Nirad C. Chaudhuri has written on this point:

> Subhas Bose as party leader failed to create a solid party behind himself. . . . Bose had nothing behind him beyond unorganized popular support. He never acquired any strong or lasting hold on the party bosses of Bengal. . . . The lower ranks of the career nationalists of Bengal gave their loyalty to him according to their estimate of his power to serve or harm their interests. . . . Thus he was never able to

knock his party enemies on the head and was paralysed all along by the factious squabbles in which he became enmeshed.[139]

Several authorities have suggested that Bose was supported by the Jugantar revolutionaries and J. M. Sen Gupta, and by Anushilan revolutionaries during their 1929 struggle.[140] Dilip Roy has written in his memoir that Bose was a lonely man constantly betrayed in politics by his supposed friends.[141] Bose did have the support of his brother Sarat, who often acted as a kind of alter-ego for the more dynamic and charismatic Subhas, and the two worked in a kind of flexible tandem that made Subhas Bose's political career possible. Beyond this solid family support were close associates such as Satya Ranjan Bakshi and later Hemanta Kumar Basu, as well as a wide popular following. But he never developed a party structure or recruited a cadre of very talented lieutenants, as did C. R. Das for the Swaraj Party in the years 1922–1925. Those groups and leaders in whom he should have found firm allies simply because of a close ideological concurrence often proved to be his most hostile critics.

The Gandhians were weakened by the death of Sen Gupta in 1932. The rural Gandhians, who had been at work since the early 1920s, continued as one group within the Bengal Congress under P. C. Ghosh and Suresh Banerjee,[142] but they did not seem to have forceful enough leadership or enough popular support to become the most powerful faction in the Bengal Congress. In the 1930s, Dr. B. C. Roy and Nalini Ranjan Sarker grew closer to Gandhi and became in time two of the most important links that the Congress High Command had with the Bengal political scene. Dr. Roy had first come in contact with Mahatma Gandhi in 1925, and the latter helped to have him made secretary of the Deshbandhu Memorial Trust.[143] Dr. Roy remained friendly with Sarat and Subhas Bose for some years, even in the 1930s when he grew closer to the Gandhian High Command and became one of Gandhi's personal physicians. In the 1920s, he served under Sen Gupta as deputy leader of the opposition in the Bengal Legislative Council. He was elected mayor of Calcutta for the years 1931–1933. Dr. Roy had tried to mediate the 1929 Bengali election dispute and in the end appeared to side more with Bose than with Sen Gupta.[144] The first time he ran for mayor, he was nominated by Subhas Bose, and there is a friendly reference to him in a personal letter written by Bose in 1937.[145] But the split with the Boses seems to have been widening by 1934, when with Gandhi's support Dr. Roy helped to revive the Swaraj Party. In 1935 Dr. Roy was elected president of the BPCC over Subhas Bose, who spent most of that year in Europe. The same year, Sarat Bose was released from detention and a controversy erupted with the other members of the Big Five, partly over who was to run the elections in Bengal. Eventually Sarat Bose did run the elections on behalf of the Congress for seats in the Bengal Legislative Council and Assembly, but Dr. Roy was selected as president of the BPCC and as a member of the Congress Working Committee for 1937.[146] Just how strained relations were at this point between the Boses and Dr. Roy is not clear.

Another member of the Big Five who moved out in his own direction from the late 1920s was Nalini Ranjan Sarker. Sarker's career and actions must be seen in connection with those of other Indian businessmen who may be called the "nationalist business interest." In Calcutta, some nationalist businessmen were non-Bengalis, the most prominent of whom was G. D. Birla. In describing his political affiliation in 1940, Birla said, "I am not a Congressman. But I *am* a Gandhi-man." [147] This may also have been true for other Indian businessmen in varying degrees. For the most part, many of them hedged their bets and gave money to the Congress while appearing loyal to the government. They wanted protection for the private sector and eventually assistance for Indian business interests over foreign business interests in India. They also wanted some assurance against nationalization of the private sector. Gandhi's theory of trusteeship, if carried out, would seem to offer some assurance that their property would not be suddenly expropriated. Some insight into their viewpoint may be gained from this passage in a letter from G. D. Birla to the secretary of state for India in 1932:

> I need hardly say that I am a great admirer of Gandhiji . . . I have liberally financed his Khaddar-producing and untouchability activities. I have never taken any part in the Civil Disobedience movement. But I have been a very severe critic of the Government and so have never been popular with them. . . . I wish I could convert the authorities to the view that Gandhiji and men of his type are not only friends of India but also friends of Great Britain, and that Gandhiji is the greatest force on the side of peace and order. He alone is responsible for

keeping the left wing in India in check. To strengthen his hands is, in my opinion, therefore, to strengthen the bond of friendship between the two countries.[148]

Birla and a whole network of business connections who were principally fellow Marwaris came to play an increasing role in Indian politics.[149] Birla evidently had Gandhi's ear from the late 1920s; one version of events in Bengal that came personally to Gandhi's attention came through G. D. Birla, and sometimes through Nalini Sarker.[150]

Nalini Ranjan Sarker began his political career as a lieutenant of C. R. Das; but as he rose in the business world, Sarker seemed to become less attached to the Congress and more a go-between connecting the government and the nationalists. Sarker moved from his base as successful manager of the Hindustan Cooperative Insurance Company to the inner councils of the Bengal National Chamber of Commerce and the Indian Federation of Chambers of Commerce by the early 1930s. He resigned from the Bengal Legislative Council in 1930 with other congressmen, but at the same time he was serving as a member of the Central Banking Enquiry Committee. In 1933 Sarker was nonofficial adviser to the government of India on the Indo-Japanese trade negotiations and in 1934 he was elected mayor of Calcutta. He was president of the Bengal National Chamber of Commerce and the Indian Federation of Chambers of Commerce in 1933 and was elected representative of the former to the Bengal Legislative Assembly in 1937.[151] His part in the Bengal Ministry question from 1937 to 1939 will be discussed later. From the late 1930s, Sarker served in increasingly important official positions and was a minister of the central government during World War II. Nalini Sarker and Dr. Roy, G. D. Birla, and the "pure-Khadi" Gandhians were Gandhi's allies against the leftists and revolutionaries. Although none of the Gandhians had the popular appeal of Subhas Bose or the widespread organization of the revolutionaries, they did represent a de facto coalition of considerable strength.

The revolutionaries moved gradually toward one of several leftist groups that were beginning to crystallize. A few formed a group within the Bengal Congress. Although revolutionaries have often been identified as either Jugantar or Anushilan, these organizations began to split up and become several among many revolutionary groups. Jugantar was disbanded, and men such as Surendra Mohan Ghose and Bhupati Majumdar moved into positions of importance in the Congress. Others joined leftist groups operating within the Congress in the later 1930s. For example, Bhupesh Gupta and Ganesh Ghosh joined the Communist Party of India (CPI), A few other Jugantar men, such as Amarendra Nath Chattopadhyay and Jibal Lal Chatterjee, joined the Royists. Tridib Chaudhuri and Jogesh Chatterjee from the Anushilan Samiti went into the Congress Socialist Party (CSP).[152] With the suppression of the Chittagong revolt and the wave of revolutionary actions in the early 1930s, the revolutionary phase ended, except for actions in connection with the 1942 movement. With their long political experience, their openness to new ideologies, and their devotion to politics as a career, the revolutionaries were prime recruits for leftist parties seeking to grow in the 1930s.

The leftist parties in Bengal were hampered by a factionalism that pervaded other parts of the political terrain as well. The parties described here all recruited from the same groups: students, factory workers, and educated high-caste Hindus, particularly the intellectuals. The parties—the CPI, the Royists, and the CSP—had small memberships, but the influence of a vague, socialist ideology was much wider than the party lists. This ideological line was also taken by Subhas Bose and his supporters, by the Bengal Labour Party, which was part of the CPI and the CSP for some time, and by the two Krishak Praja Parties.

After the success of the Bolshevik Revolution in 1917, Western and Russian communists founded the Third Communist International or Comintern. The failure of communist revolts in Western and Eastern Europe drove Lenin and his colleagues to paying greater attention to nationalist struggles and revolutionary possibilities in Asia.[153] From among the Indian émigrés scattered throughout the world, the Comintern chose M. N. Roy as their premier theoretician and organizer for India.[154] In the discussion of the colonial question at the Second Congress of the Comintern in Moscow in 1920, Roy placed the movements in colonial countries in the forefront of his plan for world revolution, while Lenin remained more European-centered and more aware of organizing difficulties than did the confident young Roy.[155] A critical issue, unresolved today, concerned the relationship between communists and bourgeois nationalists. Roy described differing views of Gandhi in his *Memoirs:*

> we could not agree about the role of Gandhi, whose name was just coming to be known in Russia. Lenin regarded the new leader of Indian Nationalism as objectively revolutionary like the great heretics of mediaeval Europe. I held that such an estimation of the role of Gandhi was precluded by his religious and social ideas, which were positively reactionary. . . . As a disciple seeking light from the Master, I enquired whether an anti-imperialist movement inspired by reactionary social ideas and burdened with obscurantist religious beliefs, could be politically revolutionary.[156]

To support his views Roy undertook the first thorough Marxist study of Indian nationalism, *India in Transition*, published in 1922. It included a class analysis of Indian society and an effort to show the relationship of this class structure to nationalism. Gandhi, who he thought embodied revolt and reaction, posed a problem. Roy admired Gandhi's mobilization of the mass in 1921, but thought the masses were moved by objective economic forces, not the magnetism of a man he considered a religious fanatic. Gandhi, Roy decided, was the expression of petty bourgeois as well as bourgeois interests, for he had called off the Noncooperation movement when the seething proletariat was about to capture it.[157]

Roy realized many years later that he had gravely overestimated the strength of the proletarian movement in India, but through the 1920s he called for the formation of a peasants' and workers' party within the Congress. Roy sent a stream of political pamphlets and propaganda, a number of agents, and some funds back to India to organize an Indian communist party.[158] He wrote to men like C. R. Das who he thought might be sympathetic, but in organizational terms the CPI had hardly begun in the 1920s. The government of India nevertheless held two show trials, at Cawnpore in 1924 and at Meerut in 1929.[159]

One contact in Calcutta was Muzaffar Ahmad, who began to correspond with Roy in Europe and served as chief contact and organizer in Bengal. Although he was arrested several times and was a central figure in the Cawnpore conspiracy case of 1924, Ahmad always returned immediately upon release to his political work. Together with Naresh

Sengupta, Atul Gupta, Kazi Nazrul Islam, Hemanta Sarkar, and Nalini Gupta, he formed the Bengal Workers and Peasants Party in Calcutta in 1924 or 1925.[160] They published a weekly paper, *Langal* (Plow), and began the effort to spread Marxist ideas among workers and intellectuals in the industrial areas of western Bengal.

During this same period, Roy tried to resume contact with his old revolutionary colleagues. The Intelligence Branch reported in 1922 that

> Since Nalini Gupta's return to Germany Roy has written several letters to prominent members of the old revolutionary party in Bengal, and in August he was reported to have secured the consent of Pulin Das to co-operate with him. In consequence of warnings received from Muzaffar Ahmad he appears since to have been making further inquiries regarding the reliability of these revolutionaries.[161]

Through almost a decade of efforts to organize the Communist Party of India from Europe, and even with numerous agents and funds, Roy was constantly hampered by severe handicaps. He could not tell who was a spy and who could be trusted. His letters were constantly being intercepted by the Intelligence Branch even when he took precautions. He was trying to convince men at a distance that a foreign-derived ideology was relevant to the Indian struggle and Indian conditions, and he had to compete with the nationalist leadership headed by Gandhi. Roy appeared to dislike Gandhi intensely; it is difficult to tell how much he owed this hatred to his Bengali youth and how much to his subsequent secularization and conversion to communism.

The CPI shifted with the Third Communist International to an ultraleft line from about 1928.[162] This meant concentration on the organization of the CPI itself rather than cooperation with the other nationalists through the peasants' and workers' parties. For this reason the CPI split from the All-India Trade Union Congress and formed the Red Trade Union Congress, which was in operation from 1931 to 1934.[163] Although the CPI benefited from publicity they received through the Meerut conspiracy case, they lost the services of Muzaffar Ahmad until his release from prison in 1936.[164]

With the Comintern's official shift to the "united front" line in 1935, the CPI also shifted its work and moved into the CSP and the Congress. Among the Bengali communists who worked in the Congress were Muzaffar Ahmad, Promode Dasgupta, Hare Krishna Konar, Somnath Lahiri, Hirendranath Mukherjee and Biswanath Mukherjee. During the period 1935 to 1940, several of these men served in the executives of the Bengal Provincial Congress, of district Congress committees, and of the CSP.[165] One of their goals was to capture control of the CSP and eventually the Congress and after independence to make India into a communist country. They maintained a secret organization within the CSP until 1940, when after a grave crisis within that organization, they were expelled.[166] The CPI, although illegal and underground at the time, broke with the Congress on the issue of participation in the World War II effort once the CPI switched to the "people's war" line in 1941.[167] But between 1935 and 1941, the CPI was a small and determined group within the Congress. It supported Subhas Bose at one crucial moment in his career (see below), but ridiculed him after that.

The Royists were a small political group which was committed to the leadership and ideology of M. N. Roy. Roy lost favor within the Comintern from 1927 and was expelled in 1929. He joined the Communist International Opposition, which included August Thalheimer in Paris and Jay Lovestone in New York.[168] They thought that they had a more truly communist perspective and strategy. Against the advice of his friends, Roy returned to India secretly in 1930 after a fifteen-year absence. He was helped by Tayab Shaikh and Sunder Kabadi and slowly began to collect a number of political and trade-union workers around him who formed the nucleus of the Royist group, later called the League of Radical Congressmen (1937–1940) and the Radical Democratic Party (1940–1946).[169]

While the Comintern and the CPI were veering to the left (1928–1934) and viewing the Congress as an enemy rather than a potential ally, Roy was moving from his former left, sectarian position toward a much more positive view of the Congress. He argued for leftist work within the Congress and the trade unions, but he was against forming an autonomous left-wing party until 1940, when he split with the Congress on the war issue.[170] Although the Royists became known as a definite group, they were members of the Congress as individuals and did not maintain the same secrecy as the CPI during 1937 to 1940.

After doing underground political work for about seven months in

1930–1931, Roy was finally captured by the police, prosecuted under an old conviction in the Cawnpore conspiracy case, and sentenced to 12 years' imprisonment.[171] The term was later reduced to 6 years, during which Roy secretly continued his political work. Instructions and articles were smuggled out of prison, usually to his associate V. B. Karnik in Bombay; they were then copied and sent out to the members of the Royist political and labor network in India and to the headquarters of the Communist International Opposition in Paris.[172] During 1931 to 1936, while Roy was still in prison, Calcutta served as the publication center and Tayab Shaikh and others turned out a journal called *Masses*, as well as the pamphlets *Party Programme*, *Appeal to the Students*, and *Appeal to the Railway Workers*. Some later Royists in Calcutta included a few old associates from the Jugantar revolutionary organization, such as Amarendra Nath Chattopadhyay and Jibin Lal Chatterjee. Roy hoped that more of his Jugantar comrades would opt for the Royist group, but they preferred to follow their own line in the Congress or to join another leftist group.[173] Roy was hampered by his professed low opinion of Gandhi, his atheism, his antipathy to many aspects of Indian culture, and perhaps by his arrogance and his lack of any strong local support.

The Congress Socialist Party (CSP) was formed in 1934 as a group of leftist members within the Congress who were critical of its political strategy and ideology. Their program included: power to the masses; state planning and ownership; elimination of the princes and landlords; redistribution of and to the peasants; and the establishment of cooperatives and collectivization.[174] M. N. Roy's writings and those of other Marxists had considerable impact on the CSP. At first they decided to let Royists and communists join, but severe internal conflicts forced them to expel the Royists in 1937 and the communists in 1940. They recruited a number of ex-revolutionaries in Bengal, but none of their most important or most influential members was a Bengali. Thomas Rusch has explained the relationship of the Bengal Labour Party and the CSP:

> the Bengal Labour Party had merged with the C.P. and thereby entered the C.S.P in that Province as part of the Communist merger with the Socialists. In the period between 1939–1940, it left the C.P. to become an independent party again, and aligned itself with the Forward

Bloc of Subhas Chandra Bose. Thus, this section, although small, was also lost to the C.S.P.[175]

The CSP was thus another small group in the Bengal Congress, partly merged with the CPI during 1934–1940, that competed with the Bose group, the Royists, and other Congress factions for support inside the Congress organization and outside among the students, workers, intellectuals, revolutionaries, and peasants.

While the CPI, the Royists, the CSP, and a number of other small leftist groups were working in Bengal and other parts of India during the 1930s, Subhas Bose was forced to spend almost the entire period from 1932 to 1938 in prison or in Europe. Sarat Bose was also imprisoned and was only released in 1935, after more than three years behind bars. Sarat, according to his brother Subhas, preferred to be a backbencher and to avoid public honors and offices.[176] Nevertheless, when Subhas, the family's full-time politician, could not be active on the local scene because of imprisonment, ill-health or enforced exile, Sarat Bose came more into the open and acted for his brother. Meanwhile, Subhas Bose went to Europe to seek treatments for his health.

SUBHAS BOSE IN EUROPE

The major work Bose allotted to himself in Europe was that of a spokesman for Indian nationalism and culture. In the years from 1933 to 1938, he visited and established contacts in Austria, Germany, Czechoslovakia, Poland, Switzerland, Hungary, Yugoslavia, Bulgaria, Turkey, Belgium, Holland, and Ireland. He attended an International Conference for India in Geneva during 1933; he attended the opening of the Italian Oriental Institute in Rome during the same year, where he noted that Mussolini made a fine speech; and he maintained contact with the Federation of Indian students in Europe.[177] At the same time, he made a number of new friendships with Indians and Europeans, especially in central Europe (mainly Vienna), where he spent the largest part of his time. Among those friends were Mr. and Mrs. Vetter, Mrs. Fulop-Muller, and Miss Emilie Schenkl, who served as his assistant in writing *The Indian Struggle*. In Berlin Bose became acquainted with Mr. and Mrs. Kurti, and had a number of discussions and exchanges of letters with Mrs. Kurti, particularly about psychoanalysis.[178] He reestablished old ties and made some new friendships with Indians, including

S. K. Chatterjee, Nathalal Parikh, Amiya Chakravarty, and Vithalbhai Patel. Bose stayed with the latter during his last months and issued a joint statement with him criticizing Gandhi in 1933.[179]

Through these years, Bose showed a lively interest in political and intellectual currents in Europe. He visited municipal institutions in Berlin, Dublin, and Vienna, seeking knowledge which would help affairs in Calcutta. Although Bose did speak kindly of the positive aspects of fascism from the 1920s until the end of his life, he was also aware of the dark and brutal side. He urged Mrs. Kurti and her husband to flee Berlin,[180] and he wrote a letter about the Nazis to Dr. Theirfelder of the Deutsche Akademie after a visit to Berlin.

> To-day I regret that I have to return to India with the conviction that the new nationalism of Germany is not only narrow and selfish but arrogant. . . . The new racial philosophy which has a very weak scientific foundation, stands for the glorification of the white races in general and the German race in particular. Herr Hitler has talked of the destiny of the white races to rule over the rest of the world. But the historical fact is that up till now the Asiatics have dominated Europe more than have the Europeans dominated Asia . . . I am saying this not because I stand for the domination of one people by another, but simply because I want to point out that it is historically false to say that Europe and Asia should not be at peace with one another.[181]

Bose was developing his views on world politics at first hand and he finally decided that the internal politics of other states should be of no concern to India.[182] Jawaharlal Nehru and a number of other congressmen who were interested in the international scene did not agree with this detached viewpoint, which stressed nationalist interests above any overriding human and political values. Bose could see the dangers to the Kurtis and condemn Nazi racism, particularly as it applied to India, but he was willing to seek support for India in any camp, fascist, communist, or capitalist.

While in Europe, Bose did a good deal of writing, completing two books, *The Indian Struggle* and his autobiography, *An Indian Pilgrim*. In addition he wrote a number of essays that were collected in *Through Congress Eyes*. *The Indian Struggle* is Bose's effort to give his version of the recent political history of India and his assessment of the nationalist movement both to outsiders and to Indians. The book was originally published in Europe and was banned in India for some years.[183] It has a political focus and is concerned especially with the changing strategies of the Congress; it does not attempt to give a more penetrating sociological, psychological, or historical analysis of Indian nationalism. It is important not only as Bose's view but also for its impact later on nationalist leaders who were finally able to read it. The book contained praise as well as sharp criticism of Gandhi. Bose saw Gandhi as the head of an older, reformist group of nationalists backed by wealthy capitalists. He saw a dichotomy partly between the haves and the have-nots among Indian nationalists.[184] It was as if he were indirectly borrowing Marxist categories, identifying his political allies and himself with the masses of Indians, and seeing Gandhi, whom he admitted was accepted by the masses as their leader, as the leader of the oppressive forces. He viewed Gandhi, the High Command, and the government of India as restraints on the radical and militant nationalist forces with which he identified. This is yet another example of what Bose later called the "rebel mentality" which he had had since his youth. He not only rejected the authority of the government of India but also questioned the authority and wisdom of the controlling group within the nationalist organization with which he worked.

The one feature of the Congress to which Bose most objected was the lack of criticism of Gandhi. He wrote:

> Besides the influence which the first three leaders [C. R. Das, Motilal Nehru, and Lajpat Rai] had in their own provinces, their importance was also due to the fact that they were the three outstanding intellectual stalwarts of the Congress. Many of the blunders committed by the Mahatma as a political leader could have been avoided if they had been in a position to advise him. Since the death of these three giants, the leadership of the Congress had fallen to a low intellectual level. The Congress Working Committee today is undoubtedly composed of some of the finest men of India—men who have character and courage, patriotism and sacrifice. But most of them have been chosen primarily because of their 'blind' loyalty to the Mahatma—and there are few among them who have the capacity to think for themselves or the desire to speak out against the Mahatma when he is likely to take a wrong step.[185]

Bose did not name any others who were willing to criticize the Mahatma, but he obviously thought he was one of the few following in the steps of Das, Motilal Nehru, and Lajpat Rai. Bose was also concerned with the character of Gandhi's relationship with the masses, and he wrote:

> As we have already seen, a large and influential section of the intelligentsia was against him, but this opposition was gradually worn down through the enthusiastic support given by the masses. Consciously or unconsciously, the Mahatma fully exploited the mass psychology of the people, just as Lenin did the same thing in Russia, Mussolini in Italy and Hitler in Germany. But in doing so, the Mahatma was using a weapon which was sure to recoil on his head. He was exploiting many of the weak traits in the character of his countrymen which had accounted for India's downfall to a large extent. After all, what has brought about India's downfall in the material and political sphere? It is her inordinate belief in fate and in the supernatural—her indifference to modern scientific development—her backwardness in the science of modern warfare, the peaceful contentment engendered by her latter-day philosophy and adherence to Ahimsa (Non-violence) carried to the most absurd length. In 1920, when the Congress began to preach the political doctrine of non-co-operation, a large number of Congressmen who had accepted the Mahatma not merely as a political leader but also as a religious preceptor—began to preach the cult of the new Messiah.[186]

So Bose saw himself on the side of reason, science, and modern values against the most deplorable traits of enfeebled India, which Gandhi was exploiting. Later in his book, Bose condemned numerous blunders of the Mahatma, especially Gandhi's lack of planning for the Second Round Table Conference. At the root of Gandhi's errors was confusion between the Mahatma's two roles of political leader and world preacher.[187] Perhaps Bose never thought to consider that Gandhi's very success may have resulted in part from the Mahatma's effective fusion of religion and politics, or that his own popularity in Bengal may have been in part related to a religious aura that surrounded him because of his sacrifices and his years of imprisonment. Bose felt that in her struggle against the British, India needed a strong, vigorous, military-type leader—perhaps even himself—and not a hesitating, confused reformist guru.[188] Showing admiration for strong leaders, among whom he listed Hitler, Stalin, Mussolini, and even Sir Stanley Jackson, the governor of Bengal, Bose claimed that India wanted and needed a strong party, strict discipline, and dictatorial rule.[189] At the end of *The Indian Struggle*, Bose offered an ideological blend of fascism and communism and promised that all his energies would be used for the proper leadership of his country.[190] The passages and ideas mentioned above also exhibit Bose's forthright style, his blunt manner of speech, and his outspoken criticism of colleagues, none of which were to do him any good in the Congress political struggles which lay before him.

NINE
The Crisis of Bengal and Congress Politics

In the late 1930s there were two major issues for Bengali politicians: a crisis of leadership in the Congress in 1939, and the controversy surrounding the Bengal Ministry which had taken power under the regional autonomy provisions of the Government of India Act of 1935. The first issue was primarily an internal one for the Congress; the second involved all those participating at the highest levels in Bengali politics.

The roots of the antagonisms and conflicting positions behind the Congress confrontation reach back to the late 1920s. The growth of the left gradually led to differences on significant issues between the Gandhian High Command and the younger leftists. The differences became sharpened from 1934 when the Congress Socialist Party was formally founded as an organization within the Congress. At this time, followers of M. N. Roy and the CPI were temporarily working within the CSP.[1] The issues over which there was disagreement with the Gandhian leadership included the Congress' agrarian program, its positions on labor and industrial disputes, its perspectives on economic planning, its work in the princely states and on the question of federation, and finally, its organization and leadership.[2] Through the 1930s there were internal divisions among leftists on these issues and also dividing lines between the left and the right within the Congress. The Gandhian old guard was wary of the socialist ideas beginning to make their impress in India and resistant to the challenge of the leftists to its continued control of the Congress.[3]

Jawaharlal Nehru and Subhas Bose, the two prominent young leftist leaders, were more often rivals than allies. Nehru had formed close personal and political ties with Gandhi early in his career and Gandhi placed enough trust in him to have him chosen president of the Congress three times during this period. The last two terms were consecutive ones, 1936 and 1937. Nehru had persuaded several Congress Socialists to join the Working Committee during his presidency. But even these conciliatory gestures by Nehru and shrewd tactics by the Gandhians did not prevent the strain from growing.[4]

Subhas Bose was in Europe for almost the entire period between 1933 and 1937, and so was not intimately involved in the controversies. Although he was usually identified as a leftist, Bose did not form close ties with Nehru or with the leaders of the CSP. Such ties would have been of great value to him in the coming crisis. For although the leftists were bracketed together by the old guard then, and are today by some historians, distrust runs through the relations between Nehru and Bose, M. N. Roy and the Congress Socialists, the Congress Socialists and Bose, M. N. Roy and Nehru. In the case of M. N. Roy and the CPI, suspicion turned to hatred.[5]

Perhaps following the same strategy of blunting opposition by incorporating it that had worked so effectively with Nehru, Gandhi privately offered Subhas Bose the Congress presidency when Bose returned to India briefly in 1937. Bose was unanimously chosen president for 1938, and he flew back to India to deliver his presidential address to the Haripura Congress.[6] Some Bengali nationalists had been harboring bad feelings against the national Congress leadership for several reasons: no Bengalis had been selected for the Congress Working Committee in 1935; Bengalis were experiencing growing employment discrimination in Bihar; and the terms of the Communal Award and the Poona Pact cut most directly into the number of caste Hindu members in the Bengal Legislative Assembly and the council.[7] To assuage some of these regional grievances, Gandhi may have felt that it was intelligent politics to have a Bengali president of the Congress, who would be the first since C. R. Das had resigned in early 1923.

In his Haripura address, Bose put forth his position on a wide range of issues. Some of his stands are in line with the policy of the Congress Socialists; some may be said to represent a Bengali view; and still others were worked out independently by Bose. He spoke in general terms in favor of socialism and agreed with the Congress Socialists on the issues of collective affiliation of unions and Kisan Sabhas, increased Congress pressure in the princely states, opposition to federation and to office acceptance under the provincial autonomy provisions of the 1935 Government of India Act.[8] Bose opposed the Communal Award because he said it was antinational. Although his reasoning differed, he ended up on the same side of the issue as the Nationalist Party, which had gained a significant victory over the Congress candidates in the 1934 elections for Bengali members of the Central Legislative Assembly.[9] Gandhi, Nehru, and other Congress leaders supported Bose's view of this problem. Bose also said he adhered to the national Congress position on the rights of minorities and the use of the Satyagraha method.[10]

Bose turned some of his attention to foreign affairs and to the shape India should assume after independence, and on these issues, he was stating his own view rather than that of any particular group. Bose maintained that in foreign relations Indian self-interest was to be the single criterion for relationships with other states; [11] the internal politics of other states were of no concern to India. Bose said he expected the Congress to rule independent India; a national economic policy and industrial development under state ownership would be necessary; and a lingua franca for the nation was essential. He said that he looked at the Working Committee as a shadow cabinet for free India. Under his presidency, he formed a planning group headed by Nehru so that the Congress could prepare itself for the coming transfer of power.[12] In several areas, Bose has been given less credit than is his due for specifying some of the crucial problems of free India in the decade before independence.

During Bose's presidency Acharya J. B. Kripalani continued to serve as Congress secretary, and much Congress business continued to flow through the small secretariat under him. Bose was not particularly orderly in his correspondence, perhaps because he had been moving from country to country for a few years and was not prepared to handle the considerable chores associated with the Congress presidency. Keeping the secretary's office in the hands of Kripalani allowed the Gandhians to insure that no issue arose without their being fully aware of it.[13]

On several of the important issues that he had to handle, Bose worked closely with the Gandhian leaders on the Working Committee. For some years the various presidents of the Congress had been carrying on a fruitless correspondence with Jinnah, now more or less permanent president of the Muslim League. Jinnah insisted that the league spoke for all Muslims and demanded parity for the league with the Congress in many contexts. The Congress view, as propounded by Prasad, Nehru, Gandhi, and Bose, was that the league represented many Muslims, but that other Muslim organizations and the Congress represented other sections of the Indian Muslim community. Jinnah raised the same fourteen points that the league had put forward in 1929. Nehru agreed to some but held that others were out of date. The correspondence finally ended during Bose's presidency when it became clear to Jinnah that he could not persuade any Congress leader to recognize the league as the organization speaking authoritatively for all Indian Muslims. On this issue, at least, Bose was completely in accord with his Gandhian colleagues.[14]

Bose was also called upon during 1938 to settle a controversy between members of the Congress ministerial group in the Central Provinces. Working with Rajendra Prasad, Maulana Azad, and Sardar Patel, all members of the Congress Parliamentary Board, Bose finally ruled against N. B. Khare, who lost his position as chief minister. Khare violently denounced the Congress leadership.[15]

Although some leftists walked out of a meeting of the AICC in September 1938 over several of their differences with the old guard, Bose himself does not seem to have had any serious break with the Gandhians until he made it clear that he would seek another term as Congress president.[16] Bose's term as president had served to put off a more serious break between left and right in the Congress, but the political and ideological differences had not been removed.

CONTEST FOR THE CONGRESS PRESIDENCY

In the usual informal fashion in which the Gandhians chose the candidates for the presidency, they met and decided on Maulana Azad. Azad declined to run. Sardar Patel said in a public statement at the time,

At informal consultations at one stage or other at which Moulana Azad, Mr. Jawaharlal Nehru, Babu Rajendra Prasad, Mr. Bhulabhai

Desai, Mr. Kripalani, Mahatma Gandhi and myself were present, not by design but by accident, it was agreed that if perchance the Moulana remained adamantine in his resistance, according to the constitution Dr. Pattabhi Sitaramayya was the only choice left, since we were clearly of opinion that it was unnecessary to re-elect Subhas Babu.[17]

Bose, who had been seeking a left coalition within the Congress during his first year back in active politics, said he would only stand aside in favor of another leftist candidate. On January 24, 1939, six members of the old guard in a public statement questioned the idea of a competition for the presidency and said that the Congress president had always been selected unanimously.[18] This was the same line of argument that the entrenched moderates used against the insurgent Extremists in 1906 and 1907. Bose, in reply to the Gandhians, said that democratic procedures allowed competition for office. In his opinion, it was a question of ideology and platform. Among the issues was that of federation under British rule, which Bose strongly opposed. Although officially the Congress was with Bose on this issue, there were rumors that the Gandhians were wavering on it.[19] Bose also stood by socialism as he had defined it in his Haripura address, including national planning and industrial development under state control. Bose also advocated that a national demand or ultimatum be issued to the British with a six-month time limit. Gandhi was against this.[20] Bose often described the ideal national worker and leader as selfless, absorbed in a strong and active social movement; but he was not personally reticent. One of his coworkers remembered Bose's desire to "remain in history." [21] Nehru had preceded Bose and served two terms; so Bose, for personal and political reasons, may have felt that he should have a second term. For his part, Nehru seemed to side with the Gandhians, although by ideological criteria, Bose was closer to Nehru's own views than was Sitaramayya. With no other prominent leftist put forward, Bose ran and to the surprise of many, was elected by 1,580 votes, as against 1,375 for his opponent.[22] Sitaramayya had said before the election, "I am an ardent devotee of the cult of Gandhism." [23] A number of factors combined to produce Bose's triumph. The left had been growing throughout the 1930s and given a choice of Bose and Sitaramayya, almost all leftists, including the Congress Socialists, M. N. Roy's League of Radical Congressmen, the communists, and the unattached leftists apparently voted for Bose. Bose was also much more widely known than Sitaramayya. Bose's strength in the vote was in Bengal, the United Provinces, the Punjab, Kerala, and the Karnatak. Sitaramayya was stronger in Gujarat, Orissa, Andhra, and Bihar. Both had considerable support in Madras and Bombay.[24]

After the election, Gandhi announced that "the defeat is more mine than his [Sitaramayya's]." Gandhi, however, was against rash moves because, he said, "After all Subhas Babu is not an enemy of his country." [25] Bose issued a statement answering Gandhi, which said in part:

> I do not know what sort of opinion Mahatmaji has of me. But whatever his view may be, it will always be my aim and object to try and win his confidence for the simple reason that it will be a tragic thing for me if I succeed in winning the confidence of other people but fail to win the confidence of India's greatest man.[26]

This passage embodies the follow-up to Bose's usual desire to challenge authority. He wanted to beat the Gandhian candidate and did; but at the same time he wanted Gandhi's approbation. He wanted the satisfaction of victory over authority and approval from the vanquished as well. Gandhi and Bose met on February 15, 1939, and Bose came away satisfied that he would have the Mahatma's cooperation.[27]

Before the election in January, Bose had said to the press, "It is widely believed that there is prospect of a compromise on the Federal Scheme between the Right Wing of the Congress and the British Government during the coming year." [28] On February 22, twelve Gandhian members of the Working Committee resigned after Bose's retraction of the above "aspersion" was not forthcoming. Although Bose was not aware of it, the Gandhians were at work preparing to put him in his place. They wanted a homogeneous Working Committee and a policy based on the "will of the majority." They saw the forthcoming Congress session as a test of leftist and rightist strength, and an opportunity to assess Congress confidence in Bose's or in Gandhi's leadership.[29]

This period was also a crucial test of the internal cohesion and strength of the left. M. N. Roy, writing to Bose in February, 1939, said:

I have little more to add to the suggestion I made after your election last year. This year, there is absolutely no reason for you not to assert yourself. . . . The significance of the result of this year's presidential election has been correctly and clearly characterised by Gandhiji himself; *he has been defeated.* There can be little doubt regarding what is to be done in the given situation. The Congress must be given a new leadership, entirely free from the principles and pre-occupations of Gandhism which until now determined Congress politics. Gandhist principles cannot be reconciled with honest anti-imperialist politics. . . . it will be suicidal if any consideration is permitted to interfere with your selecting an Executive according to the verdict of the majority expressed in the presidential election. What is of still more importance, is that the new leadership of the Congress should have the courage and conviction of acting independently even of the wishes of Gandhiji, when these run counter to the objective revolutionary urge of the movement.[30]

Although the left had given Bose solid support for the presidency, the victory itself brought a jostling for places and second thoughts by some. M. N. Roy wanted a homogeneous leftist Working Committee and the position of general secretary of the Congress for himself.[31] The CPI wanted a large block in the Congress Executive, while the Congress Socialists, who wavered between national unity and leftist unity, thought that the Working Committee should be divided among leftists and rightists, with the leftists having the edge.[32] Bose himself was apparently undecided but seemed to feel that he needed the Gandhians to run the Congress organization; and he did not want to split the Congress. Some, like Roy and several of Bose's closer followers, wanted him to complete the split and form a leftist Working Committee. One adviser to Bose, Sardar Sardul Singh Caveeshar, told Thomas A. Rusch in 1954 that Bose "did not have the courage" to split the Congress. He also felt that the British would not allow the Congress to function if Bose and the left had completely captured it.[33]

With this matter still undecided, the annual Congress session convened at Tripuri in Mahakoshal in the present state of Madhya Pradesh. Bose fell ill with fever, attending some sessions on a stretcher but for the greater part of the time confined to his tent. Under such circumstances, Sarat Bose served as his younger brother's spokesman. Gandhi was not present, since he had what he felt to be pressing work to do in the princely state of Rajkot.[34]

The confrontation between left and right at Tripuri came down to a controversy over the wording and passage of a resolution put forth by one of the old guard. This was the Pant Resolution, which was worded as follows:

> In view of various misunderstandings that have arisen in the Congress and the country on account of the controversies in connection with the Presidential Election and after, it is desirable that the Congress should clarify the position and declare its general policy.

> (1) This Congress declares its firm adherence to the fundamental policies which have governed its programme in the past years under the guidance of Mahatma Gandhi and is definitely of opinion that there should be no break in these policies and they should continue to govern the Congress programme in future. This Congress expresses its confidence in the work of the Working Committee which functioned during the last year and regrets that any aspersions should have been cast against any of its members.

> (2) In view of the critical situation that may develop during the coming year and in view of the fact that Mahatma Gandhi alone can lead the Congress and the country to victory during such a crisis, the Congress regards it as imperative that the Congress executive should command his implicit confidence and requests that President to nominate the Working Committee in accordance with the wishes of Gandhiji.[35]

This resolution was first put forward in the closed meeting of the Subjects Committee, and Bose supporters, including M. N. Roy, made an attempt to dilute the resolution. In his amendment Roy changed the two points to one, deleted the instructions to the president to consult Gandhi about the formation of the Working Committee, and transformed Pant's Resolution into a meaningless tribute to Gandhi and Bose.[36] But Roy's amendment was beaten, as were other attempts by the left. Mr. Niharendu Dutt Mazumdar, a labor leader, leftist, and member of the Bengal Legislative Assembly, said that the resolution showed "a spirit of vindictiveness on the part of the members of the Working Committee." [37] He regarded it as a "backdoor method" of attacking the Congress president.

It was reported that, "When the discussion on the resolution was going on in the Subjects Committee a news [report] appeared that through telephonic communication the approval of Gandhiji had been secured for it." [38] This event may have been stage-managed, since Gandhi later said that he had not participated in the formulation and passage of this resolution. Even the Congress Socialists seem to have moved amendments to weaken the Pant Resolution in the closed session. But the amendments failed by a margin of 218 to 135.[39]

The most effective speech for the resolution was given by its mover, Pandit Pant. He said that if the delegates wanted Gandhiji back they had to prove it to him. The *Indian Annual Register* reported,

> Digressing for a while, Pandit Pant said that wherever nations had progressed they had done so under the leadership of one man. Germany had relied on Herr Hitler. Whether they agreed with Herr Hitler's methods or not, there was no gainsaying the fact that Germany had progressed under Herr Hitler. Similarly, Italy had risen because of Signor Mussolini and it was Lenin that raised Russia.[40]

The Pandit reminded the delegates that "we have Gandhi. . . . Then why should we not reap the full advantage of that factor?" [41] Pandit Pant denied the suggestion that the resolution savored of vendetta and he disarmed some of the opposition by saying, in effect, that the resolution was for Gandhi, not against Bose. The resolution was adopted by the Subjects Committee and brought before the open session. The Congress Socialists decided to remain neutral on the resolution, and the margin of passage was even greater than it had been in the Subjects Committee.[42] Conflicting accounts have been given of the position taken by the communists on the resolution.[43] They were caught in the dilemma of having to choose between left unity and nationalist unity. For the moment, both groups chose Gandhi and left Bose to his fate. The Congress Socialists had disagreed with Bose about setting a time limit on the national demand to the British. The Gandhians agreed to pass the national demand resolution in the form desired by the Congress Socialists, and this may have obtained the neutrality of the Congress Socialists on the vote.[44]

Subhas Bose had made yet another challenge to authority, this time within the Congress, but in the end showed his familiar ambivalence. He wanted to defeat the Gandhians and control them, and yet to retain their support for his program. The passage of the Pant Resolution put Bose in a very difficult position. The "wishes of Gandhiji" were interposed in the usual Congress procedure of having the president nominate the Working Committee. A long, sometimes embittered, correspondence between Subhas and Sarat Bose, Nehru, and Gandhi followed the Tripuri Congress and lasted until the end of April.[45] In conciliatory tones, Bose pleaded with Gandhi to compromise on the selection of the Working Committee. Bose said he would nominate half the members, while Sardar Patel for the Gandhians could choose the other half. Bose argued that a heterogeneous Working Committee was what circumstances required, and he was willing to go more than half way.[46] Nehru was in favor of some sort of compromise, but Bose was furious at Nehru, for he felt that Nehru had betrayed the left and the future of socialism in India by not taking his side. Nehru later admitted that he had let Bose down, but he claimed that there would be no movement in India without Gandhi.[47] Gandhi, for his part, was adamant and seemed determined to oust Bose. He argued that it would be impossible for a heterogeneous Working Committee to operate effectively and he refused to nominate anyone, since he said that his nominees would be men with whom Bose could not work. Gandhi urged Bose to select his own committee.[48] Bose answered that this would go against the Pant Resolution. Although Bose maintained that the Pant Resolution was unconstitutional, he felt bound by it.[49]

Gandhi was, in effect, challenging Bose to select a Working Committee of leftists. Bose, feeling his lack of strong support from the left and unable to confront the danger of splitting the Congress, did not select a Working Committee. Although Bose believed in the socialist ideology that he expounded, he also felt that the mass support for the Congress among millions of Indians was due to Gandhi's charisma and the organization which had been built in large part by Gandhians.[50] There were a number of other issues which entered into the correspondence with Gandhi, and they may be summarized as follows:

1. Gandhi said he "smelled violence in the air"; Bose said Gandhi had a bogey about violence and there was no such smell.[51]
2. Gandhi, Nehru, and the Gandhians felt the moment was inopportune to put an ultimatum before the British.[52]
3. Bose had established a National Planning Committee; he favored land reform, including the abolition of landlordism, and state control of the economy. The Gandhians disagreed with many parts of Bose's economic program.[53]

4. Bose's "aspersion" on some former members of the Working Committee, for which he had never apologized, and remarks in *The Indian Struggle*. A writer in the *Indian Annual Register* noted that this book had been banned in India until 1938. "The correspondence published in the Press on May 14, 1939, after his [Bose's] resignation, bears unmistakable evidence of his spirit of accommodation, of his eagerness to propitiate and reconcile. This eagerness failed to win confidence, because the book stood in the way." [54]

Bose failed because the left which united to elect him president continued to disintegrate. M. N. Roy, although he had thought the Pant Resolution undemocratic and had opposed it, called for Bose to resign.[55] Nehru and the Congress Socialists may not have been happy about the evidence of the weakness of the left or about the treatment given Bose, but they flowed with the Gandhian tide. Bose's victory in the presidential election proved to be hollow and he and his brother were outwitted and outmanned by the Gandhians in the ensuing contests.

Bose and Gandhi could not come to an agreement about the composition of the Working Committee, and the stalemate continued until a meeting of the AICC in Calcutta during late April and early May. Nehru, trying to prevent a damaging split, moved that Bose continue as Congress president. But after some discussion Nehru withdrew his resolution. Another attempt to keep Bose in office was also abortive, and finally, seeing no other course open to him, Bose resigned as Congress president.[56] Rajendra Prasad wrote this description of the events just before and after the meeting:

> As Subhas Bose's position was now untenable, we began to think of his successor. The brutal frankness of Sardar Patel was not liked by Bose and other people. Jawaharlal, who was disgusted with the state of affairs, did not want to take up the Presidentship. Maulana Azad, who would have been the best choice had an accident. . . . My name was suggested. I did not want to take it up. . . . But all my arguments had to be waived when Gandhiji directed me to take up the responsibility.[57]

Outside one of the sessions of the AICC, Pandit Pant and Bhulabhai Desai were roughly handled and Acharya Kripalani was threatened with violence. Observers believed that Bengali supporters of Bose were responsible for these incidents.[58] There was undoubtedly much hostile feeling in Bengal against the national leadership of the Congress at this time. The choice of Rajendra Prasad, a Bihari, to succeed Bose just at a moment of some ill-feeling between Bengalis and neighboring Biharis may have added to the charged atmosphere. With Bose's exit, a new Gandhian Working Committee was formed, and it included Dr. B. C. Roy and Prafulla C. Ghosh, two of Bengal's foremost Gandhians.[59]

After Bose's capitulation, he was subjected to much criticism from other members of the amorphous left. Among the most severe critics were those who had wanted him to choose a solid left-wing Working Committee. The following example of this criticism is from *Forward*, which by 1939 was edited by a faction of former Jugantar revolutionaries.

> Then entered Subhas Babu into the arena with the passport of thorough obedience to Gandhiji. Throughout the year he was perfectly submissive even on the Federation and the political prisoners' release issues. He never attempted, he never thought of increasing the organization strength of the Congress. . . . when the revolt was a *fait accompli* and the split was brought about that should have been postponed until some organisational strength had been built up, an attempt was made to make the best of a bad job by the real revolutionary elements in the country. . . . The advice was to replace the representatives of the conservative sections on the Working Committee by those who might in a way and for the time being represent the interests of the masses. . . . But Subhas Babu, having revolted for nothing other than the Presidentship, carried a blank mind as far as a plan or a programme was concerned. . . . He had not the courage to accept the plan of action placed before him. . . . When asked why he was not acting in this situation, he replied that his supporters were "shaking in their shoes." . . . The fact of the matter . . . is that Subhas Babu is no radical. . . . When it became obvious that he had no lead to give and no plan of action to put forward, he could no longer keep his supporters together. In the last resort, his mainstay was Bengal's Provincial feeling. As a result, Bengal tended to be isolated as it once before had been during the Assembly elections of 1934. . . . Luckily for the Province, at long last he calls off the revolt. He ought not to find a chance to repeat a like experiment by which . . . he has landed the country in confusion and demoralisation.[60]

With the debacle of the left at Tripuri and Calcutta, Bose decided later in 1939 to form a leftist group and called it the Forward Bloc.[61]

But finding that several groups like the Royists and the communists would not submerge their identities in a new organization, Bose called for a more amorphous left-wing grouping called the Left Consolidation Committee. Even this looser alliance, however, was not able to bring together the warring factions of the left.[62]

In the same period in 1939 and 1940 when the left and the national Congress were passing through a crisis, the Bengal Provincial Congress Committee was also affected. Subhas Bose was the reigning president of the BPCC and the annual general meeting of the committee was held in late April 1939 in Calcutta. Some 420 members out of a total of 544 attended. But more important than the general meeting was a small gathering of 15 representatives of the different groups in the BPCC. These included Sarat and Subhas Bose, Kiran Sankar Roy, Prafulla Ghosh, Monoranjan Gupta, Arun Chandra Guha, Bhupen Kumar Datta, Surendra Mohan Ghose, Satish Chakravarty, Amar Ghosh, Bijoyendra Palit, Rajkumar Chakravarty, Sushil Banerjee and Pandit Jeewanlal. It was decided that the executive council of the BPCC was to be formed in consultation with all groups, that Subhas Bose was to continue as president, and that the BPCC would have 5 vice-presidents and 5 assistant secretaries.[63] Starting with the hypothesis that there were five main factions to be represented, some suggestions may be offered about the ones gathered in the smaller meeting. Sarat and Subhas Bose headed the Bose faction, and Amar Ghosh was with their group. Kiran Sankar Roy, J. C. Gupta, and Rajkumar Chakravarty were known as official congressmen, usually following the national Congress line. Prafulla Ghosh was a pure Gandhian and had been since about 1921. Surendra Mohan Ghose, Bupen K. Datta, Arun Guha, and Monoranjan Gupta were all ex-Jugantar revolutionaries; but there may well have been divisions between them, since Jugantar members had moved into different groups.[64]

When Subhas Bose announced his executive council for the BPCC early in June, some factions felt that they had been underrepresented or left out. *Forward*, edited by Bhupen K. Datta, maintained that Bose had gone back on the April agreement about the composition of the executive body. It was argued that Bose had blocked participation of the opposition in the regional Congress in the same way that Gandhi had neglected Bose and other leftists in forming the Working Committee of the national Congress.[65]

Shortly, however, an even more serious crisis arose for the regional Congress when Gandhi selected Dr. B. C. Roy to reorganize the BPCC.[66] Dr. Roy was thwarted, but the Working Committee shortly found a way to get at the Bose-dominated BPCC. In July 1939 Bose called for a demonstration opposing a move by the Congress to gain greater control over provincial committees. As punishment for this action, Bose was suspended from Congress executive positions for three years. The Working Committee called for new elections to the BPCC and when Bose refused to hold them, a new, ad hoc BPCC was appointed.[67] Bose resisted the Working Committee efforts. He wrote in a letter to M. N. Roy in January 1940:

> I have already used my moderating influence to the extreme limit. As a result, the B.P.C.C. toned down the resolution of the Executive Council. This could be done with great difficulty, and members were on the point of revolting against my moderation. But if the W.C. does not reconsider the ad hoc committee affair, then I am afraid that the B.P.C.C. will defy the W.C. Bengal has certain traditions (which cannot be ignored) in its relation with the W.C. of the Congress. Consequently it will not take lying down what other provinces possibly may.[68]

In July 1940, Bose was arrested by the Bengal government for leading a demonstration demanding the removal of a memorial to Black Hole of Calcutta victims. He was also held for sedition. After some time in prison, he undertook a fast and, fearing for his health and possibly his life, the government released him, placing him under house arrest in his home on Elgin Road. Early on January 17, 1941, Bose slipped secretly from his house; and he soon left India never to return.[69]

During his final year of freedom in India, from the summer of 1939 to the summer of 1940, Bose toured the country trying to rouse support for the Forward Bloc. Although he was greeted by large crowds in some parts of the country, he did not build a viable organization. But he did get a large percentage of the Congress Socialists in Bengal, the Central Provinces, Berar, and some Congress Socialists in the Punjab, the United Provinces, and Orissa, to switch to the Forward Bloc.[70] Bose's legacy to this small party was his own charisma and his eclectic program.[71]

BENGAL MINISTRY QUESTION

Through this account of the Congress, the left, and Subhas Bose from 1926 to 1940, Bengali Muslims and Bengal legislative bodies have been neglected. In general, communal relations in Bengal and in India regressed during these years. Bengali Muslim leaders such as H. S. Suhrawardy and the Muslim Swarajists, who had cooperated with the Swaraj Party and defended many Congress moves, now took more of a Muslim separatist line. Virtually all Muslim leaders in Bengal now advocated separate electorates and wanted seats reserved for Muslims commensurate with their percentage of Bengal's population.[72] Communications between Bengali nationalists and important Muslim leaders seem to have been minimal, and even the term "nationalist" began to take on a Hindu communalist connotation. A group calling themselves the Bengal Nationalist Party challenged the Congress for Bengal seats in the Central Legislative Assembly in 1934 and won a surprising victory. They played upon caste fears over the small share of seats given caste Hindus by the Communal Award of 1932.[73] This event assisted those Muslim leaders who believed in manipulating Muslim communal feelings to gain preeminence.

But it would be misleading to dwell only upon communal difficulties and neglect communal cooperation. There were a number of small Muslim groups, including the Bengal Nationalist Muslim Conference and some Muslim leaders, who were still willing to work with the Congress and Hindu leaders and would remain so until independence and partition. These efforts deserve attention in order to counteract an ahistorical view that by this period communalism and eventual partition were inevitable.

Among Bengali Muslim leaders there were some of the same problems that Congress leaders faced. Difficulties arising from endemic factionalism, personal ambition, and strains between national and regional organizations are apparent among the Muslims.[74] From the late 1920s up to about 1937, and perhaps later, the Muslim League was weak as a national organization and particularly feeble in the Muslim majority areas. In the late 1920s and early 1930s, the Bengal Muslim Party and annual Bengal Muslims' Conference had considerable strength. The Bengal Nationalist Muslim Conference and the Bengal Presidency Muslim League leaned towards the Congress and had less support.[75] In this period, the Krishak Praja Party was formed under the leadership of A. K. Fazlul Huq. Humayun Kabir, who was associated with the party and worked with Huq for some time until the party split, wrote this sympathetic description of its aims in 1944.

> The Krishak Praja party has already been mentioned as a party with a future. Though non-communal in aim and objective, the party is dominantly Muslim in composition and leadership and is continually trying to organise the masses on the basis of an economic programme. The conviction that political democracy cannot be made real and effective without a fundamental reconstruction in the economic framework of society serves as the cornerstone of the Praja movement and organisation. Aiming at agrarian revolution through parliamentary and constitutional methods, it has grown out of the peasantry's fight for rights and is bound to increase in strength with the growth of political consciousness among the masses.[76]

The wide support given the Krishak Party in the 1937 elections, the presence of a few Muslims—most notably Muzaffar Ahmad—in the inner circles of the communists, and the growing fame of the leftist poet Kazi Nazrul Islam, indicate that socialist and communist ideas were spreading among Bengali Muslims as well as Hindus.[77] A socialist program offered the opportunity to appeal to Hindu intellectuals and Hindu and Muslim peasants, though it might alienate business and landholding interests which were cagily working between the government, the nationalists, and the communal groups. The Congress, which had been incorporating a number of socialist items into its program, did not make a major effort to gain Muslim support until the 1937 elections showed how little Muslim backing it had.[78]

In the period 1927–1936, Muslim members and ministers played an important role in the working of the Bengal Legislative Council.[79] By 1929 the Swaraj Party had been severely weakened in the legislative councils and that year, in an effort to put pressure on the government of India for significant constitutional advances, Congress members resigned from these bodies. This left the Bengal Legislative Council completely in the hands of Hindu loyalists or liberals and the Muslim members. The Muslims, with the support of the officials and the Europeans, were able to run the transferred departments.[80] Although there was some shuffling of ministers, the Muslim leaders were able to pass some measures of importance to them, especially concerning elementary education, local self-government, and peasant indebtedness.[81] One Hindu leader has suggested that this long experience of power and the opportunity to pass measures of value to the Bengal Muslims made some difference in the support the idea of partition eventually gained among them.[82] They developed a sense of their growing importance in Bengal and a determination to benefit from their numerical majority in the province.

The importance of the work of the Bengal Legislative Council itself, however, was undercut by the continuing discussions of the next step of constitutional advance.[83] These talks within the government of India and the British Parliament, at round table conferences, and between Indian leaders, formally began with the formation of the Indian Statutory (or Simon) Commission, and culminated with the Government of India Act of 1935. Though almost all political organizations, including the Congress and the Muslim League, disliked most or many of the provisions of the act, all groups eventually decided to participate in the elections for provincial legislative bodies to be held early in 1937.[84]

Many leftist leaders of the Congress, including Subhas Bose and Jawaharlal Nehru, opposed the formation of ministries by the Congress under the provisions for provincial autonomy in the 1935 Act. The Congress as a whole decided to wait until after the actual elections and then evaluate its position.[85] The league, although it rejected the federal provisions of the act, seemed willing to implement the provincial provisions in those areas where they were strong enough to form a government or to be an important element in a coalition government. In the elections, the Congress gained an absolute majority in 6 states, while it was the largest single party in 2 others, Bengal and Assam.[86] The Congress demanded the assurance from the government of India that governors would not interfere with the work of Congress ministries. Negotiations with the government dragged out over several months. The bargain finally struck did not actually give the Congress what it wanted, but it was accepted anyhow. The Congress formed governments in 6 provinces but did not participate in coalitions in those provinces in which it did not have an absolute majority.[87]

In Bengal there had been considerable wrangling over an allotment of seats which greatly changed the strengths of the different castes and communities from those of 1919 Act. Under the new Act, Bengali Muslims had 117 of the total 250 seats in the Bengal Legislative Assembly reserved for them. Of the remaining seats, 78 were in the general non-Muslim category, but of these, 30 were reserved for scheduled caste members. The Communal Decision had raised the number of scheduled caste seats from 10 to 30, and this action is what had given the Bengal Nationalist Party strong support among caste Hindus in the 1934 election for the Central Legislative Assembly. There were 55 other seats, divided in the following way: Europeans, 11; Anglo-Indians, 4; commerce and industry, 19; landholders, 5; labor, 8; universities, 2; Indian Christians, 2; women, 4. Much controversy had accompanied this allotment.[88]

In 1934, the Swaraj Party had been reconstituted, and after some controversy between Dr. B. C. Roy and Sarat Bose, the latter became head of the Congress Parliamentary Board in Bengal responsible for running the Congress election campaigns.[89] The results of the 1937 poll for Legislative Assembly seats showed that the Congress had 60 seats, the Muslim League 40, independent Muslims 41, the Krishak Praja Party 35, Europeans 25, the independent scheduled caste group 23, and independent caste Hindus 14.[90] The Congress formed de facto alliances with scheduled caste candidates and this enabled it to win many scheduled caste seats under joint electorate voting. A government report on the elections noted that the Congress was the most "clearly defined party" and exercised a "remarkable influence" on Hindu voters.[91] The electorate numbered 6,695,483 or 13.4 percent of the population. Only 40.5 percent of the electorate voted, but there was great variation from constituency to constituency, with the extremely low percentages voting for women's and scheduled castes' seats pulling down the average. The Muslim League won only about one-third of the seats reserved for Muslims and did badly in several contests with the Krishak Praja Party.[92] The generally poor showing of the league spurred Jinnah to work energetically to build support for the league in the following years. Since the Congress was not willing to enter coalitions or form governments in the early months of 1937, other party leaders were approached in Bengal. Ram Gopal has described the fruits of this effort:

> Fazlul Huq, who was the leader of the Praja Party, and who was looking for the co-operation of another party to raise his strength to a

clear majority, preferred to approach the Congress and not the League. The Congress had declined to accept Ministerial responsibility. Huq, therefore, made common cause with the League and, instead of coalescing with that party, joined it with most of his followers. It was an event of outstanding importance. A Congress-Praja Party coalition would have put itself on a road to Hindu-Muslim understanding; the Praja Party's merger with the League made the Ministry almost wholly communal, and gave communalism a foothold to expand.[93]

Fazlul Huq had been a fringe member of the Muslim League until 1937 and had concentrated his energies on building up his own party. He did take a more active part in league activities from 1937 but often had a strained relationship with Jinnah and the national organization.[94] In these circumstances, private negotiations continued among a number of Bengali politicians, including Huq, about the possibilities of alternative coalition arrangements. By October 1937, the Bose group had decided that they would like to join with Fazlul Huq's party and oust the Muslim League from the coalition in office. Nalini Ranjan Sarker, ex-Swarajist, peripheral congressman, and friend of Gandhi, had agreed to serve as finance minister in the Bengali cabinet dominated by the Krishak Party and the Muslim League. The Boses, who had control of the BPCC, continued to apply pressure on Gandhi to have the latter ask Sarker to resign, allowing the Bengal Congress to form a coalition with the Krishak Party.[95] At the same time other talks were going on between Surendra Mohan Ghose and Khwaja Nazimuddin about the possibility of a Congress-league coalition, to which the league at first was not averse.[96] In the period 1937 to 1941, none of these negotiations bore fruit. The story of these negotiations and exchanges has not been written, and much of the evidence that may eventually be gathered must come from oral sources. There are a few documents bearing on this issue, and they include unpublished letters exchanged between Subhas Bose and Gandhi in 1938. Gandhi wrote to Bose in December 1938,

My Dear Subhas Babu,
  I must dictate this letter as I am wilfully blind. Whilst I am dictating this, Maulana Saheb, Nalini Babu and Ghamshamdas are listening [that is, Maulana Azad, Nalini Ranjan Sarker, and G. D. Birla]. We had an exhaustive discussion over the Bengal Ministry. I am more than ever convinced that we should not aim at ousting the Ministry. We

shall gain nothing by a reshuffle; and, probably, we shall lose much by
including Congressmen in the Ministry. I feel, therefore, that the best
way of securing comparative purity of administration and a continuity
of a settled programme and policy would be to aim at having all the
reforms that we desire, carried out by the present Ministry. Nalini
Babu should come out, as he says he would, on a real issue being raised
and the decision being taken by the Ministry against the interests of
the country. His retirement from the Ministry would then be dignified
and wholly justified. . . .

Yours sincerely,

M. K. Gandhi

Bose replied to Gandhi from Bombay on December 21, 1938:

My dear Mahatmaji,

The letter which Sjt. G. D. Birla brought from Wardha came as a
profound shock to me. I remember to have discussed the Bengal situation with you time and again. The other day at Wardha it was discussed between us once again. My brother Sarat also discussed the
matter with you. Both of us have the clear impression that you have
always agreed with the idea of a Coalition Ministry for Bengal. I do
not know what has happened since I left Wardha to make you alter
your view so completely that you now write—"I am more than ever
convinced that we should not aim at ousting the ministry etc." The
papers say that after I left Wardha Sjt. N. R. Sarkar, Sjt. G. D. Birla
and Moulana Azad Sahib have seen you. Evidently you have altered
your [view?] after talking to them. The position, therefore, is that you
attach more value and importance to the views of those three gentlemen than to the views of those who are responsible for running the
Congress organisation in Bengal.

You are not in the habit of writing anything lightheartedly—
hence I shall be justified in attaching the fullest weight to what is
your considered opinion. Your letter has given rise to a crisis in which
it is necessary for me to speak very frankly and I crave your pardon at
the outset for doing so.

To come straight to the point—there is a fundamental difference
between Moulana Sahib and myself on the point at issue. This became
manifest when we were confronted with the ministerial crisis in
Assam. I can perhaps now claim that I was right and Moulana Sahib
was wrong. But if Sardar Patel had not providentially come to my res-
cue, Moulana Sahib would never have given in at Shillong and perhaps
you would not have supported my view point against that of Moulana
Sahib when the Working Committee met at Delhi. In that case there
would not have been a Coalition ministry in Assam. . . .

Over Sindh, there has been a difference between Moulana Sahib on the one side and several members of the Working Committee including myself on the other. And now come[s?] the Bengal situation on which our views are diametrically opposed.

Moulana Sahib's view seems to be that in the Muslim-majority provinces like Bengal, communal Muslim Ministries should be allowed to continue in office. Moulana Sahib is evidently unhappy over our lending support to the Allah Bux Ministry in Sindh.

I hold, on the contrary, that it is imperative in the national interest that we should pull down the Huq Ministry as early as possible. The longer this reactionary Ministry remains in office, the more communal will the atmosphere of Bengal become and the weaker will the Congress grow, vis-a-vis the Muslim League. . . .

At long last early in November Sjt. Nalini Sarkar had been convinced that he should resign from the Huq Ministry. He assured me for the last time on the 9th December, before I left Calcutta for Wardha, that he would resign his office before the next Budget Session. What made him renege from the position within one week, I do not know. Your influence is going to be used not to get Nalini Babu to resign but to get him to stick to office at a time when even his closest friends want him to get out of the Huq Ministry. It has astonished me that you did not feel it necessary to even consult me before you arrived at a decision on such a serious matter.[97]

Bose went on to explain at length why he advocated a coalition ministry. He thought that Nalini Sarker's resignation would bring down the Huq ministry and then the Congress would be in a strong bargaining position for forming a coalition ministry in which it would hold decisive power. As long as Sarker would not resign, Bose and the Bengal Congress were effectively prevented from overturning the predominantly Muslim ministry which Bose thought was encouraging communalism by both Muslims and Hindus. Nirad C. Chaudhuri, who was Sarat Bose's private secretary at the time and who handled much of Subhas Bose's correspondence, has suggested that Bose felt that not only was there a difference of view with Maulana Azad, but that G. D. Birla was interfering because he feared Hindu-Muslim unity, that is, a coalition ministry, in Bengal because this would adversely affect Marwari economic domination of Calcutta. In Mr. Chaudhuri's opinion, Gandhi acted knowingly in the Marwari interest because he was against Bose and against Bengali interests, other than those of his own men in Bengal.[98]

The strains between Gandhi and the Boses in early 1939 may have had a stronger regional aspect to them than was obvious from the superficial facts of the Congress presidency campaign.

With the continuing failure of Congress-Krishak Party discussions, Fazlul Huq, who was known for frequent changes of direction and a determination to stay in power, talked and wrote publicly in ever harsher communal terms. Under his name a pamphlet was published in December 1939 on *Muslim Sufferings under Congress Rule*. Listing hundreds of violent acts by Hindus against Muslims in those provinces under Congress rule, Huq concluded, "The Muslim case remains that during the Congress regime they were condemned to live in terror and to suffer these atrocities, while the Law moved tardily or did not move at all." [99] Within two years after writing this, Huq found himself expelled from the Muslim League and began to form the Progressive Coalition, an alliance between the Bose faction of the Congress, the Krishak Party, and the Hindu Nationalists.

With the coming of World War II in September 1939, the government of India, without consulting Indian politicians or ministers, brought India into the conflict. The Congress, feeling that this step should not have been taken in such a manner, had its ministries resign in the six provinces which they controlled. Nalini Sarker finally resigned in 1939, but in 1941 he became a member of the Viceroy's Executive Council. The Bengal Ministry continued, since the Muslim League and the Krishak Praja Party supported the Indian government's war effort.[100]

Subhas Bose was under house arrest in December 1940 when he made an effort to have the viceroy step into the deteriorating communal situation in Bengal. He wrote to Lord Linlithgow, criticizing the Bengal Ministry, and continued:

> in criticising the Bengal Ministry in the above manner, I have nothing in common with the mental attitude of the Hindu Mahasabha [an organization of more communally oriented Hindus—L. G.]. People like myself are prepared to concede to the Muslims, gladly and voluntarily, their legitimate share in everything which interests them. We have already proved our *bona fides* in this matter by our action in the past —action which at times has made us unpopular with that section of the Hindus which is communally-minded. Today we represent perhaps the only party in India that can still hope to bridge the gulf be-

tween the two major communities and can still claim to possess the goodwill of a large section of Indian Muslims.

Nobody will deny that Bengal has been the cradle of Indian Nationalism since the dawn of British rule in this country. Hindu Bengal, in particular, has throughout these decades thought and striven in terms of nationalism, with the result that the Hindu Mahasabha movement has never had a strong foothold here. But today a wave of communalism is spreading over Hindu Bengal, as an inevitable reaction to Muslim Communalism. In the face of this communal vortex with its unending eddies, those who believe in Nationalism are looking on helplessly.[101]

Bose asked the viceroy to make an effort to have the support of officials and European businessmen withdrawn from the Bengal Ministry. He even suggested the suspension of the Constitution in Bengal, if necessary. About three weeks after this final act, he left India.

Bose's efforts at forming a Hindu-Muslim coalition ministry and his challenge to the Gandhian leadership in the Congress both ended in failure while he remained in India. Whatever his personal sentiments for communal harmony and leftist hegemony in the Congress, he was not able to bring about either of them. Although he probably had a larger popular following than any Bengali Hindu leader in his own province and had considerable support from Indians in other regions, he was not able to use this enthusiasm to help him make concrete political accomplishments. He was limited in what he could do by his lack of rapport with the Gandhians and by the general suspicion which characterized the Indian left.

It must have been with mixed emotions that Subhas Bose listened to Rabindranath Tagore in 1939 give a second famous address entitled "Deśanāyak." Tagore, addressing Bose, said in part,

As Bengal's poet, I today acknowledge you as the honored leader of the people of Bengal. The Gītā tells us that from time to time the eternal principle of the good arises to challenge the reign of the evil. . . . Suffering from the deadening effect of the prolonged punishment inflicted upon her young generation and disintegrated by internal faction, Bengal is passing through a period of dark despair. . . . At such a juncture of nation-wide crisis, we require the service of a forceful personality, the invincible faith of a natural leader, who can defy the adverse fate that threatens our progress. . . . I have watched the dawn that witnessed the beginning of your political *sadhana*. In that uncer-

tain twilight there had been misgivings in my heart and I had hesitated
to accept you for what you are now. . . . Today you are revealed in
the pure light of the midday sun which does not admit of apprehen-
sions. . . . Your strength has been sorely taxed by imprisonment, ban-
ishment and disease, but rather than impairing these have helped to
broaden your sympathies. . . . You did not regard apparent defeat as
final: therefore, you have turned your trials into your allies. More than
anything else Bengal needs today to emulate the powerful force of
your determination and your self-reliant courage. . . . Let Bengal af-
firm in one united voice that her deliverer's seat is ready, spread for
you. . . . Long ago . . . I sent out a call for the leader of Bengal who
had yet to come. After a lapse of many years I am addressing at this
meeting one who has come into the full light of recognition. My days
have come to their end. I may not join him in the fight that is to
come. I can only bless him and take my leave, knowing that he had
made his country's burden of sorrow his own, that his final reward is
fast coming as his country's freedom.[102]

Even the poet's vision and homage could not dispel the sense of failure
and frustration which may have filled Bose as he felt the disparity between the call for unity which Tagore sent out and the divisions
within Bengal and India which Bose could not eliminate. Tagore, as
usual, saw the dangers, and suggested a solution, unity behind Bose.
But neither could bring it about. Although both had pride in Bengal's
past and hope for her future, they saw grim sights around them. Tagore was to die within two years, while Bose was to seek new avenues
to action and India's freedom outside his native land.

POSTSCRIPT

The beginning of World War II changed the political situation in
India and Bengal significantly. Positions on the war effort determined,
to a great extent, the kinds of activity the government of India was
willing to allow each political group. Strange matings occurred. Once
the Soviet Union was in the war on the Allied side, the CPI surfaced
and quickly changed its line from "imperialist war" to "people's war."
M. N. Roy also supported the war effort and was suspended from the
Congress for his stand. He transformed his small group, the League of
Radical Congressmen, into the Radical Democratic Party. The Congress Socialists and the Forward Bloc, on the other hand, were ada-
mantly against supporting the war unless the British were ready to

hand over power to Indian nationalists. The Congress was torn between the two positions, with Nehru eager to join the fight against fascism but unwilling to do so without major concessions from the government. Prodded by the Congress Socialists and embittered by the shortcomings of a British offer made during the Cripps Mission in 1942, the Congress finally began the Quit India movement. This involved individual civil disobedience, mass action in some areas such as Midnapur district in Bengal, and acts of violence and sabotage often planned by underground Congress Socialists.[103]

The Muslim League and the Bengal Ministry supported the war effort. Fazlul Huq, perhaps seeking to have a position more independent of the Muslim League and eager for improved communal relations in Bengal, brought the downfall of the league–Krishak Party ministry and formed a new ministerial alliance, the Progressive Coalition, in 1941. Huq wrote to Jinnah in December 1940:

> It is far from my intention to bring about a disruption in the Muslim League. . . . My only desire has been for peace, because I feel that unless there is unity among all communities on the principle of give and take, there will be no constitutional advance and no prospect of a better India than we know at the present moment.[104]

It is difficult to understand what motivated Huq's changing positions and alliances. The Progressive Coalition included the Krishak Party, the Forward Bloc section of the Congress formally led by Sarat Bose, a scheduled caste group, and the Hindu Nationalists led by Shyama Prasad Mookherjee. There were 5 Muslims and 4 Hindus in the new cabinet, 8 of the 9 lawyers by training.[105] The coalition might have been a step toward improved communal relations in Bengal if its members had worked together more effectively and if tremendous outside pressures had not been applied. Jinnah took the formation of this ministry as an attempt to ruin the Muslim League. He visited Bengal and made considerable efforts to insure its prompt dissolution.[106] Khwaja Nazimuddin, who had been a member of the inner circle of Huq's earlier ministry, became the leader of the Muslim League Parliamentary Party spearheading the opposition. Natural disasters, the 1942 rebellion, the growing strength of the Muslim League, and the disfavor of the government of Bengal contributed to the fall of the Progressive Coalition in

1943. It was replaced by a Muslim League ministry headed by Nazimud-din and H. S. Suhrawardy.[107] It should be noted, however, that even before the collapse of his ministry in 1943, Huq had been privately dickering with Jinnah about dissolving the Progressive Coalition and returning to the Muslim League fold.[108]

Early in the tenure of the Muslim League ministry, Bengal suffered one of the worst famines in its history. It has been blamed on profiteering food distributors and speculators, the governments of India and Bengal, a poor administrative and distribution system, and the Huq and Nazimuddin ministries. The ministry struggled on through this crisis, but became so weak in 1945 that it was defeated in a vote in the assembly and Lord Casey, the Australian governor of Bengal, temporarily suspended parliamentary government.[109]

Subhas Bose decided, probably in 1940, to take advantage of the war situation to promote India's struggle for freedom. On January 17, 1941, Bose slipped out of his house and by car, train, plane, and foot secretly made his way to Afghanistan and then to Berlin. During World War II, he worked with the Axis powers against those who he said were enslaving India, the British. From Europe he traveled to Southeast Asia in 1943. With the assistance of the Japanese, he formed a provisional Indian government-in-exile and an army, the Indian National Army (INA), composed of captured Indian prisoners-of-war and fought with the Japanese against the British in Burma.[110]

Bose died in a plane crash in 1945 as he was trying to flee from the victorious Allied forces.[111] After the war, the government of India tried some leading members of the INA, but the trail became a *cause célèbre* and several prominent lawyers joined the defense committee, including Jawaharlal Nehru.[112] Gandhi wrote in glowing terms at that time about Subhas Bose. "Netaji's name," he said, "is one to conjure with. His patriotism is second to none. His bravery shines through all his action." [113] Bose became a greater hero in death than he had been in life. Demonstrations for the INA prisoners were a factor in making the British anxious about controlling the country, and they strengthened their determination to quit India.[114]

In the brief period between the end of World War II and the granting of independence to India and Pakistan, there was a growing polarization between the Muslim League and the Congress. The Muslim

League made rapid progress in gathering support during the war years, and the 1946 elections demonstrated that the league had so broadened its base that it could now claim to speak for most of the Muslims in India. The Krishak Praja Party had fallen apart and Fazlul Huq had gone into temporary eclipse.

The Muslim League in Bengal led by H. S. Suhrawardy, who was ably assisted by Abul Hasem, won virtually all the Muslim reserved seats in the 1946 provincial elections and Suhrawardy became chief minister, forming a Muslim League cabinet with only very minor Hindu support. Serious communal disturbances broke out in Bengal following the league's "Direct Action Day" in August 1946, the most famous of which was the Great Calcutta Killing.[115] This latter incident and riots in Noakhali District in Eastern Bengal persuaded many Hindus that they could never endure a permanent Muslim-majority government after British rule ended.

At the center, there were negotiations over possible constitutional changes which proved fruitless until the new Labour Government in London announced that British rule would terminate in 1948, and that Lord Mountbatten would be the new viceroy empowered to carry through this transfer of governmental authority. Once Mountbatten had decided that no federal system would work, he pressed for the partition of British India and persuaded Congress leaders Nehru and Patel that this was the only way out of the impasse. In Bengal some Hindu and Muslim leaders, including Sarat Bose, Kiran Sankar Roy, H. S. Suhrawardy, and Abul Hasem advocated an independent and united Bengal. This made sense to many Muslims, since they would be the majority in such an independent entity, and Jinnah is said to have given his blessing to such a move. Mahatma Gandhi, who opposed the partition of India as the destruction of his life's work, also gave some verbal support to the movement for a united Bengal.

But after the riots of 1946, many Hindus in Bengal were unwilling to accept a Muslim-majority, united Bengal. A section of the Congress in Bengal and the Hindu Mahasabha organized a majority of Bengali Hindus to demand the partition of Bengal into two separate provinces, even if there was to be no partition of India. Communal antagonism was at flood level and could not be resisted. Sardar Patel supported the demand for the partition of Bengal and wrote to Sarat Bose that the latter had become isolated from his Hindu brethren. The efforts for a united Bengal failed, and British India was officially partitioned into the independent nations of India and Pakistan on August 15, 1947. Bengal was split into the Hindu-majority area of West Bengal in India, which included Calcutta, and East Bengal, later called East Pakistan.[116]

The Congress and the Muslim League took office in the two new nations. In West Bengal, those Bengali political leaders most closely allied with the Gandhian leadership controlled the BPCC and the government of the state for two decades following independence. These men included Prafulla Ghosh, Dr. B. C. Roy, Surendra Mohan Ghose, P. C. Sen, and Atulya Ghosh.[117] They were aided for this long period by the inability of leftist forces, including Socialists, communists, and members of the Forward Bloc, to ally. Sarat Bose made an attempt to rally the leftists under one banner at the end of the 1940s, but he failed.[118] There continued to be considerable resentment against the Congress and the government of India which the leftists were finally able to take advantage of in the 1967 and 1969 elections,[119] and the Congress hold over the state was finally broken.

In East Pakistan, the Muslim League came to power under Khwaja Nazimuddin, who with Jinnah's assistance gained preeminence over H. S. Suhrawardy in the Bengal branch of the league shortly before independence.[120] But in East Pakistan as well, there continued to be resentment against the national party and the government. A temporary alliance between the two political groups headed by H. S. Suhrawardy and Fazlul Huq capitalized on this feeling and crushed the Muslim League in the 1954 general elections held in Pakistan.[121] These were the first elections conducted in that country, and they demonstrated that Bengali Pakistanis would have to be given more autonomy, economic assistance, and a greater share in the rule of Pakistan if the nation were to hold together.

Some Bengali Hindus have created a regional version of the nationalist past. They would claim that Bengalis made decisive innovations in the movement—for example, the beginning of Noncooperation during the Swadeshi period. Later, however, the Gandhians gained control of the movement and the Bengalis were exploited in the interests of North Indians. A few insist that Subhas Bose, not Gandhi or other Congress leaders, won independence for India and that the demonstrations during the INA trials were the critical factor that made the British determine to leave India.[122]

In the regional version of the past shared by some Bengalis, Mahatma Gandhi is the chief antihero. He is blamed for the Bengalis' decline within the movement, for the partition of India, and for the vanquishing of Bengal's favorite son, Subhas Bose. Many politicians, especially those who aspire to national eminence, say kind words about Gandhi.[123] But there is an underground or street culture in Calcutta which utilizes numerous references to Gandhi and the Gandhians made in vile terms.[124] Some of Bengal's outstanding men of letters, including Nirad C. Chaudhuri and Dr. R. C. Majumdar, are more critical of Gandhi and his legacy to India in their version of the past than are most writers from other parts of India.[125]

Conclusions

꿈꾸꿈 This history of the changing Bengali role in the nationalist
movement has been illustrative of the general proposition that regional
groups came into the movement at different times and at different
rates.[1] The Bengalis, especially high-caste Hindus, played a significant
part in the movement during its first two generations. They contributed
in numerous ways to the organization and ideology of the movement
and also helped to create a Bengali self-image of priority and preeminence among the regional groups comprising the Indian nation. This
image was not far out of line in the period up to the end of World
War I. Later, however, leaders from other regions, especially Mahatma
Gandhi and his closest associates, took command of the movement.

From about 1920, Bengali sentiment and leadership was often out of
step with the Gandhian cadence. This date also marks the period when
national leaders from outside Bengal, particularly Gandhi, formed alliances with some Bengali leaders who became more closely tied to the
national program and organization than to their own region. Thus at
the very time when the Congress was being reorganized and becoming
more truly a national organization, many Bengalis and their leaders
were starting to become somewhat isolated from the mainstream of the
movement. For example, although nonviolence became the official nationalist credo, revolutionaries and important leaders sympathetic to
the use of violence, such as Subhas Bose, flourished in Bengal.

There are a number of lines of continuity between the ideological
and organizational forms developed by Bengalis during the nationalist
movement and long-standing religious and political traditions. Most
high-caste Hindus in Bengal are Shaktas or have been heavily influ-

enced by Shaktism, since lines between sects in Bengal are relatively
fluid. In the writings and speeches of many Bengali nationalist leaders
there is a concern with strength and weakness. A conception of the energizing principle of the universe growing out of the Shakta tradition
seems to have mingled with quite a different and Western idea, that of
manliness and physical prowess. The British stereotype of the Bengalis
as weak and effeminate spurred the latter's cultural and political revival,
which drew upon these very different traditions stressing energy and
strength. Some Bengali leaders, including Aurobindo Ghose, M. N.
Roy, Subhas Bose, and less famous revolutionaries, would have agreed
that the Bengalis were strong and then, somehow, became weak. In
order to regain the lost strength, power, and autonomy, they argued,
explicitly or implicitly, that all means were permissible. This would fit
in with their Shakta background, no matter how secular some of them
became in later life, and with Bengali traditions of violence. They
would have agreed with Nirad C. Chaudhuri that Gandhi's was the
"morality of the *servus*." [2] Gandhi's politics did not appeal to them except insofar as they were effective in launching a militant mass movement. It is true that others, like Rabindranath Tagore, were heavily influenced by Vaishnava as well as Shakta traditions. But Tagore, too,
was concerned with the achievement of strength and vitality and with
disproving the British view of the Bengali. Tagore also had much more
understanding of the revolutionaries than had most non-Bengalis, including the Gandhians. Although he condemned the use of violence as
yet another false shortcut to freedom, he saw that all Bengalis bore responsibility for the culture and politics which brought men to such actions.

Other cultural values that are salient to the division between many
Hindu Bengalis and non-Bengali Gandhians has been the evaluation of
Bengali culture and North Indian culture. Bengali spokesmen, including Tagore, Chaudhuri, and even a political man like Subhas Bose,
have been proud of their language and literary achievements. To them
Gandhi's rejection of art and literature as well as science, reason, and
modern civilization was to be deplored. The Bengalis saw themselves as
the defenders both of a rich and living regional tradition and of the
positive aspects of Western civilization. Many Bengalis believed that
they were preventing what Nirad C. Chaudhuri has described as "a de-

scent towards the old rancorous and atavistic form of Indian nationalism." [3]

The flow of Shakta values and conceptions into the nationalist movement and the use of Hindu symbols and songs contributed to the partial alienation of Bengali Muslims. Only at a few junctures were important or large numbers of Muslims willing to join with the Bengali Hindu nationalists. Perhaps the most crucial setback to possible lasting cooperation was the death of C. R. Das, who alone seemed capable of gaining Muslim trust. The combination of religion and nationalism that helped to popularize the movement among Hindus at the same time contributed to the split with the Muslims.

Older Bengali elements can also be found in the ways in which Bengalis organized politically and in the paths by which men came to political leadership. A factional model, drawing on both modern social science and traditional Indian political patterns, was suggested in the description of Moderates and Extremists, revolutionary groups, and Gandhians versus non-Gandhians. Within political factions and perhaps in a much broader context as well, there were also several traditional models for the adherence of followers to a single leader, two important ones being the guru-shishya and raja-subordinate relationships. These patterns were at work, but combined with other elements in the modern context. For the first generation of leaders and even for later ones, high caste standing, accomplishment in Western learning, and professional status were held to be of considerable importance. Thus ascriptive and achievement criteria have been at work. Another element that helped some men to gain notoriety and political support was the sacrifice made for the movement. Thus C. R. Das gained prestige by giving up his law practice and aristocratic style of living. Subhas Bose's standing as a leader was enhanced by his ill-health, fasting, and hardships in prison and exile.

Much attention has been given to the rise of political leaders in the successive nationalist generations and to an assessment of their effectiveness. Surendranath Banerjea, who dominated the Indian Association and the Bengali contingent of the Congress for several decades, built up a small organization and a corps of colleagues and subordinates, but he left the mofussil virtually untouched. He successfully fought off challenges to his dominance until 1918, but he did not attempt to construct a mass electoral organization. The Extremists in Bengal made a serious attempt to gain control of the Congress and talked of building an organization with mass support in every district, but they failed to do so. They did succeed, however, in politicizing many Bengalis who later contributed to the movement. At the same time, Muslim notables, in reaction to the Swadeshi movement, began to enter politics, starting as the Hindus had by forming a small caucus party with no mass organization.

It was only with the Gandhian or third generation that much more systematic efforts were made to build a mass base. In Bengal, C. R. Das finally routed Surendranath Banerjea and his colleagues from their seats of power in the Bengal branch of the Congress. Heading the Non-cooperation Movement in Bengal and then leading a campaign for the Bengal Legislative Council in 1923, Das made the first transitional step from a small party of notables to a mass political organization which could turn out the vote, do relief and propaganda work, lead an effective hartal, and even serve as a base from which to challenge the national leadership and program of the Congress. Das was the most effective Bengali nationalist leader and the one leader whose ideas for action and organization did not completely outstrip his ability to carry them through. He made a pact with some Bengali Muslim leaders and had crucial Muslim support for the Swaraj Party. Unfortunately, Das died in 1925, and no other Bengali leader proved to have the organizing skill, the trust and sympathy of many sections of the community, and the wisdom in choice of subordinates that he had had.

In the period 1926 to 1940, Subhas Bose was the most popular Bengali Hindu leader, but he never gained sufficient support among Hindus or Muslims and never had an able cadre of subordinates which might have helped to bring him successes like those of Das. Bose became a leader of the leftists on the national scene and he, like Das, mounted a challenge to the Gandhian leadership. But Bose had some reservations about his challenge after he beat the Gandhian candidate in an election for Congress president. Bose did not have the whole-hearted support of a number of peers in other regions, or the solid organizational backing such an effort required. In January 1937, the *Statesman*'s political commentator could still maintain that the masses waited, unorganized, outside party politics.[4] The Bengal Provincial

Congress in the Bose years did not effectively bring the peasants and workers, still without much say in legislative politics, into the organization. Bose provided rhetoric about the masses, but not the necessary kind of leadership. The Congress remained a party of what Marxist analysts would call the bourgeoisie. It was composed of professional men, some liberal landholders, and businessmen who claimed to speak for all Bengalis. In the politics of the National Congress, Bose won a preliminary victory but then was badly beaten by the Gandhian leadership, who recaptured both the Congress presidency and, eventually, the Bengal Provincial Congress. Bose's ideas and actions far exceeded his abilities to carry them out.

Leaders from all three nationalist generations had an image of the priority of Bengal, but by the Gandhian period such a regional self-image was out of touch with political realities. The difficulty of reforming this image so that it would be more realistic was one no Bengali political or cultural leader wanted to face. Some hoped that the decline and isolation of the Bengalis in the movement was simply a transitory state before new heights. But with the coming of independence, Bengali Hindus looked more to Bengali greatness in the past than to the new dawns ahead.

Bengal, East and West, is still in the midst of upheaval and political change. West Bengal has been torn by violence during the past few years as Marxist revolutionaries or Naxalites started a campaign of violence for which they themselves (as well as others) have had to pay dearly and which has not, to date, been successful. A Congress government is again in control, but social and political forces churn beneath the surface.

In the eastern part of Bengal, now Bangladesh, the Bengalis took the opportunity of the 1970 elections to express their grievances against their exploitation by the West Pakistanis during a generation of independence. Negotiations for a political solution failed and the military regime attempted to suppress the struggle for political, economic, and cultural justice. A movement for autonomy turned into a war for independence. The Indian army came to the aid of the Bangladesh irregulars and Bangladesh government established by members of the Awami League Party, and together they triumphed over the Pakistani army.

New nationhood has brought measures of hope and despair and the possibility for a new and healthier relationship between the two Bengals. But the poverty is so great and the cultural and social cleavages so strong that there cannot be any easy solutions. Although the people in the two Bengals speak Bengali, they still harbor communal antagonisms that not even a joint military victory can eradicate. In time these hostile feelings may wane or may become stronger. Only the growth of a spirit of communal harmony will allow a common sense of Bengali identity to flourish. The economic pressures are severe in both Bengals, and what effect this will have on the communal issue, no analyst can say with certainty. Bengal is again a cynosure of South Asian politics as its people struggle to determine their future.

Notes

PROLOGUE

1. On Calcutta see, Government of India, *Census of India 1951*, ed. A. Mitra (Delhi, 1954), VI, 74–81; H. E. A. Cotton, *Calcutta Old and New* (Calcutta, 1907), pp. 250–51; O. H. K. Spate, *India and Pakistan, A General and Regional Geography* (London, 1954), pp. 542–48; Asok Mitra, *Calcutta, India's City* (Calcutta, 1963), pp. 19–29.

2. According to the 1931 census, high-caste Hindus formed 6.1% of the population of Bengal but 28.9% of the Calcutta population. Government of India, *Census of India 1931* (Calcutta, 1932), Vol. V, Part 2, pp. 225–32; Edward C. Dimock, Jr. and Ronald Inden, "The City in Pre-British Bengal," *Urban Bengal*, ed. Richard L. Park (East Lansing, Michigan, 1969), pp. 3–18.

3. Government of India, *Report on the Census of Bengal*, ed. H. Beverley (Calcutta, 1872); *Report on the Census of Bengal*, ed. J. A. Bourdillon (Calcutta, 1881) I; on demographic balance of ethnic groups see Fredrik Barth, ed., *Ethnic Groups and Boundaries* (London, 1969), p. 24.

4. Peter J. Bertocci, "Patterns of Social Organization in Rural East Bengal," *Bengal East and West*, ed. Alexander Lipski (East Lansing, Michigan, 1970), pp. 107–38; Morton Klass, "Marriage Rules in Bengal," *American Anthropologist*, Vol. 68, No. 4; Ralph W. Nicholas, "Ecology and Village Structure in Deltaic West Bengal," *Economic Weekly* (Special Number, July 1963); Ronald B. Inden, "Structure and History of the Brahman and Kayastha Castes of Bengal" (unpublished Ph.D. thesis, University of Chicago, 1969), Introduction.

5. Edward Thompson and G. T. Garratt, *Rise and Fulfilment of British Rule in India* (reprint, Allahabad, 1958; originally published 1934), pp. 409–69; S. Gopal, *British Policy in India 1858–1905* (Cambridge, 1965), section entitled "The Aftermath of the Revolt 1858–1869"; Thomas R. Metcalf, *The Aftermath of Revolt, India, 1857–1870* (Princeton, 1964), pp. 289 ff.;

on the slow and grudging acceptance, see Bruce Tibout McCully, *English Education and the Origins of Indian Nationalism* (New York, 1940), pp. 200 ff.; Hugh Tinker, *Foundations of Local Self-Government in India, Pakistan and Burma* (London, 1968), pp. 39–40, 70.

6. A. P. Thornton, *The Habit of Authority* (London, 1966), *passim*.

7. R. J. Moore, *Liberalism and Indian Politics 1872–1922* (London, 1966), pp. 63–64.

8. Francis Hutchins, *The Illusion of Permanence* (Princeton, 1967), *passim;* Wilfrid Scawen Blunt, *India under Ripon* (London, 1909), pp. 33, 51.

9. See Government of India, *Census of India 1911* (Calcutta, 1913), Vol. V. Out of a total of 37,985,581, some 165,333 had been born in Bengal and 2,294,944 were Bengali speakers. In Assam in 1911, out of a total of 7,159,857, some 191,912 had been born in Bengal and 3,224,130 were Bengali speakers. Government of India, *Census of India 1911* (Shillong, 1912), Vol. III, Assam. But what is more important than the absolute numbers involved is the fact that many of the Bengalis held important positions. In Government of India, *Census of India 1931* (Calcutta, 1932), Vol. III, Assam, pp. 50–51, the writer goes on at length about the hordes of land-hungry Bengalis and says that the lower Assam districts were becoming colonies of Mymensingh. The writer quoted the Calcutta University Commission, 1917–1919, *Report* on the Bengali "bhadrolog" in the professions and in government and clerical jobs. There are some comments on Bengalis in Orissa in the nineteenth century in R. D. Banerji, *History of Orissa* (Calcutta, 1931), II, 329–32. Bengalis in the Punjab are described in Kenneth W. Jones, "The Bengali Elite in Post-Annexation Punjab: An Example of Inter-Regional Influence in 19th Century India" (paper presented at Second Annual Bengal Conference, University of Missouri, May 1966). See also Ganendramohan Dās, *Bāṅer bahire bāṅāli* [Bengalis outside Bengal] (Calcutta, 1915); Thomas R. Metcalf, *The Aftermath of Revolt, 1857–1870* (Princeton, 1964), pp. 125–26.

10. McCully, *English Education,* p. 197.

11. Sivanath Sastri, *History of the Brahmo Samaj* (Calcutta, 1912), II, 393–437; the Indian Association also tried to spread its connections across northern India.

12. L. S. S. O'Malley, *History of Bengal, Bihar and Orissa under British Rule* (Calcutta, 1925), pp. 353, 460.

13. C. E. Buckland, *Bengal under the Lieutenant-Governors* (2d ed., Calcutta, 1902), II, 420, 426–27, 521; O'Malley, *History of Bengal,* pp. 451–55.

14. Tom G. Kessinger, "The Problem of the 'Martial Races' in the Writing

of Indian History" (unpublished seminar paper, University of Chicago, 1966), pp. 1–31, *passim.*

15. Luke Scrafton, *Reflections on the Government of Indostan* (London, 1770), p. 17.

16. Lord Thomas Macaulay, *Critical, Historical and Miscellaneous Essays* (Boston, 1860), V, 19–20.

17. R. Carstairs, *Human Nature in Rural India* (London, 1895), pp. 201–32.

18. "*Baboo.* . . . Properly a term of respect attached to a name . . . and formerly in some parts of Hindustan applied to certain persons of distinction. . . . In Bengal and elsewhere, among Anglo-Indians, it is often used with a slight savour of disparagement, as characterizing a superficially cultivated, but too often effeminate, Bengali. . . . the word has come often to signify 'a native clerk who writes English.' " Henry Yule and A. C. Burnell, *Hobson-Jobson,* ed. William Crooke (new ed., Delhi, 1968), p. 44.

19. The most complete treatments of this theme are Carstairs, "The Bengal Republic," *Human Nature,* pp. 203–32; and Rudyard Kipling, "The City of Dreadful Night," *Selected Prose and Poetry of Rudyard Kipling* (Garden City, New York, 1937), pp. 187–251.

20. Kipling, *Selected Prose,* pp. 233–51, *passim;* Carstairs, *Human Nature,* pp. 55–59; W. W. Hunter, *Annals of Rural Bengal* (reprint, Calcutta, 1965), pp. 81–136.

21. J. C. Jack, *The Economic Life of a Bengal District* (Oxford, 1916), appendices; also see J. H. Broomfield, *Elite Conflict in a Plural Society: Twentieth Century Bengal* (Berkeley, 1968); Surajit Sinha and Ranjit Bhattacharya, "Bhadralok and Chhotolok in a Rural Area of West Bengal," *Sociological Bulletin,* Vol. XVIII, No. 1 (March 1969), pp. 50–66.

22. This differentiation can be seen in the writings of one of the proponents of the bhadralok theory, J. H. Broomfield, "The Vote and the Transfer of Power—A Study of the Bengal General Election 1912–1913," *Journal of Asian Studies,* Vol. XXI, No. 2 (February 1962), pp. 163–81.

23. Pradip Sinha, *Nineteenth Century Bengal* (Calcutta, 1965), pp. 40–41; on the growth of Western education in Bengal and its significance, see McCully, *English Education,* chapters I–III; A. F. Salahuddin Ahmed, *Social Ideas and Social Change in Bengal 1818–1835* (Leiden, 1965), chapters II, VI; R. C. Majumdar, *Glimpses of Bengal in the Nineteenth Century* (Calcutta, 1960), Lecture II; Rokeya Rahman Kabeer, *Administrative Policy of the Government of Bengal, 1870–1890* (Dacca, 1965), I, 11–73.

24. Calcutta University Commission, *Report 1917–19* (Calcutta, 1919), I, 49.

25. Ellen E. McDonald, "English Education and Social Reform in Late Nineteenth Century Bombay: A Case Study in the Transmission of a Cultural Ideal," *Journal of Asian Studies,* Vol. XXV, No. 3 (May 1966), pp. 453–70; Dr. McDonald takes the formalistic approach, stressing books read as requirements rather than informal education.

26. M. Azizul Huque, *History and Problems of Moslem Education in Bengal* (Calcutta, 1917), pp. 113–44.

27. Sinha, *Nineteenth Century Bengal,* pp. 51–57.

28. Huque, *History of Moslem Education,* p. 54.

29. Calcutta University Commission, *Report,* I, 143–44.

30. Edward Shils, "The Intellectual between Tradition and Modernity: The Indian Situation," *Comparative Studies in Society and History,* Supplement I (The Hague, 1961), p. 15.

31. O'Malley, *History of Bengal,* pp. 368–69, 472–73, 521–23, 760; these career choices were probably favored for many decades thereafter; see Calcutta University Commission, *Report,* III, 276–80; on the importance of fluency in English in this period and later, see Nripendra Chandra Banerji, *At the Crossroads (1885–1946)* (Calcutta, 1950), p. 52; on the dilemma of the Western-speaking native returning from Europe see Frantz Fanon, *Black Skins, White Masks* (New York, 1967), pp. 17–40.

32. L. S. S. O'Malley, *The Indian Civil Service 1601–1930* (2d ed., London, 1965), p. 241; Kabeer, *Administrative Policy,* pp. 74–127.

33. O'Malley, *Civil Service,* p. 249.

34. Precise data is offered by Bernard S. Cohn's unpublished material on the Middle Temple, 1860–1940; of 13 Indians admitted in the 1860s, 11 were Bengalis; in the 1870s, 18 of 41 were Bengalis; in the 1880s, 30 of 127 were from Bengal; of the 11 in the 1860s, 7 were Hindus, 16 of the 18 in the 1870s were Hindus, and 19 of 30 were Hindus in the 1880s. By the 1880s, an increasing number of Muslims from Bengal and Indians from other regions were admitted to the Middle Temple. On the legal profession in India and Bengal, see Samuel Schmitthenner, "The Development of the Legal Profession in India" (seminar paper for South Asia 700, University of Pennsylvania, 1965); Dinabandhu Sanyal, *Life of the Honb'le Justice Dwarkanath Mitter* (Calcutta, 1883).

35. *Hundred Years of the University of Calcutta* (Calcutta, 1957), p. 515, on the chairs endowed by Rash Behari Ghose; *Biographies of Eminent Indians* (Madras, n.d.), p. 5.

36. K. K. Aziz, *Ameer Ali, His Life and Work* (Lahore, 1968), I, 7–12; II, 585–88.

37. R. K. Prabhu and Ravindra Kelekar, eds., *Truth Called Them Differently* (*Tagore-Gandhi Controversy*) (Ahmadabad, 1961), p. 19.

38. "Deśer swādhīnatār janne prān debo" (I will give my life for the freedom of the country); my informant for this usage is Dr. Somdev Bhattacharji, a careful student of Bengali usage.

39. See Tagore's two famous essays entitled "Deśanāyak" [Leader of the country] in *Rabīndra racanābalī* (Calcutta, 1961), XII, 799–805; XIII, 387–90.

40. For example, see Rabindranath Tagore, "Neśan kī?" [What is the nation?] *Rabīndra racanābalī*, XII, 675–78.

CHAPTER ONE. THE GOLDEN AGE OF THE MODERATES

1. *Hundred Years of the University of Calcutta* (Calcutta, 1957), p. 456–71.

2. S. N. Mukherjee, "Class, Caste and Politics in Calcutta, 1815–38," *Elites in South Asia*, ed. Edmund Leach and S. N. Mukherjee (Cambridge, 1970), pp. 71–78.

3. Karl W. Deutsch, "Social Mobilization and Political Development," *American Political Science Review*, Vol. LV, No. 3 (September 1961), p. 498.

4. Rammohun Roy, *The English Works of Raja Rammohun Roy*, ed. Kalidas Nag and Debajyoti Burman (Calcutta, 1945–51), Part I, pp. 1–9; II, 83–93; IV, 4–13; on Rammohan and the Brahmo Samaj, see Prosanto Kumar Sen, *Biography of a New Faith* (2 vols., Calcutta, 1950), especially I, 14–34; Sushil Kumar De, *Bengali Literature in the Nineteenth Century 1757–1857* (rev. ed., Calcutta, 1962), pp. 534–37.

5. Sen, *Biography of a New Faith*, I, 139–65; Sivanath Sastri, *History of the Brahmo Samaj* (Calcutta, 1912), I, 109 ff., 141–54; II, 153–54.

6. Keshub Sen, *Lectures in India* (Calcutta, 1954), pp. 26, 495–96; Sastri, *Brahmo Samaj*, I, 108–12, 147–72; Sen, *Biography of a New Faith*, I, 219 ff., 327–52; II, 116–230.

7. Sen, *Lectures*, pp. 22–23.

8. Sastri, *Brahmo Samaj*, I, 133–38, 162; II, 268.

9. David Kopf, *British Orientalism and the Bengal Renaissance* (Berkeley, 1969); Nemai Sadhan Bose, *The Indian Awakening and Bengal* (Calcutta, 1960).

10. Samuel Schmitthenner, "The Development of the Legal Profession in India" (seminar paper for South Asia 700, University of Pennsylvania, 1965), p. 48, on lawyers in politics elsewhere, see Heinz Eulau and John D.

Sprague, *Lawyers in Politics* (New York, 1964); Donald R. Matthews, *U. S. Senators and Their World* (New York, 1960), pp. 30–40, 51–64; Thomas Hodgkin, *Nationalism in Colonial Africa* (New York, 1957), pp. 14, 140, 157; Gabriel Baer, *Population and Society in the Arab East* (New York, 1964), p. 19.

11. Calcutta University Commission, *Report*, III, 259.

12. L. S. S. O'Malley, *History of Bengal, Bihar and Orissa under British Rule* (Calcutta, 1925), pp. 432, 472–73, 521–23; Arthur Berriedale Keith, *A Constitutional History of India 1600–1935* (2d ed., reprint, Allahabad, 1961), pp. 182–83.

13. This assessment is based on a reading of Government of Bengal, *Proceedings of the Council of the Lieutenant-Governor of Bengal for the Purpose of Making Laws and Regulations* (Calcutta, 1901–1907), XXXII–XXXVIII, January 1900 to December 1906. These proceedings are hereafter referred to as *PBLC*.

14. *PBLC*, XXXII, 83; references to the "people," "middle classes," "the educated," and similar terms can be found in the writings of any of the early nationalists; see, for example, Surrendranath Banerjea, *A Nation in the Making* (reprint, Calcutta, 1963), pp. 41, 62, 96, 115, 125.

15. Government of Bengal, *Report on the Working of the Reformed Constitution in Bengal 1921–27* (Calcutta, 1929), pp. 151–69.

16. Hugh Tinker, *Foundations of Local Self-Government in India, Pakistan and Burma* (London, 1968), p. 70.

17. H. E. A. Cotton, *Calcutta Old and New* (Calcutta, 1907), pp. 233–34, 440; O'Malley, *History of Bengal*, pp. 440–41; Banerjea, *Nation*, p. 152; Haridas and Uma Mukherjee, *The Growth of Nationalism in India (1857–1905)* (Calcutta, 1957), pp. 124–25.

18. Anil Seal, *The Emergence of Indian Nationalism* (Cambridge, 1968), "The Politics of the Associations."

19. Charles H. Heimsath, *Indian Nationalism and Hindu Social Reform* (Princeton, 1964), p. 133.

20. Karl Deutsch, *Nationalism and Social Communication* (2d ed., Cambridge, Mass., 1966), pp. 29–71, 129 ff.

21. Warren M. Gunderson, "The Self-Image and World-View of the Bengali Intelligentsia as Found in the Writings of the Mid-Nineteenth Century, 1830–1870," *Bengal Literature and History*, ed. Edward C. Dimock, Jr. (East Lansing, Michigan, 1967), pp. 135 ff.

22. On the British Indian Association, see Bimanbehari Majumdar, *Indian Political Associations and Reform of Legislature (1818–1917)* (Calcutta,

1965), pp. 25–39; Sujata Ghosh, "The British Indian Association (1851–1900)," *Bengal Past and Present* (Calcutta, July–December 1958), Vol. LXXVII, Part II, pp. 99–119; Loke Nath Ghose, *The Modern History of the Indian Chiefs, Rajas, Zamindars, &c.* (Calcutta, 1881), Part II, *passim*, gives accounts of almost all leading families in the associations. It is clear from these accounts that politics was merely an avocation for these men.

23. Thomas R. Metcalf, *The Aftermath of Revolt* (Princeton, 1964), pp. 249 ff.; Majumdar, *Indian Political Associations*, pp. 318–52; Surendranath Banerjea, *Speeches and Writings of Hon. Surendranath Banerjea* (Madras, n.d.), p. 412.

24. Bimanbehari Majumdar, *History of Political Thought From Rammohun to Dayananda* (Calcutta, 1934), I, 330–46; Majumdar, *Indian Political Associations*, pp. 139–40; Seal, *Emergence*, pp. 213–14.

25. Jogesh Chandra Bagal, *History of the Indian Association 1876–1951* (Calcutta, 1953), pp. 48 ff.; Banerjea, *Nation*, pp. 41, 62, 115; Samuel H. Beer, *British Politics in the Collectivist Age* (New York, 1966), pp. 36, 53.

26. Banerjea said that Ashutosh Biswas called him his guru; Banerjea, *Nation*, p. 65. Ambica Charan Mazumdar, *Indian National Evolution* (Madras, 1915), p. ii, calls Banerjea his "friend and chief."

27. The main source for Banerjea's career is his own autobiography, *A Nation in Making*, written from 1914 to 1925. At a time when he found it difficult to hand over power to a new generation with different views, he made his young manhood seem purer, more exciting, more important, and more idealistic than it had been. He does not mention the strains and rivalries within the early Congress that other sources reveal.

28. Banerjea, *Nation*, pp. 63, 143, 291, 316, 368; Daniel Argov, *Moderates and Extremists in the Indian Nationalist Movement* (London, 1967) deals with Banerjea's career, but is even less insightful than Banerjea's autobiography.

29. There were important connections between the families of Banerjea, W. C. Bonnerjee, and R. C. Dutt and the Deb family of Sovabazar, the most powerful family in nineteenth-century Calcutta. See Sadhona Bonnerjee, *Life of W. C. Bonnerjee* (Calcutta, n.d. [1944?]), p. 126; Banerjea, *Nation*, pp. 133–34, 157; J. N. Gupta, *Life and Work of Romesh Chunder Dutt C.I.E.* (London, 1911), pp. 122, 242–49.

30. Banerjea, *Nation*, pp. 2–3.

31. Banerjea, *Nation*, pp. 11–31.

32. Banerjea, *Nation*, pp. 32–35.

33. Banerjea, *Speeches and Writings*, pp. 1–10; Banerjea, *Nation*, p. 40.

34. Through fifty years, the Indian Association had 10 presidents, 2 of whom, including A. M. Bose, served for 10 years each; in this same time it had 3 secretaries, Banerjea serving from 1885 to 1920; Banerjea was president from 1920 until his death in 1925. On caucus and mass parties, see Maurice Duverger, *Political Parties* (2d ed., rev., New York, 1965), pp. 18–23, 133 ff.; Bagal, *Indian Association*, pp. 258–62.

35. Bagal, *Indian Association*, pp. 78, 117–20, 193, 211.

36. Banerjea, *Nation*, pp. 63–68.

37. Quoted in Rahman Kabeer, *Administrative Policy of the Government of Bengal, 1870–1890* (Dacca, 1965), I, 161; on the Ilbert Bill agitation, see Kabeer, *Administrative Policy*, I, 133–73; Argov, *Moderates and Extremists*, pp. 9 ff.; K. K. Aziz, *Ameer Ali, His Life and Work* (Lahore, 1968), II, 577 ff.; Wilfred Scawen Blunt, *India under Ripon* (London, 1966), pp. 96–121.

38. Aziz, *Ameer Ali*, II, 583, 591; Bipin Chandra, "Two Notes on the Agrarian Policy of Indian Nationalists." *Indian Economic and Social History Review*, Vol. I, No. 4 (April–June 1964).

39. Banerjea, *Nation*, pp. 69–78; Mukherjee and Mukherjee, *Growth of Nationalism*, pp. 86–88.

40. Seal, *Emergence*, pp. 252 ff.; Briton Martin, Jr., *New India 1885* (Berkeley, 1969), pp. 40 ff.; Annie Besant, *How India Wrought for Freedom* (Adyar, Madras, 1915), pp. 13–14; Bimanbehari Majumdar and Bhakat Prasad Mazumdar, *Congress and Congressmen in the Pre-Gandhian Era 1885–1917* (Calcutta, 1967), pp. 115–16; there is some suggestion that Banerjea was snubbed by being given a late invitation to the first Congress; he denied there was any problem.

41. Majumdar and Mazumdar, *Congress*, pp. 100–20; Besant, *How India Wrought, passim.*

42. Bonnerjee, *Life of W. C. Bonnerjee*, p. 34.

43. See, for example, Rudyard Kipling, *Selected Prose and Poetry* (Garden City, New York, 1937), *passim;* Michael O'Dwyer, *India as I Knew It* (London, 1925), pp. 12–15.

44. The presidents were: W. C. Bonnerjee (1885, 1892), Surendranath Banerjea (1895, 1902), A. M. Bose (1898), R. C. Dutt (1899), Lal Mohan Ghose (1903), Rash Behari Ghose (1907, 1908), Bhupendranath Basu (1914), S. P. Sinha (1915), A. C. Mazumdar (1916).

45. Bagal, *Indian Association*, pp. 95, 117–18, 139, 211.

46. Bipin Chandra claims that this meeting was held because the Congress would not consider the tea coolie issue, ruling it to be a purely provincial

affair; Bipin Chandra, *The Rise and Growth of Economic Nationalism in India* (New Delhi, 1966), p. 366.

47. Majumdar and Mazumdar, *Congress,* pp. 149–59; Gupta, *Romesh Dutt,* pp. 217 ff.

48. Banerjea, *Speeches and Writings,* p. 226.

49. Mazumdar, *Indian National Evolution,* pp. 426–28.

50. Banerjea, *Speeches and Writings,* pp. 225–26; Seal, *Emergence,* pp. 321–23; Lovat Fraser, *India under Curzon and After* (3d ed., London, 1912), pp. xiv, xv; Argov, *Moderates and Extremists,* p. 109; Aziz, *Ameer Ali,* II, 250.

51. Banerjea, *Speeches and Writings,* p. 265.

52. Majumdar, *History of Political Thought,* pp. 395–96; Bagal, *Indian Association, passim;* from Bagal's account it is clear that few Muslims were involved.

53. For further and more concrete views by Hindus of the Muslims, see chapters 2 and 3 below; those more sensitive to the Muslims included Rabindranath Tagore and C. R. Das.

54. On these revolts, see Blair B. Kling, *The Blue Mutiny* (Philadelphia, 1966); Pradip Sinha, *Nineteenth Century Bengal* (Calcutta, 1965), pp. 22 ff.; Lal Behari Day, *Bengal Peasant Life* (London, 1926); W. W. Hunter, *The Annals of Rural Bengal* (Calcutta, 1965, reprint); Muin-ud-din Ahmad Khan, *History of the Fara'idi Movement in Bengal (1818–1906)* (Karachi, 1965).

55. Government of India, *Report on the Census of Bengal* (1872) and *Report on the Census of Bengal* (1881), I; on the problems of reaching and organizing the peasantry, see F. G. Bailey, *Politics and Social Change: Orissa in 1959* (Berkeley, 1963); Stanley Diamond, "Who Killed Biafra?" *The New York Review of Books,* Vol. XIV, No. 4 (February 26, 1970); Eric R. Wolf, *Peasant Wars of the Twentieth Century* (New York, 1969), pp. 289–94.

56. Argov, *Moderates and Extremists,* pp. 6–11, 49, 117, 152; a number of specific comments about Banerjea by G. K. Gokhale and others are given in chapter 3.

CHAPTER TWO. IDENTITY, HISTORY, IDEOLOGY:

ROMESH CHUNDER DUTT AND SYED AMEER ALI

1. See the treatment of Dutt in Bipin Chandra, *The Rise and Growth of Economic Nationalism in India* (New Delhi, 1966) and Ameer Ali in Anil Seal, *The Emergence of Indian Nationalism* (Cambridge, 1968),

W. Cantwell Smith, *Modern Islām in India* (rev. ed., Lahore, 1963), and Aziz Ahmad, *Islamic Modernism in India and Pakistan 1857–1964* (London, 1967). The closest approximations to biographies of the two are: J. N. Gupta, *Life and Work of Romesh Chunder Dutt, C.I.E.* (London, 1911) and K. K. Aziz, *Ameer Ali: His Life and Work* (Lahore, 1968); Gupta is writing about his father-in-law and quotes from correspondence and other materials not available elsewhere; Aziz is an uncritical chronicler who has made an excellent collection of Ameer Ali's essays, letters to the press, and some other documents in Part II of his work. But, as is the case with most modern Indians, Dutt and Ali await their critical and insightful biographers.

2. Joseph R. Levenson, *Liang Ch'i-Ch'ao and the Mind of Modern China* (Cambridge, Mass., 1959), *passim.*

3. Gupta, *Romesh Dutt*, p. 394.

4. Gupta, *Romesh Dutt*, pp. 1–9. Dutt was born in 1848.

5. Romesh Chunder Dutt, *Three Years in Europe 1868 to 1871, With an Account of Subsequent Visits to Europe in 1886 and 1893* (Calcutta, 1896), p. 2.

6. See Surendranath Banerjea, *A Nation in Making* (reprint, Calcutta, 1963), pp. 9–36; Hem Chandra Sarkar, *A Life of Ananda Mohan Bose* (Calcutta, 1910), p. 54.

7. Dutt, *Three Years*, pp. 13–15.

8. Gupta, *Romesh Dutt*, pp. 26–35.

9. Dutt, *Three Years*, pp. 164–65, 174.

10. Gupta, *Romesh Dutt*, pp. 38–169; Gupta quotes many tributes to Dutt from higher officials and from public men and organizations in the districts in which he served. For the stereotype, see Rudyard Kipling, "The Head of the District," *Selected Prose and Poetry of Rudyard Kipling* (Garden City, New York, 1937), pp. 604–19.

11. Gupta, *Romesh Dutt*, pp. 50–51, 93–112, 165–69; Romesh Chunder Dutt, *The Peasantry of Bengal* (Calcutta, 1874).

12. Gupta, *Romesh Dutt*, p. 229.

13. Gupta, *Romesh Dutt*, pp. 217 ff., 495.

14. Gupta, *Romesh Dutt*, pp. 242–78.

15. Gupta, *Romesh Dutt*, pp. 237 ff.; Romesh Chunder Dutt, *The Economic History of India under Early British Rule* (reprint, London, 1956) and *The Economic History of India in the Victorian Age* (reprint, London, 1956); hereafter these volumes will be referred to as *Economic History*, I and *Economic History*, II, respectively.

16. See Dutt, *Economic History,* I, xvi, xviii, xxi; *Economic History,* II, xvii; Romesh C. Dutt, *Open Letters to Lord Curzon and Speeches and Papers* (Calcutta, 1904), Parts I and II.

17. Gupta, *Romesh Dutt,* pp. 53, 217; in the preface to *A History of Civilization in Ancient India* (3 vols., London, 1889–1890), Dutt describes his role of bringing the fruits of Sanskrit scholarship to the "general public"— Romesh Chunder Dutt, *The Early Hindu Civilisation B.C. 2000 to 320* (Calcutta, 1963), reprint of most of Books I, II, and III of *A History of Civilization in Ancient India*—and then goes on to talk about the Hindu student's knowledge of India. It is not clear how these fruits would be distributed to Indian students by having the volume published in London. Dutt implicitly, at least, seems to be aiming at the Western reading public also. His later and brief *The Civilization of India* (London, 1900) seemed to be aimed primarily at Western readers, while his school texts, *A Brief History of Ancient and Modern India According to the Syllabus Prescribed by the Calcutta University* (Calcutta, 1907) and *A Brief History of Ancient and Modern Bengal for the Use of Schools* (Calcutta, 1904) were aimed at Bengali students. For the criticism of Dutt's views on the Indian past, see Gupta, *Romesh Dutt,* p. 351, and Aurobindo Ghose [Sri Aurobindo], "The Men That Pass," in *Bankim-Tilak-Dayananda* (Pondicherry, 1955), p. 64.

18. Gupta, *Romesh Dutt,* p. 69.

19. Nirad C. Chaudhuri, *The Autobiography of an Unknown Indian* (New York, 1951), p. 226; also see Nripendra Chandra Banerji, *At the Crossroads (1885–1946)* (Calcutta, 1950), p. 24.

20. Dutt, *Brief History of Bengal,* pp. i–ii.

21. Dutt mentions reading Byron, Burns, Gray, Shakespeare, Scott, Wordsworth, Macaulay, Motley, Gibbon, Buckle, Mill, Burke, and the speeches of Bright, Gladstone, and Morley. Some of the influences on his historiography undoubtedly came from British historians of the eighteenth and nineteenth century, and a few of these will be commented upon below. Dutt, *Three Years,* pp. 138–44.

22. Dutt's assumptions are similar to those of the French writer Taine. See H. A. Taine, *History of English Literature,* tr. H. Van Laun (New York, 1872), I, 3–21.

23. Dutt, *Economic History,* I, v; Dutt, *The Peasantry of Bengal,* p. 19; several of Dutt's works are organized in terms of stages of progress, especially Romesh Chunder Dutt, *England and India. A Record of Progress during a Hundred Years 1785–1885* (London, 1897) and Romesh Chunder Dutt, *Cultural Heritage of Bengal* (reprint, Calcutta, 1962; originally pub-

lished as *The Literature of Bengal*); compare Dutt's assumptions or implicit historiography with that of European writers of the time as described by Frank E. Manuel, *The Prophets of Paris* (Cambridge, Mass., 1962), pp. 292, 298, 310; J. B. Bury, *The Idea of Progress* (New York, 1955), pp. 217 ff.; Walter E. Houghton, *The Victorian Frame of Mind 1830–1870* (New Haven, 1959), pp. 14–15, 29 ff., 250–51.

24. Dutt further divides the ancient period into smaller segments as laid out in the introduction, Dutt, *Early Hindu Civilisation*, pp. 1–22.

25. It is interesting that the earlier stages are labeled in terms of religious and literary texts and the added stages in the *Civilization of India* by the name of the ruling political power in the period. It may be that Dutt considered these later stages periods low in mental and spiritual creativity and so had no alternative but to apply political labels.

26. Dutt, *Early Hindu Civilisation*, pp. 31–32.

27. Dutt, *History of Civilization in Ancient India*, II, 311–14.

28. Dutt, *Early Hindu Civilisation*, p. 35; Gupta, *Romesh Dutt*, p. 104. His defense is similar to Rammohan Roy's defense of Hinduism and Ameer Ali's defense of Islam.

29. Dutt, *Early Hindu Civilisation*, pp. 178 ff.

30. Dutt, *Early Hindu Civilisation*, p. 247; for some inexplicable reason the Indian publishers of the reprint of *A History of Civilization in Ancient India* left out the sections on the Buddhist period; see the complete edition for Dutt's favorable treatment of the Buddhists: *A History of Civilization in Ancient India*, II, 340 ff., and III, 1–204. Compare M. N. Roy, *Materialism* (2d ed. rev., Calcutta, 1951), pp. 15–25, 82, 93–100.

31. Dutt, *Early Hindu Civilisation*, p. 3.

32. Dutt, *A History of Civilization in Ancient India*, II, 304; III, 148.

33. Dutt, *Early Hindu Civilisation*, pp. 7, 125, 173, 239.

34. Dutt, *Early Hindu Civilisation*, p. 18.

35. Romesh Chunder Dutt, *Later Hindu Civilisation A.D. 500 to A.D. 1200* (Calcutta, 1965, reprint of Book V of *A History of Civilization in Ancient India*), p. 85.

36. Dutt, *Early Hindu Civilisation*, p. 18.

37. Dutt, *Civilization of India*, pp. 97–111.

38. Louis Dumont, "The Village Community from Munro to Maine," *Contributions to Indian Sociology*, IX (December 1966), 69n, 75.

39. Dutt, *Peasantry of Bengal*, pp. 19, 77, 118–19, 179.

40. Dutt, *Civilisation of India*, pp. 51–52.

41. Dutt, *Civilisation of India*, p. 122.

42. Dutt, *Civilization of India*, p. 57. Notice throughout the ease with which Dutt assimilates terms like "confederation," "local self-government," "manufactures," so that ancient India often looks like the ideal modern Western society.

43. With the brief exceptions noted above. For an excellent introduction to his life and work and the complete Bengali texts of all his novels, see Romesh Chunder Dutt, *Rames racanābalī* [Collected works of Romesh] ed. Jogesh Chandra Bagal (Calcutta, 1960).

44. Translated by Ajoy Dutt as *Todar Mull* (Allahabad, 1947).

45. Translated as *The Slave Girl of Agra* (London, 1909).

46. Translated by Ajoy C. Dutt as *Sivaji* (Allahabad, 1944).

47. Translated by Ajoy C. Dutt as *Pratap Singh, The Last of the Rajputs* (Allahabad, 1943).

48. Translated as *The Lake of Palms* (London, 1902); Romesh Dutt himself did this translation into English.

49. Gupta, *Romesh Dutt*, p. 69.

50. Dutt, *Sivaji*, pp. 14, 17, 57, 102, 164–65; the more correct spelling, following the Bengali, would be "Bhavānī," but I have used the most common English spelling, "Bhawani."

51. Dutt, *Sivaji*, p. 99.

52. Dutt, *Sivaji*, pp. 203, 214.

53. Compare Dutt's treatment to that of Jadunath Sarkar, *Shivaji and His Times* (6th ed., rev., Calcutta, 1961), p. 44, and of Mahadeo Govind Ranade, *Rise of the Maratha Power* (reprint, Delhi, 1961, first published 1900), p. 5.

54. Dutt, *Economic History*, I, xviii; Gupta, *Romesh Dutt*, pp. 223–24.

55. Dutt, *Early Hindu Civilisation*, p. 10.

56. Dutt, *England and India*, pp. xii, 2–3, 120; Dutt, *Cultural Heritage of Bengal*, pp. 3, 6, 58, 90, 163.

57. Dutt, *Early Hindu Civilisation*, p. 10.

58. See Chandra, *Economic Nationalism, passim*, where there are dozens of references to Dutt; R. Palme Dutt, *India Today* (Bombay, 1947), pp. 84–85, 265.

59. Gupta, *Romesh Dutt*, pp. 217 ff.

60. Dutt, *England and India*, pp. xii, 2–3, 120; Dutt, *Open Letters*, II, 44–45; Dutt, *Economic History*, II, vii, 4.

61. Dutt, *Cultural Heritage of Bengal*, pp. 3, 58, 90 ff.; Dutt, *England and India*, pp. 45, 117, 120.

62. Dutt, *Peasantry of Bengal*, p. 111.

63. Dutt, *Cultural Heritage of Bengal*, pp. 58–59.

64. Dutt, *Cultural Heritage of Bengal*, p. 90.

65. Dutt, *Peasantry of Bengal*, p. 49.

66. Dutt, *Peasantry of Bengal*, pp. viii–ix.

67. Gupta, *Romesh Dutt*, p. 57.

68. Dutt, *Economic History*, II, x, 258, 263–64, 349, 427, 455, 457.

69. Dutt, *Economic History*, II, 461.

70. Dutt, *Economic History*, pp. 88–89.

71. The evidence on Madras is based on Munro's reports: Dutt, *Economic History*, I, 135–52. The statements about Bombay are based on Elphinstone's reports: Dutt, *Economic History*, II, 50. The North Indian evidence is from Holt Mackenzie's reports: Dutt, *Economic History*, I, 90–91.

72. Dutt, *Economic History*, II, 375, 384.

73. R. Palme Dutt, *India Today*, pp. 84 ff.; Barrington Moore, Jr., *Social Origins of Dictatorship and Democracy* (Boston, 1966), p. 348.

74. Dutt, *Economic History*, II, 32.

75. Dutt, *Economic History*, II, 150–51, 155, 186–87, 192, 332, 445.

76. Gupta, *Romesh Dutt*, pp. 231–49; Dutt, *Open Letters*, II, 30 ff.

77. Gupta, *Romesh Dutt*, p. 249; Dutt, *Open Letters*, II, 42.

78. Gupta, *Romesh Dutt*, pp. 212 ff.; Dutt, *Economic History*, II, 32.

79. Dutt, *Three Years*, pp. 374–75.

80. Dutt, *Later Hindu Civilisation*, pp. 100–17.

81. Dutt, *Economic History*, I, 128.

82. Dutt, *Economic History*, II, 518–19.

83. For a subtle catalog of these characteristics and some of their ambiguities, see Houghton, *Victorian Frame, passim*.

84. Dutt, *Economic History*, I, xviii.

85. Gupta, *Romesh Dutt*, p. 223.

86. Dutt, *Brief History of Bengal,* pp. i–ii, 3–21. His writings on Bengal include his two early books, *The Peasantry of Bengal* and the *Literature of Bengal* (reprinted as *Cultural Heritage of Bengal*); his school text, *A Brief History of Ancient and Modern Bengal for the Use of Schools,* and brief comments and sections in his novels, in *A History of Civilization in Ancient India,* and in *Economic History.*

87. Dutt, *Peasantry of Bengal,* p. 19.

88. Dutt, *Peasantry of Bengal,* p. 44.

89. Dutt, *Peasantry of Bengal,* p. 113.

90. Dutt, *Cultural History of Bengal,* pp. 90–163; Dutt, *Peasantry of Bengal,* pp. 120, 174.

91. Dutt, *Economic History,* II, 151, 155, 186–87, 192.

92. Ghose, *Bankim-Tilak-Dayananda,* pp. 61–66; Bipinchandra Pal, *Character Sketches* (Calcutta, 1957), pp. 30, 212–13, 219.

93. Aziz, *Ameer Ali,* II, 12.

94. Aziz, *Ameer Ali,* II, 279; Ameer Ali, *The Personal Law of the Mahommedans* (London, 1880), p. xi; also see Ali's comment on Muslims from outside Bengal living in Bengal, Aziz, *Ameer Ali,* II, 49–50.

95. Ameer Ali, *A Critical Examination of the Life and Teachings of Mohammed* (London, 1873), dedication.

96. Aziz, *Ameer Ali,* II, 527 ff.

97. Aziz, *Ameer Ali,* II, 535–38; for the memories of communal amity, see Aziz, *Ameer Ali,* II, 253, 541–42.

98. Aziz, *Ameer Ali,* II, 507, 539, 543.

99. Aziz, *Ameer Ali,* II, 547.

100. Aziz, *Ameer Ali,* II, 539 ff.; Ali, *Life of Mohammed,* p. ix.

101. Ali, *Life of Mohammed,* pp. v–vi.

102. Aziz, *Ameer Ali,* II, 555; Ameer Ali, *The Legal Position of Women in Islam* (London, 1912), pp. 5 ff.; Ameer Ali, *Islam* (London, 1914), p. vi; Ameer Ali, *The Spirit of Islam* (London, 1967, reprint of 1922 ed.), pp. xvii ff.; Ameer Ali, *A Short History of the Saracens* (London, 1899), p. v.

103. Aziz, *Ameer Ali,* II, 558 ff.; the anecdote on his "blessed life" is on p. 563.

104. Ali, *Personal Law,* p. vi.

105. Ali, *Personal Law,* pp. v ff.; Ameer Ali, *Student's Handbook of Mahommedan Law* (5th ed., Calcutta, 1906); in the latter work Ali says that

one who believes in the unity of God and the prophetic character of Muhammad is a Muslim either by birth or conversion); he stresses that one need not observe specific rites or ceremonies.

106. Ali, *Saracens,* preface; it is interesting to compare Ali's treatment with that of Edward Gibbon, *The History of the Decline and Fall of the Roman Empire* (reprint, London, 1969), Vols. V and VI, and with the modern, analytical version by Bernard Lewis, *The Arabs in History* (5th ed., London, 1950).

107. Aziz, *Ameer Ali,* II, 567 ff.; also 361, 367, 383; Ali's view is similar to that of Colonel Qadhafi, the present ruler of Libya, who "believes in a kind of instant unity for the Arabs." C. L. Sulzberger, "Returning to the Arab Womb," *Herald Tribune,* August 2, 1971.

108. Wilfrid Scawen Blunt, *India under Ripon* (London, 1909), pp. 7–99.

109. Blunt, *India under Ripon,* pp. 104–105; Aziz, *Ameer Ali,* II, 556–57.

110. Aziz, *Ameer Ali,* II, 23–40; cf. "A Cry from the Indian Mahommedans," *The Nineteenth Century,* August 1882, 193–215.

111. Aziz, *Ameer Ali,* II, 229, 381.

112. Aziz, *Ameer Ali,* II, 343–50, 592, 610.

113. Blunt, *India under Ripon,* pp. 88–121.

114. Aziz, *Ameer Ali,* II, 577 ff., 601; also see the Aga Khan, *The Memoirs of Aga Khan, World Enough and Time* (London, 1954), p. 104.

115. Aziz, *Ameer Ali,* II, 513, 552, 616.

116. Aziz, *Ameer Ali,* II, 113 ff., 190–91, 205, 261, 541, 566, 613, 621–23.

117. Aziz, *Ameer Ali,* II, 574–75, 601; Aga Khan, *Memoirs,* pp. 104, 153; Syed Razi Wasti, *Lord Minto and the Indian Nationalist Movement 1905 to 1910* (London, 1964), pp. 59 ff.; M. N. Das, *India under Morley and Minto* (London, 1964), pp. 78 ff.

118. Aziz, *Ameer Ali,* II, 592.

119. Aziz, *Ameer Ali,* II, 352 ff., 627 ff.; Smith, *Modern Islam,* p. 51n.

120. Smith, *Modern Islam,* p. 50.

121. Ali, *Saracens,* p. 436 and *passim;* Ali, *Spirit of Islam,* p. 458 and *passim.*

122. Aziz, *Ameer Ali,* II, 450–56; Ali, *Saracens,* p. vii.

123. Aziz, *Ameer Ali,* II, 98, 131 ff., 298; Ali, *Saracens,* pp. 320 ff.; Ameer Ali, "Christianity from the Islamic Standpoint," *The Hibbert Journal,* Vol. IV, No. 2 (1906), 241–59; reprinted in Syed Razi Wasti, ed., *Syed Ameer Ali on Islamic History and Culture* (Lahore, 1968), pp. 74 ff.

124. Ali, *Spirit of Islam*, pp. xxxviii ff.; Ali in Wasti, *Syed Ameer Ali*, p. 89.

125. Ali, *Saracens*, p. 563.

126. Aziz, *Ameer Ali*, II, 550, 584; Ali, *Spirit of Islam*, pp. 213, 290 ff., 353, 399, 402, 431–32, 440, 448 ff., 472–78; Ali, *Saracens*, p. vii.

127. Aziz, *Ameer Ali*, II, 279, 361, 367.

128. Of particular value are "Islamic Culture in India" and "Islamic Culture under the Moguls," first published in *Islamic Culture*, July and October 1927 and reprinted in Aziz, *Ameer Ali*, I, 457–508.

129. Ali, *Spirit of Islam*, pp. ix–xxviii, 455, 459; Aziz, *Ameer Ali*, II, 268, 290, 316–17, 513, 552, 616–24.

130. Aziz, *Ameer Ali*, II, 376.

131. Aziz, *Ameer Ali*, II, 468.

132. Aziz, *Ameer Ali*, II, 253 ff., 335, 383.

133. Aziz, *Ameer Ali*, II, 34, 59, 62, 190–91, 513.

134. Ali, *Personal Law*, pp. v–vi.

135. Aziz, *Ameer Ali*, II, 207.

136. Aziz, *Ameer Ali*, II, 566.

137. Aziz, *Ameer Ali*, II, 613, 621–23.

138. Aziz, *Ameer Ali*, II, 10.

139. Ali, *Personal Law*, p. vi; Aziz, *Ameer Ali*, II, 195, 216–17, 232, 319, 522.

140. Aziz, *Ameer Ali*, II, 252, 275.

141. Aziz, *Ameer Ali*, II, 249 ff.

CHAPTER THREE. THE SWADESHI MOVEMENT

1. For an elegant and detailed account of Curzon's reign, see Earl of Ronaldshay, *The Life of Lord Curzon* (London, 1928), II; Lovat Fraser, *India under Curzon and After* (3d ed., London, 1912), gives an even more favorable estimate of Curzon's accomplishments; for views from the Indian side, see Surendranath Banerjea, *A Nation in Making* (reprint, Calcutta, 1963), pp. 139–75; Pansy Chaya Ghosh, *The Development of the Indian National Congress 1892–1909* (Calcutta, 1960), pp. 95 ff.; Haridas and Uma Mukherjee, *The Growth of Nationalism in India (1857–1905)* (Calcutta, 1957), pp. 123–27.

2. For the connection, see Bipinchandra Pal, *Memories of My Life and Times* (Calcutta, 1951), II, 108 ff.; *Swadeshi and Swaraj* (Calcutta, 1954),

pp. 18–20, 94; and chapters 4 and 5 below. Secondary works of value are Amales Tripathi, *The Extremist Challenge* (Calcutta, 1967), an account which I saw after the present one was written, and Sumit Sarkar, "Trends in Bengal's Swadeshi Movement (1903–1908)," *Bengal Past and Present,* Vol. LXXXIV, Part I, No. 157 (January–June 1965), pp. 10–39, and Part II, No. 158 (July–December 1965), pp. 140–60.

3. Christopher Isherwood, *Ramakrishna and His Disciples* (New York, 1965), pp. 13 ff.; Romain Rolland, *The Life of Ramakrishna* (6th ed., New York, 1960); M. [Mahendra Nath Gupta], ed., *The Gospel of Sri Rama-krishna,* tr. Swami Nikhilananda (4th ed., Mylapore, Madras, 1964), pp. 64–113, 385–90, 522–29.

4. Romain Rolland, *The Life of Vivekananda and the Universal Gospel* (Almora, 1947), pp. 35–50; Sisirkumar Mitra, *Resurgent India* (Calcutta, 1963), p. 236, writes, "1893 is a landmark in the long history of India's spiritual life. . . . Swami Vivekananda goes out to the West; Sri Aurobindo comes home to the East. The one to illumine the West with the light of the East as a preparation for a greater light to follow. The other to liberate India the Mother and to liberate the world." See also Swami Vivekananda, "Lectures from Colombo to Almora," *The Complete Works of Swami Vivekananda* (9th ed., Calcutta, 1964), III, 131, 159–61, 188–89, 272–73, 277, 325–27.

5. Vivekananda, "Lectures," pp. 152–53.

6. Vivekananda, "Lectures," pp. 156–67, 243, 312, 380; we might say that he displayed ambivalence toward Western culture and national self-love and self-hate.

7. Vivekananda, "Lectures," p. 242.

8. Vivekananda, "Lectures," p. 320.

9. Hemchandra Ghose wrote in a letter to Bhupendranath Datta, *Swami Vivekananda Patriot-Prophet* (Calcutta, 1954), p. 335, "Swami Vivekananda appeared to us to be more a political prophet than a religious teacher." Mr. Datta is the younger brother of Vivekananda; he was long involved in left-wing politics, and was interested in demonstrating the political relevance of his older brother's message. For two critical views of the Ramakrishna Mission and Order, see Swami Agehananda, *The Ochre Robe* (London, 1961), pp. 89–143, and David McCutchion, "The Ramakrishna Mission: A Personal Experience," *The Radical Humanist* (Calcutta), Part I, July 21 and Part II, July 28, 1963; for a view of the order and its recruitment from among high-caste Bengali Hindus, see Dhan Gopal Mukerji, *The Face of Silence* (New York, 1926), pp. 106–107.

10. Rachel Rebecca Van Meter, "Bankimchandra and the Bengali Renaissance" (unpublished Ph.D. dissertation, University of Pennsylvania, 1964), pp. xiii–xv; Jayanta Kumar Das Gupta, *A Critical Study of the Life and Novels of Bankimchandra* (Calcutta, 1937), pp. 12–19; for the responses of several readers, see Nripendra Chandra Banerji, *At the Crossroads (1885–1946)* (Calcutta, 1950), p. 23; Nirad C. Chaudhuri, *The Autobiography of an Unknown Indian* (New York, 1951), p. 226; Rabindranath Tagore, *Reminiscences* (reprint, London, 1961), p. 115; Bankim Chandra Chatterjee, "A Popular Literature for Bengal," *Essays and Letters* (Calcutta, 1940), ed. Brajendra Nath Banerji and Sajani Kanta Das, pp. 13–18.

11. Van Meter, "Bankimchandra," pp. 82, 135 ff.; Amales Tripathi, "Bankim Chandra and Extremist Thought," *Bengal Past and Present* (Calcutta, 1965, 1966), Vol. LXXXIV, No. 158, pp. 167–79, especially pp. 169–70, and LXXXV, No. 159, pp. 82–112; Chatterjee, *Essays and Letters*, pp. 13–14.

12. Van Meter, "Bankimchandra," pp. 54–58; Chatterjee, *Essays and Letters*, pp. 95–97; Rachel R. Van Meter, "Bankimcandra's View of the Role of Bengal in Indian Civilization," *Bengal Regional Identity*, ed. David Kopf (East Lansing, Michigan, 1969), pp. 61–70.

13. Sir John Woodruffe [Arthur Avalon, pseud.], *Principles of Tantra* (Madras, 1960), pp. 8, 245 ff.; G. S. Ghurye, *Gods and Men* (Bombay, 1962), p. 258; Ernest A. Payne, *The Sāktas* (Calcutta, 1933), *passim;* Jogendra Nath Bhattacharja, *Hindu Castes and Sects* (Calcutta, 1896), *passim.*

14. Bankim Chandra Chatterjee, *Anandamath*, tr. Sree Aurobindo and Barindra Kumar Ghosh (Calcutta, *n.d.*); T. W. Clark, "The Role of Bankimcandra in the Development of Nationalism," *Historians of India, Pakistan and Ceylon*, ed. C. H. Philips (London, 1962), pp. 429–40; Das Gupta, *Critical Study*, pp. 30 ff., gives a summary of each novel; Van Meter, "Bankimchandra," *passim.*

15. Haridas and Uma Mukherjee, *India's Fight for Freedom or the Swadeshi Movement (1905–1906)* (Calcutta, 1958), p. 100.

16. Tripathi, "Bankim Chandra," LXXXV, 106, offers an intelligent defense of Chatterjee but seems to have seen many trees and not the forest; Clark, "The Role of Bankimcandra," pp. 440–45; Chatterjee, *Anandamath, passim.* That many Muslim writers saw Bankim Chandra as anti-Muslim has been pointed out in two fine doctoral dissertations by Bengali Muslims: Mustafa Nurul Islam, "Bengalee Moslem Public Opinion as Reflected in the Vernacular Press between 1901 and 1930" (unpublished Ph.D. thesis, London University, 1971), pp. 171–72, and Sufia Ahmed, "Some Aspects of the History of the Muslim Community in Bengal (1884–1912)" (unpublished Ph.D. thesis, London University, 1960), pp. 273–74.

17. Chatteree, *Anandamath*, pp. 190–204; Bimanbehari Majumdar, *History of Political Thought, from Rammohun to Dayananda (1821–84)*, Vol. I, *Bengal* (Calcutta, 1934), pp. 469–71.

18. For Chatterjee's satire on the babu, see Bankim Chandra Chatterjee, "Se kāl ar ekāl" [That time and this], *Bankim racinābalī* [Collected works of Bankim] (2d ed., Calcutta, 1960), II, 200, quoted in Van Meter, "Role of Bengal," p. 1; compare Chatterjee's views with that of Rabindranath Tagore, *Rabīndra racinābalī* [Collected works of Rabindra] (Calcutta, 1961), I, 360–64; hereafter cited as Tagore, *RR;* Chatterjee, *Essays and Letters*, p. 46, mentions that the *Spectator* has described the Bengalis as the Italians of Asia, "acclimatising European ideas and fitting them for reception hereafter by the hardier and more original races of Northern India."

19. Tripathi, "Bankim Chandra," p. 176; Majumdar, *Political Thought*, I, 462–63.

20. Ronaldshay, *Curzon*, II, 418–20; also see M. N. Das, *India under Morley and Minto* (London, 1964), p. 206; Fraser, *India under Curzon*, pp. 175 ff.

21. Banerjea, *Nation*, p. 152.

22. H. E. A. Cotton, *Calcutta Old and New* (Calcutta, 1907), pp. 233–34; Ronaldshay, *Curzon*, II, 29, 74; C. E. Buckland, *Bengal under the Lieutenant-Governors* (2d ed., Calcutta, 1902), II, 420, 426–27, 521; L. S. S. O'Malley, *History of Bengal, Bihar and Orissa under British Rule* (Calcutta, 1925), pp. 451–55; Robert Reid, *Years of Change in Bengal and Assam* (London, 1966), p. 26. On the Universities Bill, see Fraser, *India under Curzon*, pp. 175–200; Banerjea, *Nation*, pp. 161–63; Tagore, "University Bill," *RR*, XII, 734–39.

23. Ronaldshay, *Curzon*, II, 321; Mukherjee and Mukherjee, *India's Fight*, pp. 5–7; Tripathi, *Extremist Challenge*, chapter 3; Sir Bampfylde Fuller, *Some Personal Experiences* (London, 1930), p. 123. The political rationale, at least after the fact, is perfectly clear in extracts from the Minto Papers, quoted at length in Pardaman Singh, "Lord Minto and the Partition Agitation," *Bengal Past and Present*, Vol. LXXXV, Part 2 (Calcutta, July–December 1966), pp. 141 ff.

24. Government of Bengal, *Report (Part II) on Native-Owned English Newspapers in Bengal* (hereafter cited as *R (Part II of N-OENB)*) and *Report of the Native Press in Bengal* (hereafter cited as *RNPB*), 1905, from which these figures and suggestions have been extracted; these are, of course, problematic sources to use because they give government-selected snippets, but they often have information not easily found elsewhere.

25. The name of the contemporary Sinn Fein movement means the same thing as "Swadeshi," and Indian nationalists were constantly aware of

Irish developments; on Ireland, see Dorothy Macardle, *The Irish Republic* (New York, 1965), pp. 65–66; Mukherjee and Mukherjee, *India's Fight*, pp. 12 ff.; Surendranath Banerjea, *Speeches and Writings of Hon. Surendranath Banerjea* (Madras, n.d.), pp. 120, 292–99.

26. Banerjea, *Speeches and Writings*, pp. 295–99.

27. Banerjea, *Speeches and Writings*, p. 289.

28. See the suggestions about the functions of youth activities for the groups themselves and for the larger society in S. N. Eisenstadt, *From Generation to Generation* (New York, 1964), pp. 207–208, 273, 303, 314; data can be found in Mukherjee and Mukherjee, *India's Fight, passim*, and in chapter 5 below.

29. Haridas and Uma Mukherjee, *The Origins of the National Education Movement* (Jadavpur, Calcutta, 1957), pp. 44 ff., 255–66.

30. John R. McLane, "Calcutta and the Mofussilization of Bengal Politics," *Bengal East and West* (East Lansing, Michigan, 1970) ed. Alexander Lipski, pp. 70 ff.; Sarkar, "Trends," Part I, pp. 28–29.

31. Sarkar, "Trends," Part II, pp. 146 ff.

32. Banerjea, *Speeches and Writings*, p. 125.

33. Lajpat Rai, *Young India* (New York, 1917), pp. 178–79.

34. M. K. Gandhi, *The Collected Works of Mahatma Gandhi* (Delhi, 1963), X, 13.

35. Das, *Morley and Minto*, pp. 34, 81.

36. Rabindranath Tagore, "The Religion of an Artist," *Rabindranath Tagore on Art and Aesthetics* (Calcutta, 1961), p. 40; on Tagore and his family, see Krishna Kripalani, *Rabindranath Tagore* (New York, 1962), pp. 14 ff.; Debendranath Tagore, *The Autobiography of Maharshi Devendranath Tagore* (London, 1914), tr. Satyendranath Tagore and Indira Devi; Loke Nath Ghose, *The Modern History of the Indian Chiefs, Rajas, Zamindars, & c.* (Calcutta, 1881), Part II, pp. 160–223.

37. Rabindranath Bhattacharyya, ed., *Tagore Birth Centenary 1861–1961*, Supplement Issue, *The Calcutta Municipal Gazette*, Vol. LXXV, No. 21, pp. 156–57; very few of Tagore's political essays from the early period, 1890–1908, have been translated; they are collected in *RR*, XII, 673–1099 and XIII, 1–438.

38. Bhattacharyya, *Tagore Centenary*, p. 159.

39. Rabindranath Tagore, *Greater India* (Madras, 1921), p. 45.

40. Many anti-imperialist quotations from Tagore are collected in *Your Tagore for Today* (Bombay, 1945), ed. Hirankumar Sanyal, tr. Hiren-

dranath Mukherjee; this particular metaphor comes from "Britons and Indians," written in 1893.

41. Tagore, "The Way to Get It Done," *Greater India*, pp. 47–48.

42. For Tagore's concern with leadership, see the two essays entitled "Deśanāyak" [Leader of the country], *RR*, XII, 799–805 and XIII, 387–90; these essays were written in 1906 and 1939.

43. Rabindranath Tagore, *Towards Universal Man* (Calcutta, 1961), p. 59; the original Bengali version is longer and more concrete; "Swadeśī samāj," [Society and state, *or* Our own society] *RR*, XII, 683–708, 767–80.

44. Tagore was accused of ignoring the daily political crises; see Sarkar, "Trends," Part I, pp. 35–36; Aurobindo Ghose, *The Doctrine of Passive Resistance* (2d ed., Pondicherry, 1952), pp. 81–88; Bipinchandra Pal, *Indian Nationalism* (Triplicane, Madras, n.d.), pp. 16 ff.

45. Tagore, "Society and State, 2," *Towards Universal Man*, p. 51; Tagore particularly addresses such remarks on the work to be done to students; see "Chātrader prati sambhāṣan" [Address to the students], *RR*, XII, 723.

46. Tagore, *RR*, XII, 778–79; also Rabindranath Tagore, *Rabindranath Tagore on Rural Reconstruction* (Calcutta, 1962), *passim*.

47. Kripalani, *Tagore*, pp. 176–212; Edward Thompson, *Rabindranath Tagore, Poet and Dramatist* (2d ed., London, 1948), pp. 204–19.

48. Rabindranath Tagore, *Letters to a Friend* (London, 1928), p. 111.

49. A fuller account of revolutionary activity can be found in chapter 5, below.

50. Bipinchandra Pal, *Character Sketches* (Calcutta, 1957), p. 30. The idea of negative identity is developed in Erik H. Erikson, *Identity, Youth and Crisis* (New York, 1968), pp. 172–76, 195–96.

51. Haridas and Uma Mukherjee, *Sri Aurobindo's Political Thought* (Calcutta, 1958), pp. 77, 81, 84. This volume contains many of Aurobindo's early political articles.

52. *R (Part II) of N-OENB*, No. 44 of 1904, para. 8170, October 12, 1904.

53. Bipinchandra Pal, "The Shell and the Seed," *Bande Mataram*, September 17, 1906, reprinted in Haridas and Uma Mukherjee, *Bipin Chandra Pal and India's Struggle for Swaraj* (Calcutta, 1958), pp. 134–45.

54. Mukherjee and Mukherjee, *Bipin Pal*, pp. 46–49; the plan is mentioned in Ghose, *Passive Resistance*, pp. 9–10.

55. Gokhale to Krishnaswamy, September 29, 1906, Gokhale Papers, quoted in Pardaman Singh, "The Indian National Congress–Surat Split," *Bengal*

Past and Present (Calcutta, July–December 1965), Vol. LXXXIV, Part 2, p. 127.

56. R. C. Majumdar, *History of the Freedom Movement in India* (Calcutta, 1963), II, 202–209; Sisirkumar Mitra, *The Liberator, Sri Aurobindo, India and the World* (Delhi, 1954), p. 90.

57. To get a complete picture, one must read several accounts; see Amvika Charan Mazumdar, *Indian National Evolution* (Madras, 1951), Appendix B; "The Surat Papers," Annie Besant, *How India Wrought for Freedom* (Adyar, Madras, 1915), pp. 466 ff.; Mazumdar was a Moderate and Mrs. Besant leans to that side. For an account more sympathetic to the Extremists, see Majumdar, *Freedom Movement*, II, 209 ff.; participants' versions are in Banerjea, *Nation*, pp. 219–20, and Aurobindo Ghose, *Sri Aurobindo on Himself and the Mother* (Pondicherry, 1953), pp. 78–81.

58. Mazumdar, *National Evolution*, pp. 285 ff.

59. Mukherjee and Mukherjee, *Bipin Pal*, pp. 105 ff.; for comments critical of Pal when he returned, see *R (Part II) of N-OENB*, No. 42 of 1911.

60. Stanley A. Wolpert, *Tilak and Gokhale* (Los Angeles, 1962), pp. 220 ff.

61. Mitra, *Liberator*, pp. 137 ff.

62. *Nayak*, October 30, 1911, *RNPB*, No. 45 of 1911, paragraph 85.

63. Ronaldshay, *Curzon*, II, 322 ff.; P. N. Bhargava, ed., *Who's Who in India* (Lucknow, 1911), p. 26; J. H. Broomfield, *Elite Conflict in a Plural Society* (Berkeley, 1968), pp. 45–46, 65; many Bengali Muslims consider the Dacca Nawab family outsiders; they came from Kashmir, were influential at the Mughal court, and moved to Sylhet in the eighteenth century; they later moved to Dacca and held property there and in Barisal, Patna, and Mymensingh. During the revolt of 1857 they supported the Raj and thereafter they were generally loyalists to the Raj in politics.

64. See the different accounts in Das, *Morley and Minto*, pp. 147–82, and Syed Razi Wasti, *Lord Minto and the Indian Nationalist Movement 1905 to 1910* (London, 1964), pp. 59–88; also Tripathi, *Extremist Challenge*, chapter 5.

65. Sarkar, "Trends," Part II, p. 152.

66. Muin-ud-din Ahmad Khan, *History of the Fara'idi Movement in Bengal (1818–1906)* (Karachi, 1965). An organization of Namasudras also approached the government at this time in search of assistance; N. K. Bose, *Culture and Society in India* (Calcutta, 1967), pp. 255–56.

67. John R. McLane, "The 1905 Partition and the New Communalism," *Bengal East and West*, Alexander Lipski, ed. (East Lansing, Michigan, 1970).

68. Tagore, "The True Way," *Your Tagore for Today*, p. 25.

69. Tagore, "Presidential Address," *Towards Universal Man*, pp. 105–106.

70. Banerjea, *Nation*, p. 60; Government of India, Sedition Committee, 1918, *Report* (Calcutta, 1918), gives only the fruits of CID investigations and is systematically organized; a better sense of the work of the CID and of the Home Department can be gained from reading of individual files; for the Viceroy's view, see Mary, Countess of Minto, *India Minto and Morley 1905–1910* (London, 1934), pp. 374–75.

71. Minto, *India*, p. 235; on the regulations, see pp. 154, 238, 256–57, 277, 377.

72. Wolpert, *Tilak and Gokhale*, pp. 220 ff.; an account of Aurobindo Ghose's year in prison is given in chapter 4 below.

73. Lord Minto letter of March 19, 1907, in Minto, *India*, p. 109.

74. Extract from memorandum sent to Morley, March 19, 1907, Minto, *India*, pp. 110–11.

75. Minto, *India*, pp. 284, 332, 367.

76. Aga Khan, *The Memoirs of Aga Khan, World Enough and Time* (London, 1954), pp. 76–77, 93–94, 103–104.

77. Minto, *India*, p. 260; Besant, *How India Wrought*, pp. 493–95, 540.

78. Das, *Morley and Minto*, pp. 218–21.

79. Besant, *How India Wrought*, pp. 493–95, 540.

80. Aurobindo Ghose, "The Reformed Councils," *Karmayogin*, November 20, 1909, I, No. 20; although the article is unsigned, Sisirkumar Mitra, an expert on the writings of Aurobindo Ghose, has assured me that it was written by Ghose.

81. See numerous extracts from the *Bengalee* and other Indian papers on this point in R (*Part II*) of N-OENB, No. 51 of 1911, for period ending December 23, 1911.

82. Reprinted in *Nayak*, December 16, 1911, *RNPB*, No. 51 of 1911, para. 29.

83. Mary Helen Elizabeth Carmichael, *Lord Carmichael of Skirling* (London, 1929), p. 148.

84. Ronaldshay, *Curzon*, II, 259–60; Fraser, *India under Curzon*, pp. x–xxvi.

85. For example, see the statement of Bhupendranath Basu at the 1911 Congress, quoted in Besant, *How India Wrought*, p. 529.

86. *Moslem Hitaishi*, December 15, 1911, *RNPB*, No. 51 of 1911, para. 35.

87. *Comrade*, December 16, 1911, R (*Part II*) of *N-OENB*, No. 51 of 1911, para. 1547.

88. *Comrade*, December 16, 1911, R (*Part II*) of *N-OENB*, No. 51 of 1911, para. 1576.

89. Reid, *Years of Change*, p. 26.

CHAPTER FOUR. AUROBINDO GHOSE:
SECRETS OF THE SELF AND REVOLUTION

1. There are numerous government of India, Home Department, political files on Aurobindo Ghose; for example, see Home Department, Political, A. May, 1908, Nos. 104–111, which described him as the leader of the Extremists in Bengal.

2. For example, Sisirkumar Mitra, *The Liberator, Sri Aurobindo, India and the World* (Delhi, 1954), p. 3, writes, "Sri Aurobindo is a truth too vast for the mind—a truth that by its very dynamism is and will be revealing itself more and more to the world as time rolls on. . . . The subject which Sri Aurobindo is had better be approached with reverence and contemplation. Else, not even an iota of its truth and meaning can be grasped." K. R. Srinivasa Iyengar, *Sri Aurobindo* (2d ed., Calcutta, 1950) and R. R. Diwakar, *Mahayogi Sri Aurobindo* (3d ed., Bombay, 1962) are similarly reverential; A. B. Purani, *Sri Aurobindo In England* (Pondicherry, 1956) and *The Life of Sri Aurobindo (1872–1926)* (2d ed., Pondicherry, 1960), is also a disciple but he, along with Sisirkumar Mitra, has been the most energetic at gathering information systematically about Aurobindo; all these works except Iyengar's are useful as sources of information and of attitudes toward their common subject.

3. Aurobindo's description of his own life is presented in Aurobindo Ghose [Sri Aurobindo], *Sri Aurobindo on Himself and the Mother* (Pondicherry, 1953), Part I; he always describes himself in the third person, almost as if he were an object, albeit an object chosen by God; the biographies mentioned in note 2 above all view the political career as preparatory to a higher stage; an exception is Girijāśaṅkar Rāycowdhurī, *Śrī Arabinda o bāṅlāy swadeśi yug* [Sri Aurobindo and the Bengali Swadeshi age] (Calcutta, 1953); Karan Singh, *Prophet of Indian Nationalism* (London, 1963) also deals with Aurobindo's career in politics, but it adds nothing to our knowledge of Aurobindo's thought or activity.

4. Purani, *Life*, pp. 3–6.

5. Nemai Sadhan Bose, *The Indian Awakening and Bengal* (Calcutta, 1960), pp. 139–40, 170.

6. Diwakar, *Mahayogi*, p. 24; Purani, *Life*, p. 3.

7. See Aurobindo Ghose, *Kārākāhini* [Prison diary] (3d ed., Calcutta, 1930), *passim;* for the melodramatic clash of cultures, see Aurobindo Ghose [Sri Aurobindo], *The Foundations of Indian Culture* (Pondicherry, 1959), *passim.*

8. Diwakar, *Mahayogi*, p. 26.

9. Purani, *Aurobindo in England*, pp. 3 ff.

10. Purani, *Life*, pp. 6–7.

11. Ghose, *On Himself*, p. 18.

12. Purani, *Aurobindo in England*, pp. 29–32.

13. Purani, *Aurobindo in England*, p. 18.

14. Government of India, Home Department, Political File No. 13, June 1908, Note on Aravinda Acroyd Ghose by A. Wood, ICS.

15. Wood Note on Aravinda, Home Department File No. 13, June 1908.

16. Ghose, *On Himself*, p. 13.

17. Government of India, Judicial and Public File 1396 of 1892.

18. Mitra, *Liberator*, pp. 30–31.

19. Aurobindo was 11th in the open competition of 1890, 23rd in the first periodical examination, and 37th in the final examination. Government of India, Judicial and Public File 1396 of 1892.

20. Government of India, Judicial and Public Proceedings, Files 1345, 1376, 1414, 1897, 1926, and 2035 of 1892.

21. It seems that this is but one instance in which Aurobindo was trying to create a revolutionary past and attribute his difficulties to the machinations of an evil imperial power. There is not a word in the government files about his revolutionary activities while in England.

22. Government of India, Judicial and Public File 1926 of 1892.

23. Government of India, Judicial and Public File 1926 of 1892.

24. Ghose, *On Himself*, p. 13.

25. Ghose, *On Himself*, p. 17.

26. Mitra, *Liberator*, p. 36.

27. Purani, *Life*, p. 57–59; the articles have been reprinted in Aurobindo Ghose [Sri Aurobindo], *Bankim Chandra Chatterjee* (Pondicherry, 1954), and in Haridas and Uma Mukherjee, *Sri Aurobindo's Political Thought* (Calcutta, 1958), pp. 61–123.

28. Mukherjee and Mukherjee, *Aurobindo's Thought*, pp. 84, 90–92, 95.

29. Mukherjee and Mukherjee, *Aurobindo's Thought*, pp. 79–81, 107.

30. Mukherjee and Mukherjee, *Aurobindo's Thought*, p. 119.

31. Mukherjee and Mukherjee, *Aurobindo's Thought*, p. 108.

32. Ghose, *Chatterjee*, pp. 2, 17, 23, 41.

33. Joseph R. Levenson, *Liang Ch'i-Cha'o and the Mind of Modern China* (Cambridge, Mass., 1959), p. 150.

34. Ghose, *Chatterjee*, p. 35.

35. Dinendrakumar Roy, *Arabinda-prasanga*, p. 8, quoted in Mitra, *Liberator*, pp. 44–45.

36. Purani, *Life*, pp. 72–78.

37. Purani, *Life*, pp. 68–72.

38. Mukherjee and Mukherjee, *Aurobindo's Thought*, pp. 84–85.

39. Ghose, *On Himself*, p. 32.

40. Ghose, *On Himself*, p. 97.

41. See Sister Nivedita, *Civic and National Ideals*, (4th ed., Calcutta, 1948), especially "The Function of Art in Shaping Nationality," pp. 62–82.

42. Ghose, *On Himself*, pp. 36–37; Purani, *Life*, pp. 78–80.

43. Ghose, *On Himself*, p. 36.

44. See Aurobindo's *Bhawani Mandir*, reprinted in Purani, *Life*, pp. 84–97, and the analysis of it below.

45. Purani, *Life*, p. 73; Mitra, *Liberator*, p. 51; Ghose, *On Himself*, p. 42.

46. Ghose, *Chatterjee*, pp. 47–48.

47. Mitra, *Liberator*, p. 58.

48. Mitra, *Liberator*, p. 66.

49. Purani, *Life*, pp. 77, 83; Ghose, *On Himself*, p. 85.

50. R. C. Majumdar, *History of the Freedom Movement in India* (Calcutta, 1962), I, 341; Purani, *Life*, p. 76; Kees W. Bolle, *The Persistence of Religion* (Leiden, 1965), p. 10.

51. Purani, *Life*, p. 84.

52. Purani, *Life*, p. 87.

53. Purani, *Life*, pp. 88–89.

54. J. N. Farquhar, *An Outline of the Religious Literature of India* (2d ed., Varanasi, 1966), pp. 150–51; on the Tantras in general, see Sir John

Woodroffe [Arthur Avalon, pseud.], *Principles of Tantra* (Madras, 1960), pp. 212 ff.

55. Purani, *Life*, pp. 95–96.

56. Bolle, *Persistance*, p. 8; Purani, *Life*, p. 89.

57. Purani, *Life*, p. 85.

58. Although Aurobindo does not specifically say this, it would seem that a tract flooded with Hindu symbols and concepts would be anathema to the Muslims. Throughout his political career, Aurobindo showed little sensitivity to the Muslim question. He concentrated his energies and words on Hindu audiences. See Ghose, *On Himself*, p. 77.

59. For example, see Government of India, Home Department, Political, A. October 1909, Nos. 230–48, Note in the Criminal Intelligence Office on the *Karmayogin*, No. 1, June 19, 1909, by J. C. Ker, Personal Assistant to Director, C. I. Ker argues that Aurobindo would have to choose between pan-Indian or pan-Hindu nationalism and thought that at present the Muslims were placed outside nationalism as Aurobindo interpreted it.

60. According to Nalini Kanta Gupta, a disciple and publisher of Aurobindo's *Collected Poems and Plays* (Pondicherry, 1942), a large part of the first of the two volumes was written in the Baroda period; Purani, *Life*, pp. 63, 83.

61. Aurobindo Ghose [Sri Aurobindo], *Speeches* (3d ed., Pondicherry, 1952), pp. 1–2.

62. Mitra, *Liberator*, p. 73.

63. Mitra, *Liberator*, p. 74.

64. Purani, *Life*, pp. 112–13; Haridas and Uma Mukherjee, *The Origins of the National Education Movement* (Jadavpur, Calcutta, 1957), pp. 43 ff.

65. Ghose, *On Himself*, pp. 72–73.

66. These articles and speeches have, in large part, been collected and reprinted; see Ghose, *Speeches;* Mukherjee and Mukherjee, *Aurobindo's Thought;* Haridas and Uma Mukherjee, eds., *Sri Aurobindo and the New Thought in Indian Politics* (Calcutta, 1964); Aurobindo Ghose [Sri Aurobindo], *The Doctrine of Passive Resistance* (2d ed., Pondicherry, 1952).

67. Mukherjee and Mukherjee, *Aurobindo and the New Thought*, pp. 323–24.

68. Aurobindo, along with others of the "New School," thought that the earlier Indian nationalists were "denationalized." So to nationalize Indian politics, one had to bring into play native concepts and terms, and these were often religious. At the same time, Aurobindo had become increasingly religious and interested in spiritual matters since his return to India.

69. Mukherjee and Mukherjee, *Aurobindo and the New Thought*, pp. 61, 190.

70. Mukherjee and Mukherjee, *Aurobindo and the New Thought*, pp. 27–28.

71. Ghose, *Passive Resistance*, p. 70.

72. Ghose, *Passive Resistance*, p. 84.

73. Ghose, *Passive Resistance*, pp. 24, 26.

74. Ghose, *Passive Resistance*, pp. 66–68.

75. Ghose, *Passive Resistance*, pp. 27–29.

76. Ghose, *Passive Resistance*, p. 72.

77. Ghose, *Passive Resistance*, p. 29.

78. A great variety of plans were offered; see Mukherjee and Mukherjee, *National Education, passim*; for Tagore's plans see chapter 4 above.

79. Ghose, *Passive Resistance*, p. 30. For rebuke, see Franklin Edgerton, ed. and tr., *Bhagavad Gita* (reprint, New York, 1964), chapter II, verses 2–3.

80. Ghose, *Passive Resistance*, pp. 29–30.

81. Ghose, *Passive Resistance, passim.*

82. Compare Aurobindo's use of Indian traditions with the views of Tagore, Bipin Pal, and Gandhi in chapter 4 above and 6 below.

83. For a full exposition of Aurobindo's views on the *Bhagavad Gītā*, see Aurobindo Ghose [Sri Aurobindo], *Essays on the Gita* (Pondicherry, 1959). Aurobindo seems to have been much less influenced by Bengali Vaishnavism than almost any other major nationalist from Bengal.

84. Ghose, *Passive Resistance*, pp. 87–88. Although they were a scribe caste, some Kayasthas in the nineteenth century claimed Kshatriya status, and Aurobindo may have been one of them; at any rate, he seems to have identified strongly with the warrior caste.

85. There have been other twentieth-century Indians who have argued that violence is a more central Indian tradition than nonviolence; see Nirad C. Chaudhuri, "Janus and His Two Faces," *The Continent of Circe* (London, 1965), pp. 97–119; it is probable that all those involved in the revolutionary movement and all those sympathetic to it would have agreed.

86. Ghose, *Passive Resistance*, p. 4.

87. Ghose, *Passive Resistance*, pp. 4–9.

88. Ghose, *Speeches*, pp. 7–9.

89. Ghose, "Lewd-Tongued Imperialism and Soullessness," *Bande Mataram*, October 4, 1907, reprinted in Mukherjee and Mukherjee, *Aurobindo and the New Thought*, p. 83.

90. Haridas and Uma Mukherjee, *India's Fight for Freedom or the Swadeshi Movement (1905–1906)* (Calcutta, 1958), pp. 100–101.

91. Ghose, *On Himself*, p. 38.

92. Home Department, Political, May 1908, Nos. 104–11.

93. Ghose, *On Himself*, pp. 49–50.

94. Pardaman Singh, "The Indian National Congress—Surat Split," *Bengal Past and Present*, Vol. LXXXIV, Part 2 (July–December 1965), pp. 121–24.

95. Mitra, *Liberator*, pp. 79–81; Ghose, *On Himself*, pp. 51, 76.

96. Ghose, *On Himself*, p. 51.

97. Ghose, *Passive Resistance*, pp. 9–10.

98. Amvika Charan Mazumdar, *Indian National Evolution* (Madras, 1915), pp. 108–23, xxxii–lxiii; Annie Besant, *How India Wrought for Freedom* (Adyar, Madras, 1915), pp. 465–82; Majumdar, *Freedom Movement*, II, 175–213.

99. Sumit Sarkar, "Trends in Bengal's Swadeshi Movement (1903–1908)," *Bengal Past and Present*, LXXXIV, Part II (July–December, 1965), pp. 144 ff.

100. Many revolutionaries recruited from 1907 to 1915 continued to work in Bengali politics until independence. Some later moved into the Congress or one of the small leftist parties. See chapters 6 and 7 below.

101. Singh, "Congress–Surat Split," p. 129.

102. Mitra, *Liberator*, pp. 88–90; Majumdar, *Freedom Movement*, II, 175 ff.

103. Mitra, *Liberator*, p. 94; Ghose, *On Himself*, pp. 78–82.

104. Ghose, *On Himself*, pp. 81–82.

105. Mitra, *Liberator*, pp. 93–95; Purani, *Life*, photographs following p. 116; Stanley A. Wolpert, *Tilak and Gokhale: Revolution and Reform in the Making of Modern India* (Los Angeles, 1962), pp. 206 ff.

106. Purani, *Life*, pp. 120 ff.

107. Written in 1939, quoted in Purani, *Life*, p. 121.

108. Mitra, *Liberator*, p. 98.

109. Ghose, *On Himself*, p. 33.

110. Ghose, *On Himself*, pp. 31–34; Purani, *Life*, p. 118.

111. Purani, *Life,* p. 118; Nalini Kiśor Guha, *Bāṅlāy biplabbād* [Revolutionary movement in Bengal] (Calcutta, 1954), pp. 93 ff.

112. Government of India, Home Department, Political, A, May, 1908, Nos. 104–11, section 12.

113. Suprakāś Rāy, *Bhārater baiplabik saṅgrāmer itihās* [History of the Indian revolutionary struggle] (Calcutta, 1955), pp. 170–72; Ghose, *Kārākāhinī,* pp. 2–4.

114. Ghose, *Kārākāhinī.* It is noteworthy that this most revealing account is one of the few works by Aurobindo that the Sri Aurobindo Ashram and other nationalist publishers have not seen fit to reprint.

115. Hemendranath Das Gupta, *Deshbandhu Chittaranjan Das* (Delhi, 1960), pp. 10–16; one of the best biographies of Das.

116. Barindra Kumar Ghose, *The Tale of My Exile* (Pondicherry, 1922).

117. Ghose, *Kārākāhinī,* p. 7.

118. Ghose, *Kārākāhinī,* pp. 20, 28, 40.

119. Ghose, *Kārākāhinī,* p. 47.

120. Ghose, *Kārākāhinī,* p. 31.

121. Ghose, *Kārākāhinī,* p. 44; Ghose, *On Himself,* pp. 107, 115.

122. Ghose, *Kārākāhinī,* p. 23.

123. Ghose, *Kārākāhinī,* p. 33.

124. B. Ghose, *Tale of Exile,* pp. 62–63.

125. Ghose, *On Himself,* p. 61.

126. Ghose, *Kārākāhinī,* p. 2.

127. Ghose, *On Himself,* p. 90; Government of India, Home Department, Political. A. October 1909, Nos. 230–48; several officials were against making Calcutta a "proclaimed area" or arresting Aurobindo, since these steps would help a "dying movement."

128. Several of the most interesting articles have been collected in Aurobindo Ghose [Sri Aurobindo], *The Ideal of the Karmayogin* (7th ed., Pondicherry, 1950).

129. Quoted in Government of India, Home Department, Political. A. October, 1909, Nos. 230–48, pp. 6–7.

130. Quoted in Government of India, Home Department, Political. A. October, 1909, Nos. 230–48, pp. 6–7.

131. Government of India, Home Department, Political. A. October 1909, Nos. 230–48, p. 4.

132. Government of India, Home Department, Political. A. October, 1909, Nos. 230–48, p. 3.

133. Mitra, *Liberator*, pp. 137 ff.; Ghose, *On Himself*, pp. 62–63.

134. Mitra, *Liberator*, p. 139.

135. Ghose, *On Himself*, pp. 26, 83.

136. Ghose, *On Himself*, p. 113.

137. Ghose, *Karmayogin*, pp. 50–54.

138. Ghose, *On Himself*, pp. 65–66.

139. There have been many stories and rumors about overtures to Aurobindo in Pondicherry and about his influence on Indian politics from the ashram. He did have some contact with Bengali politics through Surendra Mohan Ghose, who visited him in Pondicherry from the 1930s (interviews with Surendra Mohan Ghose, New Delhi, September 20, 27, and 30, 1964). There were also stories that Aurobindo was offered the Congress presidency in the 1920s, and he was visited by C. R. Das (Purani, *Life*, p. 212). It is possible that further interviews and investigation may clarify this matter.

140. Purani, *Life*, pp. 180 ff.; in the wider world, it appears that Aurobindo is known especially for these works, including *Essays on the Gita; The Foundations of Indian Culture* (Pondicherry, 1959); *The Future Poetry* (Pondicherry, 1953); *The Human Cycle* (New York, 1950); *The Ideal of Human Unity* (New York, 1950); *The Life Divine* (New York, 1949); *On Yoga I* (Pondicherry, 1955); *On Yoga II* (Pondicherry, 1958); *On the Veda* (Pondicherry, 1964).

141. Ghose, *On Himself*, p. 434.

142. Purani, *Life*, pp. 68–69.

143. Translated and reprinted by Purani in *Life*, pp. 97–105; available in Bengali as *Śrī Arabinder patra* (Pondicherry, 1952).

144. Purani, *Life*, pp. 104–105.

145. Purani, *Life*, pp. 180 ff.; Ghose, *On Himself*, pp. 355 ff.

146. Purani, *Life*, pp. 219, 229–30, 243 ff.; Ghose, *On Himself*, pp. 216 ff.

147. Mircea Eliade, *Yoga: Immortality and Freedom* (New York, 1958), p. 112.

148. Ghose, *On Himself*, p. 26.

149. Ghose, *Foundations*, pp. 4–6, 17, 38 ff.; Ghose, *On the Veda, passim*.

150. Ghose, *Karmayogin*, pp. 5, 7, 33, 60, 63; Ghose, *Essays on the Gita*, pp. 345–46; Ghose, *The Future Poetry*, pp. 265 ff.

151. Ghose, *Human Cycle*, p. 347; Ghose, *Ideal of Human Unity*, pp. 178 ff.

CHAPTER FIVE. THE ORGANIZATION OF THE REVOLUTIONARIES

1. Suprakāś Rāy, *Bhārater baiplabik saṅgramer itihās* [History of the Indian revolutionary struggle] (Calcutta, 1955); Balshastri Hardas, *Armed Struggle for Freedom* (Poona, 1958); Government of India, Sedition Committee, 1918, *Report* (Calcutta, 1918).

2. For a corrective, see Nirad C. Chaudhuri, "Janus and His Two Faces," *The Continent of Circe* (London, 1965), pp. 97–119.

3. W. W. Hunter, *The Annals of Rural Bengal* (reprint, Calcutta, 1965), pp. 35, 98; Ronald B. Inden, "The Localization of the Hindu Elite of Bengal and its Effects on the Polity of the Southeastern Bengal Chiefdoms" (unpublished master's thesis, University of Chicago, 1963), p. 15.

4. Earl of Ronaldshay, *The Heart of Āryāvarta, A Study of the Psychology of Indian Unrest* (London, 1925), p. 125; Valentine Chirol, *Indian Unrest* (London, 1910), also gives some attention to cultural factors—for example, he writes, "In its extreme forms Shakti worship finds expression in licentious aberrations which, however lofty may be the speculative theories that gave birth to them, represent the most extravagant forms of delirious mysticism" (p. 84). See also the historical novels of Romesh Chunder Dutt, *Rames racanābalī* ed. Jogesh Chandra Chatterjee (Calcutta, 1960), *Anandamath* (Calcutta, n.d.), tr. Sree Aurobindo and Barindra Kumar Ghosh.

5. This phrase was used by Hari Kumar Chakravarty in an interview with Professor Robert C. North, Kodalia, West Bengal, August 25, 1958.

6. I have used the forms "Jatin" and "Jatin-da" throughout in referring to Jatindranath Mukherjee since I am usually quoting from English language sources which spell the name in this way. A more correct transliteration of the Bengali would be "Yatīn" and "Yatīn-dā."

7. Interviews with Lalit Bhattacharya in Calcutta during 1964. Mr. Bhattacharya and I checked the dates in a notebook kept by his father Dinabandhu Bhattacharya. Naren, later in life when he had changed his name to M. N. Roy, said that he was born some years later than the date given here and in most accounts. Naren's year of birth corresponds to the Bengali year 1293.

8. M. N. Roy, "The Dissolution of a Priestly Family," *The Radical Humanist* (Calcutta, February 1954), Vol. XVIII, Nos. 6–7, 66–68, 72–74.

9. North interview with Chakravarty, 1958.

10. North interview with Chakravarty, 1958.

11. North interview with Chakravarty, 1958.

12. See Bipinchandra Pal, *Memories of My Life and Times* (Calcutta, 1932, 1951), I, 313; Subhas Chandra Bose, *An Indian Pilgrim. An Unfinished Autobiography and Collected Letters 1897–1921* (Calcutta, 1965), pp. 34 ff. The nineteenth-century movements relevant to the revolutionaries have been discussed in chapter 3 above. See also Nirad C. Chaudhuri, *The Autobiography of an Unknown Indian* (New York, 1951), pp. 195 ff.

13. One might call this the problem of "manhood," and it had been noted by many writers on Bengal in this period; Chirol, *Indian Unrest*, p. 79; Haridas and Uma Mukherjee, eds., *Sri Aurobindo and the New Thought* (Calcutta, 1964), pp. 14, 89.

14. Interviews with Lalit Bhattacharya.

15. Sibnarayan Ray, ed., *M. N. Roy Philosopher-Revolutionary* (Calcutta, 1959), p. 65.

16. Government of India, Home Department, Political, Part A, Proceedings January 1917, Nos. 299–301, K. W. to—Decision that no *prima facie* case exists for the extradition of Norendra Nath Bhattacharji *alias* Martin, at present in the USA (includes second statement of Fanindra Kumar Chakravarty *alias* William Arthur Payne *alias* Ananda Mohan [Simla, 1916]), para. 57.

17. Nalini Kiśor Guha, *Bāṅlāy biplabbād* (Calcutta, 1954), pp. 88–116.

18. Government of India, Home Department, Political Proceedings, August 1911, Nos. 23–36, Howrah-Sibpur political dacoity gang case.

19. Sedition Committee, *Report*, pp. 101–102.

20. Richard Leonard Park, "The Rise of Militant Nationalism in Bengal: A Regional Study of Indian Nationalism" (unpublished doctoral dissertation, Harvard University, 1951), p. 238; Sedition Committee, *Report*, pp. 101–102.

21. Home Department, 1917, Nos. 299–301, Chakravarty statement, para. 4–5; Ramyansu Sekhar Das, *M. N. Roy, the Humanist Philosopher* (Calcutta, 1956), p. 26; Gopal Halder, "Revolutionary Terrorism," *Studies in the Bengal Renaissance* (Jadavpur, Calcutta, 1958), ed. Atulchandra Gupta, p. 241.

22. Home Department, 1911, Nos. 23–26.

23. Home Department, 1911, Nos. 23–36; Home Department, 1917, Nos. 299–301, Chakravarty statement, para. 8.

24. This was suggested to me in interviews with Surendra Mohan Ghose in New Delhi, September 1964, and with Dr. R. C. Majumdar in Calcutta, July 26, 1964.

25. Home Department, 1911, Nos. 23–36.

26. Home Department, 1917, Nos. 299–301 Chakravarty statement para. 3; M. N. Roy, "Jatin Mukherji," *Independent India*, Vol. XIII, No. 8 (February 27, 1949), p. 91.

27. Roy, "Jatin Mukherji," p. 91.

28. Roy, "Jatin Mukherji," p. 91.

29. S. N. Mukherjee, *Elites in South Asia* (Cambridge, 1970), pp. 71–78.

30. E. E. Evans-Pritchard, *The Nuer* (Oxford, 1940), chapter 4.

31. R. Carstairs, *Human Nature in Rural India* (London, 1895), pp. 268–71, 340; Ralph W. Nicholas, "Factions: A Comparative Analysis," in *Political Systems and the Distribution of Power* (New York, 1965), pp. 21–59.

32. Jyotirmoyee Sarma, "Formal and Informal Relations in the Hindu Joint Household of Bengal," *Man in India* (Calcutta, April–June 1951), Vol. XXXI, No. 2, pp. 51–71.

33. Sir John Woodroffe [Arthur Avalon, pseud.], *Principles of Tantra* (Madras, 1960), p. 535.

34. Sedition Committee, *Report*, p. 94.

35. Guha, *Bāṅlāy biplabbād*, pp. 89–91.

36. Ghose, *Passive Resistance*, pp. 29–30.

37. Guha, *Bāṅlāy biplabbād*, pp. 94–95.

38. Interviews with Nirad C. Chaudhuri in Delhi, May and September 1964.

39. Guha, *Bāṅlāy biplabbād*, pp. 88 ff.; Halder, "Revolutionary Terrorism," pp. 229–31.

40. Ronaldshay, *Āryāvarta*, pp. 80–87; Pal, *Nationality and Empire*, pp. 84–85, 100, 123.

41. Roy, "Jatin Mukherji," p. 91.

42. Sedition Committee, *Report*, pp. 46–114, *passim*, and 213–20; Uma Mukherjee, *Two Great Indian Revolutionaries* (Calcutta, 1966), pp. 174–78, 213.

43. Sedition Committee, *Report*, Annexure 2, p. 226.

44. Government of India, *Census of India, 1921* (Calcutta, 1923), Vol. V, Part II, pp. 165–69.

45. Sedition Committee, *Report*, pp. 111–18.

46. Home Department, 1917, Nos. 299–301, Chakravarty statement, *passim*.

47. Home Department, 1917, Nos. 299–301, Chakravarty statement, para. 3; Sedition Committee, *Report*, pp. 66–67; A. B. Purani, *The Life of Sri Auro-*

bindo (*1872–1926*) (2d ed., Pondicherry, 1960), p. 72; Guha, *Bāṅlāy biplabbād*, p. 98; Chaudhuri, *Autobiography*, pp. 238–41.

48. Sedition Committee, *Report*, p. 66.

49. Sedition Committee, *Report*, p. 103.

50. Home Department, 1917, Nos, 299–301, Chakravarty statement, para. 13.

51. Home Department, 1917, Nos. 299–301, Chakravarty statement, para. 15.

52. Halder, "Revolutionary Terrorism," pp. 242–43.

53. Home Department, 1917, Nos. 299–301, Chakravarty statement, para. 27.

54. Sedition Committee, *Report*, pp. 6–8, 119–25; Mukherjee, *Two Indian Revolutionaries*, pp. 60–96; M. N. Roy, *M. N. Roy's Memoirs* (New Delhi, 1964), pp. 313 ff.; Gene D. Overstreet and Marshall Windmiller, *Communism in India* (Berkeley, 1959), pp. 19–81.

55. Sedition Committee, *Report*, pp. 119–25.

56. Home Department, 1917, Nos. 299–301, Chakravarty statement, para. 11; Sedition Committee, *Report*, pp. 67–71.

57. Guha, *Bāṅlāy biplabbād*, pp. 109–17.

58. Guha, *Bāṅlāy biplabbād*, p. 116; Mukherjee, *Two Indian Revolutionaries*, pp. 181–82.

59. Guha, *Bāṅlāy biplabbād*, pp. 93, 116; Purani, *Sri Aurobindo*, p. 77.

60. Sedition Committee, *Report*, pp. 119–25; Home Department, 1917, Nos. 299–301, Chakravarty statement, paras. 27–49.

61. Sedition Committee, *Report*, pp. 121–22.

62. Home Department, 1917, Nos. 299–301, Chakravarty statement, para. 38.

63. Sedition Committee, *Report*, pp. 122–25; Mukherjee, *Two Indian Revolutionaries*, pp. 205–12.

64. Home Department, 1917, Nos. 299–301, Chakravarty statement, paras. 1, 50.

65. Roy, *Memoirs*, pp. 3–220; Overstreet and Windmiller, *Communism*, pp. 19–26; interview with Carleton Beals, Killingworth, Connecticut, June 1965.

66. M. N. Roy, *La India, su pasado, su presente y su porvenir* (Mexico, 1918); M. N. Roy, *La voz de la India* (Mexico, n.d. [1917?]); the second of these works includes the title essay and "Carta Abierta a su Excelencia Woodrow Wilson . . ." and "¿Por qué los soldados indios luchan por Inglaterra?"

67. Roy, *Memoirs,* pp. 59, 82, 164–65, 213–19.

68. Roy, *Memoirs,* p. 6.

69. Interview with Carleton Beals, 1965; Home Department, 1917, Nos. 299–301, Chakravarty statement, para. 11; Overstreet and Windmiller, *Communism,* p. 22; Roy, *Memoirs,* pp. 35–38.

70. Roy, *La voz,* pp. 9, 16.

71. Roy, *La voz,* p. 11.

72. Roy, *La voz,* p. 55.

73. Roy, *La voz,* pp. 56–57.

74. Roy, *La voz,* p. 67.

75. Halder, "Revolutionary Terrorism," p. 243; also see the recent account of D. M. Laushey, "The Bengal Terrorists and Their Conversion to Marxism: Aspects of Regional Nationalism in India, 1901–1942," (unpublished Ph.D. dissertation, University of Virginia, 1969).

76. Home Department, 1917, Nos. 299–301, Chakravarty statement, para. 37.

77. Sedition Committee, *Report,* pp. 126–27, 131–35; Mukherjee, *Two Indian Revolutionaries,* pp. 100–26.

78. Rabindranath Tagore, *Rabindra racanābalī* [Collected works of Rabindra] (Calcutta, 1961), XII; hereafter referred to as Tagore, *RR.*

79. Tagore, *RR,* XII, 976–78, 994.

80. Tagore, *RR,* XII, 999.

81. Tagore, *RR,* XII, 979, 981, 984, 1004.

82. Tagore, *RR,* XII, 978 ff.

83. See chapters 6, 8, 9, and 10.

84. See Bhupendranath Basu, "Why India is Heart and Soul with Great Britain," (London, 1914).

85. I. H. Qureshi, *The Struggle for Pakistan* (Karachi, 1965), pp. 16 ff.; Mohammad Noman, *Muslim India* (Allahabad, 1942), pp. 117 ff.; S. M. Ikram, *Modern Muslim India and the Birth of Pakistan* (rev. ed.,) (Lahore, 1965), pp. 108 ff.

86. B. R. Nanda, *The Nehrus, Motilal and Jawaharlal* (New York, 1963), p. 146; C. H. Philips, H. L. Singh, B. N. Pandey, eds., *The Evolution of India and Pakistan 1858 to 1947* (London, 1962), pp. 171–73; Stanley A. Wolpert, *Tilak and Gokhale: Revolution and Reform in the Making of Modern India* (Los Angeles, 1962), pp. 281–83.

87. J. H. Broomfield, "The Forgotten Majority: The Bengal Muslims and September 1918," *Soundings in Modern South Asian History* (London, 1968), ed. D. A. Low, pp. 204–207.

88. For details about Huq, see *Times of India, Indian Yearbook and Who's Who 1947* (Bombay, 1947), p. 1109; Broomfield, "Forgotten Majority," pp. 202–205; Khondakār Abdul Khālek, *Ek śatabdī* [One century] (Dacca, 1962); B. D. Hābībullāh, *Sere Bāṅglā* [Tiger of Bengal] (Dacca, 1962); Sir Robert Reid, *Years of Change in Bengal and Assam* (London, 1966), pp. 120–22; Ram Gopal, *Indian Muslims, A Political History (1858–1947)* (Calcutta, 1959), pp. 167, 174, 246–78; A. K. Fazlul Huq, *Bengal Today* (Calcutta, 1944); H. N. and N. N. Mitra, eds., *Indian Annual Register* (Calcutta, 1919–1947).

89. H. F. Owen, "Towards Nation-Wide Agitation and Organisation: The Home Rule Leagues, 1915–18," *Soundings*, ed. Low, p. 167 ff.; Surendranath Banerjea, *A Nation in Making* (reprint, Calcutta, 1963), pp. 221–22.

90. Gokhale letter enclosed with Morley letter to Minto, October 14, 1909, Morley Papers, V, quoted in M. N. Das, *India under Morley and Minto* (London, 1964), p. 103.

CHAPTER SIX. THE GANDHIAN AGE

AND THE RISE OF CHITTARANJAN DAS

1. Gopal Krishna, "The Development of the Indian National Congress as a Mass Organization, 1918–1923," *The Journal of Asian Studies*, Vol. XXV, No. 3 (May 1966), pp. 413–30.

2. For the usual treatment in which we see Gandhi and the masses, or Gandhi and India, see B. R. Nanda, *Mahatma Gandhi* (London, 1958), p. 213; on the dominance of Gandhi in the period up to World War II, see P. D. Kaushik, *The Congress Ideology and Programme 1920–47* (New Delhi, 1964); on Gandhi's loss of power in his last years, see N. K. Bose, *Studies in Gandhism* (3d ed., Calcutta, 1962), pp. 276–302.

3. Edward Thompson and G. T. Garratt, *Rise and Fulfilment of British Rule in India* (reprint, Allahabad, 1958), pp. 539–40; also see Edward Hallett Carr, *The Bolshevik Revolution 1917–1923* (Baltimore, 1966), III, 233, and Edwin Montagu, *An Indian Diary* (London, 1930).

4. A. J. P. Taylor, *English History 1914–1945* (Oxford, 1965), pp. 153–61; Subhas Chandra Bose, *The Indian Struggle 1920–1934* (Calcutta, 1948), 99; the Indian nationalist paper *Forward* had a regular column on Irish developments during the 1920s; Hans Kohn, "The Russian Revolution and the Orient," *A History of Nationalism in the East* (London, 1929); Carr, *Bolshevik Revolution*, III, 232–71.

5. Vera Anstey, *The Economic Development of India* (3d ed., New York, 1936), pp. 150, 215, 243, 280; Daniel Houston Buchannan, *The Development of Capitalistic Enterprise in India* (reprint, London, 1966), p. 295; Thompson and Garratt, *Rise and Fulfilment*, pp. 552–54; K. B. Saha, "Middle Class Unemployment in Bengal," *Calcutta Review*, Vol. XIII, 3d series (December 1924), pp. 350–72.

6. J. H. Broomfield, "The Forgotten Majority: The Bengal Muslims and September 1918," *Soundings in Modern South Asian History*, ed. D. A. Low, (London, 1968), pp. 196–220.

7. Harry Abram Millman, "The Marwari: A Study of a Group of Trading Castes of India," (unpublished master's thesis, University of California, 1954), *passim;* Government of Bengal, *Proceedings* of the Bengal Legislative Council, 1923, Vol. XI, No. 2, pp. 322–23 and 1922, Vol. X, pp. 103–105; hereafter the council proceedings are cited as *PBLC*. For an example of extreme hostility, see the letter of M. N. Das to *Forward,* September 12, 1924, in which this member of the Bengal Legislative Council charged that the Marwaris "are the local agents of the foreign exploiters."

8. M. R. Jayakar, *The Story of My Life* (Bombay, 1958), I, 219 ff., 306–12.

9. Mahatma Gandhi, *Collected Works* (Delhi, 1957–1964), XV, 516; D. G. Tendulkar, *Mahatma* (New Delhi, n.d.), I, 234 ff.; R. Kumar, ed., *Essays on Gandhian Politics: The Rowlatt Satyagraha of 1919* (Oxford, 1971), especially J. H. Kerr's report, pp. 325–43.

10. B. D. Shukla, *A History of the Indian Liberal Party* (Allahabad, 1960), pp. 198–206; Jayakar, *Life,* I, 209–10, 251 ff.; Surendranath Banerjea, *A Nation in Making* (reprint, Calcutta, 1963), pp. 281 ff.

11. The entire report is reprinted in Gandhi, *Collected Works*, XVII, 114–291; Jayakar, *Life,* I, 504 ff., describes the process of collecting the materials for it.

12. Jayakar, *Life,* I, 322.

13. See Jawaharlal Nehru's testimony on this point in *Toward Freedom* (Boston, 1968), p. 109.

14. Mahatma Gandhi, *Young India 1919–1922* (New York, 1923), pp. 134 ff.

15. For biographical details on Das, see Prithwas Chandra Ray, *The Life and Times of C. R. Das* (Calcutta, 1927); Hemendranath Das Gupta, *Deshbandu Chittaranjan* Das (Delhi, 1960); Dilip Kumar Chatterjee, *C. R. Das and Indian National Movement* (Calcutta, 1965); there are also interesting details in B. R. Nanda, *The Nehrus, Motilal and Jawaharlal* (New York, 1963) and Jayakar, *Life.*

16. Das Gupta, *Das*, pp. 4–7.

17. Das Gupta, *Das*, pp. 6–8.

18. Das's Bengali works include *Malañchā, Mālā, Sāgar saṅgīt, Antaryāmi,* and *Kishore Kishori;* the most popular of these was *Sāgar saṅgīt,* translated by Aurobindo Ghose as *Songs of the Sea;* it is reprinted in Sri Aurobindo, *Collected Poems and Plays* (Pondicherry, 1942), II, 249–73. The poems are typical of Bengali lyric verse and reflect the changing moods of sea and self. The sea is taken as an image of the cosmos and a metaphor for God. There are recurring descriptions of the one, the individual, and the merging of all. In devotional passages, Das recounts the secret trysts of lover and beloved, of friend and friend, of the king of mysteries and the seeker for fulfillment. See Das Gupta, *Das*, pp. 23–24 on other aspects of his literary career.

19. Das Gupta, *Das*, pp. 23–24.

20. Das Gupta, *Das*, pp. 13–16.

21. Das Gupta, *Das*, pp. 16–18; Nanda, *The Nehrus*, pp. 176–81. Nanda describes Das and Motilal Nehru, counsels for opposing sides in the case, spending their evenings together talking and drinking; their association later turned into a close political tie.

22. Das Gupta, *Das*, p. 30.

23. Under the first title it is reprinted in Rajen and B. K. Sen, eds., *Deshabandhu Chitta Ranjan* (Calcutta, 1926), pp. 1–83; under the second title, extracts are given in Das Gupta, *Das*, pp. 141–47. In neither case is the original Bengali title given.

24. Sen and Sen, *Das*, p. 16.

25. Sen and Sen, *Das*, pp. 16–17.

26. Sen and Sen, *Das*, pp. 46–48, 52–56, 60; the concern for regional culture can be found in Bankim Chandra Chatterjee, "A Popular Literature for Bengal," *Essays and Letters* (Calcutta, 1940), ed. Brajendra Nath Banerji and Sajani Kanta Das, pp. 13–18. See also the account of the Swadeshi movement in chapter 3 above and Aurobindo Ghose's concern for Bengal described in chapter 4.

27. Sen and Sen, *Das*, pp. 12–16, 56–62; Cf. Mahatma Gandhi's *Hind Swaraj* in *Collected Works*, X, 6–68 (first written November 1909).

28. Sen and Sen, *Das*, pp. 62–63.

29. Sen and Sen, *Das*, pp. 91–98; Chitta Ranjan Das, *India for Indians* (Madras, 1921, 3d ed.), pp. 1–15, 16–34.

30. Das, *India for Indians*, pp. 61–62.

31. Das, *India for Indians*, p. 32.

32. Sen and Sen, *Das*, pp. 97–98.

33. H. F. Owen, "Towards Nationwide Agitation and Organisation: The Home Rule Leagues, 1915–18," *Soundings*, ed. Low, pp. 172, 177–78.

34. J. H. Broomfield, *Elite Conflict in a Plural Society: Twentieth Century Bengal* (Berkeley, 1968), pp. 135–40.

35. Broomfield, *Elite Conflict*, p. 136.

36. Sen and Sen, *Das*, p. 1.

37. Broomfield, *Elite Conflict*, pp. 137–38.

38. Broomfield, *Elite Conflict*, p. 141.

39. Das Gupta, *Das*, pp. 42–45; Jayakar, *Life*, I, 374 ff.

40. Thompson and Garratt, *Rise and Fulfilment*, p. 545.

41. Nehru, *Toward Freedom*, p. 65.

42. Jayakar, *Life*, I, 374–75.

43. For the exact wording, see Rajendra Prasad, *Autobiography* (New Delhi, 1957), p. 125.

44. Jayakar, *Life*, I, 391–96.

45. Jayakar, *Life*, I, 407.

46. J. H. Broomfield, "The Non-cooperation Decision of 1920: A Crisis in Bengal Politics," in *Soundings*, ed. Low, pp. 247 ff.; because of his antipathy to the Bengali bhadralok politicians, Broomfield tries to demonstrate that Das is a mere opportunist; but the same charge could be made against Gandhi for his shift from cooperation to Noncooperation. Das was a pragmatist and a skillful politician and should not be condemned out of hand for this.

47. Mitra, *IAR*, 1921, I, 141.

48. Nehru, *Toward Freedom*, pp. 110–11.

49. Nanda, *Nehrus*, pp. 181 ff.; Das Gupta, *Das*, pp. 50 ff. The transformation in the life-styles of these two men was a topic brought up in several conversations with Indians who lived through this period. Perhaps there is a model for this kind of shift in the four stages of life in Indian traditions, particularly from *gṛhastha* or householder to *vānaprastha* or forest-dwelling ascetic, and also in the descriptions of the lives of religious men like the Buddha.

50. Bose, *Indian Struggle*, pp. 68–69; Prasad, *Autobiography*, p. 130.

51. Krishna, "Congress," pp. 413 ff.; Gandhi, *Swaraj in One Year*, p. 114.

52. Krishna, "Congress," p. 423.

53. Nripendra Chandra Banerji, *At the Crossroads (1885–1946)* (Calcutta, 1950), pp. 161–62.

54. *Young India*, June 29, 1921, quoted in Krishna, "Congress," p. 415.

55. Krishna, "Congress," pp. 425, 428.

56. Krishna, "Congress," p. 426.

57. G. D. Birla, *In the Shadow of the Mahatma, A Personal Memoir* (Calcutta, 1953), *passim*.

58. Birla, *Shadow*, p. 38.

59. Birla, *Shadow*, p. 38.

60. Bose, *Indian Struggle*, pp. 74–75.

61. For details about the Gandhians, see Banerji, *Crossroads*, pp. 141 ff.

62. Banerji, *Crossroads*, p. 254.

63. Banerji, *Crossroads*, pp. 150–52.

64. Banerji, *Crossroads*, pp. 163–66.

65. Banerji, *Crossroads*, pp. 3, 212, 224–25, 250; see also Banerji's political writings, *The Ideal of Swaraj* (Madras, 1921) and *Gandhism in Theory and Practice* (Madras, 1923).

66. Banerji, *Crossroads*, pp. 216, 300–301.

67. Banerji, *Ideal of Swaraj*, p. xiii.

68. Banerji, *Ideal of Swaraj*, pp. 4 ff.; Banerji, *Crossroads*, pp. 205–206.

69. For an account of this process, see Suprakāś Rāy, *Bhārater baiplabik saṅgrāmer itihās* [*History of the revolutionary struggle in India*] (Calcutta, 1955, pp. 391–94; Gopal Halder, "Revolutionary Terrorism," *Studies in the Bengal Renaissance* ed. Atulchandra Gupta (Jadavpur, Calcutta, 1958), pp. 249–50; Government of India, Home Department, Political File No. 61, 1924, "Note of the Connection between Revolutionaries and the Swarajya Party in Bengal."

70. Home Department, File 61 of 1924, section 1.

71. Interview with Surendra Mohan Ghose in New Delhi, September 27, 1964; Halder, "Revolutionary Terrorism," p. 249.

72. Narendra Nath Das, *History of Midnapur* (Calcutta, 1962), pp. 55–56, 64, 85, 98.

73. Das, *Midnapur*, pp. 86, 109, 115–17, 129, 170–71, 187, 203; Rāy, *Itihās*, pp. 392–94.

74. Gandhi acted several times to smooth out disputes between the Das group and the Gandhians in Bengal and Das acted to settle district Congress disputes in Bengal. Das, *Midnapur*, pp. 100–101; Banerji, *Crossroads*, p. 146.

75. Nehru, *Toward Freedom*, pp. 69–70 gives a vivid account.

76. Jayakar, *Life*, I, 422.

77. Nehru, *Toward Freedom*, pp. 65 ff.; Bose, *Indian Struggle*, pp. 74 ff.; Prasad, *Autobiography*, pp. 131 ff.; Mitra, *IAR*, 1922, I, 135–353.

78. Gandhi, *Swaraj in One Year*, pp. 43–96.

79. Gandhi, *Swaraj in One Year*, p. 43.

80. Das, *India for Indians*, pp. 164–66.

81. Bose, *Indian Struggle*, p. 78.

82. Probodh Chandra Sinha, *Sir Asutosh Mookherjee* (Calcutta, 1928), pp. 263 ff.; R. K. Prabhu and Ravindra Kelekar, eds., *Truth Called Them Differently* (*Tagore-Gandhi Controversy*) (Ahmadabad, 1961), pp. 18–23.

83. Banerji, *Crossroads*, pp. 148–49, 163–64.

84. L. S. S. O'Malley *History of Bengal, Bihar and Orissa under British Rule* (Calcutta, 1925), p. 585.

85. Anstey, *Economic Development*, p. 317. Unfortunately space does not permit an analysis of the Chandpur Affair of 1921; this was a complicated series of events in eastern Bengal involving tea coolies and strikes by transportation unions in Chittagong; there is an account in Broomfield, *Elite Conflict*, pp. 184–85, 214–19, but he has used mostly government of Bengal sources and presented the affair from the government point of view. To give a fairer analysis one has to go back to the different kinds of records of the period and compare all the available versions of the affair; Broomfield seems to have distorted the views of C. F. Andrews, *The Indian Problem* (2d ed., Madras, 1923), pp. 79 ff., who was involved; see also *PBLC*, 1921, III, 383–427, 452–85.

86. Broomfield, *Elite Conflict*, pp. 219 ff.; many Bengalis today recall the story of Mrs. Das's arrest and how it aided the movement.

87. Gandhi, *Collected Works*, XXII, 38; Mitra, *IAR*, 1922, II, 242–47.

88. Broomfield, *Elite Conflict*, pp. 233–35.

89. Broomfield, *Elite Conflict*, p. 219.

90. Jayakar, *Life*, I, 508–14; Mitra, *IAR*, 1921, II, 260 ff.; Prasad, *Autobiography*, pp. 155–57; Bose, *Indian Struggle*, pp. 99–101; Maulana Abul Kalam Azad, *India Wins Freedom* (Calcutta, 1960), pp. 17–19; Broomfield, *Elite Conflict*, pp. 229–30.

91. Quoted in Jayakar, *Life*, I, 509.

92. On the Bombay violence, see Jayakar, *Life*, I, 467–71.

93. Gandhi, *Young India 1919–1922*, pp. 993 ff.

94. Bose, *Indian Struggle*, p. 108; Nehru, *Toward Freedom*, p. 79.

95. Jayakar, *Life* I, 555–58; Gandhi, *Young India 1919–1922*, pp. 993 ff.; Prasad, *Autobiography*, p. 166.

96. Prasad, *Autobiography*, pp. 163–65.

97. For analysis of the government of India's strategy during this period, see D. A. Low, "The Government of India and the First Non-Cooperation Movement," *Journal of Asian Studies*, Vol. XXV, No. 2 (February 1966), pp. 241–59.

98. Banerjea, *Nation*, pp. 226–354, contains Banerjea's account of Non-cooperation and the Swaraj Party.

99. Bipinchandra Pal, *Non-Co-operation* (Calcutta, 1920).

100. Pal, *Non-Co-operation*, pp. 8, 20, 68–72.

101. Pal, *Non-Co-operation*, pp. 13 ff., 107–108, 145–54.

102. Pal, *Non-Co-operation*, p. 64.

103. Pal, *Non-Co-operation*, pp. 78, 85.

104. See Prabhu and Kelekar, *Truth Called*, pp. 13–14, 21, 47, 59, 69, 75–78; Homer A. Jack, ed., *The Gandhi Reader: 1* (New York, 1961), pp. 105–109; Bose, *Selections from Gandhi*, pp. 19–20, 124; Rabindranath Tagore, *Towards Universal Man* (Calcutta, 1961), pp. 49, 268, 281–83, 303, 311, 317.

105. Prabhu and Kelekar, *Truth Called*, pp. 126–28, 134.

106. Prabhu and Kelekar, *Truth Called*, p. 88.

107. Prabhu and Kelekar, *Truth Called*, p. 59.

108. Jayakar, *Life*, I, 373.

109. Prabhu and Kelekar, *Truth Called*, pp. 64–65.

110. Prabhu and Kelekar, *Truth Called*, p. 39.

111. Prabhu and Kelekar, *Truth Called*, pp. 76–77.

112. Bose, *Indian Struggle*, p. 103.

113. O'Malley, *History of Bengal*, pp. 585, 606–607.

114. Gandhi, *Collected Works*, XXII, 112.

115. Gandhi, *Collected Works*, XXII, 118.

116. Gandhi, *Young India 1919–1922*, p. 982.

117. Jayakar, *Life*, I, 604–13.

118. Jayakar, *Life*, I, 607, 612–13.

CHAPTER SEVEN. THE SWARAJ PARTY

1. Mitra, *IAR*, 1923, I, 872*n*.

2. Subhas Bose, *The Indian Struggle 1920–1934* (Calcutta, 1948), pp. 116–17.

3. "C. R. Das on Civil Disobedience Enquiry Committee," in H. N. Mitra, ed., *Indian Annual Register* (Calcutta, 1925–1947; hereafter cited as *IAR*), 1923, I, 180–81.

4. Bose, *Indian Struggle*, pp. 119–20.

5. Dilip Kumar Chatterjee, *C. R. Das and Indian National Movement* (Calcutta, 1965), pp. 225–27; *Forward*, August 20, 1924, article on the Tata Conciliation Committee; *Forward*, September 30, 1924, article on the South Calcutta Congress organizing a workers' association.

6. Mitra, *IAR*, 1923, I, 862.

7. M. R. Jayakar, *The Story of My Life* (Bombay, 1958), II, *passim*.

8. Jayakar, *Life*, II, 110, 128, 239.

9. The Madras speeches are collected in Deshabandhu Das, *The Way to Swaraj* (Madras, 1923).

10. These details are collected from a number of sources including *Times of India, Who's Who in India* (Bombay, 1925–1947); this is an annual publication which has continued after independence. Thos. Peter, ed., *Who's Who in India* (Poona, 1936); Tushar Kanti Ghosh, ed., *Deshapriya Jatindra Mohan* (Calcutta, 1933); K. P. Thomas, *Dr. B. C. Roy* (Calcutta, 1955); Subhas Chandra Bose, *An Indian Pilgrim, An Unfinished Autobiography and Collected Letters 1897–1921* (Calcutta, 1965); Hemendranath Das Gupta, *Deshbandu Chittaranjan Das* (Delhi, 1960), *passim*.

11. Jayakar, *Life*, I, 345–46.

12. See *Bamśa paricay* [Introduction to Families] (Calcutta, 1921), V, 30–33.

13. Many of these details have come from a reading of *Forward* in the years 1923–1924 and talks with Satya Ranjan Bakshi in Calcutta, 1964.

14. Home Department, File No. 61, 1924, section 5.

15. Home Department, File No. 61, 1924; interviews with Surendra Mohan Ghose, former Jugantar leader, New Delhi, September 20, 1964, and with

Kiron Das, ex-revolutionary and political worker, Calcutta, May 3, 1964; also from talks with Satya Ranjan Bakshi in Calcutta, 1964; all the interviewees claimed that Bose knew what was going on but was not directly involved in revolutionary work.

16. Earl of Lytton, *Pundits and Elephants* (London, 1942), pp. 63–66; on numerous occasions during 1924 and 1925, the Swarajists in the Bengal Legislative Council raised questions about the Swarajists who were imprisoned without specific charges for an indefinite term; on one occasion, an official said that the Government of Bengal was satisfied that there was a good case against Subhas Bose, *PBLC*, 1925, Vol. XVII, No. 1, p. 22.

17. Jayakar, *Life*, II, 131, 156–57, 160, 174–77.

18. Maulana Abul Kalam Azad, *India Wins Freedom* (Calcutta, 1960), pp. 20–21.

19. Azad, *India Wins Freedom*, p. 21; Jayakar, *Life*, I, 346.

20. The names of the members of the BPCC have been collected from *Forward*, September–October, 1924.

21. Azad, *India Wins Freedom*, pp. 20–21; Chaudhri Muhammad Ali, *The Emergence of Pakistan* (New York, 1967), p. 21; speech of Moulana Mohammad Akram Khan presiding over Bengal Provincial Conference, Serajgunge, June 1, 1924, summarized in Mitra, *IAR*, 1924, I, 665–68.

22. On the resignation of the Gandhians, see *Forward*, articles of July 23, 1924 and August 1, 1924; Chatterjee, *Das*, p. 204; Narendra Nath Das, *History of Midnapur* (Calcutta, 1962), p. 98.

23. Mitra, *IAR*, 1924, I, p. 665.

24. Government of India, *Census of India 1921* (Calcutta, 1923), V, Part II, 165–69; 2,710,206 out of 47,654,183 in Bengal and Sikkim. I have been assisted in my analysis of the BPCC by Professors Ralph W. Nicholas, Ronald B. Inden, and Moni Nag, but I alone am responsible for the results.

25. The list of names for these calculations comes from Amvika Charan Mazumdar, *Indian National Evolution* (Madras, 1915), Appendix B, pp. lxi–lxiii.

26. See *Forward*, September 7, 17, and 20, 1924.

27. J. H. Broomfield, *Elite Conflict in a Plural Society: Twentieth Century Bengal* (Berkeley, 1968), pp. 260–61; Das Gupta, *Das*, pp. 105–106; and numerous articles in *Forward* during 1924, for example, on July 11, 1924.

28. Jayakar, *Life*, II, 87, 106; I, 361.

29. Azad, *India Wins Freedom*, pp. 10–11.

30. For example, see *Forward,* August 5, 15, 1924, and September 7, 1924.

31. Rajen and B. K. Sen, eds., *Deshabandhu Chitta Ranjan* (Calcutta, 1926), pp. 264–68.

32. Mitra, *IAR,* 1924, I, 665–72.

33. Mitra, *IAR,* 1924, I, 671.

34. Quoted in Mitra, *IAR,* 1924, I, 604(a).

35. Quoted in Mitra, *IAR,* 1924, I, 608.

36. Mitra, *IAR,* 1924, I, 608–608(a).

37. It is quoted in Mitra, *IAR,* 1924, I, 606(a).

38. Mitra, *IAR,* 1924, I, 621.

39. For Paranjpye's speech, see Mitra, *IAR,* 1924, I, 608(b), 621; also see Jayakar, *Life,* I, 373, 377–78, on the resistance in Maharashtra to Gandhi, particularly among followers of Tilak, and on Maharashtra's relative loss of power from earlier days.

40. Mitra, *IAR,* 1924, I, 625.

41. Quoted in Mitra, *IAR,* 1924, I, 625.

42. Quoted in Mitra, *IAR,* 1924, I, 629.

43. Gandhi was subjected to some criticism from his own supporters for not pressing hard enough against the challenging Swarajists; see *Forward* article of September 14, 1924, and Jayakar, *Life,* II, 501–508.

44. William Roy Smith, *Nationalism and Reform in India* (New Haven, 1938), pp. 98–104.

45. Their figures are given in Government of Bengal, *Report on the Working of the Reformed Constitution in Bengal, 1921–27* (Calcutta, 1929), pp. 130–31; this report was also issued as Indian Statutory Commission, *Memorandum submitted by the Government of Bengal to the Indian Statutory Commission* (London, 1930), Vol. VIII; this report is hereafter referred to as Government of Bengal, *Report on 1921–27.*

46. Government of Bengal, *Report on 1921–27,* pp. 136–38; Smith, *Nationalism and Reform,* p. 107.

47. Government of Bengal, *Report on 1921–27,* p. 170; for a fuller account, see Broomfield, *Elite Conflict,* pp. 169 ff.

48. Smith, *Nationalism and Reform,* pp. 118–19.

49. *PBLC,* 1921, III, 383–427, 452–85; 1921, V, 98–108; 1922, VII, 321–22.

50. *PBLC,* 1921, V, 11–12.

51. For the debate and vote, see *PBLC*, 1922, VII, 544–88.

52. Ajoy C. Dutt, *Bengal Council and Its Work (1921–23)* (Calcutta, n.d. [1924?]), p. 86.

53. *PBLC*, 1921, V, 446–48, 532–33.

54. Dutt, *Bengal Council,* pp. 87–88; *PBLC*, 1921, V, 409–95, 513–42; Banerjea saw that the Muslims, the officials, nonofficial Europeans, and some nominated members were too strong a coalition to go against.

55. *PBLC*, 1923, Vol. XI, No. 2, p. 289.

56. *PBLC*, 1921, Vol. I, No. 5, p. 223.

57. *PBLC*, 1921, Vol. I, No. 5, p. 239.

58. *PBLC*, 1921, Vol. IV, pp. 313–43, 369–412, 448–76.

59. *PBLC*, 1923, Vol. XI, p. 14.

60. *PBLC*, 1922, XI, 249; 1923, Vol. XI, No. 3, pp. 9–10, 23, 109–10; Lord Ronaldshay said in early 1923 in the council that he could not accept the Meston Award and was pressing the government of India to give Bengal additional financial relief.

61. Lytton, *Pundits,* p. 40.

62. Lytton, *Pundits,* p. 40.

63. Lytton, *Pundits,* p. 34.

64. Government of Bengal, *Report on 1921–27,* p. 143.

65. Broomfield, *Elite Conflict,* pp. 240–42; Lytton, *Pundits,* p. 41, claimed that "completely unscrupulous" methods were used to defeat Banerjea, but Broomfield's account shows that Dr. Roy and the Swarajists were much better organized and more thorough in the campaign than were Banerjea's followers.

66. Government of Bengal, *Report on 1921–27,* p. 155.

67. Government of Bengal, *Report on 1921–27,* pp. 155–56.

68. Lytton, *Pundits,* p. 42.

69. Lytton, *Pundits,* p. 44.

70. Lytton, *Pundits,* p. 45.

71. Lytton, *Pundits,* pp. 45–46.

72. Lytton, *Pundits,* p. 48.

73. Government of Bengal, *Report on 1921–27,* reports that there were 21 Muslim Swarajists in the council, but the voting patterns do not seem to bear this out.

74. *PBLC*, 1924, Vol. XIV, No. 4, 55–108.

75. *PBLC*, 1924, Vol. XIV, No. 4, 106–108.

76. *Forward*, August 29, 1924.

77. See Gandhi's defense of the Swarajists for this action, *Collected Works*, XXIV, 479–80.

78. *PBLC*, 1922, VII, 215–16, 321–22; 1921, V, 98–99.

79. *PBLC*, 1923, XI, 582.

80. Mitter said of the Bengal Criminal Amendment Bill of 1925 that "the Bill proposes not a physician's treatment of the malady but a quack's remedy." *PBLC*, 1925, Vol. XVII, No. 1, p. 24.

81. Government of Bengal, *Report on 1921–27*, p. 171.

82. *Times of India, Indian Yearbook and Who's Who* (Bombay, 1947); *Forward*, September 25, 1924.

83. *Forward*, September 11, 25, 1924, reports on the formation of the Dacca District Anjuman.

84. *PBLC*, 1924, Vol. XIV, No. 5, pp. 164–84; Government of Bengal, *Report on 1921–27*, pp. 170–71.

85. *Forward*, August 26, 1924.

86. *PBLC*, 1924, 16th session, pp. 66–67.

87. *PBLC*, 1924, 16th session, p. 64.

88. Lytton, *Pundits*, p. 52.

89. *PBLC*, 1924, 16th session, p. 67.

90. Lytton, *Pundits*, pp. 54–56.

91. *PBLC*, 1925, Vol. XVII, No. 4, pp. 205–206.

92. *PBLC*, 1925, Vol. XVII, No. 4, p. 223.

93. *PBLC*, 1925, Vol. XVII, No. 4, p. 225.

94. *PBLC*, 1925, Vol. XVII, No. 4, pp. 234–37.

95. *PBLC*, 1925, Vol. XVII, No. 1, p. 17; see pp. 3–25 for the full speech.

96. *PBLC*, 1925, Vol. XVII, No. 2, p. 1.

97. *PBLC*, 1925, 19th session, pp. 422–35.

98. *PBLC*, 1924, Vol. XIV, No. 5, p. 224.

99. *PBLC*, 1924, Vol. XIV, No. 5, p. 238.

100. Government of Bengal, *Report on 1921–27*, p. 67.

101. Surendranath Banerjea, *A Nation in the Making* (reprint, Calcutta, 1963), p. 358; Government of Bengal, *Report on 1921–27*, p. 68.

102. Government of Bengal, *Report on 1921–27*, p. 69.

103. Government of Bengal, *Report on 1921–27*, pp. 69–70.

104. For example, Subhas Bose maintained an interest in the corporation even while imprisoned; see his *Correspondence 1924–1932* (Calcutta, 1967), pp. 41, 174–78, 281–83.

105. Das Gupta, *Das*, p. 118.

106. "Mr. C. R. Das's Manifesto," quoted in Mitra, *IAR*, 1925, I, 87.

107. Broomfield, *Elite Conflict*, p. 264; "The European View," quoted in Mitra, *IAR*, 1925, I, 88–89.

108. Quoted in Mitra, *IAR*, 1925, I, 88(b); Das Gupta, *Das*, pp. 119–20.

109. Mitra, *IAR*, 1925, I, 393.

110. Mitra, *IAR*, 1925, I, 394.

111. Mitra, *IAR*, 1925, I, 394–95.

112. Das Gupta, *Das*, pp. 125–37.

113. Das Gupta, *Das*, p. 138.

114. *PBLC*, 1925, 18th session, p. 2.

115. Ali, *Emergence of Pakistan*, p. 21.

116. Lytton, *Pundits*, pp. 40–56, 92–93; Broomfield, *Elite Conflict*, pp. 204 ff.

117. Jayakar, *Life*, I, 345–47.

118. Broomfield, *Elite Conflict*, p. 274.

119. Statement reproduced in *Forward*, September 9, 1924.

120. Jayakar, *Life*, I, 373.

CHAPTER EIGHT. SUBHAS BOSE
AND NATIONALIST POLITICS, 1925–1938

1. Gene D. Overstreet and Marshall Windmiller, *Communism in India* (Berkeley, 1959), pp. 101 ff.; David N. Druhe, *Soviet Russia and Indian Communism* (New York, 1959), pp. 97 ff.; P. D. Kaushik, *The Congress Ideology and Program 1920–47* (New Delhi, 1964), pp. 133 ff.; Thomas A. Rusch, "Role of the Congress Socialist Party in the Indian National Congress" (unpublished Ph.D. dissertation, University of Chicago, 1955), pp. 111 ff.; V. B. Karnik, *Indian Trade Unions* (rev. ed., Bombay, 1966), pp. 48 ff.; N. C. Ranga, *History of Kisan Movement* (Madras, 1939), *passim*.

2. Suprakāś Rāy, *Bhārater baiplabik saṅgrāmer itihās* [History of the revolutionary struggle in India] (Calcutta, 1955), pp. 448–49; also two recent studies, David Mason Laushey, "The Bengal Terrorists and Their Conversion to Marxism: Aspects of Regional Nationalism in India, 1905–1942" (unpublished Ph.D. dissertation, University of Virginia, 1969), and Marcus Franda's *Radical Politics in West Bengal* (Cambridge, 1971).

3. For a different but related view, see a recent account written independently of the present one, Bhola Chatterji, *Aspects of Bengal Politics in the Early Nineteen-Thirties* (Calcutta, 1969); an earlier version of the present study is Leonard A. Gordon, "Bengal's Gandhi: A Study in Modern Indian Regionalism, Politics and Thought," in *Bengal Regional Identity*, David Kopf, ed. (East Lansing, Michigan, 1969), pp. 87–130.

4. For example, Government of India, Home Department, Political File No. 61 of 1924, "Note of the Connection between the Revolutionaries and the Swarajya Party in Bengal"; also Political File No. 104 and K. W., 1927, letter of the Home Member, dated March 31, 1927.

5. For studies of rebellion against and acceptance of authority, see Theodore Adorno, ed., *The Authoritarian Personality* (New York, 1950), pp. 52–53 and *passim;* Phyllis Greenacre, *The Quest for the Father* (New York, 1963), pp. 13–15, 90 ff.; Robert D. Hess, "The Socialization of Attitudes toward Political Authority: Some Cross-National Comparisons," *International Social Science Journal*, Vol. XV, No. 4 (1963), pp. 542–59; the images are mentioned in Subhas Chandra Bose, *An Indian Pilgrim, An Unfinished Autobiography and Collected Letters 1897–1921* (Calcutta, 1965), p. 155.

6. Girija Mookerjee, *This Europe* (Calcutta, 1950), p. 156.

7. Bose, *Indian Pilgrim*, pp. 1–8.

8. Subhas Chandra Bose, *Crossroads, 1938–40* (Bombay, 1962), p. 149.

9. Subhas Chandra Bose, *Correspondence, 1924–1932* (Calcutta, 1967), p. 329.

10. Bose, *Correspondence, 1924–32*, pp. 81, 91–95, 139, 148.

11. Bose, *Correspondence, 1924–32*, p. 158.

12. Bose, *Indian Pilgrim*, pp. 8–10, 19–44.

13. Bose, *Indian Pilgrim*, pp. 113–31, includes letters to his mother, mainly on religious questions, written at the age of 15–16. On the influence of Beni Madhab Das, *Indian Pilgrim*, pp. 28–31, and interview with Subhas Bose's brother Sailesh Bose in Bombay, December 30, 1964.

14. Interview with Sailesh Bose, December 30, 1964.

15. Bose, *Indian Pilgrim*, pp. 117–18, 129–30, 140–43; interview with Sailesh Bose, December 30, 1964; Dilip Kumar Roy, *The Subhash I Knew* (Bombay, 1946), pp. 177 ff.

16. Interview with Sailesh Bose, December 30, 1964; Bose, *Indian Pilgrim*, pp. 39, 58–59, 143, 149, 157–58; Hemendranath Das Gupta, *Subhas Chandra* (Calcutta, 1946), p. 55; Dilip Roy, *Subhash*, refers to the "element of motherliness in him" (p. 34).

17. Roy, *Subhash*, p. 21; I am not sure of the exact year in which the Boses bought their house at 38/2 Elgin Road, Calcutta, but Subhas Bose is already writing letters from that address in 1914; see Bose, *Indian Pilgrim*, p. 142.

18. Bose, *Indian Pilgrim*, pp. 51–63.

19. Bose, *Indian Pilgrim*, pp. 59–63, 138–42.

20. Bose, *Indian Pilgrim*, p. 36.

21. Roy, *Subhash*, pp. 56–57, 61, 65, 67.

22. Bose, *Indian Pilgrim*, pp. 48–49.

23. Bose, *Correspondence, 1924–32*, pp. 137–41; here Subhas Bose identifies Basanti Devi, the widow of C. R. Das, with the nation, with Bengal, and with the Universal Mother.

24. Dilip Kumar Roy is the leader of this attempt; see Dilip Kumar Roy, *Netaji—The Man, Reminiscences* (Bombay, 1966), especially Appendix XI, "Netaji, The Mystic."

25. On the relationship of sexual restraint and power, see G. Morris Carstairs, *The Twice-Born* (Bloomington, Indiana, 1961), pp. 84–86, 167, 241.

26. Roy, *Subhash*, pp. 61, 65; about fifty unpublished letters of Subhas Bose to Mrs. Vetter were lent to me by the Netaji Research Bureau, 38/2 Elgin Road, Calcutta; they were written in the 1930s. Kitty Kurti, *Subhas Chandras Bose As I Knew Him* (Calcutta, 1966), also contains letters written by Bose in the 1930s.

27. Bose, *Indian Pilgrim*, pp. 67–71, 162–63; Suniti Kumar Chatterji, "Subhas Chandra Bose: Personal Reminiscences," *Netaji, His Life and Work*, ed. Shri Ram Sharma (Agra, 1948), pp. 125–27; Paramananda Dutt, *Memoirs of Motilal Ghose* (Calcutta, 1935), pp. 246–55; Roy, *Subhash*, pp. 46–47.

28. Roy, *Subhash*, pp. 46–67; the government of Bengal and Enquiry Committee versions are contained in Government of India, Judicial and Public Department, J. & P./1861/1916.

29. Bose, *Indian Pilgrim*, p. 69.

30. Bose, *Indian Pilgrim*, p. 163; Ashu Babu is Sir Asutosh Mookerjee.

31. Roy, *Subhash*, pp. 46–47; Rabindranath Tagore, stimulated by the evidence in the case, wrote an essay on the more general topic of "Indian Students and Western Teachers," *Modern Review* (Calcutta), April 1916.

Tagore described the usual insensitivity of Western professors to their Indian students, but maintained that there were and could be sensitive Western teachers as well and mentioned some at Santiniketan.

32. Bose, *Indian Pilgrim*, pp. 70–71.

33. Bose, *Indian Pilgrim*, pp. 78–79.

34. B. N. Chatterjee, "Netaji Subhas Chandra Bose, A Chronicle 1897 to 1945," *The Calcutta Municipal Gazette*, Vol. XLV, No. 8 (Calcutta, January 25, 1947), Subhas Bose Birthday Supplement, pp. 5–7.

35. Bose, *Indian Pilgrim*, pp. 78–82.

36. Bose, *Indian Pilgrim*, pp. 28, 78–82, 91.

37. Bose, *Indian Struggle*, pp. 428–34; Bose, *Crossroads*, pp. 58, 250–73, *passim*; Subhas C. Bose, *Through Congress Eyes* (Allahabad, n.d. [1938?]), pp. 19 ff.

38. Letter to Hemanta Sarkar, August 26, 1919 in Bose, *Indian Pilgrim*, p. 168.

39. Bose, *Indian Pilgrim*, pp. 84–103, 168–79; Roy, *Subhash*, pp. 48–53.

40. Bose, *Indian Pilgrim*, pp. 89–90.

41. Roy, *Subhash*, pp. 48–49.

42. Letter of November 12, 1919, in Bose, *Indian Pilgrim*, p. 170.

43. Bose, *Indian Pilgrim*, p. 93.

44. Bose, *Indian Pilgrim*, pp. 93–103.

45. Bose, *Indian Pilgrim*, pp. 95–100.

46. Letter of February 16, 1921, in Bose, *Indian Pilgrim*, p. 98.

47. For Bose's letters to Das, see Bose, *Indian Pilgrim*, pp. 180–86; the comment on Das's reply is in *Indian Pilgrim*, pp. 101–102.

48. Bose, *Indian Struggle*, pp. 80–81; Das Gupta, *Subhas Chandra*, p. 36.

49. Das Gupta, *Subhas Chandra*, pp. 37–73.

50. Subhas Chandra Bose, *The Mission of Life* (Calcutta, 1953), pp. 91–119.

51. During my interview with Mrs. Das in Calcutta in 1965, she said jokingly that Subhas Bose had become closer to her than to his own mother; this was also mentioned by several members of the Bose family and some political associates; see Bose's letters to Mrs. Das in his *Correspondence, 1924–32*, pp. 52 ff.

52. Das Gupta, *Subhas Chandra*, pp. 45–49, 53–54; J. T. Gwynn, *Indian Politics* (London, 1924), p. 284; Gwynn gives a description of Bose's work, but does not mention him by name.

53. Government of India, Home Department, Political File No. 61 of 1924, "Note of the Connection between the Revolutionists and the Swarajya Party in Bengal."

54. The Swarajists in the Bengal Legislative Council constantly protested against these laws and regulations; see, for example, Government of Bengal, *Proceedings of the Bengal Legislative Council*, 1924, Vol. XIV, No. 1, pp. 22–24, 52–188; hereafter these proceedings are referred to as *PBLC*. See also Earl of Lytton, *Pundits and Elephants* (London, 1942), p. 60; speech of Sir Hugh Stephenson in the Bengal Legislative Council, *PBLC*, 1925, Vol. XVII, No. 1, pp. 16–21.

55. Bose, *Correspondence 1924–32*, p. 197.

56. Interview with Surendra Mohan Ghose in New Delhi, September 27, 1964.

57. Bose, *Correspondence 1924–32*, p. 189.

58. Bose, *Correspondence 1924–32, passim;* unpublished notebooks kept by Subhas Bose while imprisoned which I read at the Netaji Research Bureau, Calcutta, numbered in pencil 1–8, especially 3, 5, 6, 7 and 8; referred to hereafter as "Prison Notebooks."

59. Bose, "Prison Notebooks," 3, containing fragments of essays and reading notes made from 1923 to 1927.

60. Bose, *Mission of Life*, p. 5.

61. Bose, *Mission of Life*, pp. 61–69, 205.

62. Bose, "Prison Notebooks," 3, translated from the Bengali by Keshub C. Sarkar and the author.

63. Bose, "Prison Notebooks," 3.

64. Bose, "Prison Notebooks," 3, translated from the Bengali.

65. Bose, "Prison Notebooks," 3.

66. Bose, *Indian Pilgrim*, p. 121.

67. Bose, *Mission of Life*, p. 123.

68. Government of India, Home Department, Political File No. 104 and K. W., 1927, letter of the Home Member, dated March 31, 1927.

69. Bose, *Indian Pilgrim*, pp. 42–44, 104–110.

70. Bose, "Prison Notebooks," 3.

71. Bose, "Prison Notebooks," 1 and 3.

72. Compare Roy, *Subhash*, with its later incarnation, Roy, *Netaji*, especially Appendix XI.

73. Bose, *Correspondence 1924–32*, pp. 88, 97; for Bose's earlier view of Aurobindo Ghose, see *Indian Pilgrim*, pp. 53–56.

74. Bose, *Correspondence 1924–32*, p. 391.

75. Bose, *Correspondence 1924–32*, pp. 97–98.

76. For this "symbolic" political activity, see Bose, *Correspondence 1924–32*, pp. 3–363, *passim*.

77. Bose, *Correspondence 1924–32*, pp. 151 ff.

78. Bose, *Correspondence 1924–32*, letters 35, 36, 75, 99, 112, 150, 192, 194, 205, 208–11, 214–17, 219–24.

79. Letter of October 1, 1927, Bose, *Correspondence 1924–32*, p. 393; Bose describes her as the Mother of Bengal in *Mission of Life*, p. 123.

80. Bose, *Correspondence 1924–32*, pp. 299, 390, 394.

81. Das Gupta, *Subhas Chandra*, pp. 94–95, 102.

82. On the endemic factionalism in Bengal, see selections from *The Bengal Administration Report 1934–35* in Mitra, *IAR*, 1936, I, 481–83; Subhas Chandra Bose, *Correspondence 1924–32* (Calcutta, 1967), pp. 299, 390.

83. *Forward*, May 27, 1939. Full-Khadi probably refers to the orthodox Gandhians like P. C. Ghose; Half-Khadi to the "official Congressmen" like Kiran Sankar Roy and J. C. Gupta; King's Own to the Bose group; CSP to the Congress Socialist Party; CP to the Communist Party; Jhowtala to the residence of Fazlul Huq; "Ranjani" to the home of Nalini Ranjan Sarker; Wellington St. to the house of Dr. B. C. Roy and Woodburn Park or Elgin Road to the homes of Sarat and Subhas Bose.

84. Das Gupta, *Subhas Chandra*, pp. 68–69.

85. Tushar Kanti Ghosh, ed., *Deshapriya Jatindra Mohan* (Calcutta, 1933), pp. 35, 45; Das Gupta, *Subhas Chandra*, p. 90.

86. Das Gupta, *Subhas Chandra*, p. 90; interview with Satya Ranjan Bakshi conducted in Calcutta, September 28, 1966 by Professor Edward C. Dimock.

87. Das Gupta, *Subhas Chandra*, p. 90.

88. Das Gupta, *Subhas Chandra*, p. 90.

89. Interview with Satya Ranjan Bakshi, September 28, 1966; Das Gupta, *Subhas Chandra*, p. 93; Mitra, *IAR*, 1926, I, 94–96.

90. Das Gupta, *Subhas Chandra*, pp. 95–96.

91. Mitra, *IAR*, 1928, I, 398.

92. Mitra, IAR, 1928, I, 399–400.

93. Das Gupta, *Subhas Chandra*, p. 96.

94. R. C. Majumdar, *History of the Freedom Movement in India* (Calcutta, 1963), III, 311–18; B. R. Nanda, *The Nehrus, Motilal and Jawaharlal* (New York, 1963), pp. 290–308.

95. Khalid B. Sayeed, *Pakistan, The Formative Phase, 1857–1948* (2d ed., London, 1968), pp. 68–75.

96. Sayeed, *Pakistan*, p. 71; Ram Gopal, *Indian Muslims, A Political History* (Calcutta, 1959), pp. 190–232.

97. Mitra, *IAR*, 1928, II, 417–20; Gopal, *Indian Muslims*, p. 207.

98. Sayeed, *Pakistan*, pp. 73–75; S. Gopal, *The Viceroyalty of Lord Irwin* (London, 1957), p. 37.

99. Mitra, *IAR*, 1928, II, 360–68.

100. Mitra *IAR*, 1928, II, 363.

101. Mitra, *IAR*, 1928, II, 366.

102. Mitra, *IAR*, 1928, II, 367.

103. Mitra, *IAR*, 1928, II, 368.

104. Nirad C. Chaudhuri, *The Continent of Circe* (London, 1965), pp. 103–104.

105. On Gandhi's tie to Jawaharlal Nehru, see Michael Brecher, *Nehru, A Political Biography* (London, 1959), pp. 58 ff., *passim*. Although Gandhi said on several occasions that he had affection for Bose this is not apparent in the letters they exchanged later during a Congress crisis; see Bose-Gandhi correspondence in Bose, *Crossroads*, pp. 126–70. Bose made some very critical statements about Gandhi in his history of recent nationalist developments, *Indian Struggle*, pp. 90–91, 162–63, 250, 280, 283; also see Nirad C. Chaudhuri, "Subhas Chandra Bose—His Legacy and Legend," *Pacific Affairs*, Vol. XXVI, No. 4 (December 1953), pp. 349–57.

106. Quoted in Mitra, *IAR*, 1929, I, 374.

107. Quoted in Mitra, *IAR*, 1929, I, 375.

108. Mitra, *IAR*, 1929, I, 378.

109. Karnik, *Trade Unions*, pp. 68, 70.

110. Das Gupta, *Subhas Chandra*, pp. 115–19.

111. Das Gupta, *Subhas Chandra*, pp. 95–101; Gopal Halder, "Revolutionary Terrorism," *Studies in the Bengal Renaissance*, ed. Atulchandra Gupta (Jadavpur, Calcutta, 1958), pp. 252–53; Mookerjee, *This Europe*, pp. 143–45; Bose, *Indian Struggle*, pp. 237, 242, 270–71, 284.

112. Interview with Nirad C. Chaudhuri in Delhi, September 22, 1964.

113. Das Gupta, *Subhas Chandra*, p. 120; K. P. Thomas, *Dr. B. C. Roy* (Calcutta, 1955), pp. 146–47; Mitra, *IAR*, 1929, II, 284–85.

114. Mitra, *IAR*, 1929, II, 284–86.

115. Das Gupta, *Subhas Chandra*, pp. 120–23.

116. Subhas Chandra Bose, speech on taking oath of office as Mayor of Calcutta, September 24, 1930; I read this speech in the library of the Calcutta Corporation.

117. Bose, speech, September 24, 1930.

118. Bose, *Through Congress Eyes*, pp. 240–43; there are references in Bose's letters to Mrs. Naomi Vetter about his interest in European city affairs, particularly Vienna; these unpublished letters are on file in the Netaji Research Bureau. Bose also visited Dublin, Rome, and numerous other European cities, always displaying an interest in civic government and experiments.

119. Nirad C. Chaudhuri, "Subhas Chandra Bose," *The Illustrated Weekly of India*, Vol. LXXVI, No. 38 (September 18, 1955), p. 18.

120. For an account of patronage and corruption in the Calcutta Corporation during the 1930s, see Nirad C. Chaudhuri, "The Day of Repentance, 15th August," *Now* (Calcutta), August 19, 1966.

121. Bakshi interview, November 14, 1964.

122. Ghosh, *Deshapriya*, pp. 49–53; Das Gupta, *Subhas Chandra*, pp. 127–28.

123. Rāy, *Itihās*, pp. 450–54.

124. Rāy, *Itihās*, pp. 452–55.

125. Rāy, *Itihās*, pp. 490–99; Halder, "Revolutionary Terrorism," p. 253; Sir Robert Reid, *Years of Change in Bengal and Assam* (London, 1966), pp. 55 ff.; Kalpana Dutt, *Chittagong Armoury Raiders, Reminiscences* (Bombay, 1945).

126. Halder, "Revolutionary Terrorism," pp. 254–55; Rāy, *Itihās*, pp. 446–48; Laushey, "The Bengal Terrorists," chapter 4.

127. Rāy, *Itihās*, pp. 470–90, 496; Halder, "Revolutionary Terrorism," p. 255.

128. Ghosh, *Deshapriya*, pp. 57–58.

129. Bose, *Indian Struggle*, pp. 280–82, 296–303, 306.

130. Interview with Surendra Mohan Ghose in New Delhi, September 27, 1964; Mr. Ghose was often a spokesman for Bengali prisoners to whom representatives of Gandhi came; he says that he always insisted, as did many other Bengali politicians, that the Bengali prisoners had to be released when

other political prisoners were; if they were not, then grave misgivings were felt among Bengalis.

131. Brecher, *Nehru,* pp. 179–80; Majumdar, *Freedom Movement,* III, 395–96.

132. Nanda, *Gandhi,* pp. 350–51.

133. Gopal, *Indian Muslims,* p. 237; Government of Bengal, Home Department, *Report of the Reforms Office, Bengal 1932–1937* (Alipore, Bengal, 1938), ed. R. N. Gilchrist, pp. 15–17; "The Bengal Hindus' Manifesto," Mitra, *IAR,* 1932, I, 323–24; G. D. Birla, *In the Shadow of the Mahatma* (Bombay, 1953), pp. 92–93, 108, 162–63; Narendra Nath Das, *History of Midnapur* (Calcutta, 1962), pp. 212–13.

134. Interview with Satya Ranjan Bakshi, September 28, 1966.

135. Das, *Midnapur,* pp. 116, 196.

136. Das, *Midnapur,* pp. 212–13.

137. Interview with Satya Ranjan Bakshi, September 28, 1966.

138. *Forward,* May 27, 1939.

139. Nirad C. Chaudhuri, "Subhas Bose," *Illustrated Weekly of India,* September 18, 1965.

140. Das Gupta, *Subhas Chandra,* pp. 111–12.

141. Roy, *Subhash,* pp. 34–40.

142. Nirmal Kumar Bose, *Modern Bengal* (Calcutta, 1959), p. 88; Ghosh, *Deshapriya,* p. 71.

143. K. P. Thomas, *Dr. B. C. Roy* (Calcutta, 1955), p. 142.

144. Das Gupta, *Subhas Chandra,* pp. 111–19; Thomas, *Dr. Roy,* pp. 146–47.

145. Bose letter to Mrs. Naomi Vetter, May 27, 1937 (unpublished letter in Netaji Research Bureau); Thomas, *Dr. Roy,* p. 110.

146. Thomas, *Dr. Roy,* pp. 182–88; Majumdar, *Freedom Movement,* III, 532–41.

147. Birla, *Shadow,* p. 307.

148. Birla, *Shadow,* pp. 56–57.

149. Birla, *Shadow, passim;* Birla was the link connecting the Marwari network and some other businessmen to Gandhi and the Congress High Command; when support was necessary, Gandhi would contact Birla, who would in turn contact his associates. Some connections were made through chambers of commerce; for example, see Federation of Indian Chambers of Commerce and Industry, *Silver Jubilee Souvenir 1927–1951* (New Delhi, 1952),

and other chamber of commerce publications. I have looked at some of these publications which are in the private collection of Professor Myron Weiner; there are some useful comments in Myron Weiner's *The Politics of Scarcity* (Chicago, 1962), pp. 102–26, and *Party Building in a New Nation, the Indian National Congress* (Chicago, 1967), *passim*, on the role of businessmen in politics, but a systematic study needs to be done on this relationship.

150. See the following account of the Bengal Ministry crisis and the role of Birla and Sarker in Bengali politics; Birla, *Shadow, passim*.

151. *The Times of India, Indian Yearbook and Who's Who* (Bombay, 1947), pp. 1206–1207; Reid, *Years of Change*, pp. 121–23; Nalini R. Sarker, "Industrialization and Planning," *What India Thinks*, ed. C. Roberts, (Calcutta, 1939).

152. Interview with Professor Niharanjan Ray, New York, February 1, 1968; Laushey, "The Bengal Terrorists," *passim* gives more complete details.

153. George Lichtheim, *Marxism* (New York, 1962), pp. 310 ff.; V. I. Lenin, *The National-Liberation Movement in the East* (Moscow, 1962), pp. 19, 38, 73, 205 ff.; Edward Hallett Carr, *The Bolshevik Revolution 1917–1923* (Baltimore, 1966), III, 232 ff.

154. Overstreet and Windmiller, *Communism*, pp. 8 ff.; M. N. Roy, *Memoirs* (New Delhi, 1964), pp. 285 ff.; Bhupendranath Datta, *Aprakāśita rājnitik itihās* [Unpublished political history] (Calcutta, 1953). The latter is an anecdotal but useful source; Government of India, Home Department, *India and Communism* (Simla, 1933), p. 108, calls Roy "the father of Indian Communism."

155. Carr, *Bolshevik Revolution*, III, 254–61; John Patrick Haithcox, *Communism and Nationalism in India, M. N. Roy and Comintern Policy 1920–1939* (Princeton, 1971), chapter 1.

156. Roy, *Memoirs*, pp. 499–500.

157. M. N. Roy, *India in Transition* (Geneva, 1922), pp. 162, 203–205, 236–37; Roy often compared Gandhi to Savanarola; see M. N. Roy and Evelyn Roy, *One Year of Non-cooperation from Ahmedabad to Gaya* (Calcutta, 1923), p. 193.

158. Roy, *Memoirs*, pp. 466 ff.; Muzaffar Ahmad, *The Communist Party of India and its Formation Abroad* (Calcutta, 1962), pp. 13, 28 ff.; Overstreet and Windmiller, *Communism*, pp. 29 ff.; Saumyendranath Tagore, *Historical Development of Communist Movement in India* (Calcutta, 1944), pp. 4 ff.; Government of India, Home Department, Political File No. 11, 1923.

159. Even though the Government of India realized that the trials gave the communist movement publicity, officials believed that the trials also offered an opportunity to demonstrate that it was a foreign-run movement; Overstreet and Windmiller, *Communism,* pp. 67–69, 135–39, 148–51; also see Lester Hutchinson, *Conspiracy at Meerut* (London, 1935) and Philip Spratt, *Blowing up India* (Calcutta, 1955).

160. David N. Druhe, *Soviet Russia and Indian Communism* (New York, 1959), pp. 70–71; Tagore, *Communist Movement,* p. 7.

161. Home Department, Political File No. 11, 1923.

162. Franz Borkenau, *World Communism* (Ann Arbor, Michigan, 1962), pp. 386–400; Overstreet and Windmiller, *Communism,* pp. 101 ff.

163. Karnik, *Trade Unions,* pp. 70–71.

164. Overstreet and Windmiller, *Communism,* p. 556.

165. Overstreet and Windmiller, *Communism,* pp. 166–70, 567; Rusch, "Congress Socialist Party," pp. 342–57; information about some of the Bengali Communists who worked in the Congress comes from interviews with these men conducted by Professor Donald Zagoria.

166. Rusch, "Congress Socialist Party," pp. 356–57; Jaya Prakash Narayan, *Toward Struggle* (Bombay, 1946), pp. 165 ff.

167. Overstreet and Windmiller, *Communism,* pp. 191–222.

168. M. N. Roy, *Our Differences* (Calcutta, 1938), pp. 44 ff.; Borkenau, *World Communism,* p. 346; there are many references to the group in files of letters in the M. N. Roy Archives, Mohini Road, Dehradun, U. P., India, especially letters to Jay Lovestone, Ruth Fischer, and to other ex-members of the Comintern.

169. Sibnarayan Ray, ed., *M. N. Roy Philosopher-Revolutionary* (Calcutta, 1959), pp. 69–72.

170. For Roy's changed views in the 1930s, see M. N. Roy, *Letters by M. N. Roy to the Congress Socialist Party—Written in 1934—*(Bombay, 1937); see also Roy's weekly paper, *Independent India* (Bombay, Delhi, 1937–40), *passim.* Roy's experience in Europe during the period of rising fascism made him put antifascism ahead of nationalist unity and of his own success in Indian politics; my views on this point have been shaped by reading hundreds of unpublished letters by Roy for the period 1937–45 on file in the M. N. Roy Archives.

171. Roy, *M. N. Roy,* p. 70.

172. Interview with V. B. Karnik, in Bombay, December 24, 1964; in addition, I found copies of some of the letters smuggled out of prison by Roy

in the M. N. Roy Archives and have reconstructed the network from information contained in the letters; details were checked with V. B. Karnik, who was a key operator in the network.

173. Roy correspondence with Amarendra Nath Chattopadhyay, Jiban Lal Chatterjee, Surendra Mohan Ghose, Bhupendra Kumar Datta, and Jadugopal Mukherjee in the M. N. Roy Archives.

174. Rusch, "Congress Socialist Party," pp. 146 ff.

175. Rusch, "Congress Socialist Party," p. 357.

176. Bose, unpublished letter to Mrs. Naomi Vetter, October 1, 1935.

177. Bose, *Through Congress Eyes*, pp. 140 ff., gives a record of some of his travels and observations; there are many comments on his travels in the letters to Mrs. Vetter in the 1930s; Hugh Toye, *Subash Chandra Bose, The Springing Tiger* (Bombay, 1962), pp. 41–44.

178. Kurti, *Subhas Bose, passim*.

179. Nathalal D. Parikh, "Reminiscences," *Life and Work of Netaji Subhas Chandra Bose*, ed. P. D. Saggi (Bombay, n.d.), Section II, pp. 37–43; S. K. Chatterji, "Subhas Bose," pp. 129–73; Subhas Bose unpublished letters to Amiya Chakravarty, 1935 to 1939 lent to the author by Mr. Chakravarty; Bose, *Indian Struggle*, p. 363.

180. Kurti, *Subhas Bose*, p. 48.

181. Subhas Chandra Bose, letter of March 25, 1936, printed in H. O. Günther, ed., *Indien und Deutschland* (Frankfurt ain Main, 1956), pp. 154–55.

182. Bose, *Through Congress Eyes*, p. 44.

183. The book was published in London in 1935 and was banned in India until 1937; it was not published in India until 1948.

184. Bose, *Indian Struggle*, pp. 250, 280, 283, 413–14. There are elements of a Marxist interpretation of Gandhi in *The Indian Struggle* as well as in the interpretation of the Bengali Gandhians by Satya Ranjan Bakshi that I have drawn on for my account of the Bengal Congress in the 1930s. A fuller and fairer interpretation would draw on accounts from Bengal's Gandhians as well; this is not to say that Bose's interpretation may not have considerable validity.

185. Bose, *Indian Struggle*, pp. 90–91.

186. Bose, *Indian Struggle*, pp. 162–63.

187. Bose, *Indian Struggle*, pp. 298–99, 306, 317.

188. Bose, *Indian Struggle*, pp. 105, 160, 320, 409.

189. Bose, *Indian Struggle*, pp. 428–29.

190. Bose, *Indian Struggle*, pp. 430–31.

CHAPTER NINE. THE CRISIS OF
BENGAL AND CONGRESS POLITICS

1. Thomas A. Rusch, "Role of the Congress Socialist Party in the Indian National Congress" (unpublished Ph.D. dissertation, University of Chicago, 1955), pp. 152 ff.; John Patrick Haithcox, *Communism and Nationalism in India: M. N. Roy and Comintern Policy, 1920–1939* (Princeton, 1971), chapter 9.

2. Rusch, "Congress Socialist Party," pp. 296–97 *et passim;* Nirmal Kumar Bose, *Studies in Gandhism* (3d ed., Calcutta, 1962), pp. 131–32.

3. Rajendra Prasad, *Autobiography* (New Delhi, 1957), pp. 419–20.

4. Prasad, *Autobiography*, p. 420; Rusch, "Congress Socialist Party," pp. 360–68.

5. Rusch, "Congress Socialist Party," *passim;* see the letter exchanged between Bose and Nehru in Jawaharlal Nehru, *A Bunch of Old Letters* (New Delhi, 1958), pp. 317–84; letters between M. N. Roy and Subhas Bose in File on "Bose and Forward Block," in Indian Renaissance Institute, Dehradun; also Roy's unpublished letters to many other political associates on file in Dehradun; interview with P. C. Joshi, former General Secretary of the CPI, New Delhi, February 6, 1965; Subhas Chandra Bose, *Crossroads* (Calcutta, 1962), *passim.*

6. Bose mentioned in an unpublished letter of November 25, 1937, to Mrs. Naomi Vetter that he expected to be Congress president; Prasad, *Autobiography*, p. 480; Hemendranath Das Gupta, *Subhas Chandra* (Calcutta, 1946), p. 150.

7. Prasad, *Autobiography*, pp. 395, 398, 413, 522; see Prasad's report on the Bengali-Bihari dispute in *The Statesman*, January 18, 1939; on the opposition to the Communal Award in Bengal, see pamphlets and letters collected by Marquis of Zetland, Zetland Collection, Vols. 21, 22, India Office Library MSS. EUR. 0.609.

8. Subhas Chandra Bose, *Through Congress Eyes* (Allahabad, n.d. [1938?]), pp. 5–21, 41–43.

9. Bose, *Through Congress Eyes*, p. 14; "The Bengal Hindu Conference," report in Mitra, *IAR*, 1936, II, 262–68.

10. Bose, *Through Congress Eyes*, pp. 11–17.

11. Bose, *Through Congress Eyes*, pp. 44–45.

12. Bose, *Through Congress Eyes*, pp. 18–22.

13. Nirad C. Chaudhuri, who handled some of Subhas Bose's correspondence at this time, has mentioned that Bose kept few letters or records; see references to the controversy over whether Bose was an active or a passive president, Nehru, *Old Letters*, pp. 319, 339–40; Shri Ram Sharma, *Netaji, His Life and Work* (Agra, 1948), p. 226.

14. *Re: Hindu-Muslim Settlement, Correspondence between Mr. Gandhi and Mr. Jinnah, Pandit Jawaharlal and Mr. Jinnah and S. Bose and Mr. Jinnah* (Delhi, n.d. [1938?]), *passim;* Matlubul Hasan Saiyid, *Mohammad Ali Jinnah* (2d ed., Lahore, 1962), pp. 280–87; Prasad, *Autobiography*, pp. 400 ff.

15. For details from the side of Bose and Congress officials, see All-India Congress Committee, C. P. *Ministerial Crisis* (Allahabad, n.d. [1938?]), *passim;* Prasad, *Autobiography*, pp. 475–78; for Khare's version, see N.B. Khare, *My Political Memoirs or Autobiography* (Nagpur, 1959), pp. 7–23, 48.

16. B. Pattabhi Sitaramayya, *History of the Indian National Congress (1935–1947)* (Bombay, 1947), II, 104–105.

17. Mitra, *IAR*, 1939, I, 44.

18. Mitra, *IAR*, 1939, I, 43.

19. Mitra, *IAR*, 1939, I, 42; see Bose's statements, *Statesman*, January 25, 1939; on the federation issue see John Glendevon, *The Victory at Bay* (London, 1971), *passim;* it was a major concern at Linlithgow's viceroyalty.

20. Bose, *Crossroads*, pp. 143, 159; Nehru, *Old Letters*, p. 333; Das Gupta, *Subhas Chandra*, p. 167.

21. Girija Mookerjee, *This Europe,* (Calcutta, 1950), p. 156.

22. Mitra, *IAR*, 1939, I, 45–46; *Statesman*, January 30, 1939.

23. Quoted in Bose, *Crossroads*, p. 94.

24. Mitra, *IAR*, 1939, I, 45–50.

25. Mitra, *IAR*, 1939, I, 46; *Statesman, February* 1, 1939.

26. *Statesman*, February 4, 1939.

27. Mitra, *IAR*, 1939, I, 48.

28. Mitra, *IAR*, 1939, I, 44.

29. Mitra, *IAR*, 1939, I, 50–51; Nehru, *Old Letters*, p. 332.

30. M. N. Roy letter of February 1, 1939, in file, "Bose and Forward Block," Indian Renaissance Institute, Dehradun; John Patrick Haithcox recounts this story in *Communism and Nationalism in India,* chapter 11, but apparently has not seen the relevant files in the M. N. Roy Archives.

31. Roy letter of February 1, 1939; Thomas A. Rusch interview with Ellen Roy, June, 1954, referred to in Rusch, "Congress Socialist Party," p. 378.

32. Rusch, "Congress Socialist Party," p. 378; Rusch bases some of his information on an interview with M. R. Masani, July 7, 1953.

33. Rusch, "Congress Socialist Party," p. 378; I have seen no mention of the last point in government of India records or in the correspondence of the governor of Bengal, the viceroy, or the secretary of state at the time.

34. Mitra, *IAR,* 1939, I, 53; *Statesman,* January–March 1939, *passim* on Gandhi's activities in Rajkot and Jaipur.

35. Bose, *Crossroads,* p. 152; Sitaramayya, *Congress,* II, p. 110.

36. Several versions of Roy's motions, together with the signatures of seconders and supporters of his motions and amendments are contained in the file "Tripuri Congress," Indian Renaissance Institute, Dehradun.

37. Mitra, *IAR,* 1939, I, 51, 335.

38. Mitra, *IAR,* 1939, I, 51.

39. Rusch, "Congress Socialist Party," pp. 379–91.

40. Mitra, *IAR,* 1939, I, 335.

41. Mitra, *IAR,* 1939, I, 335.

42. Rusch, "Congress Socialist Party," pp. 379–91.

43. Gene D. Overstreet and Marshall Windmiller, *Communism in India* (Berkeley, 1959), pp. 168–69; David N. Druhe, *Soviet Russia and Indian Communism* (New York, 1959), p. 150; *Forward,* March 25, 1939. These accounts all imply that the communists were united with the CSP in refusing to stand up against the Pant Resolution, but there was apparently some disagreement between Bengal communists and non-Bengal communists.

44. Rusch, "Congress Socialist Party," pp. 380–81; some communists were still in the CSP at this time.

45. Much of this correspondence is contained in Nehru, *Old Letters,* pp. 317–84, and Bose, *Crossroads,* pp. 126–70.

46. Bose, *Crossroads,* pp. 127, 144–47.

47. Michael Brecher, *Nehru, A Political Biography* (London, 1959), p. 251; Nehru's unwillingness to take a clear stand is evident in his public statements at the time: e.g., *Statesman,* February 4, 1939.

48. Bose, *Crossroads*, pp. 133, 140, 157.

49. Bose, *Crossroads*, pp. 128, 131; Nehru, *Old Letters*, p. 335.

50. Bose, *Indian Struggle*, pp. 255, 298, 406–7.

51. Bose, *Crossroads*, pp. 138, 141, 151.

52. Bose, *Crossroads*, pp. 143, 159; Nehru, *Old Letters*, p. 333.

53. Nirmal Kumar Bose, *Studies in Gandhism* (3d ed., Calcutta, 1962), pp. 218–21; Bose, *Crossroads*, p. 162.

54. Mitra, *IAR*, 1939, I, 53; on publication of the book, see *Statesman*, January 24, 1939.

55. Statement of the Co-ordinating Committee of the League of Radical Congressmen issued to the press by M. N. Roy, April 23, 1939, in Tripuri File, Indian Renaissance Institute, Dehradun.

56. Mitra, *IAR*, 1939, I, 345–46; Bose, *Crossroads*, pp. 171–73.

57. Prasad, *Autobiography*, p. 485.

58. *Forward*, May 6, 1939.

59. Mitra, *IAR*, 1939, I, 250; Prasad, *Autobiography*, p. 486.

60. *Forward*, April 8, 1939.

61. Bose, *Crossroads*, pp. 174 ff.

62. Hugh Toye, *Subhash Chandra Bose, The Springing Tiger* (Bombay, 1962), pp. 59–60; Rusch, "Congress Socialist Party," pp. 375, 397–408; M. N. Roy file, "Subhas Chandra Bose and Forward Block," Indian Renaissance Institute, Dehradun.

63. *Forward*, April 29, 1939; earlier in the year, a writer in the *Statesman*, January 21, 1939, suggested that there were four groups: the Bose group, the P. C. Ghosh group, the Kiran Sankar Roy group, and the Congress Socialist group headed by Dr. Suresh Banerji.

64. This suggestion is partly based on my reading of *Forward* and M. N. Roy's unpublished correspondence with several of these men during this period; Dr. M. K. Halder has made several suggestions about these factions, but I am responsible for the hypothesis about group membership.

65. *Forward*, May 27, 1939.

66. K. P. Thomas, *Dr. B. C. Roy* (Calcutta, 1955), pp. 192–94.

67. Brecher, *Nehru*, p. 255; Toye, *Subhash Bose*, p. 60; Mitra, *IAR*, 1939, II, 212, 224–25, 239, 250–52, 271–75.

68. Subhas Bose unpublished letter to M. N. Roy, January 14, 1940, in Roy file, "Forward Block," Indian Renaissance Institute, Dehradun.

69. Toye, *Subhash Bose*, pp. 61–64.

70. Rusch, "Congress Socialist Party," p. 408.

71. Myron Weiner, *Party Politics in India* (Princeton, 1957), pp. 174–77.

72. For examples, see Mitra, *IAR*, 1928, II, 417–21; Mitra, *IAR*, 1927, I, 432–33; Mitra, *IAR*, 1930, II, 351–54; Mitra, *IAR*, 1931, I, 309–16; Mitra, *IAR*, 1932, I, 312–19; Mitra, *IAR*, 1932, II, 329–33.

73. Prasad, *Autobiography*, p. 398; Mitra, *IAR*, 1932, I, pp. 312–13; Mitra, *IAR*, 1932, II, pp. 329–33.

74. On strains between the regional and national Muslim leadership, see Ram Gopal, *Indian Muslims, A Political History* (Calcutta, 1959), pp. 272–79; Sharifuddin Pirzada, ed., *Quaid-e-Azam Jinnah's Correspondence* (Karachi, 1966), pp. 55–67; Khalid B. Sayeed, *Pakistan, The Formative Phase 1857–1948* (2d ed., London, 1968), pp. 213–16; Glendevon, *Viceroy*, pp. 202–13; there were also strains between the government of Bengal and the government of India, particularly over financial issues. Bengal governors from Lord Ronaldshay in the 1920s to Lord Casey in the 1940s argued at the center for the rights of "their" province. Bengali officials like Sir John Anderson, governor from 1932 to 1937, and native politicians thought that Bengal was indirectly paying for development schemes in other parts of the country while Bengal became even more impoverished. The combination of economic difficulties, labor unrest, and sporadic revolutionary activity led Anderson to describe Bengal as a "running sore," keeping India from health. King George V asked Anderson, "What is *wrong* with Bengal?" See John W. Wheeler-Bennett, *John Anderson, Viscount Waverly* (London, 1962), pp. 128–32, 147–48, 171–72; Lord Casey, *Personal Experience 1939–1946* (London, 1962), pp. 182–83, 209–10.

75. Matlubul Hasan Saiyid, *Mohammad Ali Jinnah* (2d ed., Lahore, 1962), p. 265; Gopal, *India Muslims*, pp. 199–245, *passim*; Mitra, *IAR*, 1931, I, 309–16; Mitra, *IAR*, 1932, I, 312–13; Mitra, *IAR*, 1932, II, 329–33.

76. Humayan Kabir, *Muslim Politics (1906–1942)* (Calcutta, 1944), p. 36.

77. On Kazi Nazrul Islam, see Buddhadeva Bose, *An Acre of Green Grass* (Calcutta, 1948), pp. 36–42; S. Sajjad Husain, ed., *East Pakistan, A Profile* (Dacca, 1962), pp. 125–27; Nazrul Islam, *Selected Poems*, tr. Kabir Chowdhury (Dacca, 1963).

78. Kabir, *Muslim Politics*, p. 12.

79. J. H. Broomfield, *Elite Conflict in a Plural Society: Twentieth-Century Bengal* (Berkeley, 1968), pp. 284 ff.

80. Reginald Coupland, *The Constitutional Problem in India* (3 vols., London, 1945) I, 58, 71; Broomfield, *Elite Conflict*, p. 284.

81. Sir Robert Reid, *Years of Change in Bengal and Assam* (London, 1966), pp. 52–53; Broomfield, *Elite Conflict*, p. 285.

82. Interview with Satya Ranjan Bakshi, Calcutta, November 14, 1964.

83. Government of Bengal, *Report on Bengal, 1932–37*, pp. 1–17; this is not stated explicitly, but is implied by the elaborate steps taken for the next constitutional advance.

84. Prasad, *Autobiography*, pp. 392 ff.; Saiyid, *Jinnah*, p. 243; Reid, *Years of Change*, pp. 120–24; Coupland, *Constitutional Problem*, II, 27.

85. Prasad, *Autobiography*, pp. 418, 426, 433.

86. Prasad, *Autobiography*, p. 436; Coupland, *Constitutional Problem*, II, 26 ff.

87. Prasad, *Autobiography*, pp. 436–41; Coupland, *Constitutional Problem*, II, 26 ff.; Brecher, *Nehru*, pp. 226–31.

88. Government of Bengal, *Report of Bengal, 1932–37*, pp. 16–17.

89. Thomas, *Dr. Roy*, p. 188.

90. Coupland, *Constitutional Problem*, III, 27.

91. Government of Bengal, *Report of Bengal, 1932–1937*, pp. 212, 138.

92. Government of Bengal, *Report of Bengal, 1932–1937*, pp. 124, 357; Gopal, *Indian Muslims*, p. 245.

93. Gopal, *Indian Muslims*, p .246; a fuller account of the ministerial question will be given in a book, now in preparation, on Bengal politics in the decade before partition and independence.

94. Gopal, *Indian Muslims*, pp. 202–79, *passim*; Pirzada, *Jinnah's Correspondence*, p. 55–67; Sayeed, *Pakistan*, pp. 213–14.

95. Interview with Nirad C. Chaudhuri, Delhi, September 22, 1964; Nehru, *Old Letters*, p. 328; see the letters between Bose and Gandhi quoted below.

96. Interview with Surendra Mohan Ghose, New Delhi, March 1965.

97. From unpublished letters in the possession of Nirad C. Chaudhuri; quoted with his permission. Mr. Chaudhuri was at the time private secretary to Sarat Bose.

98. Interview with Nirad C. Chaudhuri, Delhi, September 22, 1964; see Sarker's speech on the continuance of and necessity for Muslim supremacy in Bengal's ministry, reported in *The Statesman*, January 21, 1939.

99. A. K. Fazlul Huq, "Muslim Sufferings Under Congress Rule" (Calcutta, 1939), p. 18.

100. Brecher, *Nehru*, pp. 257 ff.; Coupland, *Constitutional Problem*, II, 208 ff.; B. Pattabhi Sitaramayya, *History of the Indian National Congress* (Bombay, 1947), II, 124 ff.; Sayeed, *Pakistan*, pp. 183–84.

101. Bose, *Crossroads*, pp. 356–57.

102. Sharma, *Netaji*, pp. v–vii; I have compared the translation with the original in Rabindranath Tagore, *Kālāntar* [End of an era] (Calcutta, 1962), pp. 371–76, and made several changes in the English version.

103. Brecher, *Nehru*, pp. 257 ff.; Overstreet and Windmiller, *Communism*, pp. 171–222; Rusch, "Congress Socialist Party," pp. 420 ff.; Govind Sahai, *'42 Rebellion* (Delhi, 1947), *passim*; M. N. Roy and others, *India and War* (Lucknow, 1942), *passim*; *Independent India, 1939–1945*; Satish Chandra Samanta, Syamdas Bhattacharya, Ananga Mohan Das, and Prahlad Kumar Pramanik, *August Revolution and Two Years National Government in Midnapore* (Calcutta, 1946), Part I.

104. Pirzada, *Jinnah's Correspondence*, p. 58.

105. Coupland, *Constitutional Problem*, II, 29–31; Mitra, *IAR*, 1941, II, 143–51; *Statesman*, December 1941.

106. Saiyid, *Jinnah*, pp. 357, 487–503; Gopal, *Indian Muslims*, pp. 275–79.

107. Gopal, *Indian Muslims*, p. 278; A. K. Fazlul Huq, *Bengal Today* (Calcutta, 1944), *passim*; Mitra, *IAR*, 1943, I, 90–98; II, 43–49, 126–33.

108. Pirzada, *Jinnah's Correspondence*, pp. 62–68.

109. Henry Knight, *Food Administration in India 1939–47* (Stanford, 1954), pp. 67–105; Casey, *Personal Experience*, pp. 182–216; Mitra, *IAR*, 1943, I, 99–103; II, 59; Mitra, *IAR*, 1945, I, 194–98.

110. Toye, *Subhash Bose*, pp. 63–183; Das Gupta, *Subhas Chandra*, pp. 195–254.

111. Toye, *Subhash Bose*, pp. 182–83. There are quite a few Bengalis who do not believe that Bose died in the crash, and rumors circulate frequently in Calcutta that Bose is returning shortly to set Bengal's and India's troubles right.

112. Brecher, *Nehru*, pp. 305–309.

113. Quoted in Chaudhuri, "Subhas Bose," *Pacific Affairs*, p. 351; "Netaji," a term meaning respected leader, was first used by Bose's associates in Berlin.

114. Toye, *Subhash Bose*, pp. 190–91; Francis Tuker, *While Memory Serves* (London, 1950), pp. 51–72, 293.

115. Tuker, *Memory Serves,* pp. 152–65; Gopal, *Indian Muslims,* pp. 304–17; Sayeed, *Pakistan,* pp. 148–56; Mitra, *IAR,* 1946, II, 66–96.

116. Tuker, *Memory Serves,* pp. 256 ff.; Nirmal Kumar Bose, *My Days with Gandhi* (Calcutta, 1953), pp. 105–106, 217, 228 ff.; Pyarelal, *Mahatma Gandhi, The Last Phase* (2d ed., Ahmadabad, 1965), I, 24 ff. During the 1940s Hindu communalism was also rising in Bengal; the most important figure in this movement was Shyama Prasad Mookherjee; see Balraj Madhok, *Dr. Syama Prasad Mookerjee* (New Delhi, 1954); J. A. Curran, Jr., *Militant Hinduism in Indian Politics* (New York, 1951), *passim;* Weiner, *Party Politics,* pp. 164–222; Syama Prasad Mookerjee, *Awake Hindustan!* (Calcutta, n.d. [1944?]); B. D. Graham, "Syama Prasad Mookerjee and the Communalist Alternative," *Soundings in Modern South Asian History,* ed. D. A. Low (London, 1968), pp. 330–66; Sarat Chandra Bose, *I Warned My Countrymen* (Calcutta, 1968), pp. 183 ff.; C. H. Philips and Mary Doreen Wainwright, *The Partition of India, Politics and Perspectives 1935–1947* (London, 1970), *passim.*

117. Weiner, *Party Politics,* pp. 85 ff.; Thomas, *Dr. Roy,* pp. 204 ff.; Marcus F. Franda, "The Politics of West Bengal," *State Politics in India,* ed. *Myron Weiner* (Princeton, 1968), pp. 273–75.

118. Weiner, *Party Politics,* pp. 117–63.

119. *Statesman* (New Delhi and Calcutta, 1967–1969, Weekly Air Edition).

120. Tuker, *Memory Serves,* pp. 286–96, 380–82.

121. Khalid B. Sayeed, *The Political System of Pakistan* (Boston, 1967), pp. 85–91.

122. See the prominence given to the role of the INA in Majumdar, *Freedom Movement,* III, 700–45; I have heard this version of the past from several Bengalis in Calcutta and London.

123. For example, see Atulya Ghosh, *Ahimsa and Gandhi* (Calcutta, 1954).

124. There is a special term of abuse in Bengali for Gandhi; it is *gĕdośālā;* the word *śālā* in Bengali means brother-in-law, but if you are not married to someone's sister and call him your *śālā,* it is a term of abuse for obvious reasons; *gĕdo* refers to Gandhi; the whole term might be freely translated as "Gandhi-bastard." I heard a number of highly inventive stories about Gandhi's sex life in Calcutta while I was living there in 1963–1965.

125. See Majumdar, *Freedom Movement,* III, xv–xxxi, 4 ff.; Nirad C. Chaudhuri, *The Autobiography of an Unknown Indian* (New York, 1951), pp. 428 ff.

CONCLUSION

1. The most direct parallel to the changing position of the high-caste Bengalis is that of the Maharashtrian Brahmans; see J. A. Curran, Jr., *Militant Hinduism in Indian Politics* (New York, 1951); Dhanajay Keer, *Savarkar and His Times* (Bombay, 1950); Balshastri Hardas, *Armed Struggle for Freedom* (Poona, 1958); Stanley A. Wolpert, *Nine Hours to Rama* (New York, 1963); J. C. Jain, *The Murder of Mahatma Gandhi* (Bombay, 1950); John Frederick Muehl, *Interview with India* (New York, 1950), pp. 152–213.

2. Nirad C. Chaudhuri, *The Autobiography of an Unknown Indian* (New York, 1951), p. 430.

3. Chaudhuri, *Autobiography*, pp. 431–32.

4. *Statesman*, January 17, 1939, column of "An Indian Observer," who was B. B. Roy.

Selective Bibliography

The bibliography is arranged under the following main headings:
I. Primary Sources
  A. Manuscript Collections
  B. Official Records and Reports
  C. Newspapers and Periodicals
  D. Interviews
  E. Other Works
II. Secondary Works
  A. Books, Articles, Unpublished Theses and Papers
  B. Reference Works

I. PRIMARY SOURCES

A. Manuscript Collection

All-India Congress Committee Files, 1927–1947. Jawaharlal Nehru Memorial Library, New Delhi.

Subhas Chandra Bose Papers. Letters and Prison Notebooks (numbered 1–8), 1923–1940, by courtesy of the Netaji Research Bureau, Calcutta.

M. N. Roy Papers. Letters and Political Papers, 1931–1953, by courtesy of the Indian Renaissance Institute, Dehradun, U.P.

Sir B. P. Singh Roy Collection. Jawaharlal Nehru Memorial Library, New Delhi.

Correspondence of Subhas C. Bose, by courtesy of Nirad C. Chaudhuri, Amiya Chakravarty, Mrs. Naomi Vetter.

Zetland Collection, India Office Library, London.

B. Official Records and Reports

Government of Bengal, Appointments Department, Reforms. *Report on the Working of the Reformed Constitution in Bengal 1921–27.* Calcutta, 1929.

Government of Bengal, Bengal Legislative Council. *Proceedings of the Bengal Legislative Council.* Calcutta, 1900–1939.

Government of Bengal. *Governors' Fortnightly Reports,* 1936–1945.

Government of Bengal, Home Department. *Report of the Reforms Office, Bengal 1932–1937.* R. N. Gilchrist, ed. Calcutta, 1938.

Government of Bengal. *Report of the Native Press in Bengal.* Calcutta, 1907–1915.

Government of Bengal. *Report (Part II) on Native-Owned English Newspapers in Bengal.* Calcutta, 1904–1912.

Government of India, Calcutta University Commission, 1917–1919, *Report,* 13 vols. Calcutta, 1919.

Government of India. *Census of India,* vols. for Bengal and for Calcutta, 1872, 1881, 1901, 1911, 1921, 1931, 1951.

Government of India, Home Department. *Political Proceedings and Files,* 1907–1945.

Government of India, Home Department, Political. *India and Communism.* Simla, 1933.

Government of India, Judicial and Public. *Proceedings,* 1892, 1916, 1927–1945.

Government of India, Sedition Committee, 1918. *Report,* Calcutta, 1918.

C. Newspapers and Periodicals
Amrita Bazar Patrika

Bande Mataram

Bengal Past and Present

Forward (Calcutta)

Independent India

Karmayogin

Modern Review

The Statesman (Calcutta)

The Times (London)

D. Interviews
Bakshi, Satya Ranjan, political worker, Calcutta, July and November 1964 and September 1966.

Bhattacharya, Lalit, brother of M. N. Roy, Calcutta, 1964.

Beals, Carleton, associate of M. N. Roy in Mexico, 1917–1919, Killingworth, Connecticut, 1965.

Bose, Nirmal Kumar, Gandhian worker and anthropologist, Calcutta, February 1964.

Bose, Sailesh, brother of Subhas Bose, Bombay, December 1964.

Bose, Mrs. Subhas, *see* Schenkl-Bose, Mrs. Emilie.

Brockway, A. Fenner, political leader, London, May 1965.

Chaudhuri, Nirad C., writer and former private secretary to Sarat Bose, Delhi, May, September, and October 1964.

Das, Mrs. C. R. (Basanti Devi), widow of C. R. Das, Calcutta, 1965.

Datta, Bhupendra Kumar, ex-revolutionary and political worker, Calcutta, 1964.

Dutt, R. Palme, leader of the Communist Party of Great Britain, London, May 1965.

Ghose, Surendra Mohan, ex-revolutionary and Congress leader, New Delhi, September 1964 and March 1965.

Joshi, P. C., former general secretary of the Communist Party of India, New Delhi, February 1965.

Karnik, V. B., former associate of M. N. Roy and trade union leader, Bombay, December 1964 and April 1965.

Khan, Shah Nawaz, former officer of the INA, New Delhi, February 1965.

Majumdar, Bhupati, ex-revolutionary and political worker, Calcutta, July 1964.

Mukherjee, Hirendranath, a leader of the Communist Party of India, New Delhi, September 1964.

Ray, Niharranjan, former political worker and historian, New York, February 1968.

Schenkl-Bose, Mrs. Emilie, widow of Subhas Bose, Vienna, May 1965.

Sinha, K. K., former associate of M. N. Roy and writer, Calcutta, 1965.

Tagore, Saumyendranath, political leader and writer, Calcutta, September 1964.

Tarkunde, Justice V. M., former associate of M. N. Roy and former judge of the High Court, Bombay, Mussoorie, May 1965.

Vetter, Mrs. Naomi, friend of Subhas Bose, Vienna, May 1965.

E. Other Works

Aga Khan. *The Memoirs of Aga Khan, World Enough and Time*. London, 1954.

Ameer Ali. *Ameer Ali, His Life and Work*. K. K. Aziz, ed. Lahore, 1968.

——. *A Critical Examination of the Life and Teachings of Mohammed*. London, 1873.

——. *Islam*. London, 1914.

——. *The Legal Position of Women in Islam*. London, 1912.

——. *The Personal Law of the Mahommedans*. London, 1880.

——. *A Short History of the Saracens*. London, 1899.

——. *The Spirit of Islam*. London, 1967. Reprint of 1922 ed.

——. *Student's Handbook of Mahommedan Law*. 5th ed., Calcutta, 1906.

——. *Syed Ameer Ali on Islamic History and Culture*. Syed Razi Wasti, ed. Lahore, 1968.

All-India Congress Committee. *C. P. Ministerial Crisis*. Allahabad, n.d. (1938?).

Andrews, C. F. *The Indian Problem*. 2d ed. Madras, 1923.

——. *To the Students*. Madras, 1921.

Aurobindo, *see* Ghose, Aurobindo.

Azad, Maulana Abul Kalam. *India Wins Freedom*. Calcutta, 1960.

Banerjea, Surendranath. *A Nation in Making*. Calcutta, 1963. Reprint of 1925 ed.

——. *Speeches and Writings of Hon. Surendranath Banerjea*. Madras, n.d.

Banerji, Nripendra Chandra. *At the Crossroads (1885–1946)*. Calcutta, 1950.

——. *Gandhism in Theory and Practice*. Madras, 1923.

——. *The Ideal of Swaraj*. Madras, 1921.

Basu, Bhupendranath. *Why India is Heart and Soul with Great Britain*. London, 1914.

Birla, G. D. *In the Shadow of the Mahatma, A Personal Memoir*. Bombay, 1953.

Blunt, Wilfrid Scawen. *India under Ripon*. London, 1909.

Bonnerjee, W. C., ed. *Indian Politics*. Madras, 1898.

Bose, Nirmal Kumar. *My Days with Gandhi*. Calcutta, 1953.

Bose, Sarat Chandra. *I Warned My Countrymen*. Calcutta, 1968.

Bose, Subhas Chandra. *Correspondence 1924–1932*. Calcutta, 1967.

——. *Crossroads*. Calcutta, 1962.

——. *Impressions in Life*. Lahore, 1947.

——. *An Indian Pilgrim, An Unfinished Autobiography and Collected Letters 1897–1921*. Calcutta, 1965.

——. *The Indian Struggle 1920–1934*. Calcutta, 1948.

——. *The Indian Struggle 1920–1942*. Calcutta, 1964.

——. *The Mission of Life*. Calcutta, 1953.

——. *Through Congress Eyes*. Allahabad, n.d. (1938?).

Carmichael, Mary Helen Elizabeth, Baroness Carmichael, ed. *Lord Carmichael of Skirling*. London, 1929.

Carstairs, Robert. *Human Nature in Rural India*. London, 1895.

——. *The Little World of an Indian District Officer*. London, 1912.

Casey, Lord. *Personal Experience 1939–1946*. London, 1962.

Chatterjee, Bankim Chandra. *Anandamath*. Sree Aurobindo and Barindra Kumar Ghosh, trs. Calcutta, n.d.

——. *Essays and Letters*. Brajendra Nath Banerji and Sajani Kanta Das, eds. Calcutta, 1940.

——. *Letters on Hinduism*. Brajendra Nath Banerji and Sajani Kanta Das, eds. Calcutta, 1940.

Das, Chittaranjan. *India for Indians*. 3d ed. Madras, 1921.

——. *Songs of the Sea*, in Aurobindo Ghose, *Collected Poems and Plays*, Vol. II. Pondicherry, 1942.

——. *The Way to Swaraj*. Madras, 1923.

Datta, Bhupendranath. *Aprakāśita rājnītik itihās* [Unpublished political history] Calcutta, 1953.

Dutt, Kalpana. *Chittagong Armoury Raiders, Reminiscences*. Bombay, 1945.

Dutt, Romesh Chunder. *A Brief History of Ancient and Modern Bengal for the Use of Schools*. Calcutta, 1904.

——. *A Brief History of Ancient and Modern India According to the Syllabus Prescribed by the Calcutta University*. Calcutta, 1907.

Dutt, Romesh Chunder. *The Civilization of India.* London, 1900.

——. *Cultural Heritage of Bengal.* Calcutta, 1962 (originally published under the title, *The Literature of Bengal*).

——. *Early Hindu Civilisation, B.C. 2000 to 320.* Calcutta, 1963. (originally published as part of *A History of Civilisation in Ancient India*).

——. *The Economic History of India under Early British Rule.* London, 1956. Reprint.

——. *The Economic History of India in the Victorian Age.* London, 1956. Reprint.

——. *England and India. A Record of Progress during a Hundred Years 1785–1885.* London, 1897.

——. *A History of Civilization in Ancient India.* 3 vols. London, 1889–1890.

——. *The Lake of Palms.* London, 1902.

——. *Later Hindu Civilisation A.D. 500 to A.D. 1200.* Calcutta, 1965 (originally *A History of Civilization in Ancient India*).

——. *Lays of Ancient India.* London, 1894.

——. *Open Letters to Lord Curzon and Speeches and Papers.* Calcutta, 1904.

——. *The Peasantry of Bengal.* Calcutta, 1874.

——. *Pratap Singh, The Last of the Rajputs.* Ajoy C. Dutt, tr. Allahabad, 1943.

——. *The Ramayana and the Mahabharata.* New York, 1963. Reprint.

——. *Rames racanābalī* [Collected works of Rames]. Jogesh Chandra Bagal, ed. Calcutta, 1960.

——. *Sivaji.* Ajoy C. Dutt, tr. Allahabad, 1944.

——. *The Slave Girl of Agra.* London, 1909.

——. *Todar Mull.* Ajoy Dutt. tr. Allahabad, 1947.

——. *Three Years in Europe 1868 to 1871, With an Account of Subsequent Visits to Europe in 1886 and 1893.* Calcutta, 1896.

Fazlul Huq, A. K. *Bengal Today.* Calcutta, 1944.

Fraser, Andrew H. L. *Among Indian Rajahs and Ryots.* London, 1911.

Fuller, Sir Bamfylde. *Some Personal Experiences.* London, 1930.

Gandhi, Mohandas K. *An Autobiography, The Story of My Experiments with Truth.* Boston, 1959.

——. *The Collected Works of Mahatma Gandhi.* 28 vols. Delhi, 1958–1968.

——. *Selections from Gandhi.* Nirmal Kumar Bose, ed. Ahmadabad, 1957.

——. *Swaraj in One Year.* Madras, 1921.

——. *Young India 1919–1922.* New York, 1923.

Ghose, Aurobindo (Sri Aurobindo). *Bankim Chandra Chatterji.* Pondicherry, 1954.

——. *Collected Poems and Plays.* 2 vols. Pondicherry, 1942.

——. *The Doctrine of Passive Resistance.* 2d ed. Pondicherry, 1952.

——. *Essays on the Gita.* Pondicherry, 1959.

——. *The Foundations of Indian Culture.* Pondicherry, 1959.

——. *The Human Cycle.* New York, 1950.

——. *The Ideal of Human Unity.* New York, 1950.

——. *The Ideal of the Karmayogin.* 7th ed. Pondicherry, 1950.

——. *Kārākāhinī.* [The story of prison] 3d ed. Calcutta, 1930.

——. *The National Value of Art.* 3d ed. Calcutta, 1946.

——. *On the Veda.* Pondicherry, 1964.

——. *The Renaissance in India.* Chandernagore, 1927.

——. *Speeches.* 3d ed. Pondicherry, 1952.

——. *Śrī Arabinder patra* [Sri Aurobindo's letters] Pondicherry, 1952.

——. *Sri Aurobindo on Himself and the Mother.* Pondicherry, 1953.

Ghose, Barindra Kumar. *The Tale of My Exile.* Pondicherry, 1922.

Ghose, Lalmohun. *The Natives and the Government of India.* London, 1879.

Ghosh, Atulya. *Ahimsa and Gandhi.* Calcutta, 1954.

Ghosh, Rashbehary. *Speeches and Writings.* 3d ed. Madras, 1921.

Günther, H. O., ed. *Indien und Deutschland.* Frankfurt am Main, 1956.

——. "Muslim Sufferings under Congress Rule." Calcutta, 1939.

Ispahani, M. A. H. *Qaid-e-Azam Jinnah as I Knew Him.* Rev. ed. Karachi, 1967.

Jayakar, M. R. *The Story of My Life.* 2 vols. Bombay, 1958, 1959.

Khare, N. B. *My Political Memoirs or Autobiography.* Nagpur, 1959.

Kipling, Rudyard. *Selected Prose and Poetry of Rudyard Kipling.* Garden City, New York, 1937.

Kurti, Kitty. *Subhas Chandra Bose As I Knew Him*. Calcutta, 1966.

Lytton, Earl of. *Pundits and Elephants*. London, 1942.

"M" [Mahendra Nath Gupta], comp. *The Gospel of Sri Ramakrishna*. Swami Nikhilananda, tr. 4th ed. Mylapore, Madras, 1964.

Mazumdar, Amvika Charan. *Indian National Evolution*. Madras, 1915.

Minto, Mary, Countess of. *India Minto and Morley 1905–1910*. London, 1934.

Mohammed Ali, Moulana. *Selections from Moulana Mohammed Ali's Comrade*. Syed Rais Ahamd Jafri, ed. Lahore, 1965.

Montagu, Edwin S. *An Indian Diary*. Venetia Montagu, ed. London, 1930.

Mookerjee, Syama Prasad. *Awake Hindustan!* Calcutta, n.d.

Morley, John, Viscount. *Recollections*. Vol. II. London, 1917.

Mukherjee, Hiren. *Gandhiji, A Study*. 2d ed. New Delhi, 1960.

Narayan, Jaya Prakash. *Towards Struggle*. Bombay, 1946.

Nehru, Jawaharlal. *A Bunch of Old Letters*. New Delhi, 1958.

——. *The Discovery of India*. London, 1956.

——. *Soviet Russia*. Allahabad, 1929.

——. *Toward Freedom*. Boston, 1958.

Nivedita, Sister. *Civic and National Ideals*, 4th ed. Calcutta, 1948.

Pal, Bipinchandra. *The Brahmo Samaj and the Battle for Swaraj in India*. Calcutta, 1945.

——. *Character Sketches*. Calcutta, 1957.

——. *Indian Nationalism: Its Principles and Personalities*. Madras, n.d.

——. *Memories of My Life and Times*. 2 vols. Calcutta, 1932 and 1951.

——. *Nationality and Empire*. Calcutta, 1916.

——. *Non-Co-Operation*. Calcutta, 1920.

——. *The Soul of India*. 4the ed. Calcutta, 1958.

——. *The Spirit of Indian Nationalism*. London, 1910.

——. *Swadeshi and Swaraj*. Calcutta, 1954.

——. *Writings and Speeches*. Vol. I. Calcutta, 1958.

Pirzada, Syed Sharifuddin, ed. *Quaid-e-Azam Jinnah's Correspondence*. 2d ed. Karachi, 1966.

Prabhu, R. K. and Kelekar, Ravindra, eds. *Truth Called Them Differently (Tagore-Gandhi Controversy)*. Ahmadabad, 1961.

Prasad, Rajendra. *Autobiography*. New Delhi, 1957.

Rai, Lajpat. *Young India*. New York, 1917.

Re: Hindu-Muslim Settlement, Correspondence between Mr. Gandhi and Mr. Jinnah, Pandit Jawaharlal and Mr. Jinnah and between S. Bose and Mr. Jinnah. Delhi, n.d. (1938?).

Reid, Sir Robert. *Years of Change in Bengal and Assam*. London, 1966.

Ronaldshay, Earl of [The Marquess of Zetland]. *'Essayez'*. London, 1956.

———. *The Heart of Āryāvarta*. London, 1925.

Roy, Dilip Kumar. *Netaji—The Man, Reminiscences*. Bombay, 1966.

———. *The Subhash I Knew*. Bombay, 1946.

Roy, M. N. *Crime and Karma: Cats and Women*. Calcutta, 1957.

———. "The Dissolution of a Priestly Family," *Radical Humanist*, Vol. XVIII, Nos. 6–7 (February 7, 1954), pp. 66–68, 72–74.

———. *India in Transition*. Geneva, 1922.

———. *La India, Su pasado, su presente y su porvenir*. Mexico, 1918.

———. *India's Message*. Calcutta, 1950.

———. "Jatin Mukherji," *Independent India*, Vol. XIII, No. 8 (February 27, 1949).

———. *Jawaharlal Nehru*. Delhi, 1945.

———. *Letters by M. N. Roy to the Congress Socialist Party—Written in 1934—*. Bombay, 1937.

———. *M. N. Roy's Memoirs*. New Delhi, 1964.

———. *Materialism*. 2d ed. Calcutta, 1951.

———. *Our Differences*. Calcutta, 1938.

———. *The Problem of Freedom*. Calcutta, 1945.

———. *Politics, Power and Parties*. Calcutta, 1960.

———. *La Voz de la India*. Mexico, n.d.

Roy, M. N. and Roy, Evelyn. *One Year of Non-Cooperation from Ahmedabad to Gaya*. Calcutta, 1923.

Roy, M. N. and others. *India and War*. Lucknow, 1942.

Roy, Rammohun. *The English Works of Raja Rammohun Roy*. Kalidas Nag and Debajyoti Burman, eds. 6 parts. Calcutta, 1945–1951.

Sarker, Nalini R. *Economic Policy and Programme for Post-War India.* Patna, 1945.

——. "Industrialization and Planning," *What India Thinks.* C. Roberts, ed. Calcutta, 1939.

Sen, Keshub. *The Brahmo Samaj, Discourses and Writings.* Part I. 2d ed. Calcutta, 1917.

——. *Lectures in India.* Calcutta, 1954.

Sen, Rajen and B. K. Sen, eds. *Deshabandhu Chitta Ranjan.* Calcutta, 1926.

Sinha, Satyendra Prasanna. *Speeches and Writings of Lord Sinha.* Madras, n.d.

Sondhi, G. C., ed. *To the Gates of Liberty, Congress Commemoration Volume.* N.p., n.d.

Spratt, Philip. *Blowing Up India.* Calcutta, 1955.

Tagore, Debendranath. *The Autobiography of Maharshi Devendranath Tagore.* Satyendranath Tagore and Indira Devi, trs. London, 1914.

Tagore, Rabindranath. *Collected Poems and Plays of Rabindranath Tagore.* London, 1961.

——. *Creative Unity.* London, 1959.

——. *Gora.* London, 1961.

——. *Greater India.* Madras, 1921.

——. *The Home and the World.* London, 1961.

——. "Indian Students and Western Teachers," *Modern Review,* (April, 1916).

——. "Introducing Oneself," *Quest* (May 1961), pp. 9–17.

——. *Itihās* [History]. Calcutta, 1955.

——. *Kālāntar* [End of an era]. Calcutta, 1962.

——. *Letters to a Friend.* London, 1928.

——. *My Boyhood Days.* Marjorie Sykes, tr. Calcutta, 1955.

——. *Nationalism.* New York, 1917.

——. *Rabindra racanābali* (Collected works of Rabindra). 14 vols. Calcutta, 1961.

——. "The Religion of an Artist," *Rabindranath Tagore on Art and Aesthetics.* Calcutta, 1961.

——. *Reminiscences.* London, 1961.

———. *Towards Universal Man.* Calcutta, 1961.

———. *Your Tagore for Today.* Hirankumar Sanyal, ed., and Hirendranath Mukherjee, tr. Bombay, 1945.

Tagore, Saumyendranath. *Historical Development of Communist Movement in India.* Calcutta, 1944.

Thompson, Edward J. and Arthur Marshman Spencer. *Bengali Religious Lyrics, Śākta.* London, 1923.

Tuker, Sir Francis. *While Memory Serves.* London, 1950.

Vivekananda, Swami. "Lectures from Colombo to Almora," *The Complete Works of Swami Vivekananda.* Vol. III. 9th ed., Calcutta, 1964, pp. 103–464.

II. SECONDARY WORKS

A. Books, Articles, Unpublished Theses and Papers
Ahmad, Kamruddin. *The Social History of East Pakistan.* Dacca, n.d.

Ahmad, Muzaffar. *The Communist Party of India and its Formation Abroad.* Calcutta, 1962.

Argov, Daniel. *Moderates and Extremists in the Indian Nationalist Movement 1883–1920.* London, 1967.

Bagal, Jogesh Chandra. *History of the Indian Association 1876–1951.* Calcutta, n.d. (1953?).

Bertocci, Peter. "Patterns of Social Organization In Rural East Bengal," *Bengal East and West.* Alexander Lipski, ed. East Lansing, 1970.

Besant, Annie. *How India Wrought for Freedom.* Adyar, Madras, 1915.

Bhattacharja, Jogendra Nath. *Hindu Castes and Sects.* Calcutta, 1896.

Biographies of Eminent Indians. Madras, n.d.

Bolle, Kees W. *The Persistence of Religion.* Leiden, 1965.

Bonnerjee, Sadhona. *Life of W. C. Bonnerjee.* Calcutta, n.d. (1944?).

Bose, Nemai Sadhan. *The Indian Awakening and Bengal.* Calcutta, 1960.

Bose, Nirmal Kumar. *Modern Bengal.* Calcutta, 1959.

———. *Studies in Gandhism.* 3d ed. Calcutta, 1962.

Brecher, Michael. *Nehru, A Political Biography.* London, 1959.

Broomfield, J. H. *Elite Conflict in a Plural Society: Twentieth-Century Bengal.* Berkeley, 1968.

Broomfield, J. H. "The Vote and the Transfer of Power—A Study of the Bengal General Election 1912–1913," *Journal of Asian Studies*, Vol. XXI, No. 2 (February 1962), pp. 163–81.

Buckland, C. E. *Bengal under the Lieutenant-Governors*. 2 vols. Calcutta, 1901.

Chandra, Bipan. *The Rise and Growth of Economic Nationalism in India*. New Delhi, 1966.

——. "Two Notes on the Agrarian Policy of Indian Nationalists," *Indian Economic and Social History Review*, Vol. I, No. 4 (April–June 1964).

Chatterjee, B. N. "Netaji Subhas Chandra Bose, A Chronicle 1897 to 1945." *The Calcutta Municipal Gazette*, Vol. XLV, No. 8. Subhas Bose Birthday Supplement (January 25, 1947).

Chatterjee, Dilip Kumar. *C. R. Das and Indian National Movement*. Calcutta, 1965.

Chatterji, Bhola. *Aspects of Bengal Politics in the Early Nineteen-Thirties*. Calcutta, 1969.

Chaturvedi, Benarsidas and Marjorie Sykes. *Charles Freer Andrews*. London, 1949.

Chaudhuri, Nirad C. *The Autobiography of an Unknown Indian*. New York, 1951.

——. *The Continent of Circe*. London, 1965.

——. "Subhas Chandra Bose." *The Illustrated Weekly of India*, Vol. LXXVI, No. 38 (September 18, 1955).

——. "Subhas Chandra Bose—His Legacy and Legend." *Pacific Affairs*, Vol. XXVI, No. 4 (December 1953), pp. 349–57.

Chirol, Valentine. *Indian Unrest*. London, 1910.

Clark, T. W. "The Role of Bankimcandra in the Development of Nationalism." *Historians of India, Pakistan and Ceylon*. C. H. Philips, ed. London, 1962, pp. 429–45.

Cohn, Bernard S. "Political Systems of Eighteenth Century India: the Banaras Region." *Journal of the American Oriental Society*, Vol. 82, No. 3 (1962), pp. 312–19.

——. Unpublished Material on the Middle Temple, 1860–1940.

Cotton, H. E. A. *Calcutta Old and New*. Calcutta, 1907.

Coupland, Reginald. *The Constitutional Problem in India*. 3 parts. London, 1945.

Crane, Robert I., ed. *Regions and Regionalism in South Asian Studies: An Exploratory Study.* Duke University, 1967.

Das, M. N. *India under Morley and Minto.* London, 1964.

Das, Narendra Nath. *History of Midnapur.* Part Two. Calcutta, 1962.

Das Gupta, Hemendranath. *Deshbandhu Chittaranjan Das.* Delhi, 1960.

———. *Subhas Chandra.* Calcutta, 1946.

Dasgupta, Shashibhusan. *Obscure Religious Cults.* Rev. ed. Calcutta, 1962.

De, Sushil Kumar. *Early History of the Vaisnava Faith and Movement in Bengal.* 2d ed. Calcutta, 1961.

Deutsch, Karl W. *Nationalism and Social Communication.* 2d ed. Cambridge, Massachusetts, 1966.

———. "Social Mobilization and Political Development." *American Political Science Review.* Vol. LV, No. 3 (September 1961), pp. 493–514.

Dimock, Edward C., Jr. and Ronald B. Inden. "The City in Pre-British Bengal." *Urban Bengal.* Richard L. Park, ed. East Lansing, 1969.

Diwakar, R. R. *Mahayogi Sri Aurobindo.* 3d ed. Bombay, 1962.

Druhe, David N. *Soviet Russia and Indian Communism.* New York, 1959.

Dutt, Ajoy C. *Bengal Council and its Work.* Calcutta, n.d. (1924?).

Dutt, Paramananda. *Memoirs of Moti Lal Ghosh.* Calcutta, 1935.

Duverger, Maurice. *Political Parties.* Rev. ed. New York, 1965.

Erikson, Erik H. *Gandhi's Truth.* New York, 1969.

———. "Identity and the Life Cycle." *Psychological Issues,* Vol. I, No. 1 (1959).

Evans-Pritchard, E. E. *The Nuer.* Oxford, 1940.

Farquhar, J. N. *Modern Religious Movements in India.* New York, 1915.

Fibbertigibbet [Niranjan Majumdar]. "A Calcutta Diary." *Economic Weekly.* Bombay, 1956–1964.

Fraser, Lovat. *India under Curzon and After.* 3d ed. London, 1912.

Franda, Marcus F. "The Politics of West Bengal." *State Politics in India.* Myron Weiner, ed. Princeton, 1968. Pp. 245–318.

———. *Radical Politics in West Bengal.* Cambridge, Massachusetts, 1971.

Ghose, Loke Nath. *The Modern History of the Indian Chiefs, Rajas, Zamindars, & c.* Part II. Calcutta, 1881.

Ghosh, Pansy Chaya. *The Development of the Indian National Congress 1892–1909*. Calcutta, 1960.

Ghosh, Sujata. "The British Indian Association (1851–1900)." *Bengal Past and Present*. Vol. LXXVII, Part II, No. 144 (July–December 1958).

Ghosh, Tushar Kanti, ed. *Deshapriya Jatindra Mohan*. Calcutta, 1933.

Gopal, Ram. *Indian Muslims, A Political History*. Calcutta, 1959.

Guha, Nalini Kiśor. *Bānlāy biplabbād* [Revolution in Bengal]. Calcutta, 1954.

Gunderson, Warren. "The Self-Image and World-View of the Bengali Intelligentsia, 1830–1870." *Bengal Literature and History*. Edward C. Dimock, Jr., ed. East Lansing, 1967.

Gupta, Atulchandra, ed. *Studies in the Bengal Renaissance*. Jadavpur, Calcutta, 1958.

Gupta, J. N. *Life and Work of Romesh Chunder Dutt, C.I.E.* London, 1911.

Haithcox, John Patrick. *Communism and Nationalism in India. M. N. Roy and Comintern Policy 1920–1939*. Princeton, 1971.

Heimsath, Charles H. *Indian Nationalism and Hindu Social Reform*. Princeton, 1964.

Hundred Years of the University of Calcutta. Calcutta, 1957.

Hunter, William Wilson. *The Indian Mussalmans*. Lahore, 1964. Reprint.

Huque, M. Azizul. *History and Problems of Moslem Education in Bengal*. Calcutta, 1917.

Ikram, S. M. *Modern Muslim India and the Birth of Pakistan (1858–1951)*. 2d ed. Lahore, 1965.

The Indian Nation Builders. 3 vols. Madras, n.d.

Isherwood, Christopher. *Ramakrishna and His Disciples*. New York, 1965.

Jack, J. C. *The Economic Life of a Bengal District*. Oxford, 1916.

Kabeer, Rokeya Rahman. *Administrative Policy of the Government of Bengal 1870–1890*. Dacca, 1965.

Kabir, Humayun. *Muslim Politics (1906–1942)*. Calcutta, 1944.

Karim, Abdul. *Social History of the Muslims in Bengal*. Dacca, 1959.

Karunakaran, K. P. *Continuity and Change in Indian Politics*. Delhi, 1964.

Kaushik, P. D. *The Congress Ideology and Programme 1920–47.* New Delhi, 1964.

Khan, Muin-ud-din Ahmad. *History of the Fara'idi Movement in Bengal (1818–1906).* Karachi, 1965.

Kling, Blair B. *The Blue Mutiny.* Philadelphia, 1966.

Kripalani, Krishna. *Rabindranath Tagore.* New York, 1962.

Krishna, Gopal. "The Development of the Indian National Congress as a Mass Organization, 1918–1923," *Journal of Asian Studies.* Vol. XXV, No. 3. (May, 1966), pp. 413–30.

LaPalombara, Joseph and Myron Weiner, eds. *Political Parties and Political Development.* Princeton, 1966.

Laushey, David Mason. "The Bengal Terrorists and Their Conversion to Marxism: Aspects of Regional Nationalism in India, 1905–1942." Ph.D. thesis, University of Virginia, 1969.

Leach, Edmund and S. N. Mukherjee, eds. *Elites in South Asia.* Cambridge, 1970.

Levenson, Joseph R. *Liang Ch'i-Ch'ao and the Mind of Modern China.* Cambridge, Massachusetts, 1959.

Low, D. A., ed. *Soundings in Modern South Asian History.* London, 1968.

McCully, Bruce Trebout. *English Education and the Origins of Indian Nationalism.* New York, 1940.

McLane, John R. "Calcutta and the Mofussilization of Bengali Politics." *Urban Bengal.* Richard L. Park, ed. East Lansing, 1969.

——. "The 1905 Partition and the New Communalism." *Bengal East and West.* Alexander Lipski, ed. East Lansing, 1970.

Majumdar, Bimanbehari. *History of Political Thought from Rammohun to Dayananda.* Vol. I. Calcutta, 1934.

——. *Indian Political Associations and Reform of Legislature (1818–1917).* Calcutta, 1965.

—— and Bhakat Prasad Mazumdar. *Congress and Congressmen in the Pre-Gandhian Era 1885–1917.* Calcutta, 1967.

Majumdar, R. C. *Glimpses of Bengal in the Nineteenth Century.* Calcutta, 1960.

——. *History of the Freedom Movement in India.* 3 vols. Calcutta, 1962, 1963.

Mehrotra, S. R. *The Emergence of the Indian National Congress*. Delhi, 1971.

Metcalf, Thomas. *The Aftermath of Revolt, 1857–1870*. Princeton, 1964.

Misra, B. B. *The Indian Middle Classes*. London, 1961.

Mitra, Sisirkumar. *The Liberator*. Delhi, 1954.

Mookerjee, Girija. *This Europe*. Calcutta, 1950.

Moore, R. J. *Liberalism and Indian Politics 1872–1922*. London, 1966.

Mukherjee, Haridas and Uma Mukherjee. *'Bande Mataram' and Indian Nationalism (1906–1908)*. Calcutta, 1957.

——. *Bipin Chandra Pal and India's Struggle for Swaraj*. Calcutta, 1958.

——. *The Growth of Nationalism in India 1857–1905*. Calcutta, 1957.

——. *India's Fight for Freedom or the Swadeshi Movement (1905–1906)*. Calcutta, 1958.

——. *The Origins of the National Education Movement*. Calcutta, 1957.

——, eds. *Sri Aurobindo and the New Thought*. Calcutta, 1964.

——. *Sri Aurobindo's Political Thought*. Calcutta, 1958.

Mukherjee, Uma. *Two Great Indian Revolutionaries*. Calcutta, 1966.

Nanda, B. R. *Mahatma Gandhi*. London, 1958.

——. *The Nehrus, Motilal and Jawaharlal*. New York, 1963.

Nicholas, Ralph W. "Factions: A Comparative Analysis" in *Political Systems and the Distribution of Power*. New York, 1965. Pp. 21–61.

Noman, Mohammad. *Muslim India*. Allahabad, 1942.

O'Malley, L. S. S. *History of Bengal, Bihar and Orissa under British Rule*. Calcutta, 1925.

Overstreet, Gene D. and Marshall Windmiller. *Communism in India*. Berkeley, 1959.

Park, Richard L. "The Rise of Militant Nationalism in Bengal: A Regional Study of Indian Nationalism." Ph.D. thesis, Harvard University, 1951.

Purani, A. B. *The Life of Sri Aurobindo (1872–1926)*. 2d ed. Pondicherry, 1960.

Ray, Prithwis Chandra. *The Life and Times of C. R. Das*. Calcutta, 1927.

Rāy, Suprakaś, *Bhārater baiplabik saṅgrāmer itihās* [History of the revolutionary struggle in India]. Calcutta, 1955.

Ronaldshay, Earl of. *The Life of Lord Curzon.* Vol. II. London, 1928.

Rusch, Thomas A. "Role of the Congress Socialist Party in the Indian National Congress, 1931–1942." Ph.D. thesis, University of Chicago, 1955.

Saggi, P. D. *Life and Work of Netaji Subhas Chandra Bose.* Bombay, n.d.

Saha, K. B. "Middle Class Unemployment in Bengal." *Calcutta Review,* Vol. XIII, 3d series (December, 1924), pp. 350–72.

Sarkar, Hem Chandra. *A Life of Ananda Mohan Bose.* Calcutta, 1910.

Sarkar, Sumit. "Trends in Bengal's Swadeshi Movement (1903–1908)." *Bengal Past and Present,* Vol. LXXXIV; Part I, No. 157 (January–June 1965) pp. 10–39; Part II, No. 158 (July–December 1965) pp. 140–60.

Sastri, Sivanath. *History of the Brahmo Samaj.* 2 vols. Calcutta, 1911, 1912.

Sayeed, Khalid B. *Pakistan, The Formative Phase 1857–1948.* 2d ed. London, 1968.

Seal, Anil. *The Emergence of Indian Nationalism.* Cambridge, 1968.

Sharma, Shri Ram, ed. *Netaji, His Life and Work.* Agra, 1948.

Shils, Edward. "The Intellectual between Tradition and Modernity: The Indian Situation." *Comparative Studies in Society and History.* Supplement I. The Hague, 1961.

Shukla, B. D. *A History of the Indian Liberal Party.* Allahabad, 1960.

Sinha, Pradip. *Nineteenth Century Bengal, Aspects of Social History.* Calcutta, 1965.

Sitaramayya, B. Pattabhi. *History of the Indian National Congress.* 2 vols. Bombay, 1935 and 1947.

Smith, William Roy. *Nationalism and Reform in India.* New Haven, 1938.

Thomas, K. P. *Dr. B. C. Roy.* Calcutta, 1955.

Toye, Hugh. *Subhas Chandra Bose, The Springing Tiger.* Bombay, 1962.

Tripathi, Amales. *The Extremist Challenge.* Calcutta, 1967.

Wasti, Syed Razi. *Lord Minto and the Indian Nationalist Movement 1905 to 1910.* London, 1964.

Weiner, Myron. *Party Politics in India.* Princeton, 1957.

——. *The Politics of Scarcity.* Chicago, 1962.

Wheeler-Bennett, John W. *John Anderson, Viscount Waverly*. London, 1962.

Wolpert, Stanley A. *Tilak and Gokhale*. Los Angeles, 1962.

B. Reference Works

Bhargava, Prag Narain, ed. *Who's Who in India*. Lucknow, 1911.

Buckland, C. E. *Dictionary of Indian Biography*. London, 1906.

Mitra, H. N., ed. *The Indian Annual Register*, 1919–1924. Calcutta, published annually.

Mitra, Nripendra Nath, ed. *The Indian Annual Register*, 1925–1947. Calcutta, published annually (also called *The Indian Quarterly Register*).

Times of India, Indian Yearbook and Who's Who. Bombay, published annually.

Yule, Henry and A. C. Burnell. *Hobson-Jobson*. William Crooke, ed. New ed. Delhi, 1968.

Index

Abdul Kasim, 34
Abdul Latif, 35, 65
Abdur Rashid Khan, Maulvi, 209
Abhay Ashram, 180
Abul Hasem, 291
Aga Khan, 67, 92, 95
Afghanistan, 290
Afghans, 48, 49, 51, 61, 70
Adda (meeting places), revolutionaries', 146
Adi Brahmo Samaj, 23
Age of Consent bill, 43
Aggression: control of, 24; expression of, x, 120, 123
Agra, 4
Ahimsa, *see* Nonviolence
Ahmadabad, 112, 164, 182, 198
Ahmed, Muzaffar, 255–56, 257, 280
AICC (All-India Congress Committee), *see* Congress, Indian National
Akbar, 50, 52
Akram Khan, Maulana, 192
Ali, Ameer, *see* Ameer Ali
Ali, Mohammad, *see* Mohammad Ali
Ali Chaudhuri, Nawab Saiyid Nawab, 202, 210, 213
Aligarh: Mohammadan Anglo-Oriental College, 210
Alipore: bomb case, 116, 126–27; Alipore jail, 180
All-India Trade Union Congress (AITUC), 190, 245, 256
All-Parties Conference, 242, 243
Ameer Ali, 10, 17, 18, 34, 35, 37, 39–41, 61–74, 92, 159; assessment of Hinduism, 69; career, 63–65; comparison with Romesh Dutt, 73–74; defense of Islam, 68–70, 315–16*nn*105, 106; family background and education, 61–62; political activity, 65–68; view of Bengal, 72–73; view of British Raj, 71–72; view of Indian history, 70–71
American revolutionaries, example of, 109, 138, 155
Amrita Bazar Patrika, 28, 36, 90
Amritsar, 164, 170, 230
Ānandamaṭh, 52, 80, 81, 112, 113
Andamans, prison in, 127
Andrews, C. F., 88, 343*n*85
Anglo-Indians, 202, 203, 210, 218, 282
Anstey, Vera, 180
Anushilan Samiti, 140, 143, 145, 149, 156, 251, 253, 254
Arms: plans to obtain, 150, 151, 194; theft of, 147
Aryans, 30, 53, 70, 113, 114
Ashrams, 128, 129, 131, 134, 174, 175
Asia: revolutionary possibilities in, 254; spirituality of, 116, 121
Assam, 4, 5, 59, 82, 172, 281, 284
Atmiya, Sabha, 22
Aurangzeb, 52, 71
Aurobindo, *see* Ghose, Aurobindo
Authority, x, 142, 225, 227, 245, 261, 270, 273, 291; ambivalence toward, x, 225, 273; habit of, 2, 3; political, 5, 66, 77, 121, 138, 250, 291
Autocracy, 94